D1588746

Legends of the Open Road

MaRT

Legends of the Open Road

The History, Technology and Future of Automobile Design

SKIRA

Cover
Alfa Romeo, 8C 2900 B Berlinetta Aerodinamica Le Mans, 1938

Back cover
Chevrolet, Corvette convertible, 1958 detail

Graphic supervision
Pierluigi Cerri

Design
Marcello Francone with Luigi Fiore

Editing
Silvia Colombo

Layout
Enrico Alvarez

Translations
Lucian Comoy, Language Consulting Congressi, Milano

First published in Italy in 2007 by
Skira Editore S.p.A.
Palazzo Casati Stampa
via Torino 61
20123 Milano
Italy
www.skira.net

Printed and bound in Italy. First edition

ISBN-13: 978-88-6130-066-8

Distributed in North America by Rizzoli International Publications, Inc., 300 Park Avenue South, New York, NY 10010, USA.
Distributed elsewhere in the world by Thames and Hudson Ltd., 181A High Holborn, London WC1V 7QX, United Kingdom.

Printed on
GardaPat 13 KIARA - 135 g/m^2

**Provincia autonoma
di Trento
Comune di Trento
Comune di Rovereto**

**Museo di Arte
Moderna e Contemporanea
di Trento e Rovereto**

Board of directors
Franco Bernabè
President
Isabella Bossi Fedrigotti
Vice-president
Lino Dainese
Massimo Egidi
Giampaolo Fabris
Mariangela Franch
Michelangelo Lupo
Paolo Mattei

Director
Gabriella Belli

Scientific committee
Salvatore Settis
Co-ordinator
Achille Bonito Oliva
Manuel J. Borja-Villel
Guy Cogeval
Alanna Heiss
Rolf Lauter

Board of auditors
Carlo Delladio
Luigi Matassoni
Giovanni Zani

Direction
Gabriella Belli

Chief-curators
Roberto Antolini (*Library*)
Nicoletta Boschiero
(*Collections of 20th-century art*)
Paola Pettenella
(*Historical archives*)
Alessandra Tiddia
(*Collections of 19th-century art*)

Curators
Beatrice Avanzi
Elisabetta Barisoni
Clarenza Catullo
Margherita de Pilati
Julia Trolp
(*Temporary exhibitions*)

Curators
Lara Sebastiani
(*Art collections*)

Mariarosa Mariech
Carlo Prosser
Francesca Velardita
(*Historical archives and Library*)

Research Projects
Alice Bordin
Melania Gazzotti
Alexandra Obukhova
Francesco Samassa

Registrar
Davide Sandrini

Photographic archive
Attilio Begher
with the assistance of
Serena Aldi
Maurizio Baldo

Director's secretary
Ilaria Calgaro
Roberta Galvagni

Administrative sector

Supervisor
Diego Ferretti

Administration
Marina Cindolo
Tiziana Cumer
Angela Gerosa
Arianna Gionta
Barbara Gober
Lina Mattè
Francesco Presti

Technical and IT office
Giusto Manica
Claudio Merz
Walter Pancin
Cristian Pozzer
Sonja Sottopietra

Maintenance and installations
Vladimiro Benoni
Mario Divina
Arturo Kuer

Storage
Giampiero Coatti

**Public relations
and Comunication sector**

Supervisor
Flavia Fossa Margutti

Press office
Luca Melchionna
with the collaboration of
Clementina Rizzi

Marketing
Chiara Andreolli
Lara Facco
Carlotta Gaspari
Vanessa Vacchini

Educational Department
Denise Bernabè
Annalisa Casagranda
Daniela Ferrari
Carlo Tamanini
with the collaboration of
Maurizio Defant
Brunella Fait
Sabina Ferrario
and of
Fulvia Cantagallo
Karin Cavalieri
Ornella Dossi
Stefania Fogolari
Amina Pedrinolla
Barbara Santi
Katjuscia Tevini

Events and Merchandising
Camilla Palestra

Co-ordination of public services
Silvia Ferrari

The first edition of this volume has been published for the exhibition Mitomacchina, Motor Car Design: History, Technology and Future

Rovereto, Museo di Arte Moderna e Contemporanea
di Trento e Rovereto
2 December 2006 – 1 May 2007

Scientific director
Gabriella Belli

Scientific committee
Gabriella Belli
Gian Piero Brunetta
Pierluigi Cerri
Emilio Deleidi
Giampaolo Fabris
Giorgetto Giugiaro
Tomás Maldonado
Adolfo Orsi
Sergio Pininfarina
Mauro Tedeschini

Scientific contributors
Gabriella Belli
Donatella Biffignandi
Gian Piero Brunetta
Enrico De Vita
Helen Evenden
Giampaolo Fabris
Tomás Maldonado
Giuliano Molineri
Adolfo Orsi
Sergio Pininfarina
Lorenzo Ramaciotti
Mauro Tedeschini
Paolo Tumminelli

Technical curators
Elisabetta Barisoni
Julia Trolp
with the collaboration of
Pietro Caccia Dominioni

Registrar
Davide Sandrini

Historical, scientific and biographical notes
Raffaele Gazzi, Adolfo Orsi,
with the supervision
of Gianni Cancellieri (H.S.)
Ralf J.F. Kieselbach (R.J.F.K.)
Elisabetta Barisoni (E.B.)
Pietro Caccia Dominioni (P.C.D.)
Julia Trolp (J.T.)

Cinema section
Gian Piero Brunetta, *subject and screenplay*
Mirco Melanco, *database, screenplay and direction*
Federico Massa e Denis Brotto, *database, screenplay and editing*
Matteo Buzzanca, *original music*
Erika Fasan e Mara Nardin, *database*
Lorenzo Ronzoni, *digital technology*

Graphic design and layout
Studio Cerri & Associati

Translations
Giacomo Barsanti, Lucian Comoy
Maurizio Guerri

Photographic archive
Attilio Begher
with the assistance of
Serena Aldi, Maurizio Baldo

We wish to thank all those who made the exhibition possible. Our particular thanks to the car manufacturers, collectors, museums and archives who have provided materials, recommendations, skills and precious loans for the exhibition and catalogue.

Museums
Arese (Milan), Automobilismo Storico Alfa Romeo, Museo Storico, Centro di Documentazione Storica
Dearborn, Collections of the Henry Ford
Gaydon, British Motor Industry Heritage Trust
Ingolstadt, Museum für Konkrete Kunst
Lucerna, Verkehrshaus der Schweiz
Maranello (Modena), Galleria Ferrari
Munich, Deutsches Museum
Munich, Die Neue Sammlung
Pinakothek der Moderne
Mulhouse, Cité de l'Automobile – Musée National – Schlumpf Collection
San Martino in Rio (Reggio Emilia), Scuderia San Martino Museo dell'Auto
Sochaux, L'Aventure Peugeot
Turin, Collezione Storica Lancia
Turin, Centro Storico Fiat
Villafranca di Verona, Museo Nicolis dell'Auto, della Tecnica, della Meccanica
Zaventem, Fondazione Swaters

Archives
Archivio Anselmi
Archivio Leonardo Bertoni
DaimlerChrysler Classic Archives
Archivio Storico Fiat
Archivio Fotografico Italdesign Giugiaro
Archivio Edgardo Michelotti
Archivio Adolfo Orsi
Archivio Rèvelli di Beaumont
AUDI AG – Unternehmensarchiv
BMW AG Konzernarchiv
Dr. Ing. h.c.f. Porsche AG

Car manufacturers/Design centres
Auto Union GmbH
Autostadt GmbH
Bertone_Direzione della Comunicazione
Centro Ricerche Fiat S.C.p.A.
Citröen
DaimlerChrysler Advanced Design Italia
Fiat Auto Spa
Fioravanti srl

General Motors
Italdesign Giugiaro
Lamborghini
Maserati srl
Nissan Motor Company LTD
Pagani Automobili Spa
Pininfarina spa
Porsche
Renault / Renault communication
Smart GmbH

Private collections
Lawrence Auriana
Davide Bassoli
Bianchi Anderloni
Federico Bonomelli
Gino Coen
Paolo Fraulini
Francesco e Mietta Gandolfi
Johan Jonsson, RCA
Arturo Keller
Ralf J.F. Kieselbach
Marco Makaus
Philipp Moch
Adolfo Orsi
Uros Pavasovic, RCA
Pininfarina Collection
Private collection - Member of the Registro 356 Porsche Italia
Jonathan Punter, RCA
Quattroruote Collection
Roberto Rigoli
Fabrizio Sama
Giovanni Sandri
Kenny Schachter/ROVE
Richard Spelberg
IED, Istituto Europeo di Design, Turin site, Transportation design
Lions Club International Le Bourget – Christian Wannyn
Pforzheim, University of Applied Sciences Transportation Design Department
Verein Internationales Trabant Register e.V. 'InterTrab'

Special thanks to those who have contributed to our project, either through loans or precious advice:

Giovanni Accongiagioco
Stefano Agazzi
Bruno Alfieri
Angelo Tito Anselmi
Silvana Appendino
Emmanuel Bacquet
Nino Balestra
Chiara Barbieri
Gilian Bardsley
Philippe Barre
Filippo Beraudo di Pralormo
Giovanni Bianchi Anderloni
André Binda
Clive Birch
Sandra Bitter
Alessandro Bonini
Cristina Bonisolli
Jens Borstelmann
Lorenzo Boscarelli
Christine Bösiger
John Bowen
Nick Brändli
Thomas Bscher
Aline Calla
Paolo Canevari
Lorenza Cappello
Diego Cassetta
Massimo Castagnola
Stefano Chiminelli
Lynda Clark
Philippe Cousseau
Luca Cordero di Montezemolo
Daniele Cornil
Ermanno Cozza
Andrew Cross
Luca Del Monte
Massimo Di Carlo
Pietro Di Cremonini
Stefan Dierkes
Niklas Drechslers
Philipp Eberl
Wolfgang Egger
Tina Eggert
John Elkann
Annegret Ernst
Helen Evenden
Monica Faccini
Patrick Faulwetter
Maria Feifel
Stefan Felber
Paolo Ferrini
Leonardo Fioravanti
Luca Fioravanti
Sergio Fontana
Thomas Fuhrmann
Wilhelm Füssl
Alberto Fumagalli
Rodolfo Gaffino Rossi
Renato Ghiano
Antonio Ghini
Philippe Gras
Francesco Guasti
Maurizio Guerri
Antonio Gurrieri
Bettina Gundler
Zaha Hadid
Philip Hall
Edgar Haschke
Jakob Hirzel
Gro Höeg
Tobias Hoffmann
Petra Hölscher
Andreas Hornig
Florian Hufnagl
Denis Huille
Fred Hurst
Michele Jauch Paganetti
Gregory John Paul
Johan Jonsson
Bernhard Joseph
Arturo Keller
Richard Keller
Ralf J.F. Kieselbach
Christoph Knecht
Harald Kneitz
Cynthia Korolov
Lisa Kozzetz
Martin Kukowski
Darcy Kuronen
Erika La Rosa
Stephen Laing
Sylvie Lallement
Gerd Langer
Minoo Larson
Katja Lauffer
Ezio Lendaro
Michele Lucente
Andreas Maenner
Antonio Magro
Franco Majno
Monika Markert
Naomi Martin
Enrico Masala
Roberto Mastrostefano
Jim McCabe
Sophie McKinlay
Cesar Mendoza
John Metz
Wolf Meyer zu Bargholz
Cynthia R. Miller
Sylvia Minem-Christophe
Leslie Mio
Dieter Mnich
Luca Monaco
Daniele Moro
Enzo Moro
Silvia Nicolis
Xavier de Nombel
This Oberhändli
Pasquale Olivieri
Jim Orr
Horacio Pagani
Simon Parris
Paola Pastorelli
Uros Pavasovic
Giovanni Perfetti
Lorenza Pininfarina
Herbert Poetter
Wanda Polanski
Catia Pramazzoni
Jonathan Punter
Karam Ram
Silvia Rebuli
Susanne Reinhardt
Bethel Revelli
Mario Righini
Bernard Rignault
Uliana Ronchi
Joris Rosmolen
Pablo Rother
Elvira Ruocco
Patrizia Sala
Enrico Saroldi
Kenny Schachter
Patrik Schumacher
Petra Secunde
Alberta Simonis
Tapio Snellman
Richard Spelberg
Florence Swaters
Jacques Swaters
Fabrizio Taiana
Mike Teske
Maurizio Torchio
Ettore Trentadue
ElisabettaTruffelli
Massimo Vallotto
Volontari UGAF
Sylvie Vivo
Norbert Weber
Christian Wannyn
Henry Wydler

A thank you also to those private collectors who have preferred to remain anonymous

We thank the following for the help they have given in various ways:

Apt di Rovereto
Associazione Amatori Veicoli Storici
Associazione Nazionale fra Industrie Automobilistiche
Casse Rurali Trentine per le attività didattiche
Cineforum Trento
Compagnia Giardino Chiuso, San Gimignano
Comune di Rovereto
Consorzio Rovereto In Centro
Funivie Folgarida Marilleva
Movimento Turismo del Vino Trentino Alto Adige
Nuovo Cineforum Rovereto
Scuderia Trentina Storica

Special thanks to Ferrari for having made available the models of the 'Ferrari: New Concepts of the Myth' 2005 international contest and to Carrozzieri ANFIA for the loan of the plates for the 'Mostra Stile Italiano Giovani' competition 2006

Contents

Art and Design

Gabriella Belli

It is apparent today that the exhibition choices of many museum institutions, especially with regard to museums of modern and contemporary art, are increasingly geared towards areas of research that even in the recent past did not fall within the nevertheless broad scope of their cultural and scientific exploration.

This for many reasons. The main one, I believe, is the shift of major art criticism in the early 1950s into social, anthropological, political and economic fields, which has resulted in it being considered impossible nowadays to produce high-profile scientific studies without constant recourse to comparison with other disciplines, by which I mean not just the other fields in which art has a share, but the entire complexity of the socio-economic and political universe around us.

A second reason lies in the acquired awareness that the aesthetic 'game' is now played in every aspect of economic production, which place new objects and arguments of particular critical interest at the disposal of the old history of art.

The proposal of an exhibition dedicated to car design is thus wholly pertinent not only to Mart's cultural policy, which since its foundation has always sought to present broad-ranging work, in which a shared need was to include the various languages of art and, above all, explore fields in the margins of artistic experience *tout court*, but also to respond to public demand, which today sees culture as a broadened knowledge base, able to reflect all the complexity of today's society, and in which the most desired, hated, mystified, criticized and venerated myth is without a doubt that of the motor car.

The introductory essays in the catalogue, by Tomás Maldonado and Giampaolo Fabris, cover much of this ground; they are essays in which careful social, economic and anthropological analysis of the present helps to explain the meaning and sense of this cult object, omnipresent in our daily lives. And it is from their analysis that the profound debate within the catalogue takes its cue, in which the voice of celebrated scholars and designers, such as Sergio Pininfarina, Giorgetto Giugiaro, Mauro Tedeschini, Adolfo Orsi, Enrico De Vita and others, lead to fresh reflections, which enable us to better understand the history and development of 'mitomacchina,' a phenomenon that belongs undoubtedly to the area of industrial production, but which has insinuated itself into our lives as a constant with an absolute social significance and strong cultural overtones.

As may be seen in the catalogue and in the exhibition, this analysis, although having filled pages and pages of critical literature, seems nevertheless to require constant focusing: a century of history has not sufficed to understand this phenomenon of the car, which never appears with a single facet, but changes constantly with the changing of the economic and cultural state of our society.

There is no doubt that for its unusual nature, the proposal of 'mitomacchina' — the first exhibition dedicated to the car to be offered by a museum of modern and contemporary art — must be considered a great novelty as regards the Museum's usual programme.
Quite aside from the aspect of show or curiosity that is evident in the actual object displayed, the exhibition stresses a new state in the cultural mission of Mart.

For our institution, indeed, the exhibition marks an important turning point as to its museological definition, which more than ever today refers to a cultural universe in which the references to contemporary society, its understanding and, in a broader sense, its focusing on its complexity no longer remain residual to the aesthetics of the art to which Mart duly owes its mission. This means that in the cultural policy of the museum, alongside exhibitions of more evident art-historical bent, increasing space will be given over to exhibitions understood as the exploration of the world surrounding us, with a consequent focusing on the macrocosms or microcosms of production in every field of doing and knowing, as long as these have close connections with the aesthetic dimension of life. An aesthetic dimension which we intend in an extremely broad sense, as a place in which social events and measures can recompose differences and contradictions through culture and knowledge.

It is no coincidence that *Mitomacchina* should by a few months anticipate another exhibition dedicated to Italian design, co-produced by Mart with the Royal Ontario Museum of Toronto and the Musée des Beaux-Arts of Montreal, in which the key to understanding a century of Italian design will for the first time take the form of the close relationship between crafts and industrial design, and the visual arts: an exhibition that will itself introduce the major Mart event for the 2006–07 season, coinciding with the reopening of Fortunato Depero's Casa d'Arte Futurista, enabling the public to gain access once more to the house following a long restoration. The house will be opening in time for the celebrations promoted by the museum for the centenary of Futurism.

It is quite evident, therefore, that the common thread running through these coherent overviews of the production section that Mart offers today with *Mitomacchina*, and which it will continue to propose in future years with other exhibitions, will close the loop of the pact made by Futurist aesthetics at the start of the last century. And we refer here not solely to the colourful expressions of Marinetti, which had the undoubted merit of stamping the name of Italy on the aesthetic value of the new-born motor-car, thanks to the well-known reference to the *Nike* of Samothrace, so much as the clear declarations set out in the *Manifesto of the Futurist Reconstruction of the Universe*, signed by Balla and Depero in 1915.

It is in these two simple little pages that the dream is given material expression of an aesthetic able to address the material production of small and large-scale industry towards a dimension that a perhaps utopian but certainly to be hoped-for harmonic correspondence between art and life. In other words, towards a dimension that presented itself at the time as a saving grace for the very condition of daily life.

Are not economic production and artistic creation, today as yesterday, the two faces of a single problem? So why not believe that the cultural function of the museum be also that of considering its capacity to determine an aesthetic measure of the world through a critical reflection, or a point of reference for the most urgent cultural and spiritual problems?

Mitomacchina and Other Myths

Tomás Maldonado

In the crowded galaxy of myths rooted in contemporary society, the myth of the motor car has a central position. Central in the sense of dominant. The truth is that the myth of the car towers over all the myths which in one way or another condition our current lifestyle. Without excluding those that have developed in recent years around the computer, digital technology and mobile telephony. Despite the fact that these emergent myths exercise an increasing influence, it does not appear that they are able to match the symbolic hegemony of the car (or, at least, not for the moment). This can, in part, be explained by historical reasons. The fact cannot be overlooked that, for about a century, the car has held a privileged position in the collective imagination. Many generations have been born and lived in function of the pleasures (and sometimes displeasures) linked with the car, and there is no doubt also that its obsessive, bulky presence has profoundly marked the way of doing and thinking of millions (indeed, billions) of men and women. There has even been mention of an 'absolutism of the car,' of a sort of 'Autocracy.' Which, if we think about it, is not such a wild claim. With this in mind, however, we must also admit that there is a 'TVcracy' and a 'Computercracy.'

Of course, as with all myths, the car is both fiction and reality. In this specific case, it is hard to establish when the car is fiction and when reality. Indeed, the car is now one of the most symbolic of assembled materials and the most material of symbolic constructions. A veritable symbiosis. That artefacts are often symbols and symbols often artefacts is nothing new. As ethnologists and anthropologists know full well, the phenomenon appears in all cultures. A proof lies in the artefacts — utensils, equipment or tools — to which are attributed a magical property, a role as fetish, amulet or talisman. However, the car is a kind of artefact that, for its omnipervasive nature, for its influence at a global level, has no precedents in history. Never, truly never, has an artefact succeeded in becoming a guiding icon, the symbolic reference of a whole society. And, moreover, of a society which, for better or for worse, dreams of universal hegemony.

As far as the relationship between the car and its most assiduous user, the driver, is concerned, here too there is a link of reciprocal dependency: the symbolic condition of the car in society depends largely on the symbolic condition of the driver, and vice versa. Put differently: the car as object-icon presupposes the existence of the driver as subject-archetype, and vice versa.

Obviously, the car is a vehicle used to transport people and things, but it is also a vehicle of desires, aspirations and driver preferences. This marks a relationship of reciprocal dependence and in some ways of common destiny, one not without conflict. Very often, the environmental context, the particular situation in which car and driver are forced to operate, contribute to upsetting the balance between the two. To the point that neither is able to fulfil his/its functions in an optimal manner.

In the driver, this provokes a feeling of resigned frustration. Resigned frustration that leads him to accept with relative stoicism the psychic and physical sufferings the environmental setting forces upon him (traffic jams, interminable queues, accidents, air pollution, etc.), and all this merely to taste the ambiguous (and ephemeral) pleasure of feeling a part of the grand symbolic scenario of car-powered mobility.

From Structure to Form

In the beginning, as with all machines, the car had no true form. It had the appearance of a strongly self-referential mechanical structure, one that placed its own functional performance above all else. And other functions only in second place. In the first phase, the car was a naked, essential machine, devoid of all covering (consider Cugnot's steam wagon of 1796, for example). To use an anatomical metaphor, we might say that the car in this phase was all skeleton. A body made up entirely of bones but without flesh. But one thing is clear: a naked mechanical structure is not, usually, user friendly. Indeed, it can hurt, wound or even kill. But not only: it is a potential threat for the mechanical structure itself. It is too vulnerable to the harmful effects of accidental or climatic factors (knocks, shocks, temperature, rain, dust etc.), factors able to compromise its correct operation and, in the worst scenario, render it definitively unusable.

The need to offset these two risks, and namely to safeguard the health of the user and functional survival of the machine, is one of the principal reasons that led to the creation of the car body. In the last 20 years of the 19th century, various countries (Austria, Germany, Britain and France) established the requirement to cover the mechanisms of machines with a shell, in order to prevent accidents in the workplace. In this way, a casing hides the mechanical structure from view, thereby establishing a dichotomy that would not limit itself to work tools in general. Indeed, it would become the dominant characteristic of almost all the types of technical objects used in the industrial society. Thus, the world of products was transformed into one — still current — of a prevalence of casings. From the point of view of goods, the products are still classified by the function they fulfilled, but in the market they are perceived, recognized, identified by the actual form they acquire.

In this specific case, the bodywork which is nothing other than a casing, directly or indirectly heads any theoretical reflection on the car. We might discuss its functional performance, its social and economic implications, its environmental sustainability, but we always, sooner or later, end up by tackling the formal aspects of the bodywork. Whether right or wrong, since 1925 these aspects have played a fundamental role in the strategy of the international car manufacturing industry.

In English, the bodywork is called 'car body' to distinguish it from the mechanical structure beneath, which is not deemed a body, but a non-body. In this way, the mechanical structure, and everything this includes, is declassified to a supporting role. It is no coincidence that for a long time, the designer responsible for 'giving form' to the bodywork has been called the 'car body designer.' Later, in 1930, the term 'stylist' was adopted, and the activity undertaken by him 'styling.'

Adventures and Misadventures of the 'Elephant Style'

Naturally, the progressive emphasis placed on the formal aspects of the car body has been a rather linear process, if we except a few 'relapses' which we will examine later. There is a clear line of development leading from the underestimation of these aspects by Henry Ford to their frenetic exaltation by 'stylist' Harley Earl of General Motors and Virgil Exner of Chrysler. There is no doubt that the cars designed by these two designers mark a radical change in the formal treatment of car bodies. If we take things to their logical conclusion, we might say that with Earl and Exner, the car body — or better, its form — becomes autonomous. Now it is form that 'sets down the rules' for the underlying structures and not the other way around.

It should also be remembered that this line of development was in contrast with what was being backed at the same time by the exponents of the modern movement in architecture. While the car body designers followed the road of exuberance of form, the architects postulated a formal parsimony and preferred to show, render transparently explicit all the structural details of their buildings.

In this sense, with all due precautions, we can state that the car body designers anticipated the shift that occurred in the 1980s with post-modernism and deconstructivism in architecture. A shift which aims — or so their supporters claim — to free the forms of buildings from limitations constraining design freedom and creativity. Limitations that supposedly result from a real (or presumed) 'rationalist ideology' with its preference for the notorious 'less is more.'

In this regard, the arguments used in the 1930s by Alfred S. Sloan, President of General Motors, against Henry Ford's philosophy, is eloquent: namely, against the latter's refusal to change his models, against his obstinate defence of standards he had created, against his refusal to use different colours and rounded forms in his cars. These are very similar, in their substance, to the arguments we hear today with regard to so-called 'rationalist architecture.' And this should be no surprise, because Fordism had a considerable influence on the way of perceiving and practising architecture. One need only recall the oft-reiterated admiration of Le Corbusier, perhaps the most archetypical representative of rationalist architecture, for Ford's work and thinking.

Already in 1937, the dadaist Hans Arp, with his colourful and provocative way of expressing himself, had sensed what is happening in our times: 'Le non-sens logique a de nouveaux dû céder au non-sens illogique [...] Sur les ruines de l'architecture rationnelle s'élève l'architecture de style éléphant, paon, cloche, œuf et cœtera.'

Of the four metaphors suggested by Arp to characterize the new style, the first seems the most effective to me. Adopting an ironic tone, it well describes the connotations of that architecture that was destined, according to Arp, to arise 'from the ruins of rational architecture.' An architecture favouring a massive, heavy ('pachidermal') image of buildings and a firmly sculptural treatment of the facades. The best example of this new style is the Guggenheim Museum by Frank Gehry at Bilbao.

We cannot help but be struck by the fact that the type of relationship that exists today between the forms of buildings and the forms of cars is exactly the opposite of that of the 1930s. The 'elephant style,' at the time disapproved of and mocked by architects of the modern movement, has become the style practised by many of the protagonists of today's architecture. On the other hand, this same style that, especially in the United States, was almost *de rigueur* among designers of recent decades, is no longer the dominant trend in the international car manufacturing industry. More or less everywhere, it is possible to sense a growing disaffection with eccentricities, with formal aberrations. In other words: bold flourishes are no longer flavour of the month.

In general terms, we may say that cars resemble each other more. This should be seen as proof of a lack of creativity, as something negative, but on the contrary as the proof of a change in the very idea of creativity in this sector. Creativity is no longer identified, as in the past, with frantic research at any cost, with the spectacular breakthrough, but rather with that subtle research into a few characterizing details. In my opinion, this has been the major contribution of the European designers, Italian and French above all. Commenting on the launch of the Citroën DS in 1955, Roland Barthes stated that with this innovative model, there was a shift 'from a heroic form to a classical one.'

'Hot-rodders'

In historic summaries of the development of the car, a linear, consecutive disposition of the facts is usually preferred. This choice has the undoubted merit of favouring an easier understanding of events. On the other hand, however, it overlooks the many incidents on the way, the rethinkings, the retreats, the controversies between the major players and, last but not least, the failures. These are all situations forming part of a subordinate history, but which it is necessary to take into account in order to understand some delicate passages of this development. One of these is the movement founded in the United States after the war, above all in California, known as 'Hot-rod,' supported by the 'Hot-rodders.' We need here to distinguish between one period, which we may dub 'heroic' and culminating in the 1950s, and the following period. As of 1960, the movement lost most of its original interest although maintaining the same name, and was transformed into a community of designers, still active today, involved in 'artful bodywork' and made-to-measure 'luxury car bodies.'

The phase which interests us here is the one we have dubbed 'heroic'. In this phase, the activity of the 'Hot-rodders' consisted of taking an out-of-production car and submitting it to a drastic change in form and structure, disassembling, removing or replacing original components (radiator, headlights, wings, bumpers, engine, transmission, etc.) with others borrowed from other out-of-production vehicles. The 'Hot-rodder' is thus a *bricoleur* a 'do-it-yourselfer.' The result of his work: a 'made-to-measure' custom car.

The American poet and sociologist, Reuel Denney, was one of the first, in *The Plastic Machines*, to focus on the important part played by the 'Hot-rodders' in the history of the car. In the activities of the 'Hot-rodders,' Denney sees an element of protest, even of revolt, against the nascent 'elephant style' of the 1950s. 'The Hot-rodders,' observes Denney, 'maintained that a mass-produced car from Detroit was anti-economical and too unsafe for modern fast roads. And uglier than it had any right to be; and they added that, for its symbolic class and status values, it was too expensive, too heavy and complicated to be a good car.'

The Car System

Even though doubts and uncertainties about the future of the car industry as we know it today may be advanced, it would be unrealistic to suppose that in the near future its influence on our society may diminish (or even evaporate into nothing). Even those, such as the most intransigent environmentalists, who maintain that the world that the 'car system' has created is unsustainable, have to accept that a drastic abandonment of this system would have unpredictable social and economic consequences. It is now a fundamental and inseparable part of the order (or disorder) of the world economy.

The appearance of the 'car system,' the chief author of which was Alfred P. Sloan, mentioned above, arose from the need to regulate, so to speak, the role of the car. A role which, under the aegis of Ford, had characteristics that sat ill with the demands for dynamism in the market economy. Indeed, Fordism contained ingredients of a strategic rigidity that were not adapted — especially after the financial crisis of 1929 — to the requirements of market flexibility.

But what does the still-current 'car system' actually consist of? According to the outline given by Sloan, it is based above all on five strategic choices: 1. instalment selling; 2. used-car trade-in; 3. closed body; 4. annual model; 5. road improvements. Points one and two are of relevance to the commercial and financial aspects. Points three and four have direct design, technical and production implications. Point five concerns the concrete possibility of managing the construction of the road network or of influencing the public or private bodies able to do so.

It thus comprises a system of five sub-systems that are all closely linked. This confers upon the car industry a complex availability of functional resources, but at the same time, paradoxically, a certain vulnerability. Vulnerability that is always lying in wait. It is sufficient for just one of the five sub-systems to be administered in a less than optimal manner for the overall stability (or efficiency) of the entire system to be affected.

The Car as a Literary Subject

In an article published in *Le Figaro* in 1907, Marcel Proust did not hide his exultation concerning his first experience in a car: 'The most precious thing the car has given us is this admirable independence enabling us to leave at the time we wish and stop where we please' (with hindsight, this comment seems excessively optimistic to us).

Two years later, *Le Figaro* published the celebrated *Manifesto of Futurism* by Filippo Marinetti, in which we read: 'We declare that the magnificence of the world has been enriched by a new beauty. The beauty of speed. A racing car with its bonnet adorned with large tubes similar to snakes with explosive breath [...] a roaring car that seems to race with the sound of machine guns is more beautiful that the Victory of Samothrace.'

And yet, with the advent of the Second World War, when the machine gun was no longer a metaphor but a reality, the car became the symbol of a disappearing peace. The poet Guillaume Apollinaire wrote these disconsolate, melancholic and premonitory verses:

'31st August 1914
I left Deauville a little before midnight
In Rouveyre's little car
Counting the chauffeur there were three of us
We said farewell to an entire epoch
Angry giants stood up on Europe.'

With the war over, once the 'angry giants' had annihilated each other, a new epoch began. The car, camouflaged during the war as a tank, once more picked up the line of development inaugurated by Ford who, with the Model T of 1908, had opened the way to mass distribution of the car. In the United States, the car became a sort of symbolic catalyst for all the aspirations (and frustrations) of the middle class. It should be no surprise to discover that in American literature of the 1920s and 1930s, notoriously critical (sometimes pitilessly so) of the alienating behaviour of the middle class, the car should in one way or the other always be present.

According to the literary critic John Wickersham the car appears in three great novels of the period: in Scott Fitzgerald's *The Great Gatsby* (1925), in *The Big Money* (1936) by John Dos Passos and, above all, in *Babbit* (1920) by Sinclair Lewis. In this last case, observes Wickersham, the central character, Babbit, has 'far more respect and admiration for his car than for anyone or anything else. Indeed, his relationship with his car was little short of a religious [...] For Babbit, driving was both a sacred privilege and a ritual therapy. Starting up his engine was seen by Babbit as being something "epoch-making," parking it as being "dramatic."'

In a text of 1930, Walter Benjamin tackled the subject from a different critical viewpoint. For him, the car was perhaps the best example for examining the complex relationship between engineering and society. Benjamin wrote: 'Léon Daudet [...], leader of the French monarchal party, published a comment on the Car Salon in *Action Française* in which, although not precisely in these words, he set out the phrase: "L'automobile c'est la guerre." The idea underlying this surprising assertion was that the increase in technical instruments [...], which cannot in our private lives find appropriate or full use, seek a justification for themselves outside [in the car]. A justification implying the renouncement of a harmonic collaboration; in other words, war. A war which, with its destruction, would demonstrate how the social reality was not ready to absorb a technical world, and that this was not strong enough to govern the most elementary social forces.'

In the 1970s, we find some novelists — and not only writers of science-fiction — who sought to take the idea of the car as 'object of desire' to its logical conclusion. This is not exactly the 'Olimpian syndrome' described by E.Th.A. Hoffmann in his splendid *Der Sandman*, in which Nathanael falls in love with Olimpia, a robot with human features. In this case, instead, we are dealing with a passion — amorous, or almost — for a car, that is, with a machine resembling a machine, not a human. The best example of this genre is J.G. Ballard's *Crash* (1973). In it, he describes a person who wishes to transform the metal object into one made of flesh, and in this play at the limit of the imaginable, the subject destroys the object of his desire and destroys himself too. When all is said and done, fifty years later, this is how the secret dream of the lower-middle class Babbit comes to a tragic end.

On Fleeting Aesthetics

There is an entrenched custom of making 'aesthetic' evaluations of cars. Usually, these are evaluations that concern the form of the car body in particular. In other words: a car's external beauty (or lack of it), and this quite apart from any consideration of their technical and ergonomic performance. The tendency to render 'form' independent of 'content' — or as it used to be put, 'form' of 'function' — is nothing new. In the modern history of machines (and I refer to these in an inclusive sense), the adoption of the casing has introduced a substantial change: all of a sudden, machines can be an object attracting aesthetic judgements. Before the casing was introduced, positing the problem of the beauty of a machine would have seemed absurd.

In most cases, one might imagine, machines without a protective cases were not well-received. Quite the contrary. They were usually seen as terrifying and absolutely outside the aesthetic sphere. When enclosed within a casing and thus rendered invisible, they acquired form, at least vicariously, and so became the object of aesthetic evaluation. In the case of the car, this is certainly true. However, we must admit that our aesthetic opinions on the form of cars, as with all aesthetic opinions, cannot have a universal character. The models the managers of General Motors, Chrysler and Ford (in the post-Henry Ford era) considered to be 'beautiful cars,' were regarded by many in Europe as being of an almost perverse ugliness. And, on the other hand, these same managers, assisted by a considerable crowd of marketing experts, considered European cars to be anti-aesthetic. And, which was worse as far as they were concerned, the expression of an elitist and decadent taste.

However it may be, recalling the relativism of human judgements in this field does not wipe out the obvious fact that the question of the beauty of a car has nevertheless a certain relevance. So, for instance, when we are spectators at a race of classic cars, it is hard not to be struck by the formal refinement of these vehicles. For example, I have in mind such cars as the Hispano-Suiza (1919), the Isotta Fraschini (1920) and the Bugatti 57 (1937). Usually, these are perfectly operational (or almost), doubtless thanks to the almost maniacal care and maintenance of their owners.

A this point, the question arises spontaneously: if these cars, which we now consider to be captivatingly beautiful, were to cease to work tomorrow, would their aesthetic value remain unchanged? I believe that they would maintain at least a relevant part, if not all, of their charm. I recognize, however, that this bears a risk that should not be undervalued. Namely, unwittingly supporting an aberrant formalism that is much in vogue today: the idea that cars are nothing more than 'fine sculptures on four wheels.' This is the idea supported by the ineffable Tom Wolfe, who once described a car as 'a pure piece of abstract, curvilinear sculpture,' adding: 'If Brancusi is worth anything, then this [the car] should also be placed on a pedestal.'

Bibliography

Guillaume Apollinaire, 'La petite auto,' in *Poésie* (French and Italian facing text), Newton Compton, Rome 1974, p. 220.
Jean (Hans) Arp, 'Le Style Eléphant contre le Style Bidet' (1937), in Jean Arp, *Jours effeuillés. Poèmes, Essais, Souvenirs, 1920-1965*, Gallimard, Paris 1966, p. 109.
J.G. Ballard, *Crash*, Jonathan Cape, London 1973.
Gene Balsley, 'Detroit versus the Hot-Rod' (1950), in Richard Rhodes (editor), *Visions of Technology*, Simon and Schuster, New York 1999.
Roland Barthes, 'La nouvelle Citroën,' in Roland Barthes, *Mythologies* (1957), Seuil, Paris 1970, p. 150.
Walter Benjamin, 'Theorie des deutschen Faschismus' (1930), in *Gesammelte Schriften*, vol. III, Suhrkamp, Frankfurt am Main 1972, p. 238.
Reuel Denney, 'The Plastic Machines,' in Reuel Denney, *The Astonished Muse*, The University of Chicago Press, Chicago 1957, p. 147.
Jane Holtz Kay, *Asphalt Nation. How the Automobile Took over America and how We Can Take it Back*, University of California Press, Berkeley (California) 1997.
Sinclair Lewis, *Babbit*, Bantam Books, New York 1998.
Tomás Maldonado, 'Disegno e le nuove prospettive industriali,' Conference held at the Grande Exposition Universelle held in Brussels (Expo '58), 18 September 1958, in Tomás Maldonado, *Avanguardia e Razionalità*, Einaudi, Turin 1974.
Tomás Maldonado, 'L'automobile: merce regina' (1972), in Tomás Maldonado, *Avanguardia*... cit.
Tomás Maldonado, *Disegno industriale un riesame*, Feltrinelli, Milan 1976, pp. 25-26.
Marcel Proust, 'Impressions de route in automobile,' in *Le Figaro*, 19 novembre 1907.
Kenneth R. Schneider, *Autokind versus Mankind*, W.W. Norton and Co., New York 1971.
Coco Shinomiya, *Hot Rods & Custom Cars*, Vintage Speed Graphics, Introduction by Tony Thacker, Taschen, Cologne 2004.
Alfred P. Sloan, *My Years with General Motors* (1963), Doubleday, New York 1990, p. 246.
Lawrence J. White, *The Automobile Industry since 1945*, Harvard University Press, Cambridge (Massachusetts) 1971.
John Wickersham, Introduction to Sinclair Lewis, *Babbit*, Bantam Books, New York 1998, p. XVII.
Tom Wolfe, *The Kandy-Kolored Tangerine-Flake Streamline Baby*, Farrat, Strauss & Giroux, New York 1965, p. 83.

My Dream Cars

Giampaolo Fabris

'When one could afford to abandon the Lambretta, the great love of the average Italian in those years was the "machine" [commonly used antonomastically in Italy to refer to a motor car; translator's note]. More even than one's football team. More than one's girlfriend. More than one's wife and children.' Thus did Dino Risi,[1] director of the cult film, *Il sorpasso*, evoke a time in which 'the dream of every Italian was a light-silver, Lancia Aurelia convertible; a model that had just come out.'

We are in the early 1960s, and the economic miracle, which changed the country's face over the past decade, is still in the air. Perhaps it is unfair to recall only the Lambretta and not the Vespa; just as the country was divided into fans of Coppi and fans of Bartali (two world-class cyclists), so it was divided and took the side of the two scooter brands. Me for Bartali and the Lambretta. The car had from the start of the century been the focus of great admiration and reverence, of a respectful but distant, unattainable astonishment. It provoked more wonder and envy than any true emotive involvement, but in these years it began to become an object of shared love, of collective appeal, of desire. Because, with the more economical models (typified by the success of the Seicento), it became accessible to more than a restricted circle of wealthy individuals; increasingly wide sections of the population could aspire to a car. It is true that the purchase of a car is the item — even today — that weighs most on a family's budget after that of the home, and it implies a disbursement requiring some hard thought. However, it increasingly became part of that 'standard package' (Riesman) that Alberoni and I defined as 'consumption for citizenship' in just those years. In other words, goods that one 'must' have in order to feel oneself fully a citizen of society in the historic period in which we live.

A vehicle that confirms one's entrance into the world of drivers, the initiation into such a different way of travelling, the ability to move freely without the constriction of timetables, the access into the mythical world of free time needed no further legitimization: and yet it obtains it fully thanks to a world that is extremely rich and varied in terms of symbolic meanings determining their use. Not only cultural — such as the social duty of possession — but also emotive and in terms of affection. Initially, it was notions of status and the prestige of owning a car that prevailed — in later years, these same meanings would no longer be conveyed by the simple possession of a car, but would be qualified and promoted by the brand/model — as it conferred social respectability in a historic period in which mechanisms of emulation or ostentation associated with status — 'keeping up with the Jones,' in other words — were strongly rooted. In the semeiotic imagination, the car had an ambiguous range of meanings, sharing male/phallic significance (witness the mythical black E Type Jaguar of Diabolik, a cartoon character criminal) and feminine/maternal ones. These were often accentuated by the manufacturers in designing streamline forms, and in the attribution of characteristics of robustness and power (breaking down was not just objectively tiresome, but deep down it came to be regarded as even more disturbing as it was regarded as the public display of one's impotence). The car was not only male, but also maternal, bearing notions of care and giving, and it stimulated a sort of intrauterine regression into a space in which one could feel safe, protected, at

[1] Interview in *La Repubblica* by Irene Bignardi, 9 August 2006.

home even when far away. It was both alcove and work tool, and part of the domestic landscape to the point of becoming a sort of family member with which processes of projected identification are activated: the car was given affectionate nicknames, became the object of constant attention, of care verging on cuddling. The fact that the largest company in Italy was a car manufacturer, and that other major marques — from historical ones such as Isotta Fraschini and Bugatti to today's Alfa Romeo and Lancia — were also Italian, that the great protagonist of Grand Prix racing — Ferrari — was Italian too, as are the best designers in the car sector, certainly helped to spread increasing goodwill with regard to the car in this country. These were the years in which major infrastructure changed the geography of Italy — with the north-south *Autostrada del Sole*, for instance — in order to enable improved circulation of traffic. Such motorways gave access to the new cathedrals, the *Autogrill* motorway service areas, which were the confirmation of modernity and appeal; this in a country of taverns and little restaurants.

The car, the Italian car, would become an important icon at MoMA; it represents the ideal expression of the best of industrial design. Through cinema first of all, and subsequently through television, it became an integral part of the star system. Gradually, almost without anyone noticing, Italians became car-dependent: a car was used even to buy cigarettes at the street corner. It became common practice for all to spend Saturday morning dedicated to the car: it would be washed, polished, beautified in the garage at home or by some fountain out in the suburbs. It was by now indispensable for any journey, to highlight one's independence, but it also took on overtones of practising a sport: the ability to drive stimulated pride and increased self-respect.

However, half a century after these first exciting years — now that mass motorization is a thing of the past — what remains of all this? Plenty. The consolidated relationship of love between Italians and their car — Italy is second only to Luxembourg in the ratio of cars to inhabitants — is showing no signs of fading. Much time has passed since the period when the car lost its position of being reserved for a wealthy few, and nor is it a status symbol conferring prestige any more, and yet it continues to exert a strong attraction on the majority of Italians. 70% of drivers agree with the statement: 'A car for me is not just a means of transport, but also a pleasure.' This percentage has remained substantially unchanged in the past ten years, and a not much lower percentage (62%) states that 'I greatly enjoy driving' (the highest figure in the past 15 years: source, GPF). It is certainly true that the statement, 'If I could, I would get by without a car,' is also at its historical peak at the moment, but there is a widespread awareness that the use of the car is unavoidable. This datum should thus be seen in terms of a reaction against the cost of the car — aggravated by taxes, fuel costs, parking — and the problems of traffic congestion, rather than as a disenchantment with the car *per se*.

The prevalently functional and instrumental use — foreseen by many as the consequence of the entry of the market into a mature phase — is still to come. The car remains, despite an almost universal penetration, a widespread object of desire. Able to generate a relationship shot through with emotiveness and affectivity. We may well ask ourselves why this occurs.

A production that is particularly attentive to the evolution of manifest or latent requests emerging from the market and is so willing to satisfy them has certainly been an influence, and in this it is unlike what has occurred in many other sectors. It distributes the offer and maintains a long life-cycle for historic models with a happy mix and updates of equipment, technological innovation, iconic elements and symbols, etc. Moreover, after a long period of uniformity of models and of loss of distinctive signs — as though the wind tunnel and Cd coefficients had become the true demiurges of design — production has changed tack to satisfy the growing demand for differentiation, throwing by now consolidated aesthetic stylemes. In so doing, it has also recovered the original symbolic and semiotic capital. Comfort, ride and versatility of the car have in recent years made giant leaps forward.

Another influence has been a parallel development in a demanding, mature request. From the need for a car expressed by customers, there has been a shift to the desire for a car, or indeed a desire for more than one car. The need responds to a principle of reality, the de-

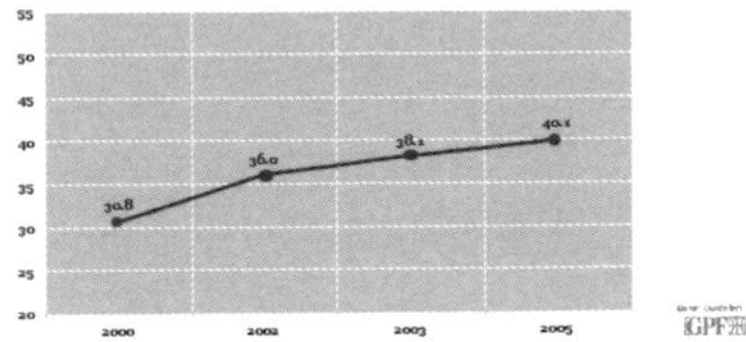

1. 'When I buy a car, I want one that makes my heart beat faster' (% in agreement)

sire to a principle of pleasure, of dream, of diversion and is more subject to emotions. The desire is one for several cars differentiated by the main modes of use (work, free time, urban traffic) and by family members (prestigious car for the head of the family, the city car mainly destined for women, the fun, sporty or cheap car for the children). Thus it is that the market ceiling — which appeared almost unbreakable: one car per family — has actually continued to rise.

The motivations for using a car have also increased in number progressively. Those associated with the symbolism of status have dropped away but those connected to free time, comfort, flexibility of use, the request for hybrid models (SUVs for town use, family coupés, coupé cabriolets, and so on) are constantly on the increase. This is a use of the car that has today lost its most naïve connotations — such as the anthropomorphism of the car – but which heightens its meanings of expression of identity, meets the strong demand for autonomy and individualism and expands its play-related significance. Important changes in production on a scale considered major and topical — safety, eco-compatibility — have accentuated the goodwill for the car and favoured the renewal of the pool.

The long-standing love affair between Italians and the car now that mass motorisation has been confirmed for some years, therefore, shows no sign of waning. Despite the growing maturity of the market, the car continues to be considered a major object of desire by a substantial part of the Italian population. In doing so, it has given lie to all the hasty but strongly entrenched and widespread forecasts that, with time, the car would be used solely in functional terms, and that there would be a substantial disengagement in terms of affectivity. The feature of the car that makes the heart beat faster when choosing a model to buy registers a growing consensus (fig. 1).

Besides, the reappraisal of many clichés once considered to be self-evident truths, has been a constant in the car world. Until some time ago, forecasts indicated that inevitable processes of concentration would have led to a substantial reduction in the number of marques. Exactly the opposite has occurred. It is hard to believe but in Italy today, some 50 marques compete, offering over 1500 different models and versions. Even the hypothesized trend towards specialization in production has proven to be wrong. The trend for a single marque is now towards making everything: from the utility car to Formula One engines, from multipurpose vehicles to roadsters. A single model embraces an increasingly vast range: from 1.6 to 3.2 litre engines, 100 to 320 hp (BMW 3/M3 – Audi A4/S4). The same car often appears in six different versions: hatchback, saloon, coupé, convertible, estate car, multipurpose vehicle. The same differentiation between general and specialized marques which used to give a basic orientation within the products offered, seems ever less distinct. On the one side, we note a downgrading of specialized marques (Mercedes Class A/Smart, Audi A3/A2), and on the other, the upgrading of general marques. This second process can take place both by using one's own marque (VW), by acquiring a prestige marque (Ford/Jaguar), or by creating a marque *ex novo* (Lexus, Infinity).

If we take a step from what is offered to what is requested, the changes — beyond the fact of continued investment in cars — are no less. Perhaps the most significant fact is a paradigm shift from factors that we might define structural to the car to superstructural dimensions. The first — reliability, traditional performance (speed, acceleration, road-holding, braking, etc.), active and passive safety, durability — are now considered to be prerequisites. A sort of *conditio sine qua non*. In the sense that we expect every vehicle — from a small utility to the top-of-the-range model — to offer these to the greatest degree. In other words, the idea that a car might have any faults in any of these departments is now completely inadmissible. Particular criticism is provoked when a marque demands a supplementary cost in this area, as it is seen as placing an essential feature at the same level as a sort of optional. For example, making one pay for a third airbag. If anything, within this structural dimension, it is other, 'softer' types of performance to focus the attention and interest of the users, such as eco-compatibility, reduced consumption, compactness, versatility, adaptability to free time.

Superstructural aspects, those we might dub 'meta benefits' to reconnect to the 'consumer benefits' the marketing efforts concentrate upon, are increasingly important. These become the true protagonists when it comes to choosing a car. First of all comes the aesthetics of the car. When we ask users to indicate the reasons for choosing a model they intend to purchase, 'a design I like' comes in first place (86% of drivers, and 90% of future drivers). For women, this is even more important than for men (89% as against 84% of men). These are followed some way behind by the structural characteristics that traditionally describe the performance of a car. There is thus a growing emphasis on the aesthetic angle, which is required to include a pleasing distinction and personality. Nothing seems less topical than the uniform styling of a recent past, when the primacy of ergonomics and the wind tunnel had produced a whole generation of cars that increasingly resembled each other. Naturally, there is a great variation in the evaluation of aesthetic appreciation, but there are nevertheless some important constants. Such as the request for coherence between design and the values of the brand/image, the primacy of form/volume on the design/line, a mistrust of a strong but gratuitous design which tends to age rapidly, a global perception which also includes the layout of the interior.

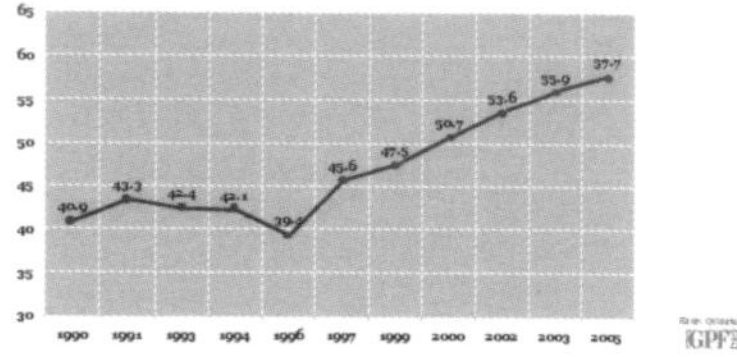

2. 'A car should express the personality of the person drving it'
(% in agreement)

Research seems to agree in highlighting the fact that the love affair with the car has never been interrupted. Even now that the honeymoon should have been over for quite some time. While some symbolic features have vanished, other new ones have appeared, and these are no less important for the individual.

The car continues to be perceived as one of the most important vehicles for conveying the sense of oneself. Not of prestige or social status as in the past but of one's personality, good taste, values, lifestyle. The car seen as expression of one's personality reaches the maximum consensus in these years (fig. 2).

The car strengthened its position as a symbol and, at the same time, as an instrument of autonomy, independence, freedom of movement. Often, this last was, in synechdotal manner, dubbed freedom *tout court*. Emotive involvement and active affective bonds remain firmly established in relationships with the car. Driving for many represents a real source of pleasure. The long-lasting interest in speed — which might be seen as being in contrast with an increasingly aware need for safety — is motivated above all in terms of power geared towards safety. Requests for comfort and improved ride are on the increase: the car is frequently seen as a second home, or indeed, sometimes as one's actual home as compared with the real one which belongs to the whole family. The greater attention paid to forms and design by today's users, is part of that more global process of aestheticisation of everyday life which involves all objects generally. Moreover, the increasing trend towards a uniform design for cars which had developed in recent decades has decreased considerably in the recent past. In recent years, manufacturers have preferred to sacrifice a few mph or the saving of a few drops per litre of petrol in favour of the insistent demands from users for cars with personality and originality in their looks. As for the prevalence of rounded forms, in *La Repubblica* Michele Serra wrote that one can sense the absence of Roland Barthes for their interpretation. I do not believe this is necessary. The explanation is actually very simple. In a social scenario of growing promotion of female values, the car also loses its male connotations of penetration to adjust to this new epochal trend. Which, besides, cuts transversally across every sector of consumption. In the food industry, it expresses itself through lightness, in clothes through soft garments, in home *décor* through soft furnishings, pastel colours and so on.

Saloon cars will continue to occupy a significant segment of the market. But their absolute primacy has been threatened. Less and less do they appear as synonyms of prestige, as they did in the past. The classy car *par excellence*, this was a model which one needed only to own for it to confer social standing and sprinkle star dust over the buyer. It still expresses social visibility and status when it is a major marque, but it is the latter that confers added value in terms of prestige. In other words, the process whereby it was the saloon that used to confer class and authoratativeness on its producer has been overturned; today, it is the producer that promotes the saloon to those levels of status it is no longer able to express by itself.

The supremacy of the saloon has marked a long period in the history of the car. That prestige which, in the 1930s, Vincenzo Lancia indicated as being measured by 'the length of the bonnet,' in the saloon seemed to migrate to the length of the boot. Three volumes had imposed themselves as the antonomastic *Gestalt* of the car sector: they provided the right form, the paradigm of excellence. Three volumes (bonnet, interior, boot) conveyed class, urbanity, elegance. One could not even imagine appearing at important social occasions except at the wheel of a saloon car.

It is with the latest generation of hatchbacks — that which was heralded by the arrival of the Golf — that the primacy of the saloon began to be openly questioned. The hatchback, previously considered little more than the equal of a utility car, seemed to assure more space and comfort for a given length. But it is on the front of cultural references, traditionally the strong point of the saloon, that the hatchbacks play their trump card. They appear more attuned to the new lifestyles and modes of use of the car. In aesthetic terms too, which had favoured the saloon and penalized all other types of car, outsiders now seem to be favoured. Besides, it is well-known that the rear of the car is one of the most problematic areas when designing a vehicle. It is here that it is hardest to maintain the tension of the lines. Where it is easiest to betray a drop in tone. For hatchbacks, it is much easier to tackle this area. Revealing just how much water has passed under the bridge since the saloon could in aesthetic terms regard itself in a self-referential manner, I remember a slogan used for the Audi A6: 'does a saloon have to look like a saloon?' Aesthetics are anyway strongly conditioned by the spirit of the time, by the types of products offered by the industry, by the success of the marques and models which, increasingly, do not include saloons as their protagonists.

While it was the modern hatchbacks to question the status of saloon cars initially, other types of vehicle would carry forward this process on a model that had once seemed the most solid guarantee of quality. In the 1990s, the estate car, once considered little more than a work horse, gained notable public success in terms of desirability. At least initially, they became the ideal car for outdoor hobbies to be cultivated far from home. Then, they were transformed into an emotionally involving car for the weekend and holidays. The car in which, with all the family, one could follow the golden roads of one's free time. The car which, without too many compromises, enabled the driver to feel comfortable at work too. Many marques offer saloon and estate versions of the same car, and the latter are aimed at a younger and more trendy public.

Other types of vehicle help to erode what used to be a clear leadership. The sports cars — coupés and convertibles — are no longer considered just a second car. Formerly uncomfortable and noisy, reserved for small niches of enthusiasts, and of no interest to the less young or those with a family, they are now clearly changing their user base. Softening their original specifications, they are transforming themselves into versatile, up-to-date cars, which interpret prestige in a more modern manner. And they also succeed in conferring connotations of dynamism and youth, which perfectly match their driving pleasure.

In the long list of new competitors, recent multipurpose vehicles are further reducing the former charisma of the saloon. Capacious and functional, of extraordinary versatility, they are now acquiring an aesthetic appreciation which had been a strong deterrent when they first came out. The multipurpose vehicle offers an excellent compromise in terms of spaciousness, 'liveability,' comfort, adaptability to all the family's requirements. It has become extremely competitive in exactly those areas that had traditionally been the strong point of the estate car. They also bring with them a hint of something new, of a greater response to new lifestyles, to the needs of the new family. They offer those emotions — and emotions play a significant role in the purchase of a car — that the estate car now finds it harder to stimulate. The Renault Scenic, the Opel Zafira, the Fiat Multipla and the Espace are successful multipurpose vehicles that have as much to offer as the classic performance of the estate car. And, more, they present themselves as the exponents of a new generation. We should not forget that the consumer is always on the lookout for novelty, both with his first purchase and then when seeking a replacement. He wishes to try out new solutions and new models even if his previous choices were by and large satisfactory.

But perhaps the most emblematic phenomenon of the new millennium is the establishment of the SUV (Sport Utilities Vehicles). These vehicles are a sort of luxury and highly flexible off-road car enabling a driver to do truly anything he wishes. They can be easily driven around town, parked on pavements, taken off road; even, at least in one's dreams, driven across deserts. The driver feels protected by a vehicle considered to be safe, enveloped in a large protective screen. Here is a muscular and elegant vehicle providing high top speeds and acceleration. Above all, it is a powerful car. The impression is that with a driving position higher than in other cars, one dominates the road and other drivers. Who are literally looked down upon from above, aware that almost certainly they cannot compete in terms of performance. This new segment is made up of vehicles such as the BMW X5, the Mercedes M Class, the Renault Grand Cherokee and, at lower price levels, the Honda HRV and the Land Rover Freelander, are all highly successful, some of them indeed, a must in terms of status symbol. For a long time, I have explored the reasons for the success of the SUVs[2] and of the hatred they provoke ('fascist,' polluting, arrogant cars, that should pay higher taxes, etc.).

It is surprising to note, given the dynamism of the car manufacturers, the process of innovation which is perhaps faster in this sector than others, and the continuous entry of new technologies, how durable many model names have proven to be. The current version of a given name has little in common with the original model. Indeed, in many cases, it does not resemble it at all. And yet the name has remained the same.

Consider the more than 30 years of the Golf. The Golf itself had an illustrious precedent, the Beetle, which dominated the markets for decades, and has now returned following popular demand, and with the same name. And yet the Golf shows no sign of old age and continues to sit at the top of its segment. Similar analogies may be made for the Ford Fiesta and the Honda Civic. Fiat has its Panda, and although in this case its origins are more recent, the Punto has given rise to a vast range of models and versions appearing over the years. In some cases, moreover, there is a nostalgic return, together with design references, to names abandoned years ago: the Cinquecento, the Seicento and the Multipla.

How is it that we see such a phenomenon, which might, after all, compromise the perception of innovations introduced with the new models? Is there not a risk of offsetting the desire for novelty, which is often one of the important reasons for abandoning/choosing a car? The reasons are many and considerable. First of all, having a tradition of continuous improvements behind one — by which the construction of the marque becomes a sort of work in progress — increases trust in the latest models. Introducing a new marque in a hyper-competitive and overcrowded market of brands, even with a powerful corporate group behind the promotion, is increasingly risky. The launch of a new product, moreover, that can make use of a consolidated brand costs only a fraction of the launch of a product with a completely new name. In the sector of major consumer goods, one study (Kapferer) indicates that after three years, only 30% of new brands survive, while this rises to 50% if the new products have been launched with the important support of a pre-existing name. Other research indicates that over a period of ten years, in American supermarkets, over two thirds of the success stories were credited to a line extension of existing brands rather than to entirely new brands.

Of course, it is possible that what takes place in the mass consumption market cannot be completely transferred to the car sector. But the general outline of the conclusions cannot be so very different. Without the protective umbrella of a prestigious name, even the most technically perfect product will find it hard to carve a foothold for itself.

As a result, the policy of some marques of planning the removal of a make when its sales start to droop — rather than to revitalize it with new engines or models — could prove a serious error. Because the risk is that of losing a symbolic heritage represented by the name of the make which, in increasingly crowded markets, can transform itself into a powerful com-

[2] Giampaolo Fabris, *Il nuovo consumatore, verso il post-moderno*, Franco Angeli, Milan 2004.

petitive asset. Naturally, there are major caveats and exceptions. The models that follow on from an original have to fit into a similar design philosophy, into an analogous product concept. The performance or symbolic benefits the consumer finds important must be carried over into the new production. The overall *Gestalt* must also remain substantially the same. If, to look back at our previous example, we observe the Golf, we can note that over the years the car has certainly changed but it continues to adhere to its original premise. Even the design maintains those stylemes that guaranteed it its early success: the same alternation of volumes, the same proportions. Naturally, the presupposition is that the archetypical product was successful. When a model differs too much from the founding characteristics, the marque may encounter difficulties (for example, the Variant for the Golf) and even destabilize the marque. So in the case of a truly different product — that is, when this is not only unlike the marque's values but also presents strongly innovative characteristics — it is better to adopt an entirely new name. This emphasizes the discontinuity introduced by the new model.

We may ask ourselves whether in a given historic period, such as that we are currently living through, in which the consumer demonstrates increasing lack of fidelity to a marque, not because of disenchantment but simply to manifest his autonomy and strong inclination to experiment, this common practice will continue to be a successful one. We believe so. Although sometimes the values of the corporate group — more important in the car sector than in most others — are in themselves sufficient to provide a certificate of credibility and value to a new product.

A last point. In the semiosphere, the space occupied by the car by far exceeds the duration of its fruition. We talk about cars — the traditional subject of men's conversations: 'women and cars' — we read about cars — a whole lively publishing sector has grown up in Italy around the institution that is *Quattroruote* — we dream about cars and our next purchase, and carefully keep track of all the main innovations in the sector (and these are many and continuous). While collecting cars is something involving only the happy few, it is because it requires plenty of space and, above all, lots of money, otherwise cars or their simulacra would have taken the place of the former Lari and Penati in many households. In reconstructing personal biographies, it is interesting how these are marked by the possession and in many cases by the nostalgic memory of cars owned. Marques and models have become clear cult objects. In the new tribes populating the post-modern society (one marque, one model), the car frequently takes on a totemic significance, a focus of identity for the tribe.

Paradoxically, the love affair we have described could, instead of heading for the sunset, be destined for a second youth and start off on a new phase of growth. Because the other half of the sky — the car has always been seen mainly in masculine terms — is impetuously breaking into the *hortum clausum* from which it had been locked out. The number of women passing their driving test — for decades the relationship was of one to four or five in favour of men — is now the same as for men. Advertising campaigns in which the (female) protagonist throws away her wedding ring but proudly holds on to her car keys (if I am not mistaken, the original of this idea was by VW, the real genius in car advertising) or similar versions, are now two a penny. If car manufacturers were to spend less resources on fantasizing about unrealistic models for women and were to start a serious dialogue with the new users, we might well witness the entry of new, major segments of the population into this world of beating hearts and love affairs.

The History of a Legend

History Belongs to the Winners

Adolfo Orsi

Given that at least so far, the internal combustion engine is the form of propulsion to have triumphed, as it has powers and continues to power virtually all the cars ever built, the history books usually credit the invention of the motor car to Benz and Daimler. The automobile[1], powered by an internal combustion engine, was invented in Germany in 1886: almost at the same time and only a few dozen kilometres away from each other although quite unaware of the existence of the other, Karl Benz and Gottlieb Daimler[2] put their machines on the road. Benz's machine had three wheels, Daimler's four.

The almost simultaneous birth of the car shows that the time was right, that the answers were in the air. Internal combustion engines, the first functioning models of which were made in Italy by Eugenio Barsanti and Felice Matteucci[3] of Lucca (fig. 1), had already been in stationary use for industrial purposes for about 20 years, but they were extremely heavy. It was thus necessary for them to be miniaturized and made more efficient and simpler to use.

Benz and Daimler had the merit of concluding a cycle or of opening a new one, if we prefer, but this was made possible by the experience, research and studies of the numerous other 'experimenters' who had preceded them.

However, if we wish to be quite accurate, the first 'auto-mobile' — machines able to move by themselves — came far earlier and were different: they were propelled by steam.

The first of all dates from France in 1769: this was 'Cugnot's wagon' (fig. 11), which was not so much a car as a military tricycle, designed to transport artillery. Bureaucratic problems, followed by the Revolution finally killed off the project.[4] By the start of the 19th century, however, steam engines were in regular use in industry and had already undergone some development. It is understandable, therefore, that enormous carriages should be made in Britain, the first country to undergo industrialization, used for regular public transport and to compete with steam-powered trains. In 1838, Walter Hancock, one of these English manufacturers, used to meander up and down Hyde Park in his personal steam-powered, four-seater Phaeton. However, these were one-off models for the use of their inventors, and not made for sale. For instance, in Italy too a two-cylinder steam engine was attached to a Landau carriage built to be horse-drawn: this was Bordino's 'Carrozza,' built at the military arsenal of Turin, and still on view today at the Museo Biscaretti in Turin.

But it was France that had the most users of steam traction in the second half of the 19th century: among these was Amédée Bollée, who built several increasingly efficient models from 1872 onwards, and Léon Serpollet, who produced about a thousand of these machines until 1907. A steam-powered Serpollet, called 'Œuf de Pâques' ('Easter Egg') beat the world speed record (until then held by Jenatzy with an electric-powered vehicle), in Nice in 1902 at over 120 kph along the Promenade des Anglais. Another Frenchman, Georges Bouton, an engineer who would later play an important part in internal combustion engines, also initially used steam engines. In 1884, Bouton, financed by Marquis Albert de Dion,[5] driving a steam-powered quadricycle, took part in what was considered to be the first car race in history, launched by *Le Petit Journal* newspaper, astonishing the public

[1] The word is French in origin and was first used as an adjective, as in the phrase 'voiture automobile.' Only in 1890 was the word used as a noun; after an animated discussion, it was decided to make it a feminine noun, as it derived from the phrase 'voiture automobile,' in which 'voiture' is itself feminine. In Italy, a male version was initially preferred, but Senator Agnelli called on Gabriele d'Annunzio to resolve the issue, and in 1926 he declared 'L'automobile è femminile' ('The car is feminine').

[2] History resulted in the two uniting their skills in 1924 to form the Daimler-Benz company.

[3] Father Eugenio Barsanti and engineer Felice Matteucci deposited a sealed report at the Accademia dei Georgofili in Florence on 5 June, 1853, concerning their trials with building an engine that was later patented in England in 1854. In 1856, an engine, which operated a drill and shears, was in use at the Officine Ferroviarie at the Maria Antonia railway station in Florence. In 2004, the Deutsches Museum in Munich recognized that Barsanti and Matteucci were effectively first with their invention.

[4] The second example built was miraculously saved and can still be seen today at the Musée Conservatoire des Arts et Métiers in Paris.

[5] In 1896, Marquis Albert De Dion founded the Automobile Club de France, the first car association in the world.

with speeds never before reached. In 1888, De Dion-Bouton began selling steam vehicles, featuring a new rear-mounted engine, a solution still adopted 120 years later in some sports cars. But the true stars in the steam-powered car sector were American twins Francis and Freeland Stanley, already inventors of the machine which revolutionized the production of photographic plates. With their marques — Locomobile (fig. 2), Mobile and, later, Stanley — the Stanley brothers outsold all the other American manufacturers of engines in 1899 and 1900. The advantages of steam were: silent running, total absence of vibration, elimination of gears. The disadvantages were the time (45 minutes) needed to heat the water and pressurize the engine, following which it had to be carefully watched, and short range, with the water tank of 85 litres needing to be filled every 20 miles or so, thus requiring a careful planning of watering stops at the homes of friends and/or public fountains for every journey.

1. The first internal combustion engine by Barsanti and Matteucci, patented in 1854

The other type of traction, which initially enjoyed great success, at least in America, was electric: New York in 1894 saw the first electric taxis, and in 1899 the first man to exceed 100 kph was the Belgian Camille Jenatzy with his electric-powered torpedo-like 'La Jamais Contente.' In 1904, no less than a third of the entire fleet of American cars was electric. These vehicles (fig. 3) were favoured by the emancipated ladies of high society, especially in large cities like New York. At the time, indeed, one of the handicaps of internal-combustion engines was the difficulty in getting the engine started, as this required use of the starting handle, which in turn needed a strong set of (male) muscles. Electric cars could instead be used independently by ladies. Moreover, the front seats could be turned to face backwards to provide a little drawing room, ideal for a chat. Double driving controls were also available as an optional extra: the vehicle could be driven from the back seats using the tiller. Another handicap faced by internal-combustion engines was the lack of petrol stations as we understand them: until around 1920 petrol was bought in tin cans from drug stores. Electricity to charge the heavy batteries, on the other hand, was available in the home. The advantages of electric traction were completely silent running, absence of gear shifts, and ease of use. The disadvantages were low speed, inability to climb hills and a range of just 80 kilometres between charges. These vehicles were thus suited to use around town, but not for voyages further afield. One of the great engineers in car history, Ferdinand Porsche of Austria, also designed a highly advanced vehicle in 1899 for Lohner, equipped with two electric motors mounted on the front wheels, thereby eliminating any loss in power resulting from the transmission. And in 1900, he built the 'Semper vivus' (fig. 4), a 'hybrid' vehicle also fitted with two petrol engines, which remained in production until 1910. So there is nothing new under the sun. But the problems of the autonomy and weight of the batteries (still a problem today) ground electric traction to a halt, to return once more only during the oil crisis.

2. The steam-powered Locomobile, designed by twins Francis and Freeland Stanley, 1899

3. An advertisement for Baker Electrics in *Life* Magazine, 1914

The electric and steam-powered cars, which had provided stiff competition to internal-combustion engines, were forced to surrender in the wake of improvements made to the petrol engines on an almost daily basis, rendering them more efficient, functional and easy to use.

The motor car was still accessible only to a wealthy few: the price was high and a full-time chauffeur was also a must. This professional figure, which today has vanished, was simultaneously driver and mechanic: at least two hours before departure, he would check and prepare the vehicle and for at least two or three hours after, would be involved in cleaning and greasing it. An outside mechanic would be called in only for major jobs; moreover, the means of transport was so new that there were no 'specialized workshops' as yet. The first repairmen were carpenters, used to fixing carriages and wagons, and bicycle repairers, supplied with the right tools (such as spanners) and a greater mechanical sensibility. Often, a carpenter would make new replacement parts completely from scratch. Indeed, the first spare parts only began to appear with the onset of mass production, at the time of the Ford Model T.

4. The Lohner 'Semper vivus' hybrid, designed by Ferdinand Porsche, 1900

As we have seen, the motor car powered by the internal combustion engine was born in Germany, but it was in France that it flourished to the greatest extent in the last decade of the 19th century. The shape of cars to come was first created by Panhard et Levassor in 1891 (fig. 5): fitted with a twin-cylinder Daimler engine, it was the first vehicle to have the engine mounted at the front, protected from the elements in a box called the 'capot.' For the first time, the engine was mounted longitudinally; in future, this solution would make it possible to fit engines with a larger number of cylinders simply by extending the length of the bonnet. Equally revolutionary was the transmission: instead of the pulleys and belts used hitherto, inherited from the stationary engines used to power machinery, Panhard presented a precursor of the gearbox, with three gears. The gears still worked in the open air, lubricated, as the English writer, Anthony Bird, wrote, 'with grease, dust from the road and optimism in equal measure.' There were two brakes, one working on the rear wheels, the other on the transmission shaft, and both were linked to the clutch, so that when they were activated, the engine would be uncoupled. There was no accelerator as yet and the engine always turned over at maximum power, which in the case of the Daimler engine meant 750 rpm! This vehicle represented the state of the art in 1891: some have written that the Old Testament of the car ends at the time in which Panhard et Levassor (and the equally innovative Peugeot) entered the car industry: from then on, it was the New Testament, with about ten years featuring not only great innovation but also, for the first time, a market in which clients sought the new products. This was still a small number of customers, an élite, but one that increasingly believed in the benefits of freedom and independence a car can provide. For example, country doctors[6], now able to reach even their furthest patients conveniently, were enthusiastic promoters of this prodigy of modernity.

5. In 1921, 30 years after its construction, the fifth example of the Panhard et Levassor of 1891 was still regularly used by abbé Gavois

In 1891, cars were still fitted with wooden wheels with metal reinforcing and a sold rubber tyre. Lighter cars boasted wire wheels with a similar solid tyre. Bicycles were just then beginning to sport the first pneumatic tyres (with an air chamber), made by John Dunlop in England. By chance, a cyclist happened to suffer a puncture a few hundred yards from the Michelin factory at Clermont Ferrand, which was already active in the manufacture of rubber articles. Brothers André and Edouard Michelin were able to witness the problems involved with repairing it, as the tyre was attached to the wooden rim with a canvas strip bearing gummed and glued linen laces. The repair took three hours, as well as a night to allow the glue to dry. As a result, the brothers developed the 'air wheel' for the bicycle, with an independent air chamber — the inner tube — and with the gummed canvas cover latched to the rim with two little circles of metal linked with bolts. Races were fundamental both to develop the product and to promote it. These appeared with the first cars and proved to be the perfect promotional tool. It was in and for races that numerous devices were developed and later used in everyday vehicles; in history, racing really has helped develop the car. The Michelin brothers also went down this road: in the Paris-Bordeaux-Paris of 1895, they fitted pneumatic tyres to their 'Eclair,' a modified Peugeot. This was the first time in history. They had to stop 50 or 60 times because of punctures, but they arrived at the finish line. Few realized that a new era was born: that of the removable tyre (fig. 6), making not only for a more comfortable ride for the passengers and more silent traffic in towns, but also and above all the possibility of building vehicles that did not need to be oversized to cope with vibration and shaking. They could thus be lighter, offer better performance and were less expensive to produce.

6. In 1900, one or more tyre changes during the course of a day's drive was quite normal

A statistic of 1899 reveals that no less than 619 manufacturers of the 888 in Europe were French, as were 1095 repair mechanics out of the 1298 around the continent. *Fin-de-siècle* Paris was the most lively of the cities, and it was here that the 'horseless carriage' was received most warmly. But beyond the ocean too, in the United States, the car found equally fertile terrain. It was in America that the car passed from a phase we might define 'craftsmanlike' to an 'industrial' one, and this thanks to Ransome Olds and Henry Ford.

Olds was one of the pioneers of this process, and in 1903, the Oldsmobile Curved Dash, a simple, reliable and cheap (it cost 600 $) vehicle (powered by a single-cylinder engine) was the best selling car in the world, with 4000 examples.

[6] There was even a popular form of coachwork dubbed the 'Doctor's coupé,' because the medical practitioners found them easy to manoeuvre, with sufficient space for their instruments, and easy to get in and out of.

Much could be written about Henry Ford (fig. 7). With his Model T, produced from 1908, he achieved several objectives: the 'Tin Lizzie' (as it was dubbed) was a car designed around its production, easy to use and to repair. Almost anyone could drive it and repair it themselves, without the need for a chauffeur or specialized mechanic (fig. 8). The explanation for this revolutionary 'new process' does not derive from the production line alone, which Ford was the first to introduce, but from the complete interchangeability of the components and the simplicity with which they were joined together, a fact which made the production line itself possible. Henry Ford had attended a race in which cars built in France were competing. He was impressed by how light they were, and he took advantage of the fact that one broke down to recover a few components and analyse the materials used. He noticed that the steel alloy used contained vanadium, which rendered it more robust[7]. This awareness was applied for the first time in the design of a car: the new Ford T contained 20 different types of steel, each with the most suitable characteristics for the specific use.

7. Henry Ford photographed in 1906 aboard his first vehicle, built in 1896

Ford also drew advantage from advances made in tooling machines, able to work pretempered metals; hitherto, the deformation that occurred during the tempering process made each piece different from the next one. The engine block of the four-cylinder Ford engine was a single cast piece. Before this, each cylinder would be cast one by one, or at the most in twos, worked and bolted together, a task requiring a skilled workforce for assembly. It also made the supply of perfectly interchangeable components impossible.

8. One of the first repair workshops in the pioneering years, England, early 20th century

Between the autumn of 1913 and the spring of 1914, a period which saw the introduction of the moving production line, Ford passed from the 750 minutes required to assemble a vehicle to just 93 minutes! And it is for this reason that from the time this process was introduced to the end of production of the T in 1927, the price of the Ford T dropped while progressively increasing the economic power of the industrialist, who became the richest man in America.

Ford's Model T was introduced in 1908; by 1920 one car in two bore his name. Up to 1927, more than 15 million examples were built. By 1928, there were 26 million cars circulating on American roads, and only 4 million in Europe, and the merit for this lies with Henry Ford and his Model T.

We can say, therefore, that the car was invented in Germany, developed in France but became adult in America; if the car has changed the way of life of humanity (as it certainly has), then we can be quite firm in stating that the Ford T was the car that changed the world.

9. The Peugeot L76, the first car to be fitted with double overhead cam shafts, being refuelled during a pit stop, Dieppe, 1912

It is interesting to note that in the early years, those of the pioneers, almost everything had already been invented — electronics apart. Almost all the solutions we find in use today were discovered before the outbreak of the First World War, during the period in which anyone considering building a car did not start with preconceived ideas, but gave free rein to his imagination and experimentation.

For example, in 1893, Rudolf Diesel patented his compression engine, which today powers one car in three; in 1912, Ernest Henry built the first car with double overhead cams (fig. 9) for Peugeot; in 1914, Ettore Bugatti built the first engines of the Type 13 (a small four-cylinder engine of 1300 cc) with four valves per cylinder; the first six-cylinder engines were built by Napier in England and Spyker in the Netherlands in 1903; the same year saw the first V8 engines from Ader in France; the first V12 engine was built by Packard in 1915.

The first systems for starting the engine and lighting were introduced by Cadillac in 1912; these were amongst the most important innovations when it came to making the motor car more 'user-friendly.'

Other innovations failed to gain the same success, for a variety of reasons: either they were too advanced, or there were insufficient funds to undertake the research and development, or the materials available were unsuitable.

Reading books about the history of the car, one cannot be but optimistic about the resolution of the problems that seem insurmountable today (fig. 10), just as others had seemed

[7] After hiring an English metallurgy expert, Henry Ford discovered that the use of vanadium required a higher temperature in the furnaces than American steelworks then provided. After obtaining a guarantee against any potential financial losses, a small steelworks in Ohio accepted the challenge and Henry Ford at last could obtain the material he desired.

10. 1940s England: will we ever have to return to this solution?

insurmountable in the pioneering days, such as electric starting or, in more general terms, the correct functioning of the progenitors of today's cars.

I would recommend that the designers of tomorrow's cars think in an unconventional manner and, if they have time and motivation, to study what had been imagined and built in the so-called pioneering years. They would be surprised.

Bibliography

Karl Benz und sein Lebenswerk – Dokumente and Berichte, Daimler-Benz AG, 1953.
Milleruote, Editoriale Domus e Istituto Geografico De Agostini, 1974.
B. de Saunier, C. Dollfus, E. de Geoffroy, *Histoire de la Locomotion Terrestre*, L'Illustration, 1936.
J. Day, *The Motor Car – its Evolution and Engineering Development*, St. Martin Press, 1975.
C. Posthumus, D. Tremayne, *Land Speed Record*, Osprey Publishing, 1985.
P. Boyer, *De l'Automobile ... De Dion-Bouton ... à l'Aéronautique*, Rétroviseur, 1995.
G.N. Georgano, *Cars – Early and Vintage 1886-1930*, Park Lane, 1985.
R. Bellu, *Toutes les Panhard*, Bellu.
G. Raimondi, *Pneumatici*, Fabbri, 1994.
K. Foster, *The Stanley Steamer – America's Legendary Steam Car*, Stanley Museum, 2004.
W. Lohner, *Lohner Automobile*, Weishaupt Verlag, 1989.
E. Borchi, R. Macii, G. Ricci, *Barsanti & Matteucci*, Fondazione Barsanti e Matteucci, 2002.
Il primo motore a combustione interna, Fondazione Barsanti e Matteucci, 2004.
M. Allen, *Ford Model T Super Profile*, Foulis/Haynes, 1987.
I. Beattie, *Automobile Body Design*, Haynes, 1977.

11. The 'Cugnot wagon:' the first self-propelled vehicle in history

Car Design from the Origins to the 1940s. From Benz to Cisitalia, and from the Carriage to the Integral Form

Lorenzo Ramaciotti

Seeking an Identity

There have been inventions in history that have opened up dimensions and possibilities to mankind that were completely unknown beforehand, of doing desired things that had always been impossible: the steam locomotive made it possible for many social classes to travel long distances and the aeroplane opened up unexplored perspectives not only as regards its use but also in terms of design: there was no precedent from which to make a flying machine heaver than air evolve; the sheet was blank.

In the case of the car, which remains one of the inventions that has most profoundly modified the way of life in the 20th century, the situation was different: this was not a case of a new, unexplored dimension in mobility, as man was already able to move around the surface of the planet at will. What was changing was not the thing in itself but the 'how:' the way of generating the energy used to move.

When Benz constructed his tricycle in 1886, the year generally accepted as the date of birth of the car, the least of his problems was that of giving it a specific formal connotation, and the same was true of his numerous immediate competitors. The most obvious solution, the one offering least complications, was to use the type of means of transport already existing and simply replace the propulsion unit: so horseless carriages were 'borrowed,' aboard which it was not hard to find space in which to house the true innovation: the internal combustion engine.

The ingenuity of the designers in the period of pioneering development was clearly geared to the solution of the technological and mechanical problems than to the study of a specific form. These included the kinematics of the steering, resolved adopting Ackermann's geometry, the cardanic or chain-driven transmission, the control of the direction resolved using handlebars or tillers and progressively smaller and rubber-clad wheels. The engines, which constituted the central feature — the most innovative and technologically important element — obviously underwent continuous improvements and interpretations to every component: number and disposition of the cylinders, fuel supply, ignition, lubrication, cooling. The design and construction efforts of the numerous workshops participating in the gold rush promised by the new means of transport concentrated on these aspects, as these formed the 'know-how' and competitive advantage of the various companies. The vehicle to which they were applied was usually supplied by an external workshop, usually a builder of carriages. This not only in Italy, but also in Germany and France, where technical development was more rapid and tumultuous, and in the United States, which in a few years bore the new vehicle forward to the status of a widely available product. It is comprehensible, therefore, that underlying the origins of names that are still famous today, such as Bertone and Farina, there was an activity of a 'carriage maker.'

Until the end of the 19th century, in these early years of development the engine did not have a morphologically definitive position within the motor car: the height off the ground and the general size of the vehicles made it possible to fit the relatively small engines within the vehicle beneath the seats or bench; only the presence of the cooling coils or radiator and tiller gave them a specific connotation. Indeed, if we look at a photograph of a street at the end of the century, the cars seem like carriages awaiting the arrival of the horse. There were various types of these new vehicles, as many as there types of carriages from which they were derived, but it is possible to recognize two main types: a lighter one, in substance consisting of seats laid on a chassis, derived from the gigs and velocipedes (fig. 1), and the more protective, solid ones with a proper cabin, derived from carriages (fig. 2). The design of these vehicles was necessarily hybrid and unbalanced: the lack of a horse at the front required to complete the overall balance of the carriage, created a feeling of temporariness, incompleteness, almost of amputation. The accessories, too, were totally derived from the functionality of a horse-drawn vehicle: lanterns, oversized mudguards, large wheels.

The construction techniques and materials could only be the same as those used by the coach-builders for the vehicles they had always produced and in many cases continued to produce: wooden chassis suspended on leaf springs, curved and painted wooden panelling, and metal used sparingly. It should be remembered that wood was technically suited to the making of light, hard-wearing vehicles, and that the new-born, forward-looking aeronautical industry used wood for most of its machines until the 1920s.

In the early 20th century, the shift towards an optimal configuration came upon a solution that won general consensus: the engine, which was now larger in size and capacity, was set towards the front of the vehicle and longitudinally, together with the radiator, exposed to the flow of air. Transmission was applied to the rear axle via a transmission shaft and differential. In the beginning, the seats were set extremely high; this was a clear derivation from the carriage as the driver had to sit high up to see over the horse. Likewise, the steering system, based on a central hinge, had needed to be high, but now the seats could be lowered, which resulted in reproportioning the entire vehicle. The beehive radiator definitively replaced the cooling coil thanks to its clear technical superiority, and became the focal point in the creation of the identity of the new means of transport. The car manufacturers began to produce car chassis with all the necessary mechanical components, but almost always 'naked:' the bodywork was usually entrusted by the customer to whichever coach-builder he chose. In this second phase, the motor car had a recognisable morphology and volume, but it still lacked any homogeneousness: the two components, engine and bodywork, although seen as being of equal importance, were still opposing features speaking different languages: a functional engineering model for the first, with vertical radiator and folding bonnet in hinged sheet metal; an aesthetic decor for the second, with decoration in relief, shaped surfaces and ground glass. Observing the image of the Benz Double Phaeton (fig. 3), this odd combination is clear and made all the more obvious by the break in continuity of the surfaces resulting from the driver's seat (the chauffeur was a technical evolution of the coachman, and would for many years accompany the motor car, then reserved for the wealthiest classes).

Towards an Accomplished Form

Ten years after the car established itself as a practical and reliable means of transport, gaining the general social acceptance that had evaded it when it first appeared, the formal aspect of the vehicle gained its final look: 'The torpedo form (that is, with an uninterrupted line from bonnet to rear) was the first bodywork design to be independent of the formal tradition of the horse-drawn carriage, and the first in which the motor car appears as a finished object.'[1] Its introduction dates to the period 1908–10.

The Fiat Zero (fig. 4) well exemplifies this typology: the vertical radiator, with a characteristic tympanum form (the form of the radiator immediately became the simplest and most immediate, and hence strongest, indicator of identity for the manufacturers), conditions the surface of the bonnet which, in turn, links to the cabin. The link is resolved with an elegant, simple concave-convex surface developed three-dimensionally. The sides are

[1] *Carrozzeria Italiana Cultura e Progetto*, Alfieri edizioni d'Arte, 1978, p. 30.

1. Oldsmobile Curved Dash, 1899

2. Fiat 3.5 HP, 1899

3. Benz Double Phaeton, 1908

continuous and finely-shaped, without mouldings or frivolous trim. From the line emerge the characterizing functional elements: the fold-down windscreen, the steering wheel, the comfortably upholstered seats, the hood to protect from rain. The cycle-wing mudguards, linked together by a running-board, although basically two-dimensional in form, have a curved outer lip and are connected to the outer chassis rails for maximum protection. The robust wire wheels are fitted with tyres and are of the right size for the specific requirements of the vehicle. These elements — the visible radiator above the front axle, the single bodywork unit, and the separate mudguards — were to last for decades as the main elements in the composition of international car design.

This consolidation coincided with the need for series production in far greater volumes than the hundreds of units produced hitherto: an open body that was very simple in construction terms and fitted at the outset in a single version without variants. Between 1908 and 1913, the formula gained ground: Ford, Fiat, Mercedes, Peugeot began producing vehicles of this type, varying in size and prize but similar in the makers' ambition to produce them in significant numbers. I have mentioned these makers amongst the many names present in the early years of the 20th century because their models were the eponyms of a century-old continuity of production. The main difference between Europe and America was the market potential and hence the numbers and production systems. The car was the perfect product for a country/continent such as the United States, a nation that was rich, uniform and characterized by distances. With its Model T, Ford invented not only the right product: simple, indestructible and relatively cheap, but also the industrial method to produce it in appropriate quantities with relative economies of scale. Between 1908 and 1926, more than 15 million Ford Ts were produced in a continuous evolution of the one project. Thus was born Fordism; the car became a product for the masses. In Europe, the numbers remained at a far lower level and the production of major series of models did not exceed the hundreds of thousands of units until after the Second World War.

While on the one hand, the constructors clearly saw a future associated with sizeable production runs, on the other the car was still a strongly elitist product and, in parallel with projects of a rational simplicity such as those mentioned above, there was also a production of cars of high complexity and costs, with bodywork made for the customer by specialized workshops. The formal value of these models depends on the skills of the single companies, but in general a certain traditionalism on the part of the customers and the natural association of luxury and exclusivity with the old world of horse-drawn carriages led to more conservative results in style and exceptional ones in terms of craftsmanship. Not all clients, however, were backward-looking: the Alfa Romeo Castagna made for Conte Ricotti in 1913 shows how important a strong vision was to be able to produce results outside the consolidated formulae. Having abandoned any link with not only the more noted forms but also with functional limitations, design concentrated solely on the ideal aerodynamic form, the drop, with obvious similarities with a flying machine: the airship. The radiator was fitted within the bodywork and the engine within the interior (with problems of heat and noise we can barely imagine today). The windows were boldly shaped and enveloping, a feat of considerable technological skill for the time, and the mudguards rectilinear. The whole seems to predict the multipurpose vehicles of today were it not for the fact that the driver is seated midway between the axles two metres from the windscreen; instead, it marks an overly premature attempt to produce an integral aerodynamic car.

Speed, however, was a siren song that it was impossible to resist, and from the very earliest days, the lucky few who could afford the new means of transport began racing their mechanical steeds. Regular competitions were started and 1906 saw the Automobile Club de France organizing the first Grand Prix. However, the race to be fastest in the world on a road had started some years before. In 1899, Jenatzy exceeded 100 kph in an electric car, the Jamais Contente, whith aluminium bodywork in an aerodynamic cigar shape. It should be noted that when Monsieur Jenatzy took up his position with his vertical tiller handle, half of his torso emerged from the vehicle.

From the point of view of design, racing cars until the 1920s were very basic: a bare chassis with seating for the driver and his mechanic. Nothing else was needed and so was left out in the interests of weight and simplicity.

The First World War was responsible for an initial selection of the fittest (a second trimming followed with the economic crisis of 1929): makers who had taken advantage a taking part in the war effort, enlarging their factories and consolidating production methods, found themselves in a position of unassailable strength to tackle the market in the years following. The other manufacturers rapidly disappeared.

The Maturity of the Classic Car

'The coach-builders of the major national schools produced what we may define as the "classical car" between 1920 and 1930 in the wake of a motor vehicle by now configured and consolidated. The equilibrium of the masses and fine workmanship reached new heights in the great luxury vehicles of this period.'[2]

Every country had imposing machines by Isotta Fraschini, Hispano-Suiza, Mercedes, Rolls-Royce, Duesenberg on which to build moving monuments to the motor car. It is hard to identify a single unifying line because the multiplicity of the companies involved and the singularity of the customers' taste gave rise to an almost infinite number of possibilities to explore individual taste, and this within a strong cultural and thus formal characterization associated with the national context. Thus, while in Britain there was a tendency towards austere lines, customers in Italy preferred a classical balance suggesting a dynamic tension, and in France more vigorous, racy lines marked by a characteristic use of two-tone paint, clearly influenced by trends in contemporary decorative arts.

The types of vehicles began to delineate themselves into defined families: the large, showy saloon cars, the formal convertibles, the more agile and compact coupés, the open, essential roadsters; each with their proportional dimensions, with the latter appearing more compact and hugging the ground, and bonnets generally playing an important part in the general balance of the volumes. Each of these families had its own specific aesthetic code communicating its specific use: while the attainment of a specific formal identity for the motor car had proved a success with the standardization of the torpedo, the aim now was to go further, to communicate the sense of the car not only as category, but also as type of car, type of use, type of owner. The use of saloons and limousines left little space for the introduction of innovative content, with the design being personalized above all in terms of details, use of colour, size of the windows, in a play of an individual interpretation of consolidated standards. The design of more sporting and personal cars — coupés and roadsters — lent itself better to the introduction of dynamic elements and lines clearly suggesting speed, fun.

The result of a decade of developments leads to a complete integration of the engine bonnet and cabin: the upper line is aligned with the beltline and there is no longer any discontinuity between the surfaces containing the engine and the side of the passenger interior. The body of the car is designed as a single volume, its section increasing from radiator to windscreen, outlined by surfaces (side, upper, rear) that blend together. The amount of curvature of the surfaces and the type of radius used define the general appearance of the car. Seen in plan view, there is considerable diversity in the design solutions chosen — more oval forms contrast with flatter, more prismatic shapes. The mudguards are an independent addition; they are two-dimensional but could be freely interpreted: from the fleshy, massive consistency of some heavy saloons to the geometric lightness of cars like the Lambda, and on to the curvilinear dynamism and reduced size of some quick roadsters.

The construction technology was fairly generalized: a robust chassis with steel members and a coachwork on top of this formed of a load-bearing structure in wood on which were applied sheet-metal panels shaped by hand.

[2] *Ibid.*, p. 28.

4. Fiat tipo Zero, 1912
Archivio museo dell'auto

5. Alfa Romeo, 1925

6. Styling centre in the 1930s

There was no lack of variants, such as the Weymann method for example, which involved covering a specially reinforced wooden structure with pegamoid, a sort of artificial leather. This was used under licence by a number of coach-builders throughout Europe and the United States.

A special example of a happy synthesis of engineering and design was the Lancia Lambda, in which the bodywork for the first time played a structural role. This was not a three-dimensional, thin-walled structure as we find in modern cars, but instead a thick framework integrated within the sides. Nevertheless, the concept was innovative in terms of product and production methods. The result was a light and low car, as there was no need to place the cabin on top of the chassis, with a highly geometric and flat form, almost a prismatic solid, in part required because of the technology available at the time. The reverse of the medal of the innovation was the lack of flexibility, which made it hard to build the special bodywork requested by the customers of the period instead of the torpedo supplied directly by the maker. There was only a single press in all Italy able to produce the sheet-metal side panels, and ironically it belonged to competitors, Fiat. The subsequent use of this press for other processes was to put production of the Lambda at risk.

One of the most memorable models, the true arrival point for the classical car, was the Flying Star by Carrozzeria Touring. This design was produced on a chassis by Isotta Fraschini, Fiat and Alfa Romeo, and achieved the best results with Alfa. The car was compact, with perfect proportions: low, with an imposing bonnet although not massive, the principal moulding drawn back to the back of the door before dividing, and another two lines on the bonnet discreetly underlining the whole. The windscreen was merely a trifling screen held up by two tiny, almost invisible pillars. The mudguards were freely designed, like two autonomous surfaces following each other in flight and crossing over mid-vehicle. The style expresses an eclectic taste, interpreted with the sobriety and dynamism characteristic of an Italian school, of which Touring would be probably the finest interpreter in the following decade.

The perfection achieved by the formula in the different national contexts which began to show signs of being worn out, the financial crisis of 1929 and the reduction in requests for luxury cars, as well as the consequent disappearance of prestige manufacturers, presaged profound changes.

In America, mass production polarized the car world around two names: Ford, which built a dominant position based on the success of the Model T, and General Motors. In opposition to the monolithic vision of Henry Ford, for whom the process was at the centre of things, and the customer had to adjust ('any colour you like so long as it's black'), Alfred P. Sloane introduced a vision geared to the customer, giving him the possibility of choosing cars varying in price, features and, above all, style. Concepts still in use today, such as product planning, brand differentiation and planned obsolescence — the practice of the model-year — as well as anticipating fashions through dream cars, began to establish themselves. Thanks to the success of this strategic vision, General Motors became the world's largest car manufacturer. Even though this position today has been undermined by internal problems and by the growth of Toyota (which at the time was making textiles machines and only built its first motor vehicle in 1936), the important fact remains that this position was maintained for 70 years, and that one of the instruments used to maintain and defend this supremacy has been design.

In 1927, Harley Earl was put in charge of a new division called, for want of anything better, Art & Colors. Thus was born the first styling centre and with Earl, the first design director of a major car maker. He was the first and also one of the most formidable and charismatic of all, and thanks to him, the position of design within the largest car manufacturer became dominant. Competitors could do no other than fall in line, creating similar structures and positions within their companies. Ford also had to give way and offer a range of models and options and add further brands to satisfy other categories of drivers.

By the end of the 1920s, the techniques still in use today were already being applied, full colour sketches, full-size drawings, reduced scale and full-size models in clay and the presentation of projects to the directors. The corresponding professional figures were thus also in existence by then: the stylists, illustrators, model-makers. It would only be in the 1950s, however, that the European manufacturers felt the need to equip themselves in like fashion, after they found themselves wrong-footed by new construction technologies, mass motorization and consequent market laws. Almost in symmetrical manner to the importance accorded the stylistic development of American models was the establishment of a technical stereotype, apart from interesting but numerically marginal examples such as the Cord with front-wheel drive. This stereotype consisted of a front-mounted V8 engine, rear-wheel drive with live axle, separate ladder frame chassis. This formula remained popular until the 1970s; the last of these dinosaurs, the Cadillac de Ville, was taken out of production in 1984.

Even though there was a clear trend towards alignment around a successful stereotype, in Europe the smaller size of the industry and more limited production runs left greater space for the exploration of alternative concepts, whether in terms of engines, where we find highly varied interpretations of engine size and number and disposition of cylinders, or of suspension and structural solutions. Some manufacturers made of this diversity a proper planning programme: Lancia, Bugatti, Voisin. Industrial then aviation pioneer, Gabriel Voisin designed his motor cars down to the tiniest detail, including locks, handles and lights, without turning simply to consolidated solutions. His sole aim was to achieve the efficiency he learned in designing aeroplanes. For the forms too, he drew inspiration from the aeronautical industry, from the cross-section of a wing, creating objects that it is hard to define as beautiful but which are certainly unmistakable. Almost his opposite, Ettore Bugatti breathed in the culture of beauty from his family, and applied aesthetic canons not only to the bodywork of the vehicles he produced but also to the mechanical components, taking care over the form of the engines, axles, wheels, and frequently succeeding in blending form, technology and efficiency. The car as total aesthetic project, often beyond the cold logic of financial interests. For this reason Bugatti and his cars, from the essential 35 to the monumental, financially disastrous Royale and the rare, highly refined Atlantic have remained the epitome of 1920s and 1930s motor cars.

Aerodynamic Inspiration

Elements borrowed from aerodynamics were of the strongest influence on car design before the war: the body of the car took on a tapering, single, drop shape, windscreens were set at an increasing angle and divided into a V shape or curved as much as the technology of the time would allow. Radiators were no longer vertical or flat, and were hidden behind strongly three-dimensional surfaces, while wings also became three-dimensional objects and running boards were reduced or removed altogether. The headlights also lost their independence from the rest of the front and were increasingly integrated within the front wings. This process was common to both luxury vehicles and to those that began to introduce into Europe the idea if not of mass mobility, at least of popular motorization. Every country had its protagonist of the new forms: the Fiat 1500 6C and Lancia Aprilia in Italy, the Peugeot 202 in France, the Volkswagen in Germany. These were aerodynamic models more in the imagination than in scientific analysis, and their efficiency was always more suggested than real.

The radical application of Jaray and Kamm's studies was premature for a public that was not yet ready to accept it. Indeed, one of the most courageous cars in this sense, the Chrysler Airflow of 1934, was one of the greatest production fiascos of the period. It is interesting to recall that Paul Jaray sued over the use of his patented concepts in the design of this car; the dispute was later settled out of court. The Airflow was also a pioneer in being the just all-metal car. The underlying steel chassis had a tubular superstructure to which

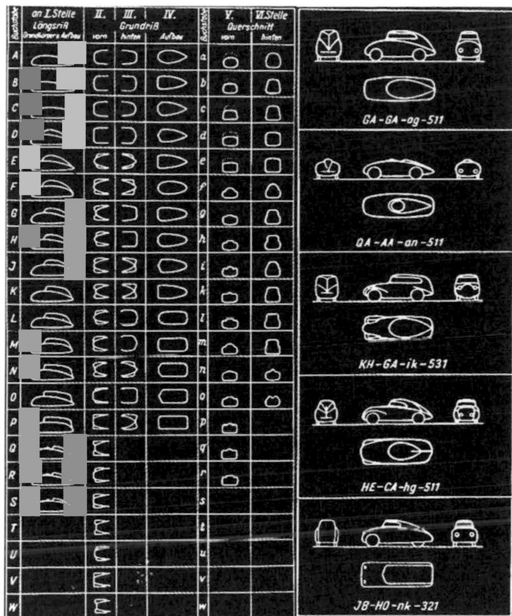

7. Jaray patent, 1921

the pressed steel panels were welded, with the engine and cabin moved forward to increase space and improve comfort, an original solution. But whereas the Airflow might appear grotesque to its potential customers, the Cord 810 combined modernity with far more consolidated proportions: a long bonnet, a small cabin set towards the rear, large wraparound wings: all were habitual and familiar features. The design by Gordon Buehrig, however, was resolutely modern and innovative: the chrome-plated details had almost vanished, including the radiator grille, replaced by a series of slits, the pop-up headlights had been recessed in to the wings, and all the surfaces smoothed and polished, without any interruptions. But the car was too expensive and unreliable and proved a failure; less than 3000 of them were made.

The spindle-shaped, three-dimensional and overall more sculptural forms opened a new, fruitful creative season for the coach-builders, who continued to dress the chassis of the cars produced with individual creations, succeeding in adopting the standardized chassis that the manufacturers were increasingly offering directly for their most common models. In every country, cars were produced in which a taste moving towards a generalized, international form was overlaid with stylistic interpretations more closely allied to the specific national contexts. In Italy, Touring used its association with Alfa Romeo to good effect, interpreting the characteristics of these light, sporty and compact cars to create a series of small saloons and convertibles of formal and constructive perfection, the forward-looking and already mature expression of the Italian-style 'Gran Turismo,' which was to acquire so much popularity and international success in the post-war years. In like manner, Pinin Farina interpreted the technical characteristics and spirit of the Lancia marque with a series of convertibles and coupés over Astura and Aprilia chassis. Without overlooking their imposing size, these succeeded in conveying dynamism and aerodynamic penetration. The sense of measure and control that the Italian school succeeded in maintaining in interpreting new forms was progressively lost by the French school. The essential volumes and in many cases lean and vigorous forms of Jean Bugatti, Ettore's son, who was responsible for the most memorable designs, were followed by emphatic, decadent designs from the school of Figoni & Falaschi and Saoutchick.

These were objects to *épater le bourgeois* rather than cars. The 'Goutte d'Eau' designs — smooth and well-proportioned, although tending towards an excessive fullness — were followed by others with fairings over the wheels, of an undue width and further laden with chrome-plated decoration suggesting second-division Art Déco. These cars were the negation of movement, of dynamism, of just measure. The appeal of their excessive forms, however, and of their abundant decoration is still strong today, given that Delage, Delahaye and Talbot continue to be favoured by collectors and judges in concours d'élégance, especially in the United States.

The theories of aerodynamics could not be applied in full to road vehicles which had to satisfy market requirements and hence the taste of customers, but they could and were to racing cars. The form (fig. 7) theorized by Jaray in 1921 (Kamm's truncated tail became topical much later) in substance foresaw a car body with wing shaped section overlaid by a drop-shaped cabin. The wheels were included within the bodywork so there were no separate wings. This was thus a single integral body with continuous sides. Pinin Farina with some Aprilia (fig. 8), Touring with the Alfa Romeo 8C 2900 Le Mans, and then with the BMW 328, were the main exponents of this form after 1935, accompanied by other coach-builders such as Savio, Boneschi and Viotti.

The integral form on the one hand met the requirements of aerodynamics, and on the other was the natural form for the best use of the construction technology of the time, with pressed steel panels spot-welded together, a technology that was progressively taking over in the United States under the constant pressure of high volume runs and extremely competitive market prices. The development of the engineering and style proceeded undisturbed beyond the Atlantic towards increasingly integrated and continuous forms, in which the separate volumes of the wings were included within the bodywork, although without vanishing altogether. Europe, instead, witnessed a singular phenomenon: the war 'froze' the state of the art for over five years, and with the return of ordinary daily life, the cars driving along the roads of Europe were the same as had been designed in the late 1930s, in some cases remaining in production for over 40 years: the Volkswagen (20 million examples made), the Citroën 2CV (7.8 million), the Fiat Topolino (fig. 9) (520,000). In these three cars, we can also witness the many-sided nature of the European design approach: beneath the common feature of an inexpensive, small car with small engine, we find two and four-cylinder engines, cooled by air or water, located at front or rear, with drive to the front or rear wheels. Even the interpretation of the bodywork design was very different, ranging from the 'classic' form of the Fiat, almost a reduction in scale of larger cars, to the determined interpretation of Jaray's theories of the Volkswagen, and the totally functional form of the Citroën, devoid of all formal preoccupations and the only one of these three to offer four doors. The first, pre-war, prototype was almost brutal, with its single asymmetric headlamp (the design was widely revamped before the car entered production in 1948).

8. Aprilia Aerodinamica PF, 1936

9. Fiat 500 A, 1936

10. Maserati A6 1500 PF, 1947

The Integral Form

While waiting for the industry to design new up-to-date models in terms of technology and style, the first post-war creations were by the same coach-builders who quickly restarted their activities, at times using a chassis that had survived or been assembled from spare parts. The forms of these vehicles showed all the uncertainty of old forms and proportions, by now worn out in terms of design, which had been revamped, with an emphatic, almost caricatural stress on some features in their striving for more radical and original solutions. The French coach-builders were slow to abandon the forms and decorations they were most comfortable with and failed to look forwards in a crisis from which they were unable to emerge.

In Germany, Ferdinand Porsche extrapolated the sports car that bears his name, the Porsche 356, from the engineering of his standard model. With perfect simplicity, this model remained unchanged for many years, as though symbolizing the virtues of German cars of the future: efficiency, technology, formal rationalism. In Italy, the situation was more varied, with some, like Stabilimenti Farina, having difficulty in assimilating change, while Touring found an interesting way forward with the Ferrari 166 MM, which it further developed with later models for Alfa Romeo. However, the high points of the 1930s were never regained. Pinin Farina was perhaps the first to find a convincing and mature expressive form, developing to perfection an intuition by Giovanni Savonuzzi and creating the archetype of the modern sports car, the Cisitalia 202. In the same year — 1947 — Pinin Farina produced a less famous car, of which only photographic records remain, but which was to my mind even more radical and innovative: the prototype Maserati A6 1500 (fig 10). It offered an essential, smooth design of exaggerated proportions; it was perhaps less perfect, but it had immense presence. These were immediately followed by a series of projects for various Italian and foreign makers, which confirmed and consolidated the perfect control of the new formal lexicon with a personal interpretation of equilibrium in the proportions and a poised tension in the surfaces.

The second half of the 1940s saw the transformation in Europe too of a form of car design leading to single-mass models, in which we no longer find features clumped together by function: radiator, headlights, the four wings, all are integrated within a single volume and the cars that started emerging in the 1950s already bore the results of this change, drawing advantage from these full, enveloping forms to make them easy, rational and efficient to manufacture in terms of panels and assembly.

'The formal research coagulated… in the direction of vehicles in which the wings were integrated with the sides of the car. This was a long conversion process… that went well beyond the aerodynamic suggestion: it meant conceiving the car as a modelled volume, rather than as a box formed by two-dimensional panels.'[3]

This was the starting point of the morphology of the classic car as we know it: a solid single mass composed of three volumes set next to each other: engine, interior and boot; the profile we learned to outline as children and which the children of today still draw to indicate a car. A sign that is universal in time and space.

[3] *Ibid.*

Design from the 'Reconstruction' to the Oil Crisis of 1973

Mauro Tedeschini

Design historians call it the 'fourth phase.' It was here, with an epicentre in the fab fifties, that what we all consider to be the modern car was born. Before this, half a century of impetuous industrialization and mass motorization had taken place: the initial phase was that of the bodywork, with a form similar to horse-drawn carriages, with internal combustion engines in the place of the horse. This was at a time that the success of the motor car was by no means assured. There were some, like Kaiser Wilhelm, who believed that the horse would dominate following the end of a passing fad. The second phase, with the advent of the torpedo body, saw the car finally take on an independent life, while the third was that of maturity and the definitive emancipation of the industry, with forms and contents adapted to mass production, in accordance with the lesson given by Henry Ford and his Model T.

We should not forget that the Fiat Balilla dates from 1932, the Cinquecento Topolino from 1936, while the Beetle was first made in 1938. Here was a model that would survive in myriad forms to the present day; from Adolf Hitler to Angela Merkel. And so we arrive at the fourth phase, which arrived late because of the shut-down of the entire sector for the Second World War. The factories were first reserved for military production and then destroyed, pretty much everywhere, by severe bombing. But when the reawakening did take place, it was impetuous and pushed along by a number of genial men, assisted in their work by the planners (the term 'designer' would be rather limiting for people of this calibre), and by courageous and enlightened businessmen, able to innovate by creating ideal conditions of work, just as the patrons of the great artists had done in earlier centuries.

There are many names that we might mention, and some omissions would be inevitable. We limit ourselves here to recalling three giants: Dante Giacosa, Alec Issigonis and Flaminio Bertoni, able to change not only the history of the car, but also that of habits in a fast-changing world. These are not names simply picked out of a hat: behind each of them are the 'visionaries' of the time, people who were quite clear as to where they wanted to go and what opportunities they wished to offer a world that, with the advent of modernity and consumption, would never have accepted being left on foot, taken as it was with an unstoppable desire to travel independently.

Giacosa is certainly a hero of this period, and the originator of the representation of the utopia of 'social capitalism' dreamed first by Giovanni Agnelli and then by Vittorio Valletta. The latter, above all, was convinced that a major company was a single corpus within which development and growth were a heritage to be protected at any cost. And that these objectives were possible only by having workers paid so well that they could themselves become the consumers and purchases of the cars produced. To do this, he was prepared even to argue with the shareholders, denying their customary dividends. In exchange, the employees were required to be disciplined and demonstrate absolute loyalty.

Giacosa was the man who made these cars, in particular the 600 in 1955 and the 500 a year later. In mind, he had objectives of cost, simplicity of use, reliability and unbeatable consumption. And yet he succeeded in impressing a totally personal style on these products; in the case of the Cinquecento, of such quality as to make it one of the most imitated cars in history, the object of a faithful remake in a modern key to be released in 2007, exactly half a century after the first launch.

Who was Giacosa? Born in 1905, he gained a degree in engineering from the Politecnico di Torino, and was an unprecedented enthusiast of the opportunities engineering offered those of his generation, but he was also an untiring creative figure, convinced that the new objects that were then being produced had to combine innovation with beauty and simplicity of use. It was no coincidence that he started his career in the aeronautical division of Fiat, which in those years was at the new frontier of the industry. But very soon, he was earmarked by Valletta for the realization of the utility vehicles that were to motorize Italy and the rest of Europe. Giacosa was a forerunner in two further aspects: he had an international vision of cars (not coincidentally, one of his points of reference was Charles Franklin Kettering, the talented American designer who invented electric starting for General Motors) and he was able to work in a team, exploiting the work of his collaborators to full effect.

Not surprisingly, the initial idea for the 500 series came from a German designer working under Giacosa in the Styling Centre Fiat had opened at Weinsberg. That absolutely original prototype convinced Giacosa far more than the idea that initially proved more popular in Fiat, that of a little car based around the idea of the most clamorous success of the time, the Vespa moped, itself designed by another talented designer 'kidnapped' from the aeronautical sector, Corradino d'Ascanio (he also designed a famous helicopter). Giacosa was convinced that the Fiat had to have an original style and that egg shape seemed the most convincing to him. He was also the author of other extremely successful and appealing models, designed over 42 years of work (such as the mechanical components for the splendid coupé made for Piero Dusio's Cisitalia). It is a mystery why Italy does not remember him as one of the men who helped make this great country.

Almost contemporary to Giacosa (1906) was Alec Issigonis, the man to whom we owe another icon of the car industry, the Mini, which was first launched on the market in 1959, and was also reproposed 50 years later, in a modern version by BMW. Issigonis shared two important characteristics with his Italian colleague: he was an all-round engineer and designer, able to create a car starting from the design table and down to the last screw; and he was a fan of simplicity of use and cheap running costs, at a time in which the car still seemed aimed at a small public. His talent for innovation did not have an easy time of it: his Morris Minor, launched in 1948, had been so controversial as to induce WIlliam Morris himself indignantly to refuse being photographed alongside his company's latest model. The Mini had an easier introduction, with a planet-wide success lasting entire generations.

Both Giacosa and Issigonis are designers of a sort that would be inconceivable today: nowadays, cars are created with the help of dozens of designers, each specialising in a microsector. There are, indeed, two major subsectors — exteriors and interiors — within which there are a number of specialized roles: the lights, the dashboard, the seats, and so on, a little like in modern medicine, with surgeons specializing in tiny areas of the human body. The requirements are completely different, too: today, there are extremely severe regulations to be respected with regard to the shapes of cars, for reasons of safety in case of accident and to reduce consumption. At the time of our heroes, there was an incomparable creative freedom, resulting in part from the fact that there were no 'family feelings' for each manufacturer (they first appeared in those years). The level of compromises, before arriving at the final line, was far lower. This explains why those years saw the creation of unforgettable models: industrial requirements were clearly reflected, but the taste for the new left plenty of space for poetry. Talent was not something Flaminio Bertoni was short of either. This Italian designer has gone down in the history books together with André Lefèbvre for having created the Citroën DS. It offered stunning lines, hydro-pneumatic suspension enabling the height off the road to be adjusted according to the surface, and the use of new materials, including plastic and aluminium... Everything seemed to make this a revolutionary and simultaneously risky machine, with those rounded shapes that clashed with the contemporary taste for angular lines.

For the interiors, too, Citroën played into the hands of sceptics who, after seeing the prototype, nicknamed the car the 'hippopotamus.' But it is incredible to note how some models, however difficult, succeeded in meeting the taste of a public that was immediately attracted to them. The DS was presented at the Paris Salon in 1955 and collected 12,000 orders on the opening day alone; it was produced for 20 years in an infinity of versions for a total of 1,456,000 examples. It enjoyed many moments of fame, including an attempt on President Charles De Gaulle's life in 1962, with the car continuing unflinchingly despite the numerous bullets that hit its various parts, including the tyres. And when *Quattroruote*, a popular Italian car magazine, on the occasion of its 50th anniversary in February 2006, asked its readers to indicate the most beautiful car of those years, the DS gained widespread approval.

These men are just a few examples drawn from an extraordinary period: among the many, how can we not mention the great Pininfarina, Nuccio Bertone and the other incredibly talented men who have created an extraordinary 'design bank,' from which designers today still borrow heavily? Many names from this extraordinary season are Italian ones, and that leadership is still recognized today, in an age in which design assumes an increasingly strategic role, given the standardization of the mechanical parts between the various manufacturers. 'But I am not at all certain, in these early years of the new millennium, that this fame is not usurped.'

'Tomorrow, Tomorrow'

Paolo Tumminelli

'Tomorrow, tomorrow, our dreams will come true, together, together, we'll make our world new'
(From the promotional short film, *Design for dreaming*, © General Motors, 1956)

Writing about the future of the car is as fascinating as it is hard. Fascinating because the car is a marvellous object. Hard because, without wishing to criticize their competence and capacity for foresight, everyone who has sought to describe the car of the future, or better, the mobility of the future, has sinned of either by being too vague or by exaggerating, in a manner often verging on the endearingly ridiculous. Sam Medway, author of a paper entitled *The Best Crystal Ball of All*, published in 1975 in *Automobile Quarterly* (in *AQ*, XIII.1, p. 4), was already aware of this. The article is worth perusing for a quick survey of visions of the future, starting with Roger Bacon, a 13th-century monk who predicted the birth of the motor vehicle, and ending with the warning from the *Scientific American*, which in 1923 declared the urgency of 'making constructors and designers understand the need to adapt the motor car to the imminent lack of fuel.' Medway's article introduced the description of three scenarios for mobility in 2020, conceived of, illustrated and commented by the Hollywood designer and futurologist, Syd Mead (*Reaching for Aquarius – A Designer Looks Ahead*, *ibid.*, p.10). Without wishing to detract from the appeal of gyro gondolas, floating personal enclosures and astral projections, with just a few short years to go before the deadline, it seems unlikely that any of these futuristic visions will come true. Overall, they take into account the high-speed evolution of society between the end of the Second World War and 1968, or between the establishment of mass consumption, on to the conquest of Space and up to the cultural revolution. The late 1960s were years of radical reflection and design, fed by atomic power, electronics and plastic, seen as the principal ingredients of a future that was believed to be behind the corner, totally new and free of cultural prejudice. In the motor car, this radicalism takes the form of a brutality in wedge-shaped lines and graphic geometric design promoted and highlighted by the style of design offered by Bertone. That the very idea of future — and not just that of the car — should be lost sight of, and that a sort of neo-romanticism of a tragically nostalgic character would take hold over the next 20 years, affecting our forms of consumption and making us prefer or re-prefer mechanical watches, whole-wheat bread and classical style, was inconceivable at the time. What is certain is that with the end of the 1970s, what arrived was not the future but a household-appliance car, perfected and rationalised but also poorer in style and sadder. The dynasty of visionary constructors was replaced by that of the 'polluting' advertisers, as Giovanni Klaus Koenig described them, exploring the theme in *Passato e futuro dell'automobile* (in *Ottagono*, 59, Dec. 1980, p. 56). For Koenig, progress was artificially slowed by the 'aberrant logic of absolute novelty' — which was naturally a fraud — and in the 'stylistic games dominated by the "optional."' Better to break free and opt for the true emotions of an old Bianchina, concluded Koenig (anticipating the 1980s cult of the classic car, the retrodesign of the 1990s and the Youngtimer-generation of 2000), and await the formation of 'that dry, rigorous mentality from which will emerge — if it emerges — the future of the car.'

Unfortunately, no new mentality has yet formed, but this does not mean that the car is not in poor, or extremely poor health. It is true that there are increasingly successful car manufacturers, often helped by the opening of new markets, presenting record accounts. But in the mature markets, which constitute the point of reference for the future, the *Stimmung* is worrying, the direction to take, uncertain. The identity of the car suffers as a result: the first signal of ill-health appeared with the arrival of the Mazda MX-5 Miata in 1989 — an appealing global fetish — created by the Japanese in the United States by copying the classic British roadster, with the aim of recharging the public's emotional fuel tanks. Helping was the soap-and-water beauty of the little roadster, an operation which proved a great success, and which gave birth to a conceptual line that guided car design in a retro direction, and which has still not come to an end. On the one hand, there are veritable remakes, like in the cinema: of the Beetle, the Mini, the Range Rover, the Ford Thunderbird, and now also the Fiat Cinquecento. On the other, a neo-classical look long on eye-catching appeal but short on substance has taken root, especially because it looks back to a period in car design, the golden period of the 1960s, already overcome in terms of affordance — the meeting point between aesthetics, semantics and performance. The conjecture of an exclusive heritage to be protected and repeated *ad infinitum* today freezes the capacity to propose something new on the part of marques historically famous for their conceptually advanced approach, such as Bentley, Lancia, Porsche, for example. What is worse is that the romantic celebration of the neo-classical ideal provides a negative influence on the powerful industry of the new Far East, with false concepts of design. Anyone hoping that this be a passing trend must revise their views. At the launch of its third series in 2006, the Miata still evokes the style of the original model of 1989, after having in part overcome it. The astonished world can now be party to the first absurd retro-retro.

A dog chasing its own tail is the vision one has of car design today. But we must not blame just the designers — or perhaps it would be more correct to call them stylists once more — who are trapped within such a powerful and complex car system as to prevent any Pindaric flight of fancy, even at a theoretical level. Touching the car, hypothesizing a different future, means interfering with a web of production and commercial interests, and hence economic and political ones too, associated with the problem of employment, energy resources and territorial infrastructure. The strategy of the car manufacturers should be no surprise: then as now, it is soft, made of little steps, often guided by legislative dispositions that are never too invasive in terms of taxation, safety, environmental impact, with California heading the list. The idea of a future-car has in some way slipped out of our hands and there is no-one, let alone a single company, apparently able to propose a winning vision. This role is given instead, in line with the idea of product placement, to the imagination of Hollywood. What comes out of this sheds very little light on the matter. For *Minority Report*, directed in 2002 by Steven Spielberg, a group of futurologists and visionaries was commissioned to hypothesize a scenario of mobility in 2054. As a result, we find a magnetic levitation system for city traffic, with improbable auto-cells that become part of the urban landscape and of the home. But for a spin in the countryside, Tom Cruise hops into a highly traditional, even though electronically super-equipped and highly performing car — sponsored by Lexus. In *I, Robot*, directed by Alex Proyas in 2004, the relationship between the human race and artificial intelligence in 2035 is explored. The Audi RSQ, belonging to the hero-cop Will Smith, moves on four spheres but, like the other cars in the film, is virtually identical to cars currently in production. In neither case is the same level of imagination reached as in the fabulous concept cars in Rocket design of the 1950s and 1960s, and it is no surprise to discover that underlying both scripts are stories from that period, respectively by Philip K. Dick and Isaac Asimov. The marketing message is clear: the car, the one we produce so much advertising for, and which costs so much money, is perfect and beautiful. Untouchable today, as desirable tomorrow. If it were up to advertising, our future would be today, as was parodied recently by a television advertisement (for coffee!) in Germany: 'If you could make a wish, what would you ask for?' asks the man,

1. In 1956, Ford dreamed up the Aquacar, a world of flying and floating vehicles
© Ford Motor Company

2. Standard vehicles for public hire system in a scenario of mobility for the year 2020
© Syd Mead (detail, from *Automobile Quarterly*, XIII.1, p. 13), 1975

3. Future-Future: the new Bertone Stratos of 1970 in front of the new BMW establishment in Munich
© Stile Bertone

elegantly standing on the stern of his yacht. 'That everything remain just the same,' she replies, beautifully dressed in white, with the Caribbean in the background. Beautiful certainly, but also ingenuous, a poor victim of the intrinsic message of marketing: deny the possibility at the outset that tomorrow, however different, might be better than today as the key to sell products and experience here and now.

4. From retro to retro-retro: the first and third series of the MX-5 in a promotional Mazda image
© Mazda Motors, 2006

5. *Aestetica cognita* in Tom Cruise's super-sports car in *Minority Report*
© Toyota – Lexus Division

6. Will Smith in a scene from *I, Robot*, today's design for cars of 2035
© Audi AG

But is it truly impossible to tackle the question of the future, especially that of the car, without descending into romanticism and utopian views? Today, nobody is astonished any more to learn that the car of the future will certainly not fly, but will move along electronic motorways controlled by a satellite system; after all, the story has been the same for the past 50 years. The monitoring system on German motorways, the invasion of speed cameras on British roads, the control of access to the centres of London and Bologna are only small, isolated experiments in electronic control applied to mobility. To complete the project, they only need to be linked into GPS, a drive-by-wire system and the autopilot already present in many cars, which follow the road, brake as needed and park by themselves. Nor does it seem to me that we are particularly worried about energy. We know, because we have been talking about it since the 1960s, that the car of the future will be powered by hydrogen, used as a medium to produce energy for electric, internal combustion or hybrid engines, thereby cancelling out the problem of ecological and economic sustainability of personal mobility (or at least shifting the goal posts). The pieces needed to manufacture cars of the future, in other words, already exist. It seems only that no-one wants to be first to put them together. The technical solutions needed to modify the industrial product, in its form and content, to the given circumstances of the moment, may be applied to any shell. The presentation in Geneva in 2006 of the prototype LAND_e was symbolic in this regard: tomorrow's technology applied to a virtually shapeless shell. An imaginary 'all and nothing' expressing the material lack of spring (or desire) in formulating future scenarios. The paradox is that there is nothing to prevent us using a Ford Model A of 1927 as the basis for the new technology. Like many of its contemporaries, this car is, in construction terms, already perfectly mature and, in its varied choice of bodywork models, compatible with today's demands. This apparent provocation serves to clarify how the problem of the car of the future has very little to do with the form of the object *per se*. If we go along with the common dialectic, it would be child's play for designers to interpret it in the preferred style: neo-classical for Jaguar, baroque for Mercedes, Pop for the Mini, Deconstructivist for BMW, Empire for Rolls-Royce, minimal for Audi, or combinations of these and others as preferred. But the concept of the future car is not expressed, as the manufacturers (would have us) believe, in an aesthetic seen as the interpretation of the brand identity, processed in relation to emerging trends. Nor will the car of the future, despite the best effort of all concerned, derive from a combination of the logical conclusions of already known typologies. The so-called crossovers are for the most part useless cars, good only for creating compromises but not for offering real alternatives to the ordinary car. The question is not one of technology or of style, but of design, and so deeply entrenched is the culture of the consumption project.

The question we should ask ourselves is instead a quite simple one: what will happen to the Myth of the Machine? What meaning, what role will the car of the future carve out for itself? Let us consider: today, cars are in good health. If chosen well, they are versatile, safe, economical, robust and reliable. The problem is that their myth on the one hand is now meaningless, and on the other is incompatible with the emerging global market — today still so heterogeneous but moving towards a tomorrow that will be more aligned. The Myth of the Machine has formed in two main thrusts, that of speed and that of status symbol. The myth of speed, the collective euphoria of the Modern Movement, wooed by the cultural avant-gardes, promoted by races and experienced personally by a population of drivers and passengers dreaming by the side of the roads of the Mille Miglia, came to an official demise on 26th November 2003, the day the supersonic Concorde was finally grounded. And was buried with the constriction of motor sports within the media circus, an experience beyond the reach of most, except sitting in front of TV screens or behind VIP lounge windows, watching the cars and their drivers as tiny, noisy dots in the distance. It has now become a commonplace experience to find ourselves in a world of inoperable infrastructures, limitations to traffic planned by and for sadists and masochists, and drivers who daily gamble their lives and penalty points. Seduced and abandoned, the public accepts a marketing technology that provides heaps of horsepower and then neutralizes it with traction and stability systems. It accepts a correctness that suggests the self-limitation of top speeds, whether a powerful BMW or little Smart, and then gives out a message like this: 'It could go at 300, but we don't trust you,' or 'we're worried that going flat out the car could fall apart.' At top speed, like in the Vasco Rossi song? If only! Cars are becoming increasingly large and the roads seem increasingly small; actual average speeds are constantly dropping. We live our experience of the car as an interminable intestinal spasm. In this dimension of quasi-immobility, the 400 kph Bugatti is no less ridiculous than a utility car with a sporty line, wedge shape and widened wheelarches. Here is an aesthetic fiction designed to give the impression of speed whilst parked, and its perception has been cancelled by technological perfection: sit in a Jeep at 200 kph, and it seems immobile; you feel nothing and no skills are needed — splendid! There is no fun in this and the myth of the racing driver, fascinating hero and at the same time a condemned soul, faded away from the collective imagination on 30th September 1955, when James Dean and his little Porsche 'bastard' crashed into a commonplace Ford coupé. So Marinetti was wrong when in his *Futurism Manifesto* he praised 'the beauty of speed' and 'the man holding the wheel' of 'a roaring motor car, which seems to race on gravel.' Proust was instead right when in 1907, in *Chronicle of a Journey by Motor Car*, he wrote that when travelling by car, he seemed to be still and see the road, the trees and bell towers of St. Etienne rushing by; the Playstation effect! And indeed, the overturning of the concept of speed has its origins in the logic real time of a computer: speed today is not perceived, it is sublimed in the instantaneous, in the imperceptible instant between a click and the download.

7. Rocket design: Harley Earl poses in front of the GM Firebird concept car, 1953–58
© General Motors

8. Technology without form: the prototype Land Rover LAND_e, 2006
© Ford Motor Company

9. Symbol of a myth: the supersonic Aérospatiale-BAC *Concorde*, 1969
© Adrian Pingston 2003

So perhaps the old myth of the status symbol still survives, the desire to show oneself to best effect, the American imperative to impress the neighbouring Jones with a bigger automobile than his. More car equals more man? This is what Cadillac used to promise, with a car that 'gives a man a new outlook' (1956), as did also the Buick Roadmaster ('it rolls out the red carpet wherever you go'), and Walt Disney with racing driver Jim Douglas in *The Love Bug* (1969): 'Without a real car I'm only half a man.' For decades, our society has been divided between drivers and aspirant drivers. Not owning a car used implicitly to mean desiring one. Possessing implied showing. And what else did Barthes intend in his *Mythologies*, comparing the Citroën DS to Gothic cathedrals, if not this? Were these cathedrals not intended to show the city to best effect, to impress the bumpkins Joneses from out of town? But nowadays, cars and their respective owners no longer impress anyone. If you turn your head, at the most you smile — or more often laugh. Possession as symbol of refinement? Jaguar produces diesel-powered baroque mini-estate cars. Possession as symbol of wealth? A used Rolls-Royce costs the same as a small Volkswagen. Possession as symbol of exclusiveness? Mercedes-Benz sells more cars in Germany than Ford. So what does possession mean? Today, (hardly) anyone buys a car any more. You can feel rich by hiring a Ferrari for a few euros from Sixt, or seem rich by taking a Porsche in leasing for a couple of years. The instalments are paid for by the company, after all, at least in the great majority of cases for the so-called prestige cars that invade our roads. The decline of the car as status symbol has also been caused by the incessant and monotonous business of brand building: all the marques, if we are to believe the brochures, offer cars that are uniformly beautiful, dynamic, elegant and prestigious. Decency, normality, defects; ugh! Long live the pimp, obscene silicon taste of the sort used by MTV to decorate a car and life (sic!). In truth, not everyone wishes to listen to these pre-digested fibs. It is from

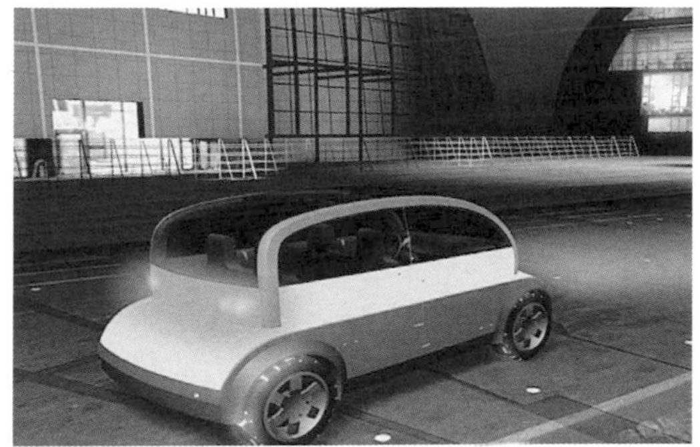

10. Future simple: prototype of a fuel cell vehicle, Glocar, 2003
© Ford Motor Company

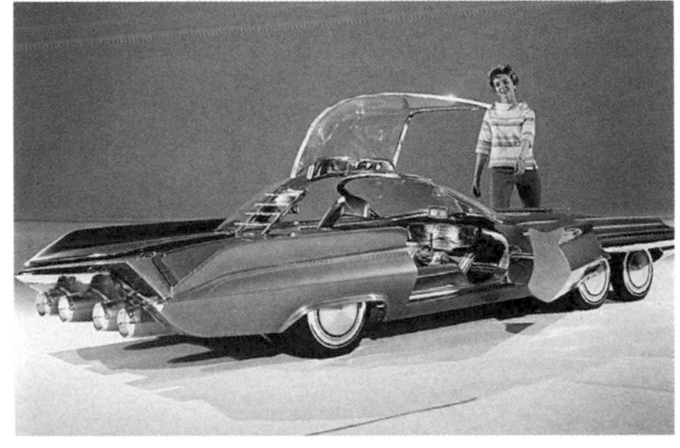

11. The Future comes from space in the prototype Seattle-ITE XXI of 1962
© Ford Motor Company

this intolerance that springs the young cult for Youngtimer cars. Everything that was once considered ugly and old — Grandad's beige Fiat, the pensioner's gold-coloured Opel, the lemon-yellow Toyota from the provincial playboy — have suddenly become 'in.' This attraction for the banal, trash and all that is out of fashion, demonstrates a courageous rejection of the monotony of the advertising image and at the same time of the popular-elitiste attempt to set up new reference values. Or should we believe that cars ought to be made to measure, as a unique model or limited series, inspired for the nth time by the myths of the past, whether contemporary status symbols or not? To paraphrase Benito Mussolini, one feels tempted to say, in defining the car status symbol today: 'it's not hard, just simply pointless.'

The car cannot cease to exist and represent, but it must change. A new myth needs to be formed. I believe that the fundamental value of the car is based on experience. The car serves to establish relationships, and not just physical ones, with ourselves and with our surroundings. Even a caustic author like Henry Miller noted in *The Air-conditioned Nightmare* (1945) that 'the automobile has been invented in order to force us to learn to be patient and kind with each other.' It is not the shell but the possibilities it offers that dictate the rules for the car of the future. I am not speaking of engines, gearshifts, numbers of doors and consumption here, but of spaces, relationships, sensations, contents, to define which new values are needed. With my childhood myths of speed and of the status symbol in tatters, let us try to take in the adult myth of the 'gettingonwelltogether' myth for a moment and hypothesize an intelligent 'slow driving.' (What would advertisers make of it, I wonder?). Acceptable? But then we have no need of a beautiful, imposing, aggressive, high-performance car! We need an appealing, light, fascinating and versatile one. It might be the prototype Ford Glocar of 2003, which not coincidentally was not planned for a motor show but for a triennial design fair, without engine and with a luminescent, sensitive skin. Of course, the car will have to sacrifice its now useless engineering in the name of other qualities; naturally, electronics will take over as the playful centre of the appearance and behaviour of the vehicle, of the on-board infotainment and communications. No longer a motorway rocket or off-road caravel, the car of the future will become a mobile space for adventure and relaxation, and again takes centre-stage as refuge-toy-telephone-cinema-eatery-cupboard-gym-discotheque... That the shell be small to take dad (or mum) to work, or large, to take a family (or friends) on holiday is not the point, as whether it be open-top or not, that it resemble Buckingham Palace, an iPod or something new. Technology is flexible and can adapt itself to everything, even style. The man-consumer will respond to this as long as good examples are set him: the valid motives are evident and urgent.

Points of View

Three 'Codes' to Decipher 50 Years of Design by Giorgetto Giugiaro

Giuliano Molineri

Summarizing the development of 50 intense, prolific years of creative, design and entrepreneurial activity of the 'car designer of the 20th century'[1] in just a few pages is as hard as it might appear impracticable for a historian to condense 50 years of history into the same space. Either one adopts a rather superfluous chronological approach or — with the excuse of summariness — one picks a few signal episodes as emblematic testimonials.

I have had the luck to follow Giorgetto Giugiaro's professional development from close up, to the point of having lived alongside a 'genius:' to bear witness to his career, I do not intend descending into hagiography but will hazard — if I am able — a cross-section of his way of tackling a car project.

Even though Giugiaro is still an active genius open to experiences and adventures that will in future require other forms of examination, I think I am able without forcing things, to describe the phenomenonology of his production as the result of some dominant parameters that follow and intersect with each other. I believe I can identify — in common with the researcher and art critic — three main codes suited to outlining his development as designer: 1. the exploitation of form as emotion and provocation; 2. the submission of form to the dictates of research and the industrial project; 3. the maturity of the contents as the result of form and function.

Giugiaro in the first place was born an artist: both his father and grandfather were painters — working in fresco — and musicians. He felt the vocation to dedicate himself to painting, going beyond the Aristotelian/naturalistic approach of his family teachers — although they were highly skilled in portraying subjects, blending colours, depicting effects — in order to try out more topical avenues justifying figurative art now being faced with overly sophisticated technical means to capture and animate a given subject: photography, cinema, television...

It was above all the use of the spatula and superimposition of broad layers of paint, reminiscent of the Impressionists (Cézanne) to intrigue him. The course he attended in Turin between the age of 15 and 17 with Eugenio Colmo — known as 'Golia' — concentrated on illustration, figure drawings, caricature and advertising images with techniques including the imitation of original works, portraits, sculptures, traditional customs, theatre sets,

There was a proposal that he go to the Accademia Albertina di Belle Arti but his father, Mario, showing considerable common sense and fearful of the risks of an artist's life, also insisted that he frequent courses of technical drawing for aspirant designers.

It was purely coincidental that the brilliant student should be invited for his end-of-course essay to work on the caricature of the most admired cars of the times, and only chance that *ingegner* Dante Giacosa, the charismatic head of style and design at Fiat (and the grandson of Golia) should visit the exhibition and stop to gaze at Giorgetto's works that revealed an uncommon skill that was more than expressive.

In September of 1955, Giugiaro found himself at Mirafiori in the Styling Office for Special Vehicles having passed a test of skill in the Technical Publications Department. He was required to do a perspective drawing of an engine, and passed thanks to the technical notions acquired during his design courses.

[1] A jury of 120 journalists and international experts met in Las Vegas in December 1999 to confer upon Giorgetto Giugiaro the nomination of 'Car Designer of the Century.'

The four years at Fiat proved an excellent apprenticeship but the essential step took place at the end of 1959, when Nuccio Bertone invited him to join his already historic coachbuilding company. The restless creativity of Franco Scaglione, who had been responsible, apart from other models, for the B.A.T. and the Giulietta SS, had seen him opte to become self-employed.

The young stylist thus arrived at the best melting-pot open to experimentation his provocative ambition could hope for. Nuccio Bertone became his teacher, inspirer and stimulus. Only in this way is it possible to explain the prototypes for the Chevrolet Corvair Testudo and the Iso Grifo Coupé (of 1963), and the Alfa Romeo Canguro (1964), along with the early projects for larger production runs, the successful Alfa Romeo Giulia GT (1963) and Fiat 850 Spider (1965).

The Testudo proved to be Giugiaro's first masterpiece: a bearer of stimuli and stylemes, it would be reutilised in the design world well beyond the 1960s. A rounded shell-shape, pop-up headlights, forward-opening canopy hinged at the base of the windscreen, a rectangular steering wheel with the first references to the aviation world: a travelling vehicle materialising a 'lunar' dream.

The Canguro, a sculpture with an original truncated tail treatment, fast-looking but not excessive to stress its racing pedigree, confirmed Giugiaro's predisposition to designing sinuous but balanced and clean volumes, helped also through the use of fixed windows to echo those aerodynamic effects which would soon — after the Yom Kippur war — make the jump to design hard points.

Giugiaro's first great gift appears in all his youthful work: a wish to experiment through technical and mechanical innovation, working through the workshop (assisted by the many experts who have worked with him in his lifetime, including Ezio Cingolani, Sergio Coggiola and Pietro Sibona), compressing and tapering the lines to form a balanced, elegant, refined whole, if we exclude the themes exploring decidedly alternative avenues, such as the Capsula (1982), Biga and Columbus (1992).

After moving to Ghia's Head of Styling and Design Centre on the suggestion of a friend, Giacomo Gaspardo Moro, director of the Turinese coachworks before the arrival of Alejandro De Tomaso, Giugiaro's creativity grew by leaps and bounds, with the De Tomaso Mangusta and the Maserati Ghibli (1966), two extreme — and today 'classic' — sports coupés, which highlight the power of their engines in the form of the bonnet and flowing tails (in the first case, the engine was set centrally and longitudinally; in the second at the front and longitudinal).

It was in this youthful, ambitious phase, open to an evident, perhaps even blasphemous, student language that Giugiaro — at the age of 28 — revealed another predisposition that became typically his throughout his career: functional research, with contents being stressed over form. The first vehicle for women was the Vanessa, based on the chassis of the Fiat 850 (1968): larger windows, a high crease line on the front wings to indicate where the car ended and facilitate parking, a second side window hinged at the top to help load a baby seat (or shopping) and a swivelling driver's seat to facilitate egress while wearing a tight skirt. The first (I believe) electric city car to be proposed by a coachwork company was the Rowan (1967), promoted by the Rowan Controller Company of Maryland, which had bought a holding in the Ghia company.

The passion for the correct dimensions for the interior, for the space for rear passengers, for reduced obstructions caused by passengers on seats, a respect for the space between head and roof and between shoulders and door were taken to their logical — and misconstrued — conclusions in an exemplary project headed by Rudolf Hruska for Alfa Romeo's Alfasud (1971), which for decades provided a point of reference for cars from Europe and further afield, despite production problems and poor quality materials and workmanship.

I cannot here dedicate the deserved space to the partnership between Giugiaro and his technological partner and friend, Aldo Mantovani, nor describe the salient phases of the Italdesign company since its foundation — as an equal partnership — in February 1968. A winning formula that for over 35 years has combined creativity and sales of engineering and technology including the handling of entire project management, feasibility, experimenting, computer testing, pre-series prototype construction for bench and road tests for international homologation requirements.

Italdesign Giugiaro (it was renamed in 1999), under the Presidency of the founder and Vice-presidency of Dario Trucco, CEO of the public company, has operational branches also in France, Spain and China. It employs 1100 people, of which 800 in the technology divisions and 200 in the design sectors, in the virtual reality centre, modelling and prototype and pre-series construction workshops.[2]

The season of cars destined for medium to large-scale production thus began with the Alfasud, Alfetta GT and GTV (1974), and the Alfasud Sprint (1976), and continued with 'epoch'-making collaborations with the Volkswagen group: Passat (1973), Golf and Scirocco (1974), the Seat Ibiza (1984), Malaga (1985), Toledo (1991), Ibiza and Cordoba (1993), the Toledo II (1998); and with the Fiat group: Lancia Delta (1979), Panda and Panda 4×4 (1980), Lancia Prisma (1982), Uno (1983), the Lancia Thema, Saab 9000 (1984) and Fiat Croma (1985), the Punto of 1993, the Idea and Alfa Romeo 156 (2003) and 147 (2004), the Fiat Croma, Grande Punto, Alfa Romeo 159 and Brera of 2005 and the Alfa Sportwagon of 2006.

Alongside work with Isuzu, Subaru, Toyota (the Lexus GS 300 of 1991) and Daihatsu, an extremely significant contribution was made by Giugiaro and Italdesign to the growth of the new brands in Korea. For Hyundai, they designed the Pony (1974), the first vehicle to be entirely produced in South Korea, and then the Stellar (1983), Excel and Presto (1985), and Sonata (1988). For Daewoo, they produced the Lanos (1996), Leganza (1997), the successful export version of the little Matiz (1998), the Magnus (2000) and the Lacetti (2003). A few years ago, China entered the picture and is proving highly prolific, and important work continues with the French and German industries.

The Golf on the one hand and the Panda on the other are, in my opinion, the most emblematic results. The German car because it featured a totally original architecture that was very different to usual practices at the time. It had a compact, rather high form, a novel crease at the top of the rear hatch, which created a 'technical-performance' effect of youthful inspiration and led the initially rather sceptical Wolfsburg company to launch two further and highly successful models: the GTI and the Diesel.

The ADI — Associazione per il Disegno Industriale, or Association for Industrial Design — conferred the Premio Compasso d'Oro on the Panda, which Giugiaro considered a joint award with Aldo Mantovani.[3] They alone were able to respect the laconic brief passed them by Carlo De Benedetti: 'A spartan but spacious utility — along the lines of the Renault 4 and Citroën 2 CV — of the same weight and industrial cost as the Fiat 126.'

In Guigiaro's incredible output from the 1970s, it is worth noting a strong formal intuition which meets, or rather precedes, market and marketing expectations. The forms — the Fiat Uno and Punto (the first edition of 1993 and the Grande Punto of 2005) are prime examples — suggest quality perceived perhaps at subliminal level by the consumer. No more gaping panel gaps between body panels and lights and windows; in shut lines between doors, pillars and roof; everything was now integrated in an organic, precise manner.

Here too, we find a forerunner — again insufficiently noted by critics — in the form of the design of the join between door and roof, with the elimination of the visible gutter (rainwater is channelled within the door frame). The smooth surface obtained in this area improves airflow and prevents aerodynamic turbulence and noise.

Applied in 1979 to the prototype Isuzu Asso di Fiori and two years later of the standard Isuzu Piazza model, this design innovation — unfortunately not covered by patent on behalf of Italdesign — was adopted in house as from the Medusa prototype, in the Fiat Uno and in the later models designed in the Moncalieri workshop, but it became a universal feature of cars by manufacturers throughout the world.

[2] The general information, most significant data and description of over 100 models put into production, and of the over 80 research prototypes made, together with information on projects in other motor vehicle, rail and product sectors can be downloaded from www.italdesign.it and www.giugiarodesign.com.

[3] In April 2005, the Politecnico di Torino conferred him an honours degree in Mechanical Engineering, with the following motivation: 'Aldo Mantovani has through instinctive passion chosen his specialization and has sat qualification exams at every step of his career. As a designer, he is a skilled promotor of knowledge: he has believed in technology and in its continuous adjustment to the signs of innovation, as a powerful stimulus towards progress...'

The passion for research led Giugiaro — assisted from 1990 by his son, Fabrizio, who is today Vice President of the Design Centre — to explore the most disparate avenues, with concept cars to be exhibit at shows, to the industry and the international public.

I shall mention a few here, in demonstration of the breadth of research. In terms of purely advanced aesthetic form: Manta, Iguana, Tapiro, Caimano, Boomerang, Maya, Incas, Aztec, Kensington, Firepoint, Bucrane, Calà, Scighera, Moray. For new forms geared to improved aerodynamic penetration: Medusa and Orca. For improved interior space and maximum versatility through increasing the height of the vehicle and shortening it — this is the most forward-looking, reiterated and clearly incisive of Giugiaro's design concept — the New York Taxi, the Megagamma, Capsula, Together, Orbit, Asgard, Buran, Kubang, Visconti, Croma V8 (the Columbus presents a case apart: a Californian shuttle constituting a prestigious vehicle that can be used as office or for public relations) and the new 2005 Fiat Croma, offering decidedly generous and highly appreciated interior space.

For research into unusual structural forms and the adoption of special materials, examined with competence and enthusiastic collaboration by Fabrizio Giugiaro: the Nazca M12, C2, C2 Spider, Structura, Twenty-Twenty, and niche projects for a young, playful or sporting public, such as the forward-looking Panda 4×4 Strip, the Machimoto, Formula 4, Formula Hammer, Tuareg, Tarek. Among the high-performance sports cars, I think it worth noting the BMW M1 (the only small-scale production series with glass-fibre body: 460 examples consigned by Italdesign to the Munich manufacturer) and the VW W12, an example of which in 2001 beat the world 24-hour speed record on the Nardò circuit for all classes.

Highly significant and in line with the content-driven research I have defined as dominating Giugiaro's production is the work started in 1967 with the electric Rowan on city vehicles with alternative hybrid engines (diesel and electric for Biga with computerized public management system, Lucciola, Toyota Alessandro Volta; battery and hydrogen for Mitsubishi Nessie). A more comprehensive researcher would dedicate much space to Giugiaro's passion for the recovery and modernization of historical stylemes: one need mention here just the attempt to revive the Bugatti brand with the superb Bugatti EB112 and latter EB118, EB218 and EB18/3 Chiron.

The Medusa (Lancia Beta Montecarlo with rear-mounted engine, 1980) represents, I believe, the 'sculpture' that more than any other is representative — *Mitomacchina* would define it his *Victory* of Samothrace — of Giugiaro's 'controlled maturity.' If we were able to be see these models circulating on today's roads, they would not cease to surprise us for their contemporary look.

The persistent quality of Giugiaro's creative vein found confirmation, 25 years after the Medusa, in the modelling of the Alfa Romeo Brera, a prize-winning coupé which convinced the manufacturer to promote this model hard to relaunch its ambitions on a worldwide scale.

Finally, an example of the granturismo from a legendary marque summarises the elegant approach, a philological material culture integrated with comfort aboard the vehicle. The car 'for me, to celebrate my 50 years as designer,' the Ferrari GG50, as authentic as it is 'personal.' If you speak of it with Giugiaro, he will have you note how it is easy to get in an out, how comfortable the passengers are in the rear seats, how the boot is able to carry a pair of skis or a golf bag.

The man seems to show little interest in his public relations office which tries to document how over 40 million cars have been built with the help of the blue pencil he has tucked into his pocket. The man has the air of one exploring the destiny of a self-propelled vehicle with curiosity and perhaps some apprehension, a vehicle that in the third millennium has to resolve the critical points it has brought forward — together with the undeniable fine points — from the 20th century.

'Silence, creativity at work.'

The Designer's Point of View

Sergio Pininfarina

Mitomacchina: Myth Machine, the title of this exhibition, has been well chosen; whoever dreamed it up has a happy gift for summary, having succeeded, with the simple fusion of two common nouns in synthesizing all that has been said and written in rivers of words in every language of the world by fans and experts.

Mart is an institution that has succeeded in gaining fame and prestige and has accorded to its praiseworthy tradition with this *Mitomacchina*, an exhibition which avoids the risks of platitude, an omnipresent risk when tackling the theme of the 'car,' invented barely more than a century ago as a means of transport and which soon became much, much more in the world's collective imagination.

Leafing through the catalogue for this exhibition is for me like leafing through a family album, not just because various Pininfarina cars are mentioned in it, but also because the history of my company and my own life are linked to that of the motor car.

I have been asked to illustrate the point of view of the designer. I would like to start by repeating what I said in 1981 to the students receiving their diplomas at the Art Center College of Design in Pasadena, California, one of the most important design schools in the world: 'you are very lucky, because not only are you preparing for one of the most fascinating and stimulating jobs in the world, but you have the possibility of creating order in the disorder of our lives.' Because producing more handsome, more efficient or functional objects means bringing order.

Even today, after a life spent — with great passion — in this magnificent job, I am deeply convinced of this.

If you look up the word 'design' in the Italian Treccani dictionary, you will find the following definition: 'in industrial production, design... aiming to reconcile technical, functional and economic requirements of mass-produced objects...'

This definition is correct in substance, but to my mind an essential requisite is missing and which I wish to add: that of the aesthetic value of the product.

Today, throughout the world, the market demands a synthesis of beauty and functional quality, style and effectiveness. This is the principal aim of the designer.

Allow me to go back a little: in the distant past, at the time of the Industrial Revolution, little importance was attributed to the aesthetics of a product. A new society was appearing, a new lifestyle: industry was frantically involved in meeting the growing demand from the market by developing new technologies; it had no time for anything else. At that time, entrepreneurs produced essentially functional, practical products that were not much appreciated by the society, especially the intellectual one, that was still tied to the Renaissance cultural model of the artist's single piece; mass-produced industrial products were seen as the antithesis of the masterpiece.

All this is true of any product and hence for the car too.

In the early post-Second World War years marked by a recovering economy, designs principally took into account economic and technical factors: the extent of the investments, facility of construction, methods of production, performance; little thought was given to aesthetics. Stylists in companies counted for almost nothing: they had only to improve the look of what had already been prepared by the technicians. Only later, in the 1950s, did the aesthetic aspect, then called 'styling,' acquire greater importance.

In truth, the industrial concept of styling appeared earlier, not in Europe but in the United States. Over 70 years ago, Alfred Sloan, at the time President of General Motors, sensed that styling would in future become the most important and aggressive feature driving sales. As a consequence, the first 'style centres' were set up for the car-manufacturing industry, which programmed an aesthetic renewal of the models, creating *ipso facto* a planned obsolescence of the products.

After a period of impetuous developments, the oil crisis of the 1970s imposed a more rational and functional rethinking of the car; a sterile stress on styling gave way to design, or to a more sensible approach to planning the form of a car. In those years, there was a new discussion of access, aerodynamics, ergonomics. In other words, the creative teams transformed themselves from poets of the pencil to true designers. Styling began to become 'design,' which term included every aspect of a project: aesthetic, technical, functional, including production and use requirements. We now enter today's phase: today, design is used in the broadest and most noble sense of the term.

As a consequence, designers are today required to offer a new culture and renewed professional training. Indeed, in a company today, the design department must work in close collaboration with other sectors of the company and share the product philosophy and targeted aims from the very start of the creative process.

The designer's role has changed considerably, therefore: we are not just asked to 'create' new forms of figurative expression, to supply a fine drawing or model: we are asked much more. We have to confer appeal and aesthetic personality on the product while respecting the functionality and technical specifications in full, including those imposed by the methods and processes of production.

This does not, however, mean transforming the designer into an engineer or seller: his principal aim remains that of striving after beauty or, better, aesthetic personality; his underlying vocation remains essentially artistic. Indeed, for a new product to be successful, it is necessary — although not of itself sufficient — that it be functional, technologically advanced and easy to produce: on top of this, it must have a strong aesthetic personality in which are blended beauty and innovation.

Even in Sloan's time, good design helped to sell, but this is all the truer today. Because today, more than ever, increasing competition has led to products that are increasingly similar in terms of price, performance and quality.

These are all important factors. However, if we examine the essential reasons for which some cars have been enormously successful for decades, we can see that one factor — aside from the technical value — is fundamental and makes the difference: their aesthetic personality. There are many examples, but I shall mention just three, all now a part of history: the Beetle, the Mini and, in Italy, the Cinquecento.

If we see two different objects which do a given job equally well, which will we instinctively pick? Certainly the one that is aesthetically more pleasing, and this admiration will transform itself into desire of possession.

I must stress that the car is an extraordinary object requiring an extremely complex design process, because it is made of an exterior and of an interior, whereas most objects are formed solely of an exterior.

With a car, we have a double problem: the emotive impact of the car exterior seen from 20 or 30 metres, and the other impact of when one sits in its interior.

In summary, the design functions in my opinion are: 1. supplying an object with beauty and aesthetic personality, an ideal man has always sought; 2. improving quality of life, in producing more functional articles; and 3. becoming a factor for economic development, since design is a vital element in the commercial success of a product.

But good design also has a highly valuable cultural function: it can help avoid a repetition of the mistakes of the past by the most industrialized nations, when very often cultural and ecological values were sacrificed. An intelligent and critical review of our experience can enable emerging countries to effect the modernization process of their society in a more far-sighted manner and within a framework of sustainable development.

I have covered the salient points in the history of design and expressed my basic convictions. I like to add that this design a typically Italian value. Why do I say this?

First of all, we live in a country that is particularly open to creative activities; I believe that over half of the world's masterpieces are to be found in Italy.

Moreover, we take strength from that ancient, tradition deeply rooted in our culture, which created the workshops of the Renaissance and that scientific, creative and artistic research of that typically Italian, multi-faceted genius that was Leonardo da Vinci. He teaches us the beauty of form is the result of a profound commitment geared to achieving high quality.

The Renaissance, the Italian artistic and literary production of the 15th century represent — and I say this without chauvinism or rhetoric — one of the greatest moments in Western civilization. This was a period that saw an exceptional development in individual creativity and craftsmanship, characteristics that are distinctive of Italian culture.

I mean by this that the exceptional upsurge of creativity in the Renaissance has influenced the history of Italy in the culture and sensibilities of the people, in industrial activities and in the way of running an activity that has lasted from then until now.

Design tends to mark the meeting point between form and technology, taste and functionality. Nothing seems to be more congenial to the so-called Italian genius as this permanent striving towards harmonizing beauty and functionality.

The excellence of Italian style is universally recognized and has become synonymous with creativity and innovative quality: hence the myth of 'made in Italy.'

I have heard it said that the golden years of design are now over, but I do not agree: perhaps the heroic years are over, but not the golden years. I am sure that the golden years of design will continue, and indeed that the importance of design is destined to increase.

The heroic period was that in which only intuition counted, the age of pioneers, in which a person could make a name for himself independently of his 'cultural' background; today, instead, it is important that method be taught and specific studies are therefore the right approach for training the young.

The role of design would not have taken on such importance were it not backed by the new methods made possible by information technology.

Let us clarify first of all that, even if this has provided an essential help to the process of manufacturing, man has nevertheless kept the noblest part for himself: creativity, judgement, approval. Machines have only taken over the most material and repetitive tasks: calculation, construction, control.

Today, however, technology has taken a truly important and revolutionary step forward, because with the invention of CAS — Computer Aided Styling — machines no longer help merely with the executive process of the design, but even with the designer's actual creativity. CAS offers incomparably greater possibilities: without even having started making a model, it makes it possible to see a project from various angles on a scale of 1:1, and set in its natural setting with a host of points of reference, such as people or objects.

Thus, with the help of a purely mathematical model, we can come closer to the sensations the final product will give, and this in a manner that could not even have been imagined in the past. We can even see it move virtually in its natural setting.

The differences in the methods of today's creative process with respect to the past are enormous, therefore, but the fundamental principles remain the same I learned from my father, my greatest teacher: a search for simplicity in lines and main proportions, for harmony between full and void, and a respect for functionality.

To conclude, I would like to dedicate a few words to the future. The car has passed through periods of strong expansion and major crises, but it has always shown itself open to renewal and able to surmount every difficulty — from the oil crisis to economic crises — with great liveliness and spirit of innovation.

It has been shown that the car can still be a young product open to new developments. Moreover, the fact that the industry continues to invest in such a massive way to renew models and the production and manufacturing technologies surely constitutes the greatest guarantee for its future.

Everyone knows that the car — perhaps the most significant product of the 20th century — has brought many benefits to all of us in our daily lives, both when we are at work and when we enjoy our leisure time. But it has also created problems for our society: atmospheric pollution, road accidents, urban congestion.

The most important challenge it must now face is that of the environment, of reducing emissions.

I feel it is only right to recognize that, of all the industrial sectors, the car industry is the one that has invested most in the ecological sector, working intensely on the development of all the technological solutions enabling the car of today to guarantee increasingly severe safety standards, to use easily recycled materials, to reduce consumption and, as a consequence, emissions.

To this end, the car industry has followed two approaches: both the improvement in the traditional systems of propulsion, in order to reduce toxic emissions drastically, and research into new systems of propulsion with low or zero pollution. Such solutions might have electric and hybrid propulsion in series or in parallel, and these are already reality.

As for the challenges of the future, I think that these more correctly concern propulsion systems based on hydrogen: both in internal combustion engines and in fuel cells.

This may well prove the final solution to all problems for a great dream to come true: that of inventing non-polluting vehicles. From a technical point of view, we may say that the problems have been substantially resolved. What remains to be solved is the economic factor, and this will still take some years before it becomes possible to sell such vehicles at competitive prices.

As a designer, however, I wish above all to stress a basic concept: I am convinced that these new propulsion systems will also bring about a revolution in the architecture of the vehicles. We all remember that when the first motor cars were built, they seemed like horse-drawn carriages with an engine where the horse ought to have been. Today, the new propulsion systems have not yet brought about such changes in weight and dimension as to change the architecture of the vehicles, but I am sure that they will, and so we will see a new generation of vehicles with new forms and new architectures.

We need only consider the possibilities offered by the joint use of fuel cells, drive-by-wire technology and the even more futuristic drive-by-light systems, in other words, in which the mechanical controls can be replaced with electric or luminous controls transmitted to the actuators by electric or fibre-optic cable (the latter are not affected by electromagnetic interference). This opens the door to incredible stylistic and design possibilities; the fuel cells can be placed anywhere and take on new forms or dimensions; the drive-by-wire/light systems will do away with the pedals, dashboard and steering wheel, so the driver will be able to sit anywhere he likes. We find ourselves before a new and exciting chapter in car construction.

The world has not yet taken stock of the infinite implications of these new prospects. Indeed, to date the cars made have been inspired by traditional mechanical vehicles, but this is destined to change.

It is up to we designers to make this cultural leap and invent new, perhaps revolutionary forms to add to the new technologies: a challenge which I am certain will open new and stimulating chapters.

Speak to Me, o Screen, of Isotta the Star...

Gian Piero Brunetta

The Evolution of Species

When Mario Morasso wrote *La nuova arma (la macchina)* in 1905, many cars had already appeared on the silver screen in a number of roles, especially as veritable protagonists of the action. There were American fire-engines miraculously managing to save endangered people, flying cars, others climbing walls, provoking accidents or overcoming obstacles of all types. While *L'arrivée du train à la gare de Lyon* was the first film to cause a trauma to the 35 spectators at the first public screening of the Lumière show in December 1895, it only took a few years for the film industry to show increasing attention to the new vehicle and its use — at times angelic and saving, at others diabolical and destructive, now dramatic, now comic.

Morasso dedicated a chapter to *The Aesthetics of Speed* and has the merit of having established the beauty of a motor car and its power as a unit of measurement four years before the *Manifesto of Futurism*. Morasso deemed a car 'beautiful the more its organs stand out and expand as much as the muscles of a hard-working athlete' and considered to be anything but irreverent the comparison between the *Victory* of Samothrace 'enthroned at the top of the stairs at the Louvre, with the wind entrapped in the folds of her drapes [...] and [...] when the iron monster shakes and stamps to the impassioned beat of the engine, it offers a magnificent revelation of virtual strength in the same way and clearly reveals the mad speed of which it is capable.'

In his *Manifesto of Futurism*, Filippo Tommaso Marinetti borrowed not just the comparison from Morasso's book, but also the motif of beauty in male terms and synonymous with power ('We declare that the magnificence of the world has been enriched by a new beauty. The beauty of speed. A racing car with its bonnet adorned with large tubes similar to snakes with explosive breath, a roaring car that seems to race on gravel is more beautiful that the Victory of Samothrace'), but seemed not to touch upon the theme of risk, of the desire for power, the defiance of death, which was instead in part tackled by Gabriele d'Annunzio in 1910 in his novel, *Forse che sì, forse che no*.

Also memorable is the start to the third section of a 1916 novel entitled *I quaderni di Serafino Gubbio operatore* by Pirandello, in which he has a car burst onto the stage of the film industry, succeeding in a single space to bring together the times of two civilizations, one burgeoning, the other declining:

> 'A slight touch of the wheel. There is a carriage trotting ahead.
>
> Beep, beep beeeeep.
>
> What? The car's horn is pulling it backwards? Yes, it really seems to be making the carriage come backwards in a comic fashion.
>
> The three ladies in the motor car laugh, turn, raise their arms to wave in lively fashion, amidst a confused, gay rush of multicoloured veils... The three ladies in the motor car are three actresses from Kosmograph and have greeted the little carriage, pulled backwards by their mechanical rush, in such a lively manner not because they have

seen a dear friend, but because the car, the machine inebriates them and provokes such an unbridled liveliness in them.'

Car and actresses are seen as a single body; although Pirandello intended neither wedding nor riding the culture of the machine, he nevertheless depicted a highly significant episode of early symbiosis.

If we turn our gaze to the entire depiction of the car in early cinema, we need to stress that although European cinema did not immediately promote the car to protagonist of the filmed action — and when it did so almost always needed a literary mediation (which we have also used and will use again), American cinema made direct use of it from the first decade of the 20th century, adopting it as a magical assistant to celebrate the advent of a new civilization and conquer space and time.

A journey back in time in the history of cinema provides an opportunity to consider together the variety of roles and functions of the car and its total adaptability and compatibility with the various dramatic and comic genres and styles, and to rediscover forms and models of cars that have for years played an important role in the collective imagination. And last but not least, it provides a way to see how, at many times, cinema has been and can still be a perfect venue for the memory of fine creativity and hybridization and intermingling with contemporary artistic processes.

Moreover, the presence of the car in leading dramatic and symbolic roles on the screen contributes to the development of the cinema as a mythopoeic machine and receives from the screen a thrust towards the development of a series of mythologies linked to this or that model of car, and to the myth of the car as symbol of modernity.

The links between cinema and the car may be divided — if we simplify a complex relationship that goes in different directions — into about four main phases, just like the stages in the operation of a four-stroke engine.

The first phase opens with wonder and a magic that is blended with science and engineering, and then with beauty and the founding of new canons reflecting the aesthetic nature of the new machine. On the one hand the paragons of the parts of the car with the golden measurements of statues from the classical world; on the other, the irresistible parallel rise of the beauty of the cars and of the first great stars of the silver screen.

Both are the object of love descended to earth to show a miracle and are soon promoted to cult status.

For example, the early Lancias appearing on the screen seem perfectly to interpret the spirit of the futurists and move to conquer the collective imagination in parallel to the birth and expansion of the diva system. From the outset, many of the models from the Turin-based company were seen not as simple means of locomotion but as characters on a stage able to play an evident diva role along with the other actors. If we observe the increasing present and progressive change of the roles of the car on the screen, which in just a few years became protagonist or co-protagonist, we may ask ourselves whether the automotive star system did not precede that of the actors, or at least moved in parallel with it and in like manner.

Starting with the films of Méliès, the car is gazed at, admired, loved, touched like an object that is fully part of the 'erosphere.'

What is there in common and what differences between the various models of Panhard, Napier, De Dietrich, Rochet-Schneider, Mercedes, Alfa Conte Ricotti, Rolls-Royce, Lancia, Itala, Isotta Fraschini and the faces and bodies of Sarah Bernhard, Asta Nielsen, Lyda Borelli, Francesca Bertini, Pina Menichelli, Lillian Gish and Gloria Swanson? The aura surrounding their bodies is quite the same and around them in a very short time grew up a similar and widely extended star cult. In some cases, we have the impression that star and car struggle to steal the scene and it is unclear if the added value comes from the one or the other co-protagonist.

1. *007 Never Say Never*, by Irvin Kershner, 1983

2. *007 For Your Eyes Only*, by John Glen, 1981

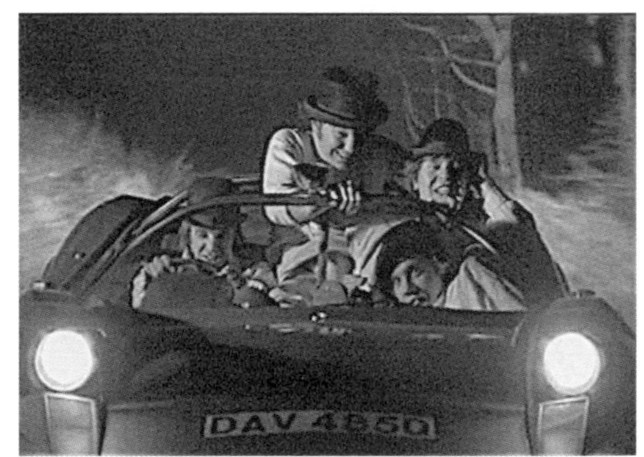

3. *A Clockwork Orange*, by Stanley Kubrick, 1971

4. *Once Upon a Time in America*, by Sergio Leone, 1984

5. *To Catch a Thief*, by Alfred Hitchcock, 1955

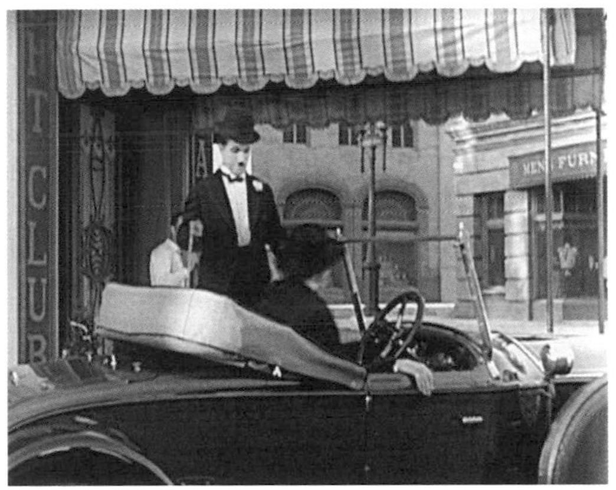

6. *City Lights*, by Charlie Chaplin, 1931

From the 1920s onwards, models of cars began to appear that imposed themselves as veritable works of art, like icons of creativity within industrial production. It is worth recalling the discovery of the Isotta Fraschini Tipo 8 A in Billy Wilder's *Sunset Boulevard* (1950), and how much appeal is exerted by the car 20 years later, Howard Hughes's 1929 Duesenberg in Martin Scorsese's *The Aviator* (2004), the Tucker prototype of 1948 in Coppola's film, *Tucker – The Man and His Dream* (1988), and Bond's Aston Martin or the Ford Mustang in *Leaving Las Vegas*, as well as the Ferrari used by Fellini in *Toby Dammitt*, one of the episodes in *Tre passi nel delirio* (1967).

The second phase is that of the metropolitan symphonies, of the accords between the rhythms of life in the city and the rhythms of the luxury cars and cars for all, of the sharing and multiplication of cars to include the widest possible range of new adepts and faithful. Beauty and power alone are no longer the absolute values. From Vertov and Ruttmann, King Vidor and Frtiz Lang to Augusto Genina, and from the great gangster films — from *Scarface* by Howard Hawks (1932) to *Public Enemy* of the year before by William Wellmann — we see how the car is above all the instrument around which the rhythms of the new urban and industrial symphonies accord. The car also became synonymous with freedom; it was the means enabling huge swarms of pioneers to move west in America in a search for new frontiers and a new promised land, as in John Ford's *The Grapes of Wrath* (1940). This was a time in which an unattainable dream suddenly became perfectly possible for the masses and within their reach. The car became an integral part of any type of landscape and millions of new devotees seemed to intone the prayer 'give us today our daily car…,' and soon succeed in realizing their dream.

The third phase was that of the hybridization and cohabitation of the two previous phases: power, beauty and multiplication of possibilities of use led to an enormous growth in the number of vehicles and progressive increase in traffic on the roads, in the cities, on motorways. The myths of progress and the symbols of a broadened well-being touching new and vast sectors of society seem to suffer a mortal blow. At the outset, the myth of the car available to all, of the utility as emblem of democratic development, seemed to take hold at the same time as the machine remaining a status symbol, marking the differences between classes and income. The explosion in the number of cars led to the formation of a veritable urban jungle, in which the distinctions disappear and the syndrome of omnipotence was replaced by that of paralysis, of blocked energy. In the latter half of the 1960s, the dizzying spell of the economic miracle over (in Italy, obviously, but also elsewhere), the car was no longer associated with the idea of progress, emancipation, freedom, but also with fear, imprisonment, constriction. The traffic jams, urban and extra-urban paralysis appearing in the films of Fellini, Tati, Godard, Comencini, became prophetic messages of the imminent collapse of industrial civilization. From these years, we witness a comparison between the speed of racing circuits and that of the city streets, chases in the dense network of urban streets or in medieval towns, but in many cases the top prize seemed to be that of being able to emerge alive from gigantic massacres of cars of all types. In the mid-1960s, Dino Risi recorded the radio report of a standard Sunday in *Ombrellone* (1965) in these terms: '150,000 Germans have crossed the border at the Brenner Pass. Numerous accidents have occurred along the French border. To the west, nothing new. Numerous crashes on the Autostrada del Sole. Twenty-five dead so far with the day barely begun.'

The fourth phase is that of absolute liberty to store the multiple possible future scenarios and changes of form, function, roles and possibilities of use of the car in a situation in which the individual in part or wholly tends to be replaced by elements derived from the car industry. From a certain moment onwards, with Cronenberg and other directors, we begin to see a reflection on a post-human condition in which a process of hybridization, symbiosis, metamorphosis of man with machine appears, almost as though their fusion were the last chapter of Darwinian evolution. The arrival point for the moment might be considered that of *Cars*, the cartoon film in which a car has all the human attributes and man is completely absent from the landscape.

We might begin with Méliès's *Voyage à travers l'impossible* of 1904 to explore all those science-fiction and other films projected into the future. Ever since the 1920s, cinema has imagined the cities and cars of the future: starting with *Metropolis* by Lang in 1927, which seemed to include the visionary designs of Sant'Elia, to the city of Everytown in the 1936 film, *Things to Come*, by William Cameron Menzies, we have been thrust forward in time well before the first space probes, predicting the future and the vehicles man will use. For the most part, we are treated to hybrid vehicles, midway between space vessels and cars, vehicles equipped with extraordinary powers but compatible in part with solutions already being explored by the car industry.

7. *Tre passi nel delirio*, *Toby Dammitt* episode, by Federico Fellini, 1967

It is worth considering the development of European and American cinema separately in that both carry a different vital, narrative and symbolic load concerning the machine culture: the first uses it in support of the creation of new canons of beauty, the second for the definition of the rhythms of a new epic suited to declaiming a nascent culture.

In common with the first stirrings and narrative movements, which focused immediately on action, American cinema organized its prosody, the matrix, syntax, times and rhythms of the era of the new machine culture that had just blossomed. While European cinema moved in tune with memory, or with Mnemosine, using yesterday's history as a model and manifestation of power to inspire the present, and staging the time of celebrations, rites, parades, the monumental time, and that of the peasant world or town life, American cinema adopted a rhythm that seemed attuned to that of internal combustion engines, and its speed became emblematic of the vital charge of an entire civilization projected ever since the early 20th century towards the conquest of the future, thanks to its new technological input.

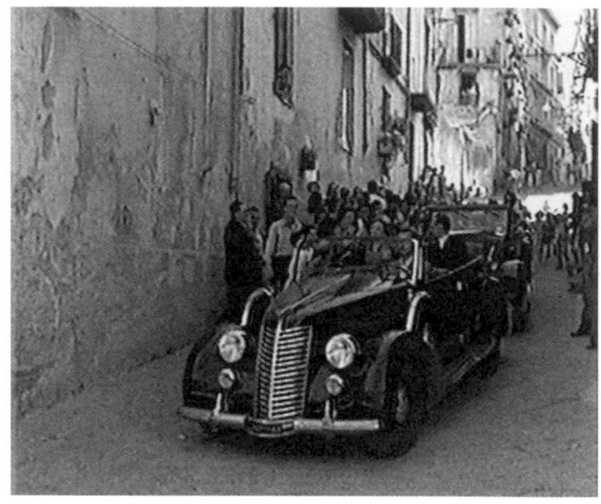

8. *Filumena Marturano*, by Eduardo De Filippo, 1951

Chronos is the protective divinity of American cinema. Its directors, from the most elementary organizing of the narrative (see Edwin S. Porter in *The Life of an American Fireman*, 1902), seem obsessed with the need to dominate time. And its first film-makers placed the camera at the heart of the metropolises to capture the motor vehicles bubbling with life and speed, dancing to the urban and metropolitan rhythms. As a consequence, they adjusted their watches to the rhythms of pistons and at all times seemed to betray an absolute faith in the possibility of spatial-temporal domination and in the power to modify individual and collective destinies thanks to the new means offered by modernity. European cinema, on the other hand, although tackling the new urban rhythms and technological marvels in the films of Ruttmann, Eisenstein and Vertov, would 20 years later not see in the speed and triumph of the machine culture any possibility of modifying the destiny of mankind and of the world.

9. *I dodici inganni*, by Alberto Lattuada, 1960

In all of the extensive work of David W. Griffith, from *The Adventures of Dollie* of 1909 to *Intolerance* of 1916, we can twist time in our favour, succeeding even in conquering the laws of destiny, thanks to instruments offered by technological progress, such as the telephone, telegraph, train and car. Without knowing, Griffith became one of the most significant popularisers of the theory of relativity, and although a man bound to 19th-century ideologies and an overall backward-looking vision of the world, he shared in an almost natural manner futurist theories, maintaining that time and space were no longer absolute quantities and it might be possible to travel rapidly through space, almost cancelling out distance. In *Intolerance*, we might gather from the finale of the modern episode that if the apostles had had a car at their disposal, or simply more rapid means of transport, they could have arrived in time to save Christ from the Cross. In the American serials (from *The Perils of Pauline* of 1914 onwards), the ways of female emancipation passed through continuous qualifying trials on the part of heroine at grips with various types of mechanical instruments, from the car to the train and aeroplane. In comic films, from Sen-

10. *Il vigile*, by Luigi Zampa, 1961

11. *Amarcord*, by Federico Fellini, 1974

12. *Il volpone*, by Maurizio Ponzi, 1988

nett onwards, the opposite process takes place and cars are the favoured vehicle for innumerable slides towards hell.

In European cinema around the First World War years, the car would become the omnipresent protagonist of serials (in particular of *Fantômas*, 1913 and of *Les Vampires* by Feuillade, 1915, but also a necessary 'assistant' in films such as *Maciste* of 1915 or *The Mechanical Man* by André Deed of 1921), and at every apparition of the car, it would be possible to associate an event, and at the same time the possibility of reaching a person in danger. In the continuous and unpredictable game of the masks of French serials, the car was an object with a multiple, deceitful identity: an ambulance was never a vehicle to carry the sick, and behind the uniforms of a driver we might find an angelic, protective figure, or a hostile, diabolical one. The doors of a car could open like holes and become the antechamber of death. Beauty was no longer the dominant attribute.

It would be a few years before one would see the legs of a young girl poking out from a car parked next to a large public swimming pool near Paris on a Sunday, as she changes her bathing costume. Very probably, when Augusto Genina filmed Louise Brooks in this scene for *Miss Europa (Prix de beauté)* in 1930, he wanted to produce a sort of modern variant of a Botticelli Venus. The bodywork of the car opens its doors to disgorge Louise Brooks in what we might see as a sort of allotrope of the large seashell.

In American cinema, there was on the one hand Griffith, celebrating the saving power of speed, showing the challenge of the car versus the locomotive in a split-second race, and making the car into an indispensable magical assistant, and on the other there was Mack Sennett, who directed a rich set of comedians, from the Keystone Cops to Chaplin, Buster Keaton to Harry Langton, Harold Lloyd to Monty Banks and Lupino Lane, and on to Stan Laurel and Oliver Hardy. With these figures, we enter more clearly into the theories of chaos, into the processes of catastrophic destruction, into the view of domestic training for the Apocalypse. The cars are on the one hand Pandora's box, from which can emerge undefined quantities of beings of various species, and on the other are beings themselves animated or antagonistic forces from which one can free oneself only with destruction. In American comic films, it was not so much beauty that captured the attention as the infinite ways a car has of transforming itself into a mass of wreckage or of provoking mayhem and a chain of disasters. These comic films could strip any car of its golden halo.

While the matrix, the prosody, the syntax of silent films, from the American to the European avant-garde, were inspired by the phases and rhythms of the internal combustion engine, with the advent of sound, the noise of cars occupied an increasingly important space in the sound track, contributing to the development of new symphonic forms.

With the arrival of sound, moreover, the film industry of Europe and America returned the car to its aura of beauty and adopted it as the favoured means of transport, as indicator of belonging to various classes and as object of desire and aspiration for social climbing, especially as regards women. Shop assistants, private secretaries, telephonists in infinite variations of the Cinderella theme, gain the chance to climb aboard not a carriage but an Isotta Fraschini, or a Bugatti, or an Alfa Romeo 8C 2900, or perhaps a Lancia with chauffeur, which in the case of Camerini's 1932 film, *Uomini che mascalzoni!*, appear emblematically as the proletarian variant of the prince charming. A marvellous open-top white car constantly appears in Italian films and was dubbed the 'white telephone.' It was chosen for its matchmaking functions and to accompany the dreams of the Italians beyond the threshold of 1000 lire a month. It should be said that the presence of cars begins to appear in 1930s films not for narrative or dramatic reason, but as the result of an evident and mature strategy of product placement on the part of Italian, European and American car manufacturers. This in similar vein to Fiat commissioning novels which had one of their cars as the protagonist (*'522.' Racconto di una giornata* by Massimo Bontempelli of 1928 tells the story of its first day of life from the viewpoint of the 522, and Pier Maria Bardi's *La strada e il volante* of 1936 tells the story of a voyage in modernized Fascist Italy of Filiberto, with fresh driving licence in his pocket, aboard a spanking new 1500 Fiat just out of the factory).

There are so many cars and they have such a necessary role in the development of the drama, in part for recognizing the year of production of a film, as to acquire fundamental functions for tracing and contextualizing the action of the film in a historical setting. Even if we do not wish to take into account the enormous quantity of material to be found in the newsreels of the time, which were often the only source of views within the factory, or of the documentaries produced by the car manufacturers for internal use (a huge number of quality films were made by masters of film making), we may say that fiction films have been able to make use of all the models of all time produced by car makers in a gigantic parade, to the exclusion of none. And all the top stars were able to climb the Olympus of stardom thanks to beautiful cars. When choosing sets, cars contend with architecture and design for the role of typifying features of a given period. The forms of the bodywork of sports cars (rather than their performance) give added value to the stars' glamour as they drive. As time passed, the roads — especially in town — became progressively more crowded with models and forms of all types. So while the world moved irresistibly towards the abyss of the Second World War, the horizon of the collective desires was constantly enriched with cars with increasingly swept-back, aerodynamic lines, from the Duesenberg to the Silver Arrow, and from the Citroën Traction Avant to Touring-bodied Alfa Romeos, which sought to carry their protagonists to various types of elsewhere, but also towards new promised lands, reviving the spirit of the pioneers of the 19th century. During the years of the New Deal, the 'Forgotten Man' and the man at the base of the social pyramid — to whom were addressed President Roosevelt's messages or those of Frank Capra — no longer identified themselves with the vagabonds: even the protagonists of Chaplin's films, the individuals struggling to avoid becoming an anonymous mass, finally manage to climb aboard a car, perhaps as guests, but in any case enjoying this opportunity. The surest and fastest method for obtaining a lift, for a pretty girl, was to hitchhike, as in Capra's *It Happened One Night* of 1934. But the car of the 1930s also appeared as a variant to the home in terms of desirability, and its interior became a love-nest, or an alternative to a conference room. These were also the years of the rediscovery of great open spaces, of a new frontier spirit, of the possibility of using cars to break the law and taste a new kind of freedom. This is what the gangster movies recounted in epic form from the early 1930s and up to 40 years later in films such as *Gangster Story* by Arthur Penn (1967).

The Second World War does not form a watershed in this process of irreversible advance of a sort of fifth estate of human beings moving no longer on foot but on four wheels. In American cinema, there was in practice no break between the periods before and after the war: the arrival of colour encouraged the proliferation of huge cabriolets from which we can discover the all-American identity and character of the small towns, huge ranches and different states, from Texas and California to Montana and Illinois. The American cowboy shifted quite naturally from holding the reins of his horse to the steering wheel of a Chrysler or Cadillac, Studebaker or Chevrolet. There were cars like the Citroën DS which in some films (for instance, Fred Zinnemann's *The Day of the Jackal* of 1975) are paraded from the Elysée Palace as the marks and attributive elements of French identity.

In Italian cinema, everything started from scratch, but some cars that survived the destruction still circulated amongst the ruins. For instance, there is a Bentley with chauffeur in *La vita ricomincia* of 1946, which takes Alida Valli to prostitute herself to be able to pay for the phials of penicillin needed to save the life of her son, and there are other luxury cars that survived the bombings, appearing as symbols of dishonesty and delinquency. With the period of reconstruction over, satisfying basic needs was matched by an increased desire for mobility, a widespread need to abandon one's own habitat and move to discover the marvels of the multi-faceted Italy. Bicycles, the most common form of transport of the post-war years, gave way to the Vespa and Lambretta and then, little by little, to the first

13. *Goldfinger*, by Guy Hamilton, 1964

14. *A Joke of Destiny Lying in Wait Around the Corner like a Robber*, by Lina Wertmüller, 1983

15. *007 The Spy who Loved Me*, by Lewis Gilbert, 1977

16. *Il sorpasso*, by Dino Risi, 1962

17. *Thelma and Louise*, by Ridley Scott, 1991

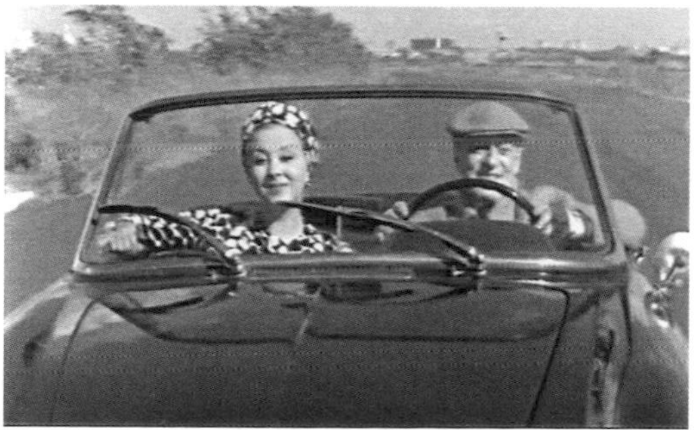

18. *Capriccio all'italiana*, episode from *Il mostro della domenica* by Steno, 1968

utility cars. Within a few years, the cinema was recording mass motorization with perfect timing. Exactly in the same ways as had occurred with the star system, the new icons were no longer unreachable objects of desire so much as something nearby and immediately familiar. At the same time (in the films of Antonioni, Lattuada, Fellini, Emmer, Pietrangeli), we find sports cars appearing ever more frequently (Alfa, Lancia, Maserati and Ferrari) making it possible to sweep through the country on the new motorways and unleash the brake horsepower to cancel out any distance in just a few hours. The Maserati in *Cronaca di un amore* (1950) by Antonioni, the Ferrari of Alberto, protagonist of *Delfini* by Maselli (1960), the Rolls-Royce of the Milanese lady in *Ieri oggi domani* by Vittorio De Sica (1963) or that of the foreign lady in *La congiuntura* by Scola (1964), the MG of Marcello in *Dolce vita* (1960) by Fellini all play a role and have a considerable weight in the action, becoming determining modifiers of the narrative. Gigantic American models — Cadillacs, Chevrolets, Oldsmobiles — burst into comic and dramatic films: from *Totò a colori* (1952) to *Un americano a Roma* (1954), *Arrivano i dollari!* by Mario Costa (1957) and *Il giovedì* by Risi (1963).

With the onset of the economic miracle, Italians began touring up and down the peninsula with increasing speed; the car became a sort of wild steed to be let loose on the motorway or on a hill-climb in some Umbrian village, or on a rough track. A Lancia Stratos would be the protagonist of a mad chase in the streets of Naples in *Napoli spara* and in similar films, it is easy to come across the finest European sports cars. Ferraris in such films were two a penny.

The proto-star system as applied to cars was now replaced with a role for the car that was far closer and more possible for the collective imagination. Together with the home, the car acquired a host of role and functions within Italian and international cinema (and in films such as Tati's *Mon oncle* of 1958, house and car were combined into a single parody of the modernization taking place in the 20 years following the end of the war. We find both men and women driving these cars (although in a film such as Marino Girolami's *Le motorizzate* of 1963, we seem to capture the spread of women drivers as it occurs). Whether a symbol of prestige, or a simple utility vehicle, the car is first of all and for quite a time an object of love (see how Cabiria in *Le notti di Cabiria*, by Fellini, 1957 caresses her Seicento, indicator of individual wealth and collective well-being). It became a means of liberation from various other slower and more antiquated means of transport, and the medium encouraging any form of socialization. It was a medium that facilitated that hunting and conquering of various types of female prey on the part of men of all ages, but also of social ascension. In *Matrimonio all'italiana* (Vittorio De Sica, 1964), Filumena Maturano considered the invitation from don Domenico to climb aboard the red soft-top Lancia to go and see the horse racing at Agnano as her first true opportunity for social legitimization.

Italian cinema celebrated the height of the irreversible change of Italian-style travelling during the first 20 years of the post-war period and mass motorization in various films, and especially in comedies. While the Lancia Aurelia convertible of Bruno Cortona in *Sorpasso* (1962) shared the lead role with Gasmann and Trentignant, attention was increasingly focused on utility and city cars, first the Seicento and then the Cinquecento. Outside Italy, but in Italian cinema too, the Mini would also play a longstanding role as protagonist; witness its fundamental part in *The Italian Job* by F. Gary Gray and in *The Bourne Identity* by Doug Liman of 2002. It was followed by the Citroën (2CV) but in all probability it is the Volkswagen Beetle that first became a myth and was further 'ennobled' thanks to the silver screen. In recent years, we have also seen attention dedicated to the Smart, in films such as *The da Vinci Code* and *The Pink Panther*. The Seicento is the car that, like an angelic creature, helped the Italian population cross the threshold of the boom period in mass. It appeared in *Belle, ma povere* di Risi (1957), while in Comencini's film of the same year, *Mariti in città*, it was bought by a woman who has just sold an antique cupboard to a dealer. In *Magnifico cornuto* of 1964, the jealous husband uses the Seicento of his wife, who is unable to drive his Alfa Romeo, in order to prevent her going out and meeting her lover. We find the Seicento again in *Mogli pericolose* (Comencini, 1958), *Il vedovo* (Risi, 1959), *Il commissario* (Comencini, 1962), and this car also marks the change of social status for Alberto Sordi in *Medico della mutua* (Zampa, 1968). The Seicento often appeared as a second car: in the episode entitled *L'automobile* (*La mia signora*, 1964), the husband accepts his wife's infidelity without batting an eyelid, but cannot bear her having allowed his Jaguar to be stolen when she could quite easily have used the utility car he had bought specially for her.

With Visconti's *Rocco e i suoi fratelli* of 1960, cinema for the first time took its cameras to the very gates of a car manufacturer (Alfa Romeo in Arese), and in the following years, Ugo Gregoretti set his science-fiction film, *Omicron* (1963) in the Fiat factory. Ettore Scola would film *Trevico-Torino. Viaggio nel Fiat-Nam* in 1973 around Fiat again.

However, in Italian cinema it was not to be the Seicento that would gain a place in the Hall of Fame alongside luxury or super cars by great designers: this place was taken by the Cinquecento. The smallest of the post-war cars, designed by Dante Giacosa, it was available in instalments and used by driving schools but at one point even became a powerful tool for the use of a secret agent: James Tont in *James Tont operazione U.N.O.* Whereas the Seicento began to disappear definitively from the screen at the end of the 1960s, the Cinquecento proved to be a durable and long-lived car: it appeared in Billy Wilder's 1972 film, *Avanti!*, and in Dario Argento's 1975 work, *Profondo rosso*, and continued to be a protagonist even in cartoon films, from *Lupin III e il castello di Cagliostro* (1979) by Miyazaki to Disney's most recent film, *Cars* by John Lassiter, of 2006.

The cinema of the past 30 years has enabled us to see the most varied models of cars undertaking the most extraordinary trials, driven by men and women with Formula 1 powers and spirit, and thanks to the cars' specifications, they seem to acquire omnipotence. The 'city chases' chapter appears as a large but separate group which has proved durable and offers some memorable sequences. The directors specializing in this, in both American and Italian cinema, use dramatic effects and unexpected endings to draw the spectator into a sort of roller-coaster effect. Witness such films as *The Day of the Jackal* and *Svegliati e uccidi* by Lizzani of 1966, *Serpico* by Sidney Lumet of 1973, and the films from The Dirty Harry series, as well as the 1995 film *Heat* by Michael Mann and Gérard Pirès's *Taxi* 1998. Alongside the increase in traffic, already mentioned from the early 1960s, in Fellini's *Dolce vita* and in many other films, we find other forms of fear that can be caused by cars making their appearance in works like John Carpenter's *Christine* on 1983, or as dark forces threatening our lives: Spielberg's *Duel* of 1971. In the present, cars seem to have saturated all the possibilities of dramatic and spectacular representation, but it is interesting to observe how in the post-human condition into which we seem destined to enter, how the relationships between man and car can become increasingly integrated and metamorphic. The logical conclusion is reached in *Cars*, in which human beings are not present and the role of absolute protagonist on the stage is taken on by the car.

The imagined future includes cars able to transform themselves into space or amphibious vehicles, into fortresses equipped with every sort of weapon, and cars made up of bits and pieces found here and there by survivors of an atomic catastrophe in what is now a regressive world (as in the medieval world shown in *Mad Max beyond Thunderdome*). The cars shown are mostly not means of transport but vehicles with which to defend oneself or attack the enemy. Also projected into the future thanks to their extreme flexibility and versatility (changing into amphibious cars, submarines or planes) are the Aston Martins or Lotus Esprits that James Bond uses in various episodes of the series. In *The League of Extraordinary Gentleman* by Steven Norrington (2003), there is a Nemomobile that races at incredible speed through the streets of Venice. The models of cars imagined for the future range from the De Lorean in *Back to the Future*, by Robert Zemekis of 1985, designed by Giugiaro, to the Batmobile from the various Batman films, a sort of armour-plated, multi-weapon fortress, to the Lexus in *Minority Report*, 2002, by Steven Spielberg, which can move horizontally or vertically, as well as the Audi RSQ in *I, Robot* (2004) by Alex Proyas, set in 2035.

The mission or the key word for those dreaming up cars for science fiction films seems to be to render possible, and soon buyable and within reach of the everyday driver, all the properties and features — from indestructible bodywork to the possibility of avoiding obstacles thanks to a special radar — enabling the super-heroes to accomplish their impossible missions successfully.

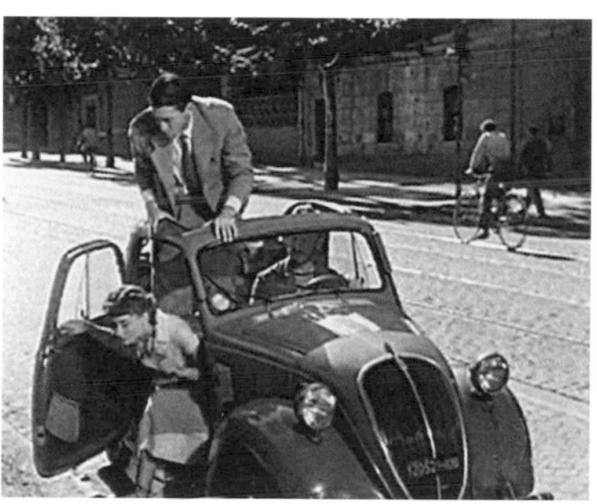

19. *Roman Holiday*, by William Wyler, 1953

20. *Sunset Boulevard*, by Billy Wilder, 1950

Words Words Words

Donatella Biffignandi

'If we take a look at modern interpretations of the bodywork of a motor car, in which art combines with knowledge, and good taste tries to blend with practicality, we find that everything that it has been humanly possible to do, has been done. All forms of bodywork have already been applied to petrol or electric engines, whether they be heavy, agile, powerful or invincible. All the forms of vehicles have been repeated, reproposed, from the vulgar era to today, and will continue to be: phaetons, double-phaetons, coupés, landeaux and landaulettes, victories, cabs, limousines: everything that was noble or elegant, soft or aristocratic, practical and even impossible; everything has been attempted, even the most bizarre, even the most illogical in enthusiastic faith, with one mobile and meritorious cause, that of achieving the ideal form… wedded to supreme comfort.' This is the peremptory opinion of a magazine called *L'auto d'Italia* in 1907, in an article with the expressive title, 'The triumph of bodywork.' So everything had already been tried and realized. There was little to hope for, then, in the new century that was just beginning…

This rather unprophetic vision was based on the conviction that the carriages, the comfortable, elegant, refined horse-drawn ones that were so functional even for long voyages, were the result of a coachbuilding art going back centuries. Coachbuilders represent an example of the incredible capacity for adaptation to different technologies as they become available and are perfected. At the end of the 19th century, this élite of craftsmen was able, throughout Europe, to assure a production that was of the very best in terms of quality and quantity. There were the berlins, so-called from their place of origin, deriving from a model made to the design of Franz Wilhelm's architect: four-wheeled vehicles with the cabin suspended from straps, windows and foldaway cover (an anticipation of the opening roof?). Another common model was the coupé, a four-wheeled, two-seater carriage, so-called because it appeared as though cut from the central cabin of a larger vehicle. An originator of this type of carriage was called the coupé-diable, because of the racket it caused on Paris's paved streets. Similar in form was the fiacre or hackney coach, and another public vehicle called gondola, which was a rounded fiacre. Then there was the break, originally a vehicle used to break in horses (in English, now called an estate, but in Italian it is still known as a break); it was heavy, and was later to be used for transporting passengers. The cab and cabriolet date from the same period (early 19th century): a light stage seat with bellows and a single horse. The cabriole was the cavorting of a horse and from this term derived the definition of a vehicle which, for its lightness, caused passengers to be jolted rather severely. The brougham, instead, derives from a carriage designed for the Chancellor of the Exchequer Lord Brougham (1834). Another coach that took its name from a person was the derby, from the name of the noble founder of the famous horse race. The tonneau was a light, two-wheeled vehicle offering two or four seats, with access from the rear and longitudinal seats. Also worth a mention is the landau, so-called in honour of the German town where it was invented: a cabin with four seats protected by a double folding top and bench for the coachman. Last to appear on the market before the advent of the engine was the wagonette (1880–90), with four wheels, low cabin, longitudinal seats; and the jardinière, for transporting objects and people. The carriage makers were not just the stylists for these carriages, frequently veritable masterpieces of carpentry and decoration, but also highly-expert engineers, as they produced not just the external shell but also the mechanics; this gave them great freedom of action and extensive independence. Only with the arrival of the engine did they become dependent on a mechanical structure built by others, and this would pose a major problem.

1. Tonneau, 1902

Let us imagine the confusion caused by the apparition of the first horseless carriages. The carriage makers of all Europe, and above all of France, Germany, Britain and Italy, suddenly found themselves faced with something 'internal' that was much more important than the exterior. Suddenly, the comfort, convenience and beauty of the carriages they had built for centuries were no longer of interest. Their wealthier clients were overwhelmed by an unexplainable brainstorm pushing them to face inclement weather, dust, rain and sun without any protection, suffer bumps and jerks, continuous breakdowns and changes of tyres; an incomprehensible torture.

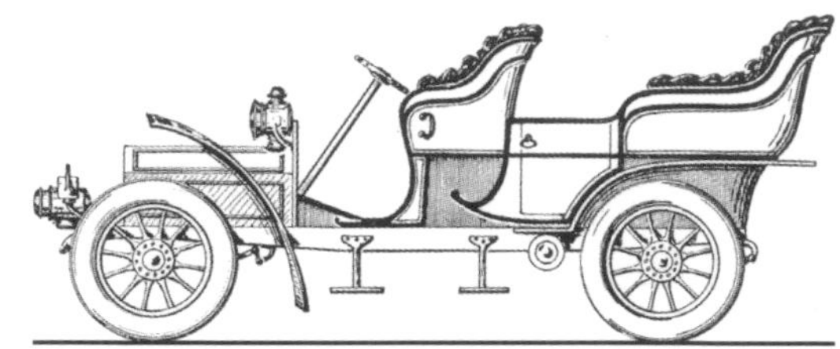

2. Double-phaeton, 1903

The coachbuilders found themselves facing electric, steam, internal combustion, hybrid, combustible and battery engines. Each was very different and carried varying weights of water, fuel, batteries, all to be distributed, hidden and made compatible with seats, doors, wheels and panels. The resulting period was one of confusion or, as historians say when faced with contradictory trends, a 'period of transition.' The carriage makers were reluctant to surrender the beautiful forms that had been their glory until a few years before, and nor could they give up the anachronistic details such as whip holder or umbrella holder. This complicated the problems to be tackled, which from the outset were themselves ill-defined: they were midway between mechanical art and coachbuilding art, having to arrange wheels, suspension, non-suspended weights, steering, distribution of the passengers and driver (and we should imagine that he was automatically at the front: on the Bedelia of 1911, the driver was located behind the passenger, in a tandem position).

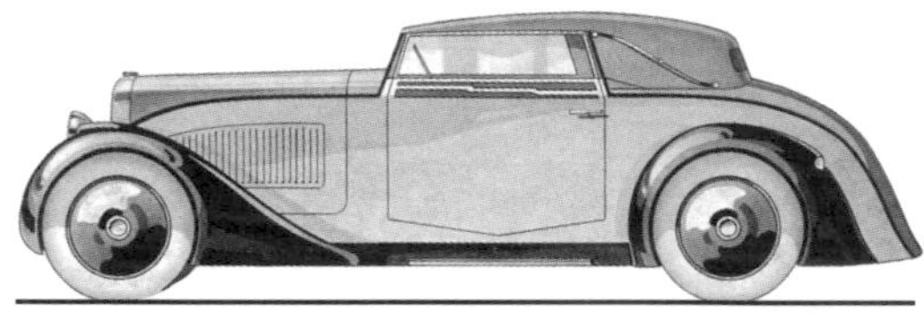

3. Cabriolet on a chassis Hotchkiss, 1931

It was a wearisome learning curve, from which emerged talented artists only when the horse-drawn carriage, with its forms and particularities, was forgotten. Paradoxically, the perfection of the carriage delayed the birth of the concept of 'motor car coachwork' in the sense of something new and different from the past. The first cars were certainly inferior to horse and carriage, and they marked a period of uncertainty, or even regression, in the construction of transport vehicles. Only in 1908, with the torpedo, equipped even with a fold-down, adjustable windscreen, and in 1910, with a hand-operated windscreen wiper (supreme refinement!), were problems tackled and resolved and 'the motor car became something serious, and no longer the exclusive domain of bold pioneers with goggles and dust coat; it now bore its "virile toga."'

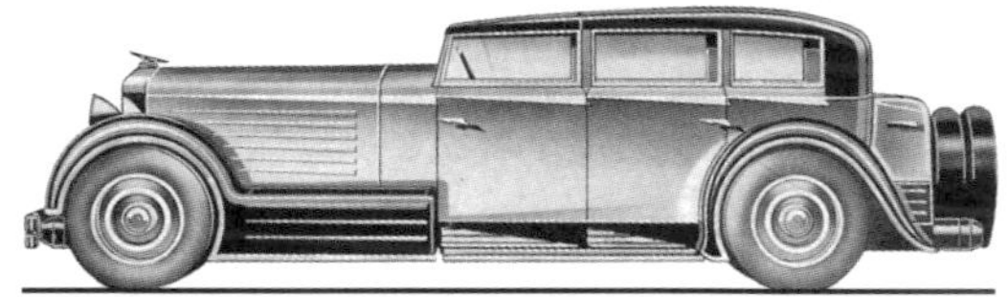

4. Convertible on a Harris-Léon Laisné chassis, 1930

5. Sports car with interior driving position on a Tracta chassis, 1931

Let us take a closer look, then, at the birth of this form of coachwork, the first to be designed wholly to be fitted to a motor-driven vehicle, and which had an English father (a certain Mr Lamplugh), a German mother (Mercedes) and French uncles (the Rheims et Auscher coach-building works). The word torpedo derives not just from the English, but ultimately from the Latin *torpedo, torpedinis* meaning 'electric ray.' In French, we find *torpilleur*, meaning 'light, slender boat,' which in car terms, sits well with *torpédo*. The latter is feminine, as is 'torpedo' in Italian, also used to designate a form of bodywork that is open, elongated and slender, and which was highly popular between 1910 and 1930. For about 20 years, therefore, the torpedo — large or small, 4 — or 6 — seater, luxury or utilitarian — was the epitome of the motor car. The only one not to derive directly from horse and carriage. It seems proven now that the first torpedo was a 45 hp Mercedes presented at the Paris Salon in 1908. In what way did this model differ from the other open models designed and produced hitherto? What made it a torpedo rather than, for example, a Roi-des-Belges phaeton?

The latter was a type of coachwork for cars. It was open and with the classic folding top or extendable hood; its lines were a little rococo, complicated and extremely luxurious. The bonnet in this version was not harmoniously joined with the rest of the body; indeed, it came to an abrupt end well before the so-called *coupe-vent* (windbreak), or panel separating the cabin from the engine bay. The result was an untidy style, with the front in which the square bonnet did not harmonize with the curves of the rest of the bodywork. More, seen from the side, the normal or Roi-des-Belges phaeton did not have an 'outline' delineating the form, as the front and rear seats protruded, while the side doors (used usually only to reach the rear seats) were reduced to little more than anonymous hatches trimmed around their edges by elaborate mouldings.

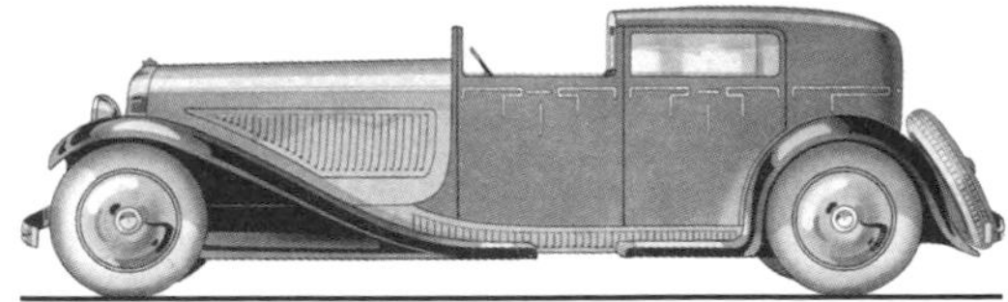

6. Convertibile front coupé on a Hotchkiss chassis, 1930

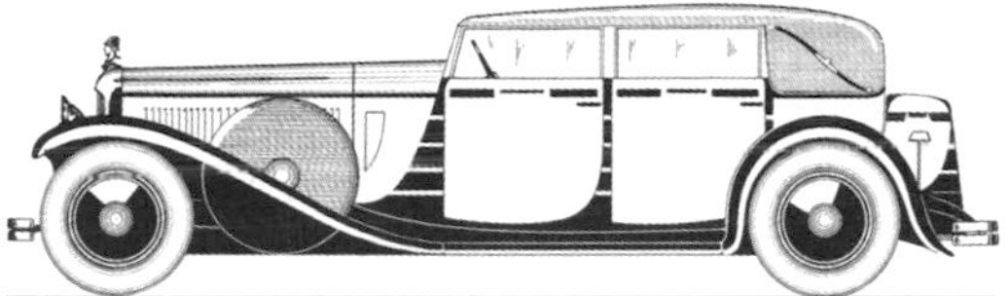

7. Cabriolet de Ville on a Minerva chassis, 1931

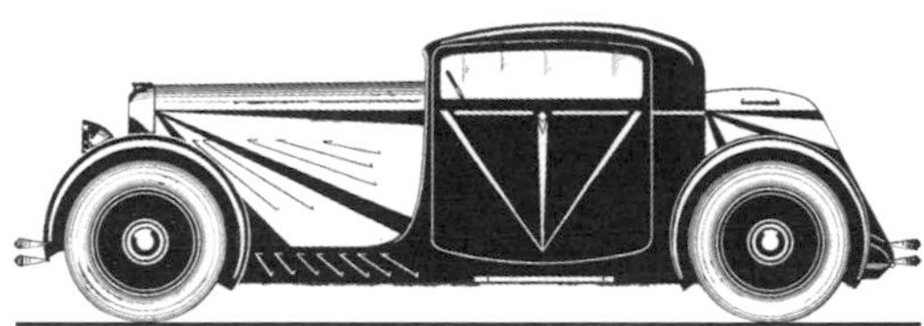

8. Petit coupé on an Amilcar chassis, 1929

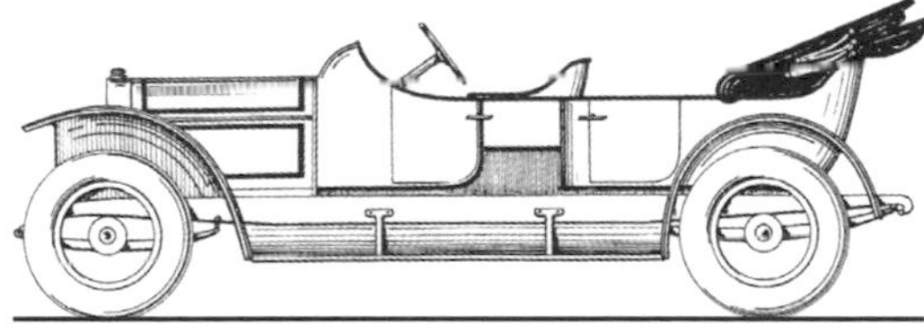

9. Torpedo, 1909

10. Cabriolet on a Mathis chassis, 1931

The Mercedes was instead a torpedo in that, although similar to earlier models, it stood out aesthetically as a result of its conceptually innovative design: the bonnet was joined to the body and this continued without mouldings or frills, incorporating the front and rear doors, while the seats, barely protruding beyond the 'outline,' were incorporated within the body itself. The result was uniform in style, with a sharp, elegant profile hinting at the performance of the vehicle. Truly a great, luxurious and simultaneously almost sporty car. The bodywork was by the Rothschild coachbuilding works (Rheims et Auscher), founded in Paris in 1838 in Avenue Malakoff 131 and with the workshops at Rue Ernest Cognacq 9 at Levallois-Perret (Seine). The Rothschild plant became the most prestigious coachbuilder in France and in 1906 opened a base in Turin in via Madama Cristina 147, called Carrozzeria Italiana Rothschild società anonima, with capital of one and a half million francs. This Italian branch was bought a few years later by Fiat and became the Fiat Coachwork Division.

In agreement with Mercedes, the Rothschild *maison* produced an improved model called the racing phaeton, which was displayed at the 1908 Salon. This model, which continued the tradition launched by Rothschild, which in 1899 had already built Jenatzy's Jamais Contente, was patented under no. 26.771.

Without a doubt, contoured coachwork had been a source of pride to Rheims et Auscher since the advent of the motor car. On top of the Jamais Contente (truly torpedo-shaped and the first car to exceed 100 kph), they had built the Bollée torpille in 1899 and the Mors racing car, which won the Paris-Madrid in 1903.

Thus was the birth of the torpedo: it emerged from the meeting between Rothschild (or Rheims et Auscher) and Mercedes, under the broad art nouveau vaults of the Salon de l'Automobile in Paris in 1908. But there was another father, too, William Alfred Lamplugh, born in Wolverhampton on 14th December 1866. After moving to France, he distinguished himself as a sportsman, or amateur racing driver, and founded Lamplugh et Cie. — Carrosserie Automobile in 1899 with capital of 280,000 francs. Lamplugh's advertising stated: '200 bodies in warehouse ready to be fitted. Rapid deliveries. Work executed with care.' It was Lamplugh that produced the racing phaeton on behalf of Rothschild for Mercedes. Why is quickly recounted: the workshops of Lamplugh were at 8 rue Ernest Cognacq in Levallois, and the company started its activity in exactly the same year as its neighbour, Rheims et Auscher: 1899. Very soon, the two companies started collaborating, in virtue of which it was Alfred Lamplugh who put pencil to paper for the outline of the innovative details of the new car.

And this is the family tree of the legendary torpedo.

In order to gain a sense of the absolute novelty of the torpedo's line, one need only compare it with the coachwork most in fashion in the years immediately before: the tonneau, a vehicle which, we have seen, derived from a horse-drawn carriage; it was open, and travellers were covered by an extendable top stretching as far as the front windscreen, and with side curtains. A step forward came with the limousine (so-called because derived from a French carriage originally made in the Limousin), as the rear compartment was closed, and so sheltered the passengers; the two front seats, however, were only protected to some extent by the roof and front windscreen.

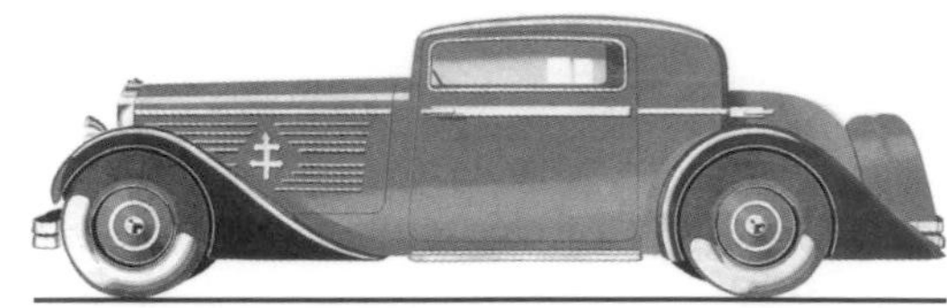

11. Coachwork with interior driving position on a Lorraine chassis, 1931

Towards 1905–06, beaten metal panels began to be applied to the wholly wooden structure, and the first sheet-metal casings began to appear. The resulting line was more elegant and complete, as it was finally free of all the little interruptions and clumsy breaks caused by the visible mechanical components. Naturally, this did not take place simply and smoothly: in 1915, a car manufacturer that had hidden the radiator cap under the bonnet was obliged, in the wake of protests from customers, to put it back where it was. The adoption of sheet aluminium, however, marked a major step forward: the metal was easier to shape than wood, was lighter and easier to work. The first panel beaters appeared: legendary figures dating from the early days of the motor car, they often symbolized the thousand skills needed to produce a car in the first 20 years of the last century.

12. Coupé-limousine on an Hispano-Suiza chassis, 1931

The benefits accruing from the spread of the torpedo from 1910 soon made themselves felt in closed vehicles, coupés and limousines. For example, with the lowering of the upper line of the car. These were years of great creative euphoria, change and invention. Another contributor to the revolution sparked off by the arrival of the torpedo was Porsche, one of the most long-lived and fecund designers of the past century. His skill lay in thinking of the aeronautical sector and working on how to reduce weight — which was simple — just when everyone else was working on how to increase power — which was harder. In 1910, he built his rounded Tulip with a slightly upward sloping bonnet, cycle wings with a sharp leading edge and with any protrusions, even of the smallest kind, such as lights and handles, reduced to a minimum. He was the first to have sensed the importance of aerodynamics and his Tulip, together with the torpedo, constituted the start of the study of form.

13. Coupé royal on a Fiat 509, 1929

1912 saw the first appearance of series production cars complete with bodywork: the result was panic amidst the coachbuilders, who saw an underhand attack on their interests. The arrival of the war distracted attention, at least in Europe, as car production, coachbuilding included, was converted almost entirely to war production.

14. Roadster on a Fiat 521 chassis, 1929

The same was not true for the Americans, who happily free of war at home, could dedicate themselves to their main objective: manufacturing standard products at low cost and accessible to most of the population. They appeared on the international markets at the end of the war with completely new vehicles, made of pressed steel, which made producing curved shapes easier. It is striking to compare the rigid, square cars of Europe from 1919–20 with those from America, which seem light-years ahead, with their fluid, elegant lines. But in 1923, Europe re-acquired a momentary supremacy with a new model destined to enjoy great success: the Weymann, named after the French manufacturer who invented it. This was a wooden skeleton covered with a material that was much easier than sheet metal to work, and namely, fake leather (pegamoid). Using this, it was possible to build an elegant, quiet, cheap car that was easy to repair. For two years, it enjoyed unprecedented success. After which, it disappeared, as it also proved itself to be fragile, anything but rot-proof, unable to protect passengers in the case of an accident, unlike the robust metal structure of other cars. Another car to be forgotten along with the Weymann was the torpedo, the very symbol of the motor car in the early 1920s. Designers were now concentrating on closed vehicles, and between 1920 and 1930, the market changed completely. While in 1920 the closed car accounted for just 10% of production, in 1928–29, open-top cars had slumped to a miserable 2-3% of sales. The enclosed driving position was first invented by Renault in 1899. It had designed a sort of tall cupboard, 1.9 m tall, with two seats and a De Dion 3.5 hp engine. The American Leland also had a go with a Cadillac in 1903; then there was silence for almost 20 years. But by 1924, there was already a car with enclosed driving position entered at the Mugello Circuit; this means that construction had reached technology level that allowed it to be need in motor sports.

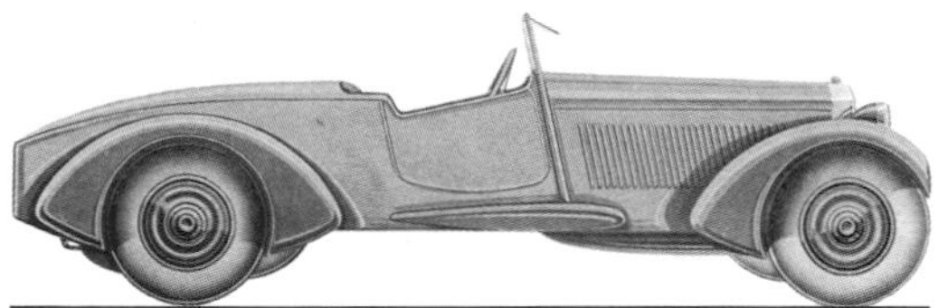

15. Drop-shaped bateau on Alfa Romeo 6C 1750 Sport chassis, 1929

This was now a period in which the horse-drawn carriage had been completely forgotten and left behind; in which the motor car was comfortable, fast, reliable, increasingly less a dream and ever more a reality; in which American competition stimulated European manufacturers to produce ever better and more attractive cars. The variety offered was enormous, with an infinity of definitions and sub-definitions, almost all originating from French or English, which the coachbuilders often added to, to bestow some fantasy on their creations. To such an extent that the country that is historically least open to standardization, Great Britain, in 1926 defined the 21 principal types of bodywork. This was an idea of the British Engineering Standards, an association of engineers seeking to unify types, materials, construction systems. They drew up a table, which was quickly reproduced by *Auto Italiana*. Here is the list:

16. Coupé touring with interior driving position, 1929

1. Two-seater;
2. Coupé cabriolet;
3. Saloon landaulette;
4. Clover leaf [a highly poetic name];
5. Open touring;
6. Single landaulette;
7. Three-quarter cabriolet;
8. Coupé;
9. Brougham;
10. Clover leaf coupé;
11. Enclosed cabriolet;
12. Clover leaf coupelette [a small clover leaf coupé];
13. Three-quarter landaulette;
14. Enclosed limousine;
15. Coupelette;
16. Saloon;
17. All-weather;
18. Clover leaf cabriolet;
19. Limousine;
20. Single cabriolet;
21. Enclosed landaulette.

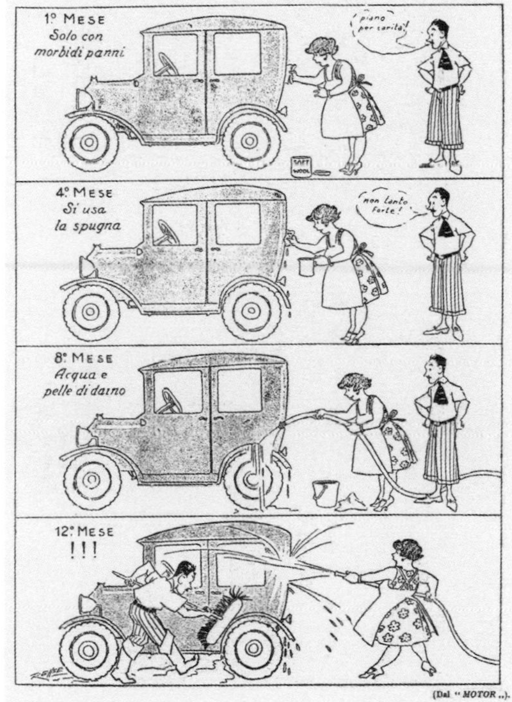

17. 'How to clean one's motor car'

How did the Italian editors of *Auto Italiana* respond in collaboration with the local coachbuilders? They dedicated some pages of the periodical to a referendum between car and coachwork manufacturers and their readers in order to attribute an Italian name to each of the forms identified by the British Engineering Standards. In reality, the authors of the referendum had few illusions about radically changing the naming of these forms, knowing full well that many Italian cars were exported and that it would thus be impracticable to adopt a linguistic hierarchy which would remain incomprehensible in much of the market. The real aim was to try and attribute a name solely and unequivocally to the coachwork itself, thus overcoming the ambiguities and uncertainties of a complicated, top-heavy lexicon.

Four years later, in 1930, in the April issue of *Carrozzeria*, appeared these words: 'A few years ago, we launched a referendum to find some Italian names... but our initiative was not successful and for their part our coachbuilders clouded the issue further by borrowing the most varied and artful names from abroad. And every year that passes, things become even more complicated, because the types of coachwork increase and, worse, mix the very characteristics that served to differentiate them.'

In France, for example, a country in which the art of coach-building had reached greater heights, it was possible to identify 23 different types of car shape, two more than in Britain. Here they are:

1. Phaeton;
2. Torpedo;
3. Torpedo-cabriolet;
4. Coupé;
5. Coupé-limousine;
6. Limousine;
7. Conduite-coupé;
8. Demi-berline;
9. Berline;
10. Conduite-limousine;
11. Landaulet;
12. Landaulet-limousine;
13. Cabriolet;
14. Cabriolet-limousine;
15. Conduite-landaulet;
16. Conduite-landaulet-limousine;
17. Conduite-cabriolet;
18. Conduite-cabriolet-limousine;
19. Berline transformable;
20. Conduite trasformable;
21. Coupé-limousine demi-conduite;
22. Phaeton sport;
23. Conduite-coupé sport.

I MISTERI DELLA NOMENCLATURA:

Le tre prime figure rappresentano tre vetture perfettamente eguali e sarebbero secondo noi tre guide interne salone con divisorio, invece i rispettivi carrozzieri inglesi le chiamano con tre nomi diversi. La quarta, che noi chiamiamo inglesemente Mylord, viene presentata da una rivista inglese quale Touring Car *a 4 posti. Proprio il tipo assolutamente inadatto pel turismo!*

18. 'The mysteries of naming'

Only someone with a maniacal eye for detail would have been able to note the subtle differences between each name. At first sight, the distinction was based on three (apparently!) easily identifiable categories: open-top cars, closed cars, openable cars. So far so good. Open-top cars might be a two-door phaeton, a four-door torpedo or a four-door torpedo-cabriolet. Closed cars were instead sub-divided into 'front torpedoes,' that is, with the front end open, and totally enclosed. Among the first, we find the four-door coupé with two windows, the coupé-limousine with four doors and four windows, and the limousine with four doors and four windows, which might be identical to the previous model but includes a hood over the front part. Totally enclosed cars were instead the conduite-coupé with two doors and two windows, the demi-berline with two doors and four windows, the berline with four doors and four windows, the conduite-limousine with four doors and six windows. Some readers will already be lost, but the worst comes with the openable or 'soft-top' cars. It is difficult to imagine how many soft-top cars there can be. Those that open totally, called transformable; those that open only above the rear seats, called landaulets, those which open at the front, called 'demi-conduites internes,' those with only the roof opening, while the tail and sides remain fixed. So in one group, we find the landaulet with four doors and two windows, the landaulet-limousine with four doors and four windows, the limousine landaulet with four doors, four windows and — why not — a hood at the front, the cabriolet with four doors, two windows, the cabriolet-limousine with four doors and four windows... In another group, there are the conduite-landaulet with two doors and two windows, the conduite-landaulet-limousine, the berline-landaulet, the conduite-limousine-landaulet, the conduite-cabriolet, the conduite-cabriolet-limousine... and we are far from exhausting all the possibilities in this wild waltz that makes us dizzy and lose sight of the shapes around us...

Who could make sense of all this? As ever, the Americans were far more pragmatic, and came up with just ten forms:

1. Roadster;
2. Phaeton;
3. Coupé;
4. Coach;
5. Closed coupled sedan;
6. Sedan;
7. Imperial sedan;
8. Landau;
9. Cabriolet;
10. Convertible sedan.

More pragmatic perhaps, but sufficiently independently-minded to use a terminology completely different to that adopted in Europe.

And the Italians? Bar one, nobody sought alternatives to this maze of definitions, one more complicated than the other. In all Italy, there was only one reply to the referendum, and it came three years later, in 1929. 'The naming of the coachwork needs to satisfy some

E se pensassimo alla visuale del guidatore?
(Dedicato ad Aldo Farinelli da Carlo Biscaretti)

19. 'What if we were to consider the driver's visibility?'

requisites... the most important is that a clearly-defined and single type of coachwork needs to be attributed to each name. Secondly, the naming must be easily accessible to both constructors and public. The third requisite... is the Italianness of the words.' In the October 1929 issue of *La Carrozzeria*, the anonymous author of these words continued, saying that it was not so much the main terms — such as torpedo, spider, coupé and cabriolet — to cause confusion, as those formed of two, three or even four words, such as the spider clover leaf coupelette, which no-one, except perhaps an old British coachbuilder, would have been able to describe fully. But in the end, wandered the writer, what is a coachwork? It is a recipient, he replied, placed on the chassis and within which people sit. So... why not denominate the coachworks on the basis of the number of seats? After all, this would merely be an extension of a concept adopted for numerous coachworks both in the English and Italian names (two-seater...). This would immediately stress the intended use of that shape, and it would be an easily accessible name for both coachbuilders and public. However, it would also be important to ensure it was clear if the seats offered were covered or not; and how many uncovered or covered with a simple hood. At this point, things become complicated again. 'It may be supposed that every coachwork has two sorts of seats: covered and uncovered and the numbers indicating how many of one and how many of the other category there are, should be noted. If there are no seats of one of the categories, these missing seats are indicated with a zero.' Here are the first examples: 'A torpedo coachwork, with all four seats open, will be called four-zero, because, as per above, the second figure indicates the covered seating, which in the case of the torpedo, is lacking; hence the zero. A berlin with four covered seats will be called zero-four... A coachwork with some covered and some open seats, as in the case of a Brougham, for example, will be indicated as one-two: Brougham with one seat for the driver and two for the passengers; two-two: Brougham with two open seats at the front and two covered seats behind; one-four: Brougham with one uncovered seat for the driver and four covered seats for the passengers.' Enough? The author thought not.

'Some coachworks have dicky seats that are normally kept folded and are opened only when required; these are not true seats, but contingency ones, or half-seats we might say. If one wishes (but did anyone?), they may be distinguished with a half set between the figures representing the covered and open seats.' A six-seater torpedo, defined a triple phaeton, would with this system be defined as a six-zero. And here, finally, are the 'Regulations for the proposed denominations:' 'First one writes the number of seats. If there are no open seats, the absence is noted with a zero. If the front seats are covered by the extension of the roof over the rear seats, one uses the half symbol. The figure corresponding to the covered seats comes next. If there are no covered seats, their absence is noted with a zero. If the roof can be folded away, the half figure is used. If, on top of the two types of seats, there are also dickies, these too can be indicated with a half.' Here then, instead of the poetic clover-leafs, is the English table described using this proposal:

- Two seater: two-zero;
- Coupé cabriolet: half-zero;
- Saloon landaulette: zero-two-half;
- Clover leaf: three-zero;
- Open touring: six-zero;
- Single landaulette: half-half;
- Three quarter cabriolet: two-half;
- Coupé: zero-two;
- Brougham: two-two;
- Clover leaf coupé: zero-three;
- Enclosed cabriolet: half-half-half;
- Clover leaf coupelette: zero-three coupelette;
- Three quarter landaulette: half-half-half;
- Enclosed limousine: zero-six;
- Coupelette: zero-half;
- Saloon: zero-four;
- All-weather: half-half;
- Clover leaf cabriolet: zero-three;
- Cabriolet limousine: half-four;
- Single cabriolet: half-two;
- Enclosed landaulette: zero-six.

Imagine the joy in the office, of declaring to your colleagues, whom you wish to see envious of your good fortune, that you have just bought a half-half; or have to suffer the complaints of your wife because instead of buying a zero-six, you allowed yourself to be tempted by a zero-two.

In short, the problem cannot be resolved. Or better, a solution did arrive in the end, but it was decreed by the market, which slowly reduced such a vast variety on offer, thanks to increasing industrialization and standardization of the coachworks. An inevitable destiny, perhaps, but certainly more acceptable and glorious than the transformation of a clover leaf into a zero.

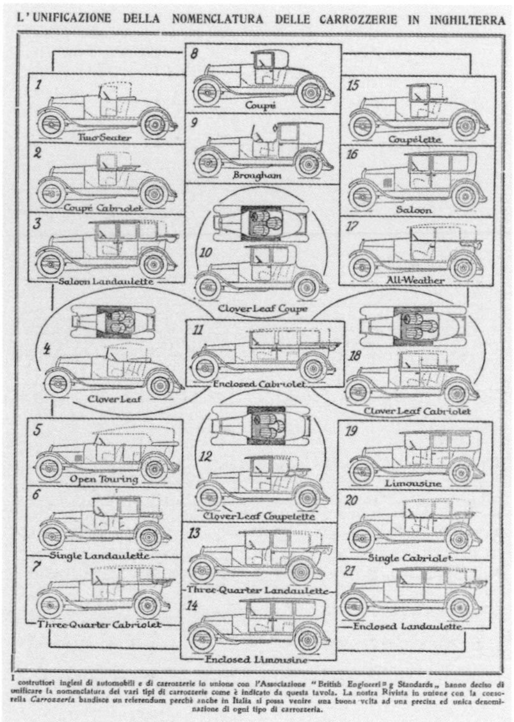

L'UNIFICAZIONE DELLA NOMENCLATURA DELLE CARROZZERIE IN INGHILTERRA

I costruttori inglesi di automobili e di carrozzerie in unione con l'Associazione "British Engineering Standards" hanno deciso di unificare la nomenclatura dei vari tipi di carrozzerie come è indicato da questa tavola. La nostra Rivista in unione con la consorella *Carrozzeria* bandisce un referendum perchè anche in Italia si possa venire una buona volta ad una precisa ed unica denominazione di ogni tipo di carrozzeria.

20. Table of English terms

21. '*Leurs joujoux*'... their toys

Bibliography

D. Biffignandi, 'Garofani e tulipani,' in *Auto d'Epoca*, November 2001.

Antonio Amadelli, '1908: nasce la torpedo,' in *Auto d'Epoca*, November 1997.

Auto d'Italia. Rivista settimanale per l'incremento dell'automobilismo, 1907.

La Carrozzeria. L'eleganza italiana dell'automobile, quarterly, 1928; 1929.

Carlo Biscaretti di Ruffia, *Carrozzieri di ieri carrozzieri di oggi*, Anfia, Turin 1963.

Automobilia. L'Automobile aux armées, fortnightly, 1931.

The Autocar. A Journal published in the interests of the mechanically propelled road carriage, weekly, 1907.

Auto Italiana, fortnightly, 1926.

Powering the Car of Tomorrow

Enrico De Vita

The first internal combustion engine was made to burn gas, but a switch was very soon made to 'mineral turpentine.' Nor were diesel engines originally made to run using diesel fuel, but coal dust. Both sorts of engine have since, and for a century, opted for liquid combustibles, which are far more convenient to transport, offer the greatest energy content (in terms of volume and weight) and, all things considered, are the least dangerous. The near future will see the use of synthetic fuels, perhaps derived from coal, but the more distant future belongs to hydrogen.

Energies of Yesterday and Tomorrow

The internal combustion engine was first created — around 1865 — to be powered using gas. An obligatory and convenient choice, given that there was no petrol to be had as yet, nor diesel, while gas — produced from coal — was already distributed in cities for street-lighting.

This was the middle of the 19th century, and it was coal that fuelled the Industrial Revolution before the arrival of electricity. Coal and water, coal and steam or just coal. It was used to provide heat, pressure, light or gas for other purposes. Steam engines are still made (with combustion outside the cylinder), fed by coal, as this works well for large locomotives weighing several tens of tons, and for ships. But in the car, 'steam' coal only made a few courageous appearances in miniature, as in the steam-powered Serpollet of 1889, weighing four tons. Coal, however, was again used to power engines — and this time in internal combustion — in the closing years of the 19th century, thanks to Rudolf Diesel. And it is certain that it will return in the future, to help give a hand with synthetic combustibles.

Let us return to 1885. Gas, already used to power internal combustion engines used in factories for stationary functions for the past 15 years, could not be easily stored and transported aboard a vehicle. So the problem facing Karl Benz and Gottlieb Daimler, the pioneers of the motor car between 1880 and 1885, was that of substituting the gas with a liquid. The choice was logical, given that nature has conferred a far greater energetic content on liquids than on gases. However, that liquid had to have clear requisites: it had to be highly inflammable, evaporate easily, able to burn without leaving residues, stable over time, non-corrosive and not mix with water.

Gasoline

In actual fact, the liquid used first of all was more akin to modern kerosene than to petrol. It was mineral turpentine, then known as gasoline (hence the American word for 'petrol' today) and was the lightest of the petroleum products, made from distilling bituminous rocks and not pumped from oil wells. It was sold in grocers for use in lamps, for medicinal purposes and as a solvent for paint.

Mineral turpentine or 'white naphta' has been known since the Middle Ages and used to make gunpowder. Its use as a fuel was invented by Karl Otto, who in 1877 built the first carburettor (more like a heated pan than a diffuser with Venturi tubes) and put into motion what is considered to be the first four-stroke petrol engine. The spread of that fuel (and of the engines) was so rapid and extensive that already by 1890 there were two functioning refineries in Italy, processing 1200 tons of crude oil a year.

If Otto's four-stroke engine had been born with petrol injection, today's petrol would be very different. Instead, a carburettor was used, and developed for over 100 years, making the engine subject to the laws of carburation: in other words, it was conditioned by the efficiency of the vaporization and spontaneous mixing of the petrol and air. So for over a century, the refineries have produced a versatile liquid, able to evaporate at temperatures close to zero, while not boiling in the summer, able to light with a simple spark, but not to self-ignite if submitted to high pressure and temperature.

With the carburettor, the vaporization of the petrol must take place spontaneously at a pressure of less than that of the atmosphere, that is at 0.6 to 0.7 bar. With indirect injection, the fuel is sprayed into the intake manyfold at a pressure of between 3 and 7 bar, pulverizing it. Finally, with direct injection — within the cylinder — values of 50 to 100 bar are attained. At these high pressures, some of the characteristics of the petrol varieties that were the stuff of novels (and advertising) in the last century are no longer required, but are preserved to power the still varied range of cars on the road. However, if we consider the problems that used to crop up as a result of poor-quality petrol, such as 'vapour lock' (bubble of vapour blocking the fuel pump in the summer), or 'icing' (crystals of ice jamming the carburettor's throttle valve in winter), we can note that the carburettor has conditioned the oil industry.

There is one characteristic of petrol, however, that was and still is independent of carburation. This is its power to resist detonation and is measured in Octanes. At the start of the 20th century, it was already clear that engine performance grew with a high compression ratio (standard production was normally around 5:1). But as soon as compression was increased further, the danger of holing a piston grew immeasurably, in part because the quality of the petrol sold was anything but uniform. It was natural that designers should seek a higher octane number from the refineries, but this could only be achieved with major investments. Until, in the 1920s, an effective and cheap solution was found: the addition of lead additives, which made it possible to arrive as high as 10.5:1, saw the octane number of the fuels increase from 60-65 at the end of the First World War to the 98 of the leaded petrol available until recently.

Banished in 1987 for rather weak health reasons (although in reality it was to pavette way for the catalytic convertor), teraethyl lead and lead alkylate — the two salts used to raise the octane rating — were replaced with benzene and other aromatic hydrocarbons, compounds that are far more hazardous and now present in petrol in greater quantities. Above all, they have proven carcinogenic effects.

1. A coal-fired diesel engine. Shown is the first engine with ignition by compression, built by Rudolf Diesel in 1893. It was extremely heavy for the meagre power output and also very noisy. It only worked for a few minutes before breaking. The glory had to wait another hundred years before erupting

Lard, Seed Oil and Coal

In 1893, Rudolf Diesel attempted a major diversification, both in the type of fuel and in the manner of igniting it. No longer a liquid, but any substance with a high calorific content, including coal dust, lard, seed oil, would be used. It would be ignited not by a spark but by a hot environment and high pressure: over 450° C, let's say, and at least 35 bar. No more would there be a close and fundamental air/fuel ratio, as required by petrol, but any ratio, even with far leaner mixtures.

In theory, it was a splendid idea and — we now know — in practice too. But at the time, they did not have the means to nebulize, dose and inject the fuel correctly. The German engineer had to satisfy himself with a compressed air system that pushed the prepared coal dust into the cylinder. His first engine did not work, and broke down immediately. And when he managed to turn the engine over, it soon showed its limitations: it was heavy, delivered little power and was noisy. Its only advantages were a high thermodynamic yield, with low consumption, conceptual simplicity and it did not need an ignition system.

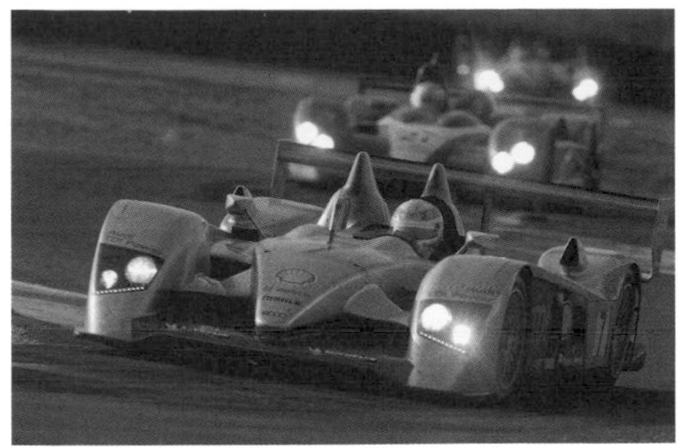

2. Victory at Le Mans. After overtaking petrol-driven cars in Europe in terms of sales, the diesel engine scored a further success here in France, a feat few would have bet on until a few years ago. In June 2006, this diesel-powered car roundly beat all the petrol-driven cars in what is considered the longest and most important car race in the world: the 24 Hours of Le Mans

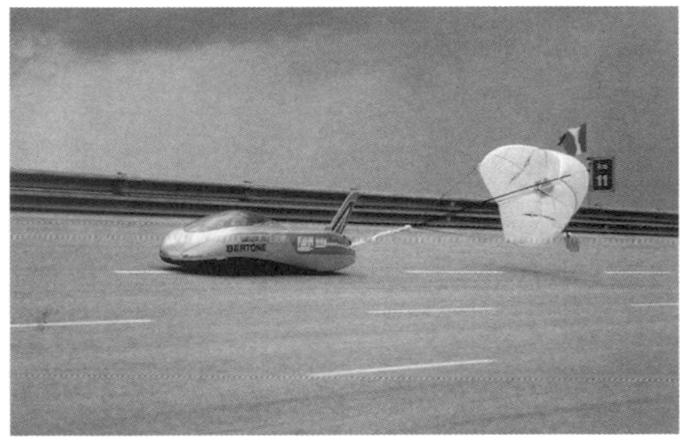

3. An electric record-breaking torpedo. It has already won numerous world records: it has been driven for an hour at 200 kph, has exceeded 304 kph over a flying kilometre, and has a range of 600 kilometres at an average of over 130 kph. It is called Zer (zero emission record), is powered with lead batteries and was built by Bertone in 1994 with the collaboration of two young Milanese engineers. In the photograph, the Zer on the Nardò track brakes with its parachute after having accelerated to over 300 kph

For over 30 years, Rudolf Diesel's offspring was used only in ships and railway engines. The heart of the system lay in the injection system. And when in 1927 Robert Bosch perfected the first hydraulic pump able to nebulize and dose diesel fuel, the diesel engine finally became more powerful, lighter, and suitable for mounting on a lorry. Ten years later, these engines were fitted to Hanomag and Mercedes trucks.

Nobody at the start of the 20th century could have imagined that 100 years later, the diesel would have won the 24 Hours of Le Mans and overtaken petrol in sales within Europe.

Electric Cars: an Old Dream

The first car to exceed 100 kph on 29th April 1899 was an electric model. It was called 'La Jamais Contente' and had been built by a Belgian, Camille Jenatzy.

The dream of using an electric engine, given that trams already existed, has for a long time been cherished by pioneers and accompanied the birth of the motor car from the outset. The battle between petrol and battery lasted about 20 years. In the early 20th century, there were over 2000 electric taxis in New York. The ease of use offered by a battery-powered car (compared with the 'manual' difficulty of getting a petrol car started) compensated for the reduced range, which rarely exceeded 50 kilometres.

Unfortunately, Mother Nature endows chemical cells with little energy, and technical progress has not improved the situation much. A hundred years ago as now, a kilo of lead battery can store 40 watt-hours of energy. A 12-kilo battery has the same energetic content as a glass of petrol. With nickel-zinc and the more modern nickel-metal hydride batteries, this content doubles but at a cost. And finally, lithium-ion batteries, commonly used for mobile telephones, can reach 160 watt-hours per kilo of battery. But these are still drops of energy, insufficient to confer decent range and performance for a modern car. The Zer (zero emission record), a record-breaking experimental vehicle by Bertone, exceeded 300 kph in 1994, and weighed 880 kg, but over 600 kg of that was batteries. These were the same sort of lead batteries as used by Jamais Contente a century earlier.

There is another dream as well, that of gathering electric energy from the sun, using photovoltaic panels. But the silicium or gallium arsenide crystals require large surface areas to provide a few horsepower. So we must then content ourselves with moving with just a little energy, as do solar-powered vehicles: 8 square metres for 1.5 kW of power, a top speed of over 90 kph, and autonomy of one day. Without consuming a drop of petrol.

Hybrid: Technological Solution or Accounting Sleight of Hand?

Modern nickel-metal hydride batteries are sufficient to give renewed lustre to hybrid cars. This is a solution that goes back to the times of Karl Benz, although both form and philosophy have changed now. In both cases, it is a case of a thermal engine plus an electric motor, which possesses its own energy store in the form of a battery pack. There is also a generator serving to recover part of the energy when braking, enabling the thermal engine to keep the batteries charged. The electric motor is used to start from traffic lights, to give added acceleration, to level off the request for power. The wheels can be turned by just one of the two engines or by both, even simultaneously.

Unfortunately, the hybrid car takes its electrical energy only from the thermal engine, that is, from the transformation of petrol, and this with a double loss as regards the thermodynamic yield of the internal combustion engine and that of the transformation into electricity, which in turn depends on the yield from the battery and from the electric motor. Given that only the petrol engine has been used so far, the production of electrical energy takes place using one of the most expensive means to transform thermal energy.

If the electricity produced in this way were to go straight to the wheels, without being stored in the batteries, we would lose only 10-15%, thanks to the yield of the electric motor. But since it is used later, it has to go to the accumulators, even if only for a few minutes. And so we have to pay the cost enforced by the batteries to convert electrical energy into chemical energy and back to electricity again. In total, another 30-35% disappears, according to battery type.

If we then add that a hybrid car carries around with it not just a thermal engine, but also a series of accumulators, an electric motor and some management systems, we also have to take into account the increased weight and consumption resulting from this. Moral of the story: analyzed from the point of view of energy, the hybrid car seems a flop, a technical contradiction, since we gain less from what we have already spent in petrol.

However, the appeal of this technology lies in the fact that it can transform part of the energy that the vehicles dissipates in the environment. In detail, this means recovering the energy lost in braking and saving of petrol in slowing down and when halted. Obviously, if travelling on the motorway at constant speed, this recovery is zero, but in city driving it can amount to as much as 20%. Which means driving 20% further for the same quantity of petrol burned. This recovery costs absolutely nothing.

But note, however, that the recovery of energy is not an unlimited and universal possibility on all hybrids. In order to transform all of the braking inertia into energy, extremely powerful electric motors are needed, able to transform themselves instantly into generators and to absorb power in the order of 350 hp (or 250 kW), representing the energy dissipated every second under hard braking in a car weighing 1300 kilos. If the electric motor is only able to absorb 60 hp, the recovery will be partial. Not only, but even if we hypothesize the availability of a hugely powerful engine, able to absorb 250 kW, once the battery is fully charged, it will be impossible to add anything more; it would be like adding more petrol to a fuel tank that is full to the brink.

This handicap can be overcome by using battery packs offering great capacity. But these are inevitably heavy, so the question arises once more: 'to what extent is it worth it?'

The reply lies in the great importance that the data concerning consumption and pollution measured in various cycles. These values are rather different to those of real-life driving, but they serve to obtain incentives, certification and approval. Indeed, these tests, which are obligatory in the USA, Europe and Japan, all include low speed or cylces require little power is required. Not only, they also include periods with the engine at idle and starting up. For this reason, a hybrid vehicle appears attractive as it can intervene with electric traction, turning off the thermal engine and making the pollution and consumption appear as nil. Never mind if that electricity has been produced just an hour before, during a trip on a motorway, at high speed, and thus burning petrol.

Leading European car manufacturers are convinced that in terms of pollution, consumption and cost, a good diesel is better than a petrol-driven hybrid car. Nevertheless, in order to pass future European anti-pollution regulations, it is probable that the technology of hybrid traction will be applied in future also to diesel cars produced in Europe.

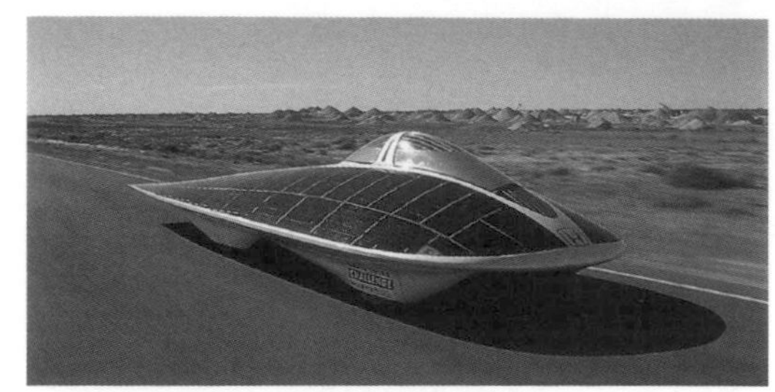

4. A solar dream. This is Dream 2, an experimental vehicle powered by photovoltaic panels and built by Honda in 1996. It won in a crossing of Australia, travelling 3000 kilometres in 33 hours 32 minutes at a speed of 89.8 kph, and drawing its energy solely from the sun via 47,000 monocrystalline silicon photovoltaic cells. It has a power output of 2.5 b.h.p., too few to be able to dream of driving every day with the sun

Today's Alternatives

Less than 1% of cars in Italy make use of fuels other than petrol or diesel. The most widespread are methane and LPG. Ethanol and methanol are not used in Italy, but thanks to considerable tax incentives, they are in others, such as Sweden and Brazil, mixed with petrol. Let us look at the advantages and drawbacks of each.

• *Methane*. This is an excellent fuel because formed of a single molecule. It pollutes little, burns well, possesses a high calorific value, high octane rating, is very common in the bowels of the earth and is still little-used. It is often to be found together in oil wells, but its presence does not necessarily depend on crude oil, and it can also be found alone. Like hydrogen, it is awkward to use in cars because of the difficulty of transportation and storage. It is a lighter gas than air (in boiler rooms and in garages with methane-powered cars, ventilation openings need to be placed high up) and needs to be compressed to 300 bar. Apart from the loss in energy that the compression process causes, accounting for 18% of its content, we need also to consider the high weight of the robust gas cylinders required to store the gas and the low range

5. Battery+petrol = hybrid. Toyota was the first company to produce and sell hybrid cars, using a complex mechanical and electronic device enabling three different power supplies to be managed without gears or clutch. The Prius, introduced in California in 1997, was the Japanese manufacturer's first hybrid model

6. Common Rail. European manufacturers maintain that a good diesel engine is even better than a petrol hybrid, in terms of consumption and emissions. An Italian diesel engine is shown in this photograph, the Turbotronic produced by VM Motori and exported to the United States. Despite the fact that diesels are not popular in America, this engine has been adopted by Ford, General Motors and Chrysler

offered by methane-powered cars. Finally, with this gas, it would be possible to obtain greater power from the engine by increasing the compression ratio, but this is impossible if it has also to run on petrol.

Methane can be easily moved from one country to another using low-pressure methane pipelines and is thus an ideal combustible for stationary use (industry, domestic heating, cooking).

In future, it will be used to produce synthetic liquid combustible more suitable for cars. And when all combustibles will be synthetic in origin, petrol and diesel cars will evolve towards a single configuration, to the advantage of both.

• *LPG*. This stands for liquefied petroleum gas. Many environmentalists love this product for its ecological virtues. In reality, it is a derivative of the oil industry (it is the lightest fraction, made up of butane and propane), and is thus available in limited quantities and is in any case linked to the production of petrol (3-4% is made per given quantity of petrol produced). It is not possible to hypothesize extending its use to the entire automotive sector, even though it has a good octane rating and does not require storage cylinders of particular robustness and weight.

• *Ethanol*. Known as ethyl alcohol, this is a combustible liquid of vegetable derivation. It contains an oxygen atom in its molecule and so has a reduced calorific content, little more than half that of petrol. This means increased consumption in terms of litres and also a different regulation of the carburation (larger jets). It is easily mixed with water and indeed attracts humidity in the tanks, causing problems of corrosion. In Brazil, it is made from sugar cane and biomass, but it is currently used only as an additive to petrol after having been transformed into ETBE, an ether produced in the laboratory offering excellent performance for car engines.

• *Methanol*. Also known as methyl alcohol, it can be made from coal, methane, heavy oil, wood. It is a little heavier than petrol and can be mixed with it up to a maximum ratio of 10%. It causes corrosion in some metal parts and in rubber membranes, so engines burning it require specific engineering. Oxygen takes up exactly half of the molecular weight, so it has a very low calorific value, less than that of ethanol (and less than half that of petrol). Methanol also can be converted in the laboratory into a fine combustible, MTBE, offering a high octane rating and easily mixable with petrol. Indeed, it is commonly used as an additive in the place of lead salts.

When the Oil Runs out

Once the oil wells dry up, there will still be petrol. Or rather, there will be no lack of substitutes for petrol and diesel. It is also probable that oil will be abandoned before all the reserves are used, because it will no longer be able to compete in terms of cost, as has already happened with the combustibles used in the 19th century — wood, peat, coal, coal gas; these were abandoned before they were exhausted because there were cheaper, more practical or less polluting alternatives. What will we be burning in future?

There are numerous options: these range from fuels of agricultural origin to those derived from biomass, and those formulated industrially from methane or synthesized from coal. The choice will depend on cost and political and local motivations. With a view to world-wide distribution, those producing less carbon dioxide will be preferred.

In any case, what is certain is that agricultural products used as such or not mixed with traditional fuels is out of the question. And they will be liquid fuels, because these contain more energy.

To finish, coal — sufficient reserves of which exist to cover energy needs for hundreds of years — could be used to produce a wide variety of made-to-measure synthetic fuels. The list includes hydrogen, because this can be made from water if a major source of heat is available.

Bio is Fashionable

Another possibility comes from biofuels, a term used to define all fuels of vegetable origin, but these have highly variable impacts on the environment and production costs. The only way to produce them in acceptable conditions — from the point of view of greenhouse effect and cost — appears to be to make them from biomass; that is, from agricultural and stock-raising waste.

Combustibles made from cultivated produce include a 'petroleum' cost resulting from the fertilisers used, diesel burned to work the soil, and heat used for distillation of the product. So at the outset, these produce an all but negligible greenhouse effect. To this, we need to add the carbon dioxide produced by the engine, which does not change much if burning vegetable fuels. The affirmation that this can be neutralized by the growth of the plant is true only if the cultivation is effected in deserts or in areas previously without plant life. Obviously, if these products are grown in Europe, where all the land is green, no benefit is achieved, as we are simply replacing one cultivation for another. The same — or worse — can be said of Brazil, where the sugar cane plantations (to produce ethanol) have taken the place of the forest, which used to capture at least double the quantity of CO_2.

Biomass, instead, is a substance that — left free in the environment — ferments and decomposes, giving off methane and carbon dioxide, and thus provoking an increased greenhouse effect. Vice versa, captured and transformed into fuel (as a gas or liquid), it cancels out in good part all the negative effects. This is why the use of biomass is always better for the environment and should be encouraged, even though the quantity of fuel obtainable is limited.

In summary, biomass apart, vegetable combustibles are not a good deal for the environment, even though some people wish to absolve 'non-fossil' CO_2, that which cars emit when burning something cultivated. As though the greenhouse effect were not produced by all the molecules of carbon dioxide. Or as though petroleum itself did not have a distant vegetable past.

7. Ethanol from biomass. Some models powered by a blend of petrol (15%) and ethanol (85%) have been on sale in Sweden since 2005. The programme — which includes considerable tax benefits — was set up more to provide an incentive to diversify sources of energy than to reduce the greenhouse gasses. Indeed, for the moment, the ethanol is bought from Brazil, which derives it from sugar cane plantations. The use of biomass would instead be less onerous for the planet and more healthy. Illustrated is the ehtnaol-powered Ford Focus

Hydrogen: Easier Said than Done

Two thirds of the atoms forming water are of hydrogen. It is present in all the hydrocarbons and in all acid substances. In short, hydrogen is the most common element on planet Earth in numerical terms. But it does not go out alone: in other words, we do not find it in a free state. To capture it, it needs to be stolen from a compound that has it in abundance, such as water or methane. But this is an expensive theft: consider that to extract hydrogen from water using hydrolysis (using electricity, in other words), the energy used to extract it is three times the amount it can yield. If, instead, we extract it from methane, a lot of heat is thrown away and a considerable dose of CO_2 has also to be dealt with.

Today, this is considered the ideal energy source for the future. In reality, this affirmation hides a trap, or a misunderstanding, according to point of view. Hydrogen is not a source of energy as it is not available in its pure state in nature. It should instead be considered an 'energy vector,' that is, a system with which to transport energy produced in a different way. Thus, hydrogen bears with it all the 'sins' of the primary source from which it derives.

Once in hand, however, it offers two fundamental benefits: 1. it burns completely and cleanly, producing only water vapour (not that this is neutral in terms of greenhouse effect; what are rain clouds, after all?); 2. it combines with oxygen even when cold to produce electricity (and water).

This second process is used in fuel cells, or combustible batteries, and forms the basis of the ecological engine of the future. Indeed, the electrical energy obtained makes it possible to run a car that resembles a battery car in every way.

Hydrogen also presents some drawbacks and disadvantages, which we must add to those of its original source. It possesses a limited energetic content if we consider it in its gaseous state (less even than methane, so it is not worth burning it in cars, especially given the limited range offered). In a liquid state, on the other hand, its energetic content (measured in calories per litre) is better than that of petrol. Sadly, to liquefy hydrogen, it needs to be compressed and taken to a temperature of -253 ° C. And this process costs about 20% of the energy possessed by the hydrogen. To transport it in a car, we need to have a cryo-

8. LPG and methane: a return to origins. The use of gaseous fuels has often been suggested as a future alternative. In reality, it marks a return to origins. The gases are clean and burn well, but their cheapness derives above all from the tax breaks they attract. If no car manufacturer has built a car powered solely by methane in over a hundred years, this is because liquid fuels offer decided advantages. Illustrated is a LPG-powered Opel

HONDA
Honda FC STACK

9. Hydrogen fuel cells. On 30th June 2005, Honda delivered the FCX, the first hydrogen-powered car for 'private' use to a family in Redondo Beach, California. In reality, the fuel cell has travelled to and from the moon several times on space missions, and it offers a technology that is already mature. However, for use in the car sector on a vast scale, there is a further need to reduce weight, volumes and costs. And then the hydrogen needs to be produced using a new source of energy, since it does not occur freely in nature

genic tank — an extremely special thermos flask — with several layers of insulation, and this is heavy and cumbersome.

This tank needs always to remain at a low temperature or the internal pressure rises and causes it to explode. For this reason, a safety valve to the exterior needs to be built in, but as a result of this, there will be a constant loss, which in summer can amount to 3% a day. Moreover, a hydrogen car cannot be parked in a closed garage for reasons of safety, but if left outside its tank will empty itself in just a month.

Today, plans are under way to store hydrogen in gaseous form, in tanks under 700 bar pressure. But the tank is heavy and despite the good yield intrinsic in the fuel cells, the range of prototypes has not so far exceeded 150-200 kilometres.

When will we have a hydrogen-powered car? Some promise it for tomorrow, but it will actually appear after 2020, although there are already experimental cars entrusted to private clients. In about ten years, it is probable that weight and size of the cells will have been reduced sufficiently to make them acceptable for use in vehicles and economical enough for industrial production. Competitiveness in costs and reliability should be achieved in the following decade, making a significant presence of these cars in private hands a possibility.

The problem of the supply of hydrogen remains. If made from methane, coal or petroleum (the only economically viable systems today, although far more expensive than petrol), there will still be a problem to solve: how to process the large amount of carbon dioxide produced in the separation from hydrogen. Some suggest liquefying it and sending it to the bottom of the oceans. But there's no guarantee that fish prefer their water carbonated.

10. Oil will exist as a fuel for cars for at least another 40 years but it will soon have to compete with synthetic liquid combustibles, made from methane, biomass and coal. Hydrogen may also be extracted from coal. For use in stationary applications, it will be soon replaced with gascous combustibles and renewable sources of energy

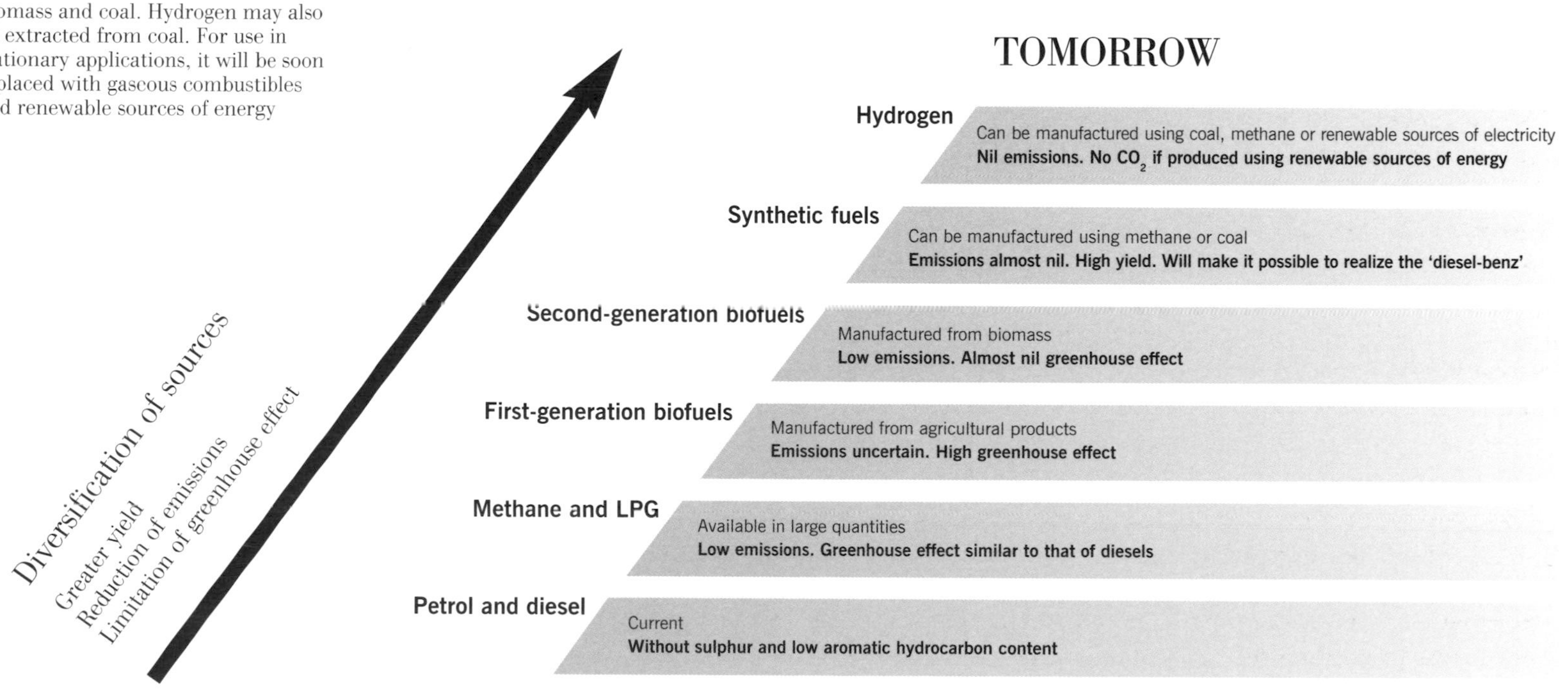
TOMORROW
Hydrogen
Can be manufactured using coal, methane or renewable sources of electricity
Nil emissions. No CO_2 if produced using renewable sources of energy
Synthetic fuels
Can be manufactured using methane or coal
Emissions almost nil. High yield. Will make it possible to realize the 'diesel-benz'
Second-generation biofuels
Manufactured from biomass
Low emissions. Almost nil greenhouse effect
First-generation biofuels
Manufactured from agricultural products
Emissions uncertain. High greenhouse effect
Methane and LPG
Available in large quantities
Low emissions. Greenhouse effect similar to that of diesels
Petrol and diesel
Current
Without sulphur and low aromatic hydrocarbon content
Diversification of sources
Greater yield
Reduction of emissions
Limitation of greenhouse effect
TODAY

Cars and Cities

Helen Evenden

As I write this essay, contemplating the relationship and tensions between the car and the city, indeed the very presence of cars in the urban domain, parking wardens patrol my London street merrily issuing £ 60 parking fines (euros 90). Red routes (no stopping routes), bus lanes, Congestion Charging, road tax, expensive imported petrol, road rage, vehicle theft, and the possibility of getting tickets for even a second over on a parking meter make it onerous to be responsible for a motor car. It is so difficult and so expensive to own a car in a city like London, or indeed any European city that the machines which democratized private transport for so many are now once again becoming the privilege of the elite.

A car is a liability in many modern cities. It is the unwelcome object, not the key to personal freedom. Yet for many of us our lifestyles, even our livelihoods depend on motor cars, vans or two-wheeled powered vehicles.

Changes to the ways in which transport services are run and maintained can be immediate, from repairing broken-down escalators at Tube stations, to increasing the price of train tickets or removing bus conductors. Changes to the moving vehicles themselves are also relatively quick and easy to implement, such as the livery of buses or the design of taxicabs. Changes to transport infrastructure — the roads, tunnels and bridges on which vehicles depend — are slow, expensive and highly politicized.[1]

In the new millennium it is fashionable to reject the very idea of private motor cars, particularly in city centres. Like many, I also believe strongly in the merits of public transport. London has historically had one of the finest public transport systems in the world: the first ever underground opened here in 1863, the iconic Routemaster bus designed by Douglas Scott and introduced in 1925 was only taken out of public service last year (due to European legislation on hanicap access) and we are still using the world-famous black cabs, albeit in the slightly modified TX1 version.

Access for motor cars is controlled by economics and policed by ever-increasing legislation. In Central London, Congestion Charge access costs £ 8 (euros 12) a day and there are threats to increase it to £ 25 (euros 37) for 4×4s. Ironically Mayor Livingstone's tax was heralded as a democratic way to improve movement in the city for all. Yet it has become a way for the wealthy to get around more quickly and more easily, while the less wealthy are denied access to private mobility and have to suffer the frustrations of overcrowded, increasingly expensive public transport.

It is an ironic situation for the very idea of the modern city, arguably of all cities is determined by ease of movement within them.

Transport Shapes Cities

From the birth of the car at the tail-end of the nineteenth century, it immediately became clear that these machines would change our landscape. Their predecessor, the horse and cart, had of course demanded streets on which to travel, fuel for the living power source, stabling for the static vehicles and yes, even the horse and cart generated a waste product that had to be disposed of. But the motor car is a very different beast, traveling at far higher speeds and capable of traveling much greater distances in shorter times.

[1] *London from Punk to Blair*, by Joe Kerr and Andrew Gibson, Reaktion Books, 2003, p. 243.

It may be said that transport infrastructure to a large extent determines the physical form of all our cities. In urban history, different cities in different parts of the world follow different patterns of transport movement, determined by geography, economics and social conditions.

Cities are the most tangible evidence of the process of civilization and the development of all cities relies upon transport links to, from and within the perimeters of the city itself. Today the shape of our cities and the experience of being in them are largely determined by how they have been affected or infected by the presence of motor cars. Streets carve their way through cities, facilitating access and connections, yet also dividing areas and creating alienating spaces, such as the voids under flyovers and the no man's land beside motorways and the roundabouts, impassable for pedestrians.

The idea of planning cities around key routes has generated many different models of urban planning. As Professor and architect Nigel Coates records, 'A spider's web was indeed a model for ideal cities up to the 20th century: radial, symmetrical, perspectival, it was a military device which placed the design at the service of projectiles drawn and directed from a central point.'[2] In Paris, Baron Haussmann brought *grandeur* and dignity to the city by the scale of his monumental boulevards, adorned with statues and monuments at key interchanges and focal points. The model was employed in part in many European cities, but was not as successful for mass car use as the American grid. The clarity of the grid system with its numeric numbering made New York, Chicago and many other American cities a cartographer's gift. A similar grid was adopted by Ildefons Cerdà whose grid-iron l'Eixample plan for Barcelona dominates the character of the city. Yet as anyone who has driven in these cities knows they are some of the most terrifying places to get lost in. Clearly the issue of driving in cities is not just determined by street layout.

Futurist City

During the 20th century, there have been many grand visions for dramatically altering cities. The idea of the functionalist city, the city that is logical and rational is often portrayed as a metropolis of straight roads containing rapidly moving vehicles, connecting to dense high-rise developments.

Marinetti, founder of the Futurist movement, wrote excitedly about the arrival of motorized transport and cars in the Foundation Manifesto of 1909; 'We all started up, at the sound of a double-decker tram rumbling past, ablaze with multi-coloured lights, like a village in festival dress that the flooded Po tears from its banks and sweeps through gorges and rapids, down to the sea. But afterwards, the silence grew deeper, and we heard only the muttered devotions of the old canal and the creaking of the arthritic, ivy-bearded old palaces until — suddenly — we heard the roar of famished motor cars beneath the windows.'[3]

Architect Antonio Sant'Elia's visions for new cities, dominated by industrial architecture and transportation infrastructure provide prophetic visions for the complexity and multi-layering of modern transport planning and particularly for the architecture of transportation terminals, or to use the contemporary terminology, interchanges.

Reyner Banham's analysis of the era is directly relevant to this discussion, for he observes that '... with the advent of the motor car, the poet, the painter, intellectual, was no longer a passive recipient of technological experience, but could create for himself. The command of vehicles of the order of 60 hp and upwards had hitherto been in the hands of professional specialists — engine drivers, ships' engineers and so forth. But the advent of the automobile brought such experiences and responsibilities within the scope of the rich amateur in the years immediately after 1900.'[4]

Perhaps the rate of progress celebrated by the Futurists has not been maintained and in the essay *The Lesson of the Motor Car* in his book *Theory and Design in the Second Machine Age*, (the sequel to Reyner Banham's *Theory and Design in the Machine Age*), Martin Pawley laments the fact that architecture remains a craft, yet car design is truly a process

[2] Brian Hatton, in *Ecstacity*, Nigel Coates, Laurence King Publishing, 2003, p. 29.
[3] Filippo Tommaso Marinetti, *Foundation Manifesto*, published in *Le Figaro*, 20 February 1909, quoted by Reyner Banham, *Theory and Design in the First Machine Age*, Architectural Press, 1960, reprinted 1982, p 100.
[4] *Ibid.*, p. 102.

of the modern age. Pawley also cites Marinetti's wonderful phrase — 'Man multiplied by the motor car.'[5]

1-3. Driving the American Landscape
Photo Andrew Cross

Modernist Cities

The infrastructure of transport, the vehicles we drive, the environments within which we commute, the terminals where we wait to embark and the destinations at which we arrive are all part of the age of Modernism.

Transportation has an intimate relationship with Modernism. Indeed the very idea of private transport for masses of individuals and mass transportation for all seems to be an embodiment of the potential of the modern ideal. So it seems perfectly logical that many Modernists, including Le Corbusier and Mies van der Rohe were interested in the things that move us — boats, planes, trains and specifically the defining machine of the 20th century, motor cars.

Corbusier's visions for new cities celebrated the possibilities of technology, what he called 'mechanical beauty' and particularly the benefits of motorized transportation, and described the 'magnificent catastrophe of the beautiful traffic patterns' of the modern city. In architectural history it is extremely rare for such grand plans to be realized. Perhaps that is a good thing, but as Corbusier himself recognized it is often the infrastructure that remains constant while the vehicles themselves evolve. In his intelligent analysis of *Le Corbusier: town-planning and aesthetics*, Reyner Banham quotes Corbusier's 1926 statement which remains true today; 'The foaming locomotive, the rearing steed that evoked the hasty lyricism of Huysmans, is rusting iron on the scrap-heap. The cars of the next Salon require that Citroën write off the model that has been all the rage. But the Roman aqueduct endures...'[6]

The pre-Second World War Beetle is a good example of Modernist ideals. The car is the ultimate mass-produced, utilitarian object, perfectly fit for its purpose. Some say Modernism reflects those who are controlling and it is interesting that many examples of its success relate to dictators, whether that be political regimes or control freak architects. The Zeppelin programme, Hitler's Volkswagen people's car and his policy to transform the German landscape with a network of autobahns do seem to add weight to this theory.'[7]

America and Motor City

Once Henry Ford had applied the principles of mass-production and created the motor industry as opposed to the craft of making motor cars, the possibility for mass consumption of cars was in place.

In America, early industrial designers and modern movement architects celebrated the possibilities of modern transportation, notably locomotives and subsequently cars. At the 1939 New York World Fair the visions are stunning, depicting free flowing highways with massive numbers of vehicles seemingly choreographed. The Ford Pavilion with its 'Highway of Tomorrow' and competitor General Motors Pavilion, containing a 'Futurama' by industrial designer Norman Bel Geddes, were both popular successes with visitors. The designer optimism for controlling flow is best illustrated by Geddes in his book *Magic Motorways*; in which he presents a detailed plan for an entirely new type of national roadway system with colour-coded highway lanes. Accordingly to the preface this 1940 text is the first work on the subject.

Although the American love-affair with the car largely continues, the Detroit story does not have a happy ending. The impact of the intense production of cars in 'Motor City' has left scars on the landscape. Detroit enthusiast Joe Kerr questions whether 'Motor City has finally run out of road?'[8] In the essay — *Trouble in Motor City* Kerr explains how 'The enormous wealth which Detroit's car plants once generated, and which helped to build it into the third most populated city in the US, has long ceased to sustain it.' The ultimate industrial landscape for the production and consumption of cars according to Fordism and the resulting American model has been shaken to its roots by competitors, firstly Japan and more recently China and India. Detroit roads are littered with abandoned buildings and no go streets that reflect the city's rapid peak and then dramatic decline.

[5] Martin Pawley, *Theory and Design in the Second Machine Age*, Blackwell, 1990, p. 55.
[6] Le Corbusier, quoted by Reyner Banham, *op. cit.*, p. 251.
[7] 'Modernism is Movement,' in *Cent Magazine*, 2006.
[8] *Autopia*, Joe Kerr and Peter Wollen (editors), Reaktion Books 2002, p. 125.

4-5. 'Autoscapes:' Los Angeles, Hong Kong
Photo Neutral

Decentralized Cities

Cars enabled commuters to travel greater distances for both work and leisure, thereby changing our lifestyles and the proximity of our homes to our places of work. The very idea of suburban living, particularly the American model of suburban areas planned about road networks (as opposed to the European examples that often developed along tram, train and tube routes) can be said to be a direct result of mass car ownership.

Historically improved transportation routes, whether by tram, train, underground or road have stretched the boundaries of cities or enabled people to imagine they live outside the city. The Arts and Crafts inspired 'Garden Cities and Suburbs,' offer a seductive way to pretend to live away from the hard-edged problems of urbanity, but actually are still economically if not socially dependent upon urbanity. Whatever the reality the idea of suburbia is facilitated by transport and the possibilities of various modes of transport in theory enables greater decentralization of the city.

In his enlightening essay *The Automobile and the City* in a seminal text on the subject of *The Automobile and American Culture*, Mark Foster makes clear that 'no pre-20th century technological advance had ever wielded so much potential for internally shaping the urban landscape as did the automobile.' Foster goes on to explain how, 'At the end of the 19th century, decentralization of the city seemed to be an imperative social goal. American cities had been growing increasingly crowded for many years, and huge influxes of immigrants and native Americans into urban areas in the late 19th century made congestion even worse.'[9]

Driving America

In America the relationship with the motor car is intense. As Jean Baudrillard observes in his book *America* and Reyner Banham studied in *Los Angeles*, the vast landscapes chartered by straight roads, the animation of vehicles on the multiple lanes of the freeway system and the ability to drive for days coast to coast or inland have created a mythology of the American road trip that is unique and enticing in fiction, film and also in reality. Yet even in America where asphalt roads link gridded cities to immense suburbs, there is a coming of age that the gas-guzzlers cannot be sustained forever.

Photographer and transport anthropologist Andrew Cross recognizes, 'Except for the few concentrated urban areas, the actual manner of driving in America is quantifiably different from that in Europe. Traffic is significantly less dense, and the pace is seemingly much more leisurely.'[10]

Differences between the American 'love affair with the car' and the European situation are interesting. Architect and public transport enthusiast Brian Richards spent a lifetime promoting a positive integration of all modes of transport in urban areas. His first book *Move-*

[9] Mark Foster, *The Automobile and the City*, essay, in *The Automobile and American Culture*, David L. Lewis, Laurence Goldstein (editors), University of Michigan Press, 1980, 1983, p. 26.
[10] Andrew Cross, in *Autopia* cit., p. 251.

6-8. 'Autoscapes:' Los Angeles, Hong Kong, Tokyo
Photo Neutral

ment in Cities was one of the first to map the then existing strategies for public transport. Richards explains the differences between the American and European models; 'in North America [...] mobility was made easy, for those with cars, to live and work in widely dispersed low density areas, and often resulted in the demise of public transport and the city centre diminishing in importance [...] In the European city, while public transport varies in quality between countries, and is mostly far from good enough to actually deter people from using their cars, the restraint imposed by the limited size of existing roads and the often high cost of parking plus lower car ownership has at least meant that people continue to use public transport.'[11]

International Language

Many of the issues relating to transport are now part of what one might call international territory and in reality much of the roadside landscape is similar if not homogenous in most of the world. Petrol stations, traffic signals, tarmac, road signs and the general identity of the driven landscape have become standardized across national boundaries and pay little respect for climate and geography. I do not regret this standardization of the dedicated roadside environment. I think it is reassuring that one can drive almost anywhere in the world and recognize a petrol (or gasoline) station and know how to get fuel there (probably without even talking to a human being).

Street graphics and the signals given to drivers travelling at speed are the subject of many fascinating semantic studies. The most enjoyable and enlightening study of the relationship between buildings and graphic signs at the edge of the road or, to use the American term, the strip is *Learning from Las Vegas*. The project and book by Robert Venturi, Denise Scott Brown and Steven Izenour developed a methodology for interpreting the architecture of the Las Vegas roadside.

Another enlightening study of the graphics of movement is included in Alison Smithson's diary of the adventures in her Citroën DS, *AS in DS: an Eye on the Road* in which she considers, 'the graphics of character of the road [...] and the mutation over the 24 hours, 52 weeks of the year's 12 months covering four seasons in all weathers.' Smithson is right to highlight differences in our driving experiences depending on weather and level of nat-

[11] Brian Richards, *Moving in Cities*, Cassell & Collier Macmillan Publishers Ltd., London 1976, p. 9.

ural or artificial light. She is also highly articulate about the way 'the car has rolled into the city like an assassin...' and that 'the car-driver's dream is spoilt by the huge number of other drivers.'[12]

Old Cities and New Cars

Ancient cities like Rome and medieval cities like London that have evolved organically and maintained many key routes that were developed centuries before even the invention of the motor car, have a problematic relationship with the machines of the modern age.

Rome, today capital of Italy and one of the largest European capital cities in land area, once the capital of the most powerful, largest and longest lasting empire of classical Western civilization, is one of the most difficult cities in which to marry contemporary demand for fast personal mobility and the limitations imposed by historic buildings, ancient remains and sensitive street planning.

Chronic congestion caused by cars during the 1970s and 1980s led to the banning of unauthorized traffic from the central part of city, the *Zona a Traffico Limitato* (ZTL), during workdays from 6 am to 6 pm. Weekend crowds and nightlife have led to the extension of this zone in the Trastevere and S. Lorenzo districts during the night, and to experimentation with a new night ZTL also in the city centre (plans to create a night ZTL in the Testaccio district as well are underway).

Mayor Walter Veltroni is well aware that the result is often frustrated drivers, grid-locked or lost in winding streets almost impossibly narrow for cars and almost impossible to park in. Italian designers have come up with a few solutions, the most important being the Vespa by Piaggio, which in Rome is less a fashion statement and more a practical tool. Fiat's Cinquento was another masterstroke, enabling four people to sit in a footprint of a tiny, yet stylish car. Lately the electric vehicle is starting to reduce urban pollution and they are popular with teenage drivers whose parents are reluctant to let them drive scooters in the city.

London is also restricted by old street organization, with the square mile of the City of London still dominated by small streets laid out in medieval times. Despite plans by Sir Christopher Wren and others after the Great Fire of 1666, London has never been subjected to something as organized as a grand plan and due to the complex ownership of land the organic development of streets remains. The nature of democracy and street planning is an interesting one.

As I stated earlier historically dictatorships have achieved greater clarity of street planning than more democratic systems. In London this situation has reached the ridiculous as is illustrated by the length of time it took to close a single street in the heart of the city. The idea to close the north of the World Heritage Site at Trafalgar Square to traffic to improve pedestrian access to one of the most photographed city squares was proposed by Foster and Partners. Despite the area's heritage it was a largely unfriendly environment, dominated by motor vehicles, its square reduced to roundabouts, providing few amenities for Londoners and fewer facilities for the thousands of people who visit each year.

A long period of research involved two major studies of traffic and pedestrian movement and consultations with more than 180 public bodies and thousands of individuals. One of the tools utilised was the plan model of London developed by Space Syntax, London, which demonstrates the potential for connectivity and pedestrian access at street level. Space Syntax are a multi-disciplinary company, established in 1989, to explore and map the nature of movement in cities and within buildings. 'The word syntax refers to the relationships between words in a sentence. It is the system by which we arrange words to create meaning. In the same way, how can public and private spaces be arranged so that they make sense to the people who use them?'[13]

This research led to the development of two possible strategies, which were launched at a public exhibition in Whitehall in November 1997.[14] The response was overwhelming support for change and today the paved area replacing the road and the subsequent new road system has redressed the balance between pedestrians and vehicles. Making this another case study of sustainable urban access for cars being controlled rather than dominating

[12] Alison Smithson, *AS in DS: An Eye on the Road*, Delft University Press, Delft 1983, Lars Muller Publishers, reprinted 2001, p. 5.
[13] www.spacesyntax.com.
[14] www.fosterandpartners.com.

the pedestrian domain. Similar changes in cities such as Barcelona, Berlin, Paris and Amsterdam have shown how the containment of traffic can contribute to the economic and cultural vitality of city centres and many other cities are looking at dramatic changes to key routes. Such as the concepts for Avenida in Lisbon where it is being considered to send cars underground.

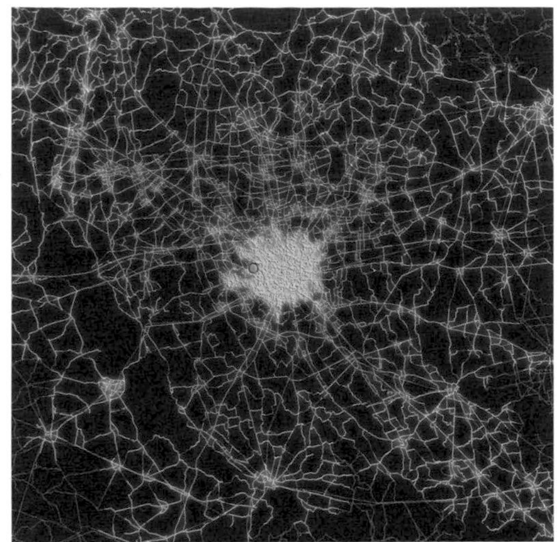

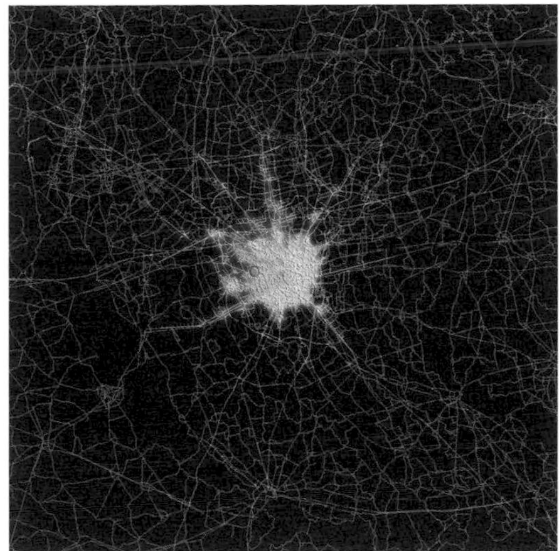

9-10. Surveys of traffic flow (research by the Laboratorio di Macrourbanistica DPA, Civil Engineering faculty, Politecnico di Milano, director Fabio Casiroli, research group Davide Boazzi, Elena Luoni, assistants Stilla Graf, Giuseppe Pepe, Luca Terragni, sponsor Systematica and Citilabs) Photo Systematica

Industrial Cities

Milan is Italy's largest city by population and a key industrial hub. The design-conscious city suffers serious traffic problems that have forced city planners to question the relationship between pedestrians and the car in an effort to improve public spaces.

Professor Fabio Casiroli, President of Systematica Spa, is a strategist, theorist and implementor of transport mapping and flow modeling. His projects include the Florence High Speed Rail Station with Foster and Partners and Genova Waterfront with Renzo Piano Building Workshop. Casiroli is based in Milan and feels particularly strongly about the problems with congestion in his hometown. 'Milan at present is a city engulfed in its own traffic and pollution. A solution must be found and this cannot be additional road infrastructure to allow even higher number of vehicles to enter the city. There are three strategic targets that must be addressed in order to tackle the traffic problem; the first one is to give consistency to urban development and infrastructure connectivity, the second is to deter the usage of private vehicles and above all Milan must strengthen the development of a sustainable public transport inside the city border but in the metropolitan area as well.'

New Cities

Integrating old and new provides unique challenges, but there are still parts of the world where the possibility for entirely new models exist. Megalopolises in Asia are reinventing themselves at alarming speed, but they still usually depend on some of the traditions if not the physical fabric of their previous incarnations. But in the desert, particularly in the states of the United Arab Emirates (UAE) there is the wealth (fuelled of course by oil), the will (from the powerful Sheiks) and the opportunity now to create new super cities as there has been little substantial development until the very recent past. In Dubai for example the centre of the country contained very few permanent buildings until very recently. Where only forty years ago camels wondered across desert planes, now tarmac highway cuts the city in two.

The American consultancy Parsons has imposed a road network and the skyscrapers are rising so high that SOM is currently building the tallest tower in the world there. The rapid development of towers and malls are all dependent upon vehicular access as there is as yet no public transport. The moment is exciting, but in terms of transport the opportunity to create a mobility solution that is not so reliant upon cars has been lost as there is currently virtually no public transport. In the UAE clearly the supply of fuel is not a problem, so the imperative to invest in public transport may not be as strong as in Europe, but the cost is not just financial and it seems crazy that the congestion is the desert is already resulting in traffic jams. The main road through the centre of the city, Sheik Zayed Road is almost uncrossable on foot and it clogs during morning and evening rush hour as the increasing volumes of traffic exceed the capacity of the bridges across the river.

Professor Casiroli of Systematica Spa is working in the region and sees new cities as exciting opportunities to get the balance right. He envisions the ideal model for future solutions for new cities, 'the private transport network should be limited and strictly restricted to zero-emission vehicles. It would be designed from scratch by specialists and form a hierarchical network with a suggested orthogonal shape. Within the urban areas bordered by the main transport network, the roads could develop freely without following any predetermined scheme. They would be able to create wide perspectives or narrow views with ancient memories.'

Way-Out Alternatives

So what are the alternatives to cities dominated by cars and congestion? Many architects have made utopian visions, but most have remained confined to the drawing board.

Perhaps we need some truly radical rethinking. What if the places in which we lived moved, or the entire city could get up and change location? That was the idea of *Walking Cities* presented by the British group Archigram in the Sixties. 'Archigram's approach to architecture was fun, as illustrated by two of the group's most memorable projects: Ron Herron's 1964 cartoon drawings of a *Walking City*, in which a city of giant, reptilian structures literally glided across the globe on enormous legs until its inhabitants found a place where they wanted to settle; and the crane-mounted living pods that could be plugged in wherever their inhabitants wished in Peter Cook's 1964 *Plug-in City*.'[15]

CarFree Cities

Walking cities and exclusively pedestranised environments are to my mind too extreme a solution and a regressive step. However, the work of the 'Carfree Cities' movement now has international momentum and the idea of annual 'Carfree days' and restricting cars during particular hours in particular locations is clearly a sensible idea.

John Crawford author of *Carfree Cities* believes, 'the industrialized nations made a terrible mistake when they turned to the automobile as an instrument of improved urban mobility. The car brought with it major unanticipated consequences for urban life and has become a serious cause of environmental, social, and aesthetic problems in cities.'[16] Crawford argues unapologetically that the car is a technology that has run wild, and that the time has come to reclaim city streets for human activities. He proposes a city planned to maximize the quality of life for individuals and communities, and gives practical suggestions for implementing this basic design in both new and existing cities. Crawford believes that sustainable development can only be achieved by ending car use within cities.

Imagine life in an environment free from the noise, pollution and stench in a city where all your basic needs, from groceries to childcare, are within a five-minute walk of every doorstep. Imagine that no commute takes more than 35 minutes from door to door, and that service is provided by a fast, cheap, safe, comfortable public transport.

The carfree vision is appealing, but fundamentally it denies us all the freedoms and pleasures of the possibility of driving when we want to.

[15] http://www.designmuse-um.org/design/archigram.

[16] There is now an annual World Carfree Day on 22 September which is a celebration of cities and public life, free from the noise, stress and pollution of cars. http://www.carfree.com/intro_cfc.html.

Bibliography

Norman Bel Geddes, *MAGIC MOTORWAYS*, Random House, 1940.
Reyner Banham, *Theory and Design in the First Machine Age*, Architectural Press, 1960, reprinted 1982.
Robert Venturi, *Learning from Las Vegas*, MIT Press, 1971.
Brian Richards, *Moving in cities*, Cassell & Collier Macmillan Publishers Ltd., 1976.
The Automobile and American Culture, David L. Lewis, Laurence Goldstein (editors), University of Michigan Press, 1980, 1983.
London as It Might Have Been, Felix Barker, Ralph Hyde John Murray (editors) Ltd, 1982.
Alison Smithson, *AS in DS: An Eye On The Road*, Delft University Press, Delft 1983, Lars Muller Publishers, reprinted 2001.
James J. Flink, *The Automobile Age*, Massachusettes Institute of Technology, 1988.
Martin Pawley, *Theory and Design in the Second Machine Age*, Blackwell, 1990.
John H Crawford, *Carfree Cities*, International Books, Utrecht 2000.
The Unknown City, Contesting Architecture and Social Space, Iain Borden, Joe Kerr, Jane Rendell with Alicia Pivaro (editors), The MIT Press, 2001.
Autopia, Joe Kerr e Peter Wollen (editors), Reaktion Books, 2002.
Nigel Coates, *Ecstacity*, Laurence King Publishing, 2003.
London from Punk to Blair, Joe Kerr and Andrew Gibson (editors), Reaktion Books, 2003.
Helen Evenden, *Moving Forward*, Victoria and Albert Museum Publications, London in progress of publication.

From the Tricycle to Design

Benz

Benz Patent Motorwagen, 1886

• *Make and Model*
Benz Patent Motorwagen
• *Year of production*
1886
• *Engine*
Single-cylinder four-stroke, horizontal
• *Engine displacement*
985 cc
• *Maximum power*
0.88 b.h.p. at 300 rpm
• *Top speed*
12 kph (7.5 mph)
• *Dimensions*
Length 2500 mm, width 1500 mm, height 1670 mm, wheelbase 1450 mm
• *Weight*
265 Kg

Villafranca di Verona, Museo Nicolis dell'Auto, della Tecnica, della Meccanica

The example on show is a replica

The Benz Tricycle of 1886 may be defined the first real motor car in history: it was designed on completely different principals to the vehicles of Daimler, who had essentially built a carriage equipped with an engine.
This three-wheeled vehicle included a brand new concept: the design was for a complete means of transport and was not merely an attempt to apply an engine to a carriage. Indeed, this aim was explicitly set out in the patent request for a 'means of locomotion equipped with engine.'
A chassis built with tubes used to make bicycles, on top of which were placed the seats, provided the basis for the coachwork and also for the chassis. Subsequently, all cars were supplied with a frame as a fundamental structure and it was thanks to this element that they were different to the concept of a carriage.
The cycles built in the 19th century — Benz himself had a model — based on the system invented by Baron Karl von Drais, had also influenced Benz from a technical point of view: to get around the problem of steering via the front axle, he built his own vehicle as a delicate tricycle.
The wire wheels were supplied by Kleyer of Frankfurt, progenitor of the Adler car company, one of the first companies to manufacture bicycles.
After the first model of car produced in 1885 — fitted with a single-cylinder engine, clutch, differential, chain transmission and tiller steering — a second version was designed and modified several times, followed by a third version with wooden spokes. In 1888, Benz's wife, driving this model equipped with a rather fragile engine, dared undertake the famous trip from Mannheim to Pforzheim, having left her husband in the dark about the project.
To this day, this journey is regularly commemorated.
The 1885-1886 prototype was preserved and later moved to the Deutsches Museum für Technik und Naturwisseschaften in Munich.
(R.J.F.K.)

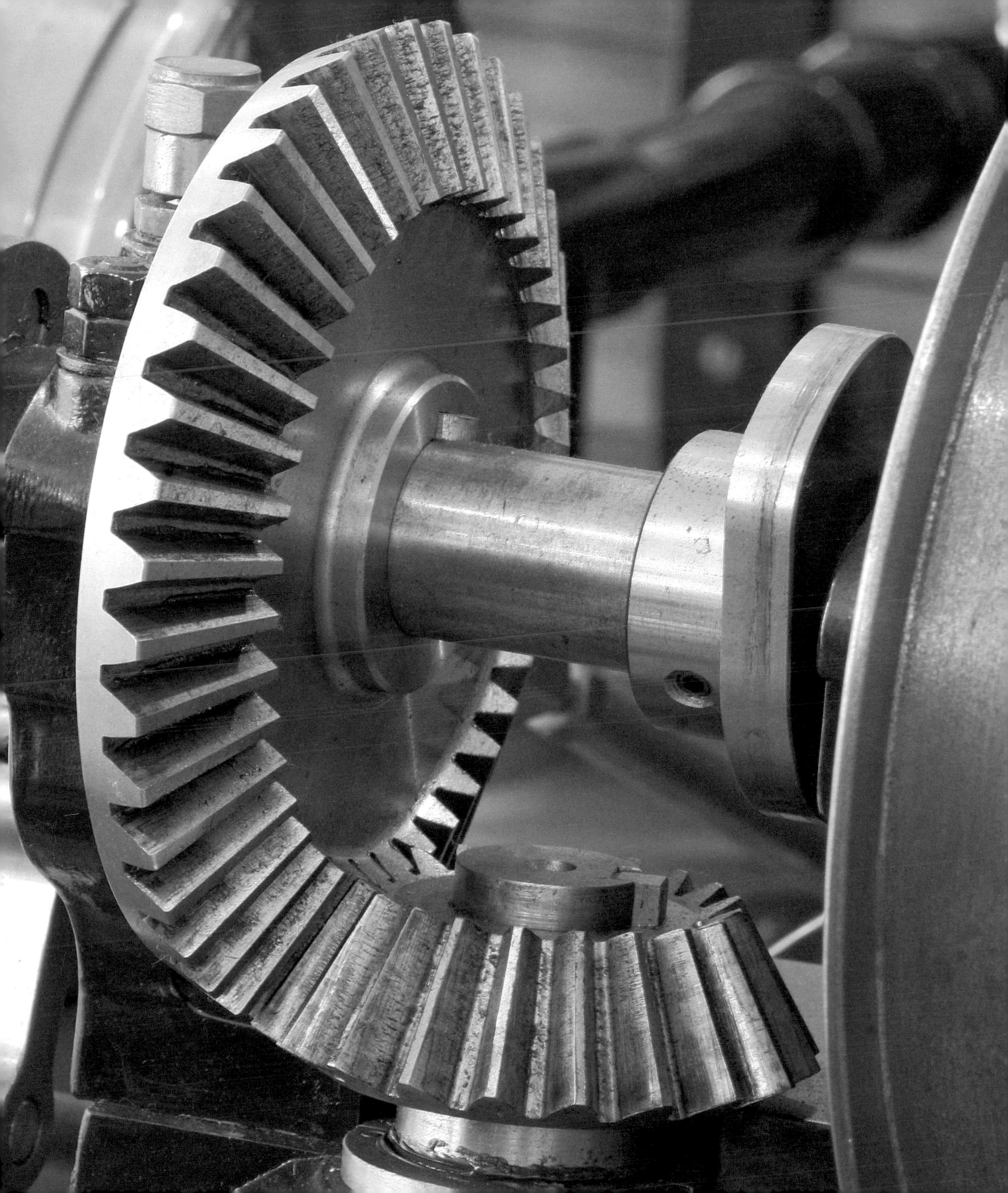

Alfa Romeo

8C 2900 B Berlinetta Touring, 1938

• *Make and Model*
Alfa Romeo 8C 2900 B
• *Year of production*
1938
• *Coachwork*
Saloon (Touring)
• *Engine*
In-line 8-cylinder, with twin superchargers
• *Bore and stroke / Engine displacement*
68 x 100 mm / 2905 cc
• *Maximum power*
180 b.h.p. at 5200 rpm
• *Top speed*
Over 180 kph (110 mph)
• *Dimensions*
Length 4900 mm, width 1770 mm, height 1500 mm, wheelbase 3000 mm
• *Weight*
1250 Kg
• *Total built*
36 to 40 (series A and B)

Arese (Milan), Automobilismo Storico Alfa Romeo, Museo Storico, Centro di Documentazione Storica
Photo: Automobilismo Storico Alfa Romeo, Centro di Documentazione Storica

The 8C 2900 gained its baptism of fire at the 1936 edition of the Mille Miglia, in which the three works cars from the Scuderia Ferrari finished first, second and third.
Vittorio Jano had designed the car especially for the Sport category in order to avoid the protests at the preceding edition of the great Italian race, in which the Milan-based manufacturer had won with a Grand Prix Tipo B camouflaged as a sports car simply by adding a seat for the co-driver, together with headlights and wings.
Success in the race was followed by commercial success and in 1937 Alfa Romeo presented the 8C 2900 B, a modified version with a short wheelbase of 2800 mm or longer wheelbase of 3000 mm to satisfy both sporty customers who intended to race, and more demanding clients who sought a car for ordinary use on the roads or for concours d'élégance.
The production run of the 8C 2900 B totalled less than 40, almost all of them still surviving, and it was certainly the most exclusive and prestigious sports car to be produced by Alfa Romeo and also, probably, 'the fastest series-production car in the world,' as it was advertised at the time.
In order to appreciate its sporty performance in full, one need only recall that after winning the Mille Miglia in 1936, 1937 and 1938, an 8C 2900 B with Touring saloon coachwork (and without supercharger) won the 1947 edition, the first of the post-war period.
A variety of body styles were fitted to the 8C 2900, from the more spartan 'Botticella' of the version A, intended purely for racing, to the sporty convertibles and more comfortable and elegant B version, built not only by Alfa Romeo but also by Stabilimenti Farina and Carrozzeria Touring.
It was Touring that produced the beautiful, aerodynamic Berlinetta, with coachwork designed for the long wheelbase version. Only five were built, each slightly different to the other, using the Superleggera method, patented only shortly before by the Milanese company. The aerodynamic research undertaken by Touring found its maximum expression in the Berlinetta and the new Superleggera technique; the curved lines of the wings and cabin are perfectly matched with the straight lines of the extremely long bonnet and short tail. The tapering tail features an arrow-like movement below the small rear windscreen which widens to almost incorporate the rear wings which remain slightly independent with separate volumes.
(H.S.)

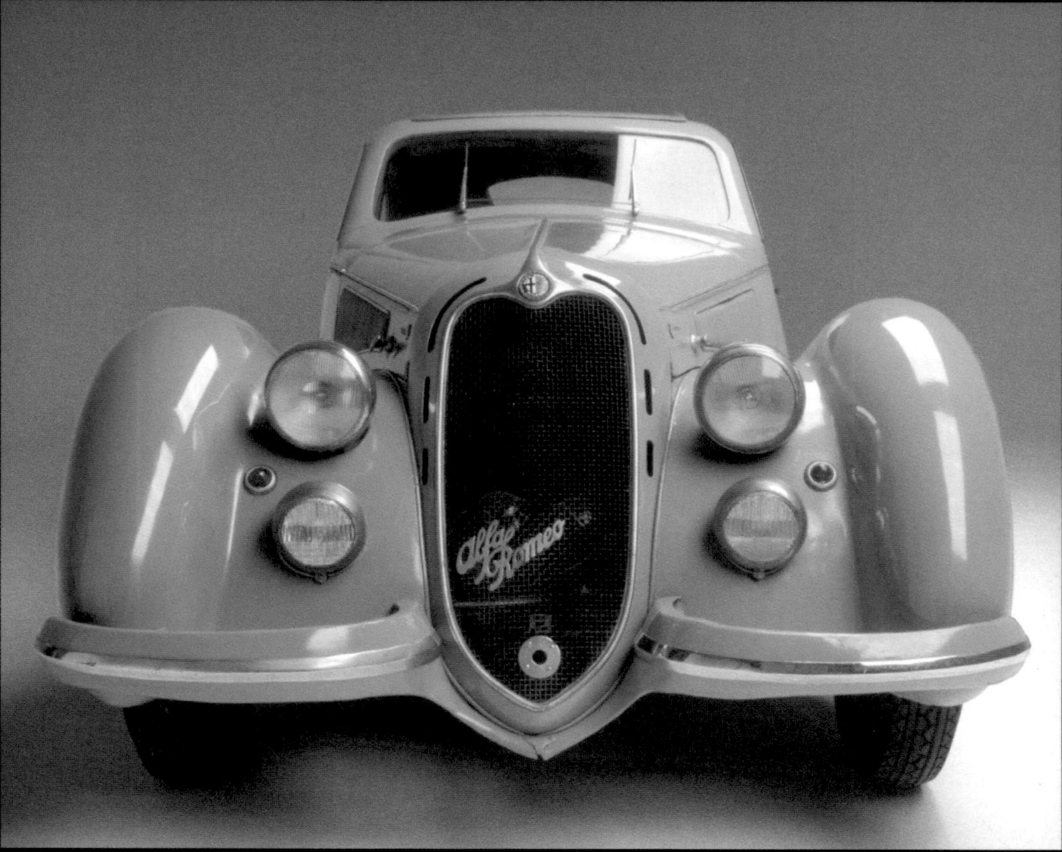
Alfa Romeo

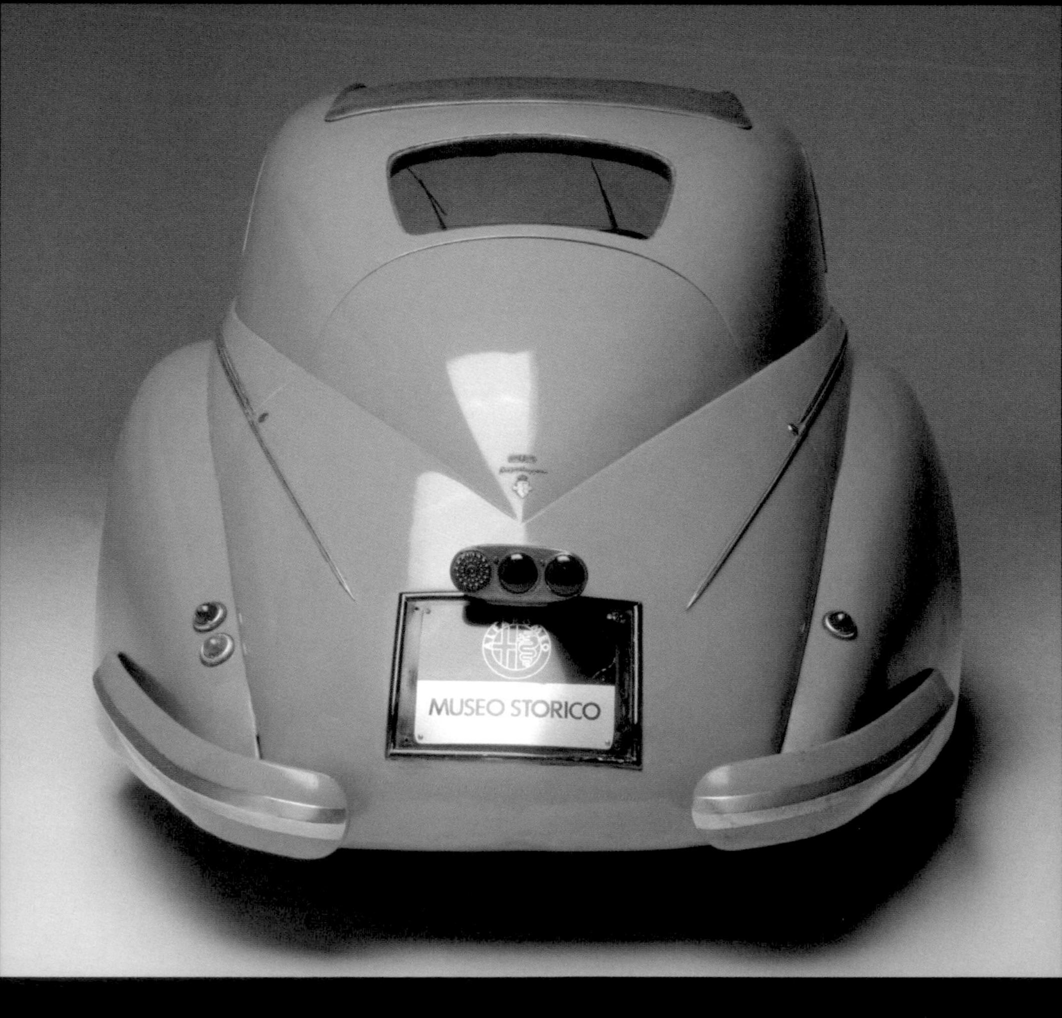
MUSEO STORICO

Alfa Romeo

ALFA ROMEO
MILANO

The Product

The Bare Necessities

Hanomag

Kommissbrot, 1925

• *Make and Model*
Hanomag Type 2/10
• *Year of production*
1925
• *Coachwork*
Cabriolet (Werk)
• *Engine*
Single cylinder
• *Bore and stroke / Engine displacement*
80 x 100 mm / 499 cc
• *Maximum power*
12 b.h.p.; continuous output of 10 b.h.p. at 2500 rpm
• *Top speed*
60 kph (37 mph)
• *Dimensions*
Length 2780 mm, width 1180 mm,
height 1440 mm, wheelbase 1920 mm
• *Weight*
370 Kg (open-top version), 430 Kg (closed version)
• *Total built*
15,520 (overall total of all versions)

Munich, Die Neue Sammlung Pinakothek der Moderne

The Hannoversche Maschinenbau AG grew from a company founded in 1885 by Georg Egestorff and was one of the first large mechanical engineering companies of the industrial era.
Following the First World War, the company sought to implement a new production programme. It was at this time that two engineers, Fidelis Böhler and Carl Pollich, presented themselves with the idea of a small motor car: a light vehicle, powered by a single-cylinder, rear-mounted engine and cheap both to produce and to maintain. From the outset, it was destined to be a success. The model was sold with a very simple coachwork, offering rounded forms both at the front and the rear, and cycle wings integrated into the bodywork — the progenitor of protruding wings — and fitted with a single headlamp on the centre of the nose. A simple metal chassis was used to support the engine and axles; later, the metal chassis would be replaced with one in wood, the front and rear parts only being in sheet metal. The engine, with three gears, powered the rear axle via a chain transmission.
In 1924, the small 2/10 Hanomag was presented at the Berlin Motor Show and, from 1925 to 1928, was produced in large numbers, thanks to the use of a production line. It was produced in convertible, coupé, sport and van versions.
Its name, Kommissbrot (army bread) evidently derives from the shape of the car, recalling that of the loaves produced by the army. In a 1933 film, starring the famous actors, Heinz Rühmann and Paul Hörbiger, the Hanomag 'plays' the part of a tiny hero struggling against a mighty 12-cylinder monster.
(R.J.F.K.)

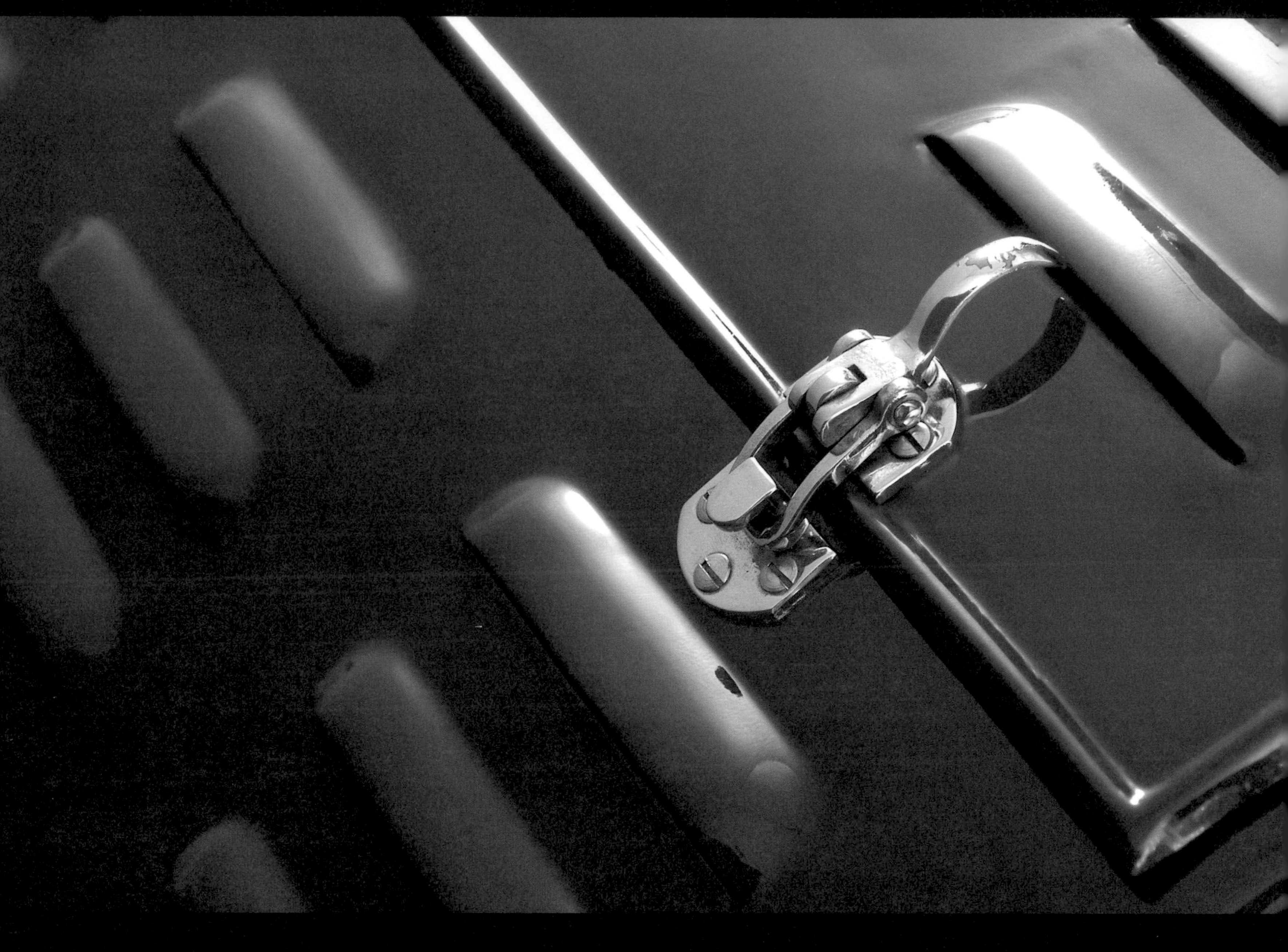

3
2
R
100
110
120
50
60

Fiat

500 Topolino, 1936

• *Make and Model*
Fiat 500
• *Year of production*
1936
• *Coachwork*
Convertible two-door saloon
• *Engine*
Side-valve 4-cylinder
• *Bore and stroke / Engine displacement*
52 x 67 mm / 569 cc
• *Maximum power*
13 b.h.p. at 4000 rpm
• *Top speed*
Approx. 85 kph (53 mph)
• *Dimensions*
Length 3210 mm, width 1270 mm,
height 1370 mm, wheelbase 2000 mm
• *Weight*
745 Kg
• *Total built*
519,646 (series A, B and C)

Turin, Centro Storico Fiat
© Photo Diego Cassetta – Mart

The model on show dates from 1937

The father of the Topolino was Dante Giacosa, an engineer who in 1934 was aged 29 and worked for Fiat as an aircraft engine designer. But that spring morning was different to any other: seated at his desk, the young designer had before him a blank sheet of paper and in his mind the instructions that Senator Giovanni Agnelli had given him for the creation of a car destined to put Italy on wheels. The brief was: a four-stroke, four-cylinder engine mounted at the front but driving the back wheels, low consumption, nominal horsepower of no more than six b.h.p., room for two adults on the front seats and for baggage or two children on the rear seats. Finally, the price: it was not to cost more than 5000 lire. This was no easy task, especially if we consider that the Balilla cost 10,800 lire at the time.
By the beginning of August 1934, the design for the engine was ready; the first complete prototype was tested on the road on 7th October and, about two years after that spring morning, on 15th June 1936, Fiat launched the Cinquecento. Only the price failed to respect the initial brief: it was fixed at 8900 lire, Obut the comfort, consumption (about 6 litres per 100 kilometres) and performance (about 85 kph) satisfied the requirements of Agnelli in every way. The lines of the 500 (subsequently called A, in order to distinguish it from the later series B of 1948 and series C of 1949), were very dynamic if we consider the vehicle was only 3,21 metres long.
They echoed those of the 1500, presented in 1935, itself a model which had introduced new concepts into the design of middle-of-the-range cars, with its long and slender bonnet, and short, rounded rear. The position of the engine is worth noting: in order to reduce size of the car and increase cabin space, Giacosa fitted it over the front axle, a solution still in use today for almost all front-wheel drive vehicles.
As a result, the radiator was positioned behind the engine.
The engine itself was remarkably simple: there was no water pump (circulation was assured by the radiator itself), and no fuel pump (the petrol being fed by gravity). Since the engine was placed over the axle, the chassis was very short, which made for lower costs; the front suspension was very modern, with independent wheels. Thanks to the low weight, performance was surprising, given that the engine size was that of a motorcycle. 'The smallest car in the world to be made in large numbers' enjoyed a great success even outside Italy and was built under licence in Germany, France, Poland and Belgium. Paintings, posters, poems and songs were dedicated to it and it was in an English poem of the late 1930s that the famous nickname 'Topolino' (little mouse) that it has carried since was used for the first time.
(H.S.)

FIAT

FIAT

OLIO
0
25
50

Iso

Isetta, 1953

• *Make and Model*
Iso Isetta
• *Year of production*
1953
• *Coachwork*
Bubblecar
• *Engine*
Two-stroke single-cylinder with two pistons
• *Engine displacement*
236 cc
• *Maximum power*
9.5 b.h.p.
• *Top speed*
Over 70 kph (43 mph)
• *Dimensions*
Length 2283 mm, width 1470 mm, height 1320 mm, wheelbase 1500 mm
• *Weight*
342.9 Kg
• *Total built*
About 6000 (excluding versions built as vans)

Bonomelli collection
© Photo Diego Cassetta – Mart

The model on show dates from 1955

In 1933, Renzo Rivolta founded Iso S.p.A. in Bolzaneto, near Genoa. After 1942, it moved to Bresso on the outskirts of Milan. The company's intention was to produce refrigerators of the Isothermos type. At the end the 1940s, the company converted to the production of motorcycles and mopeds under the name of Furetto. Refrigerators continued to be made until 1951 and mopeds until 1953.
In 1951, Rivolta met an engineer called Ermenegildo Preti who showed him an unusual design for a small, four-wheel vehicle. Rivolta took to the idea and together with Pierluigi Raggi developed the project for the production of the vehicle in series under the direction of the project manager, Gobini. The car was given a small, aerodynamic drop shape, in line with the ideas of the 1930s. The engine was mounted in front of the rear axle atop the chassis. The metal coachwork tapered to the rear and was fitted with a sliding roof. The seat was fitted behind the single front-facing door which opened outwards.
A two-stroke, single-cylinder engine with two pistons was specially developed for this vehicle. In 1952, the prototype of the little Iso, named the Isetta, was ready. After the presentation to the press in Turin in 1953, series production began in 1954 and included various commercial versions, including a little van, a model with a flat bed, a vehicle for firefighters and even a tipper version. The most important producer of the Isetta under licence, BMW which had bought the tooling, fitted the vehicle with a motorcycle engine of its own production. It modified the headlights, designed several versions of the bodywork and a more powerful engine.
The Iso Isetta, instead, remained unchanged throughout the period of production, just as Preti had designed it. The Isetta was sold in Italy and France until 1958, in Brazil until 1961, in Germany until 1964 and in Britain until 1964.
(R.J.F.K.)

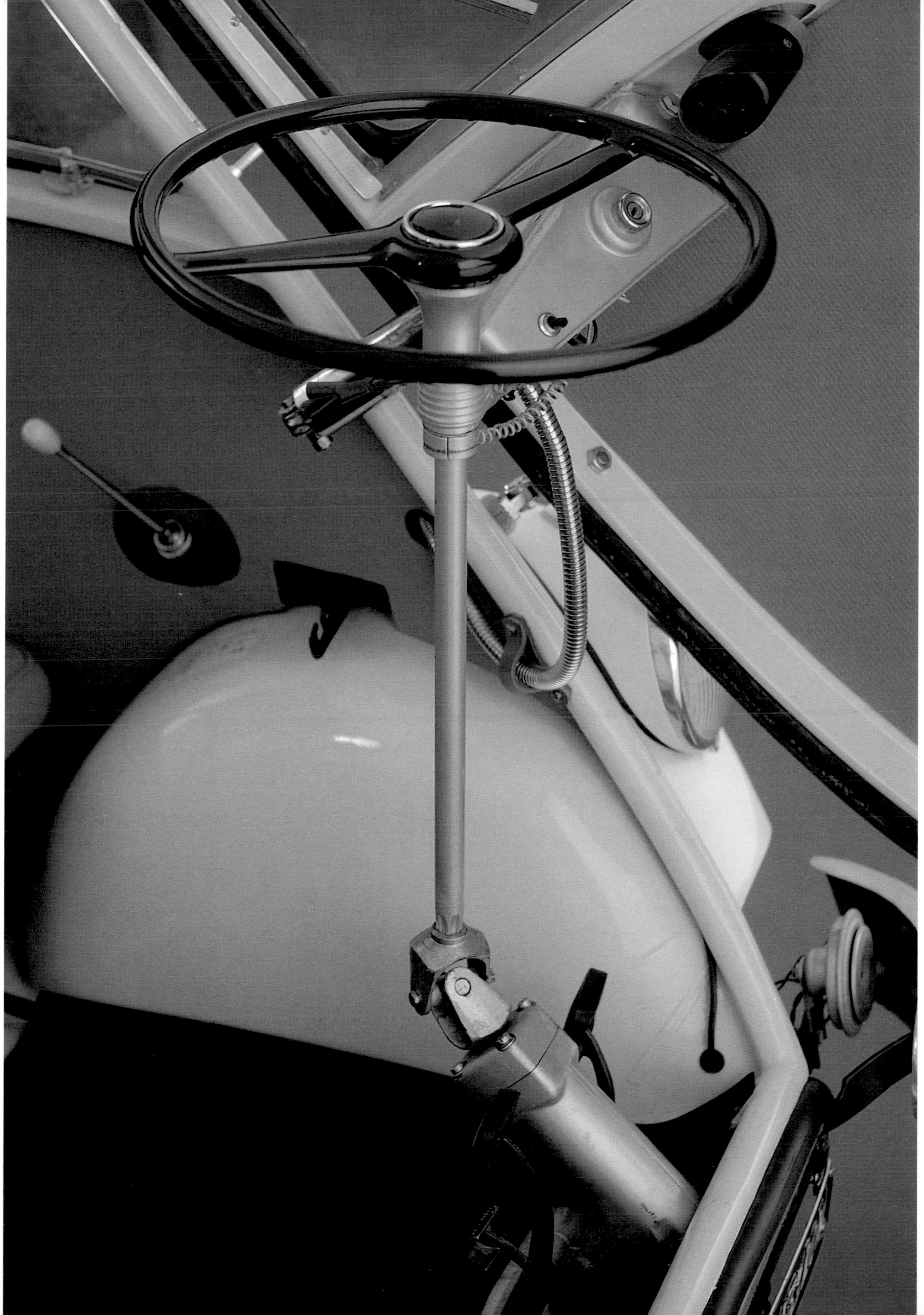

Messerschmitt

Kabinenroller KR 200, 1953

- *Make and Model*
Messerschmitt KR (Kabinenroller) 200
- *Year of production*
1953
- *Coachwork*
Three-wheeler with removable roof
- *Engine*
Two-stroke single-cylinder
- *Bore and stroke / Engine displacement*
65 x 58 mm
- *Maximum power*
10.2 b.h.p. at 5250 rpm
- *Top speed*
90 kph (56 mph)
- *Dimensions*
Length 2820 mm, width 1220 mm, height 1200 mm, wheelbase 2030 mm
- *Weight*
240 Kg
- *Total built*
About 40,000

Lucerna, Verkehrshaus der Schweiz

The model on show dates from 1955

After the end of the Second World War, aeronautical engineer Fritz Fend developed his engineless Fend-Flitzer [Fend spider], a vehicle designed for disabled ex-servicemen. A single-cylinder engine was later also fitted to this vehicle. In 1952, Fend was in touch with the Messerschmitt mechanical engineering company, which saw the possibilities of converting his machine for the small motor car sector. Fend became the manager for this project, which was developed under the direction of professor Willy Messerschmitt in the Munich design centre. The fundamental characteristic of this vehicle for two passengers was the positioning of the seats, one behind the other. Steering was effected by a sort of motorcycle handlebar. The single-cylinder engine was positioned to the rear of the vehicle. A transplant Plexiglass dome, very similar to that used for the Kabinenroller, Fend's cabin tricycles, served as roof.
The coachwork was to be produced by Spohn at Ravensburg, where the coachwork for Maybach cars had been prepared before the war. The Messerschmitt factory at Ratisbon was used to produce the Kabinenroller KR 175 from 1953, and subsequently the KR 200, built by a subsidiary company called RSM. By the summer of 1954, up to 100 vehicles a day were being built. Because of a fall in demand between the end of 1955 and the start of 1956, production ceased despite credits from the government and the merging of RSM into the parent company. The next company to be directed by Fend, FMR, continued to produce the KR 200 and — from 1958 to 1961 — the Tiger model, which was equipped with a more powerful engine and four wheels, enabling Fend to establish 25 world records.
In 1999, one year before his death, Fend presented a new Kabinenroller characterized by a small frontal area, an aerodynamic form and simplicity of construction.
(R.J.F.K.)

Fiat

Nuova 500, 1957

• *Make and Model*
Fiat Nuova 500 Economica
• *Year of production*
1957
• *Coachwork*
Two-door convertible saloon
• *Engine*
Air-cooled two-cylinder
• *Bore and stroke / Engine displacement*
66 x 70 mm / 479 cc
• *Maximum power*
15 b.h.p. at 450 rpm
• *Top speed*
75 kph (46 mph)
• *Dimensions*
Length 2946 mm, width 1220 mm, height 1325 mm, wheelbase 1840 mm
• *Weight*
470 Kg
• *Total built*
Over 3,600,000 (all series)

Paolo Fraulini collection

The 500 is part of the social history of Italy and lies in the heart and memories of generations of Italians. This is the reason why Fiat has launched a new model of the same name and similar lines.
But few remember that at the outset, the 500 looked set to become a gigantic commercial and financial flop for the Turin-based manufacturer. Let us have a look at its history. In the wake of the 600, Fiat decided to start producing an even smaller car, able to attract a clientele as yet unable to afford the purchase of a car and accustomed to making do with motorcycles and mopeds.
The person responsible for completing the design of the new car was again engineer Dante Giacosa, the father of the Topolino and of the 600. He designed a new car that differed from the 600 both in aesthetic and motoring terms. Only the basic details remained the same: a rear-mounted engine driving the rear wheels in order to provide maximum space in less than three metres' length. Everything had to be geared to respect a price that had to be much less than that of the 600: in industrial costs, weight is expensive, but the striving for lightness renders the design particularly difficult.
The engine was an air-cooled two-cylinder 479 cc unit delivering only 13 b.h.p.; the bodywork was made up of a few elements, made as light as possible; the interior was austere: fresh air could only be had by opening the quarterlights and the rear bench was covered only with a light fabric.
The presentation of the Nuova 500 Trasformabile took place on 4th July 1957: the car was not received with the hoped-for acclaim, and the price of 490,000 lire (not much more than 100,000 lire less than the 600) did not helps sales. Moreover, the car really offered very little either in terms of performance or comfort. Fiat immediately sought a solution and in November of the same year at the Turin Salon presented the Normale version, with power increased to 15 b.h.p. and, above all, greater comfort. However, interest in the new baby from Fiat truly began to grow thanks to the tuned Abarth version, used to establish speed records at Monza. Fiat subsequently included a Sport version from 1958, with engine displacement increased to 499.5 cc to deliver 20 b.h.p. The die was cast: over the years, the 500 became firmly entrenched as a family's second rather than sole car and even today is used in many city centres, where anti-smog regulations allow.
(H.S.)

Morris

Mini Minor, 1959

• *Make and Model*
Morris Mini Minor
• *Year of production*
1959
• *Coachwork*
Two-door saloon
• *Engine*
Push-rod in-line 4-cylinders
• *Bore and stroke / Engine displacement*
62,9 x 68,2 mm / 848 cc
• *Maximum power*
34 b.h.p. at 5500 rpm
• *Top speed*
116 kph (mph)
• *Dimensions*
Length 3048 mm, width 1397 mm, height 1334 mm, wheelbase 2036 mm
• *Weight*
586 Kg
• *Total built*
Over 5,000,000

Gaydon, British Motor Industry Heritage Trust

Alec Issigonis, born in Smyrna (now Izmir) in 1906 into a Greek family, moved to London in 1923 to study engineering; after finishing his studies, he worked for a number of car companies and in 1936 was taken on by Morris, for which he designed the Minor in 1948. After a period at Alvis, another historic British marque, in 1956 he returned to Morris (which in the meantime had become BMC, following its merger with Austin) and was commissioned to design a small car meeting the requirements of a typical family of 4/5 individuals. Moreover, it was to be sparing in consumption, an important point given the scarcity of petrol as a consequence of the Suez Canal crisis of that year.
The 'Mini' project contained all the best solutions in a single car for reducing volume, assuring comfort and keeping consumption down. The small wheels were located right at the four corners of the car and the chassis was fitted with simple but effective suspension. The engine, derived from one already in production at BMC for the Minor 1000, but with a smaller displacement, was mounted transversely at the front, which obviated the need for a transmission tunnel within the cabin and made it possible to maximize space for passengers and baggage. Accessories were reduced to a minimum, the front windows slid to open and the fuel tank had a maximum capacity of 25 litres.
In the end, it was possible to limit the length of the Mini to just 3.05 metres and the weight to 570 kilograms. Naturally, the smaller engine did not provide brilliant performance, but the car would cover 14 kilometres with just one litre of petrol. Presented in 1959, under both the Morris and Austin marques, the Mini was not immediately successful: quite the opposite. It was only with the Cooper version, prepared by John Cooper, builder of the single-seaters that had won the world championships in 1959 and 1960, that the Mini acquired the sporty image that enabled it to become a cult object. It was the car of choice not only for someone who could only afford a cheap car, but also for those who needed a second car for the family, and for those who needed to drive and park in the city. Moreover, many independent coachbuilders offered personalisations at every level for anyone who wanted to stand out from the crowd. For the standard models, rallies provided the most competitive means of racing. Thanks to their low weight and incredible road holding, the Mini Cooper S won the Monte-Carlo rally from 1964 to 1967, although in 1966, after finishing and winning the race, the Mini was disqualified because of a breach of the rules concerning an irregularity in... the extra headlights!
(H.S.)

AUSTIN

Smart

Smart, 1997

• *Make and Model*
Micro Compact SpA Smart City-Coupé
• *Year of production*
1997
• *Engine*
Three-cylinder turbo-charged, petrol-driven
• *Engine displacement*
599 cc
• *Maximum power*
54 b.h.p. at 5250 rpm
• *Dimensions*
Length 2500 mm, width 1450 mm, height 1550 mm, wheelbase 1880 mm
• *Weight*
680 Kg
• *Total built*
Still in production

Smart GmbH

The Smart was the result of a co-operative effort between Daimler-Benz and Nicolas G. Haydeck, a great innovator in the world of Swiss watchmaking. Haydeck hoped to do to the car sector what Swatch had done to the watch sector; in particular, he envisaged an unusual city car equipped with a hybrid engine that harked back to the idea of the utility vehicle conceived in the 1960s. In 1989 he started spreading the word about his idea until he met Daimler-Benz, which had been mulling over the project for a small Mercedes for decades.

This theme had already been explored by the talented stylist, Paul Bracq, who had designed a city car for one, two or more people back in the 1960s.

The basic design for the car-Swatch was sketched out in 1990 in California by Mercedes-Benz Advanced Design of North America, directed by Gerhard Steinle. Overall responsibility for the Mercedes City Car was taken on by Johann Tomforde in 1992, who had been with Mercedes since 1970 and had been responsible for following preparatory projects for small cars since 1972.

After a feasibility study in 1993 and the creation of a joint venture between Mercedes-Benz and the Swiss SMH Automobile in 1994, a draft design was presented in 1995 at the Frankfurt motor show. Four possible types of propulsion were proffered: electric, hybrid electric-diesel, with a three-cylinder diesel engine, or with a three-cylinder petrol engine. In 1996, one year before the official presentation of the model, the Smart won the European design award. The design was subsequently reworked a little, but the small car was finally presented at the Geneva motor show in the spring of 1998. From autumn of the same year, the Smart was produced in series.

A new sales approach assured the sale of the Smart in nine countries, in which the tiny, appealing car — equipped with luxurious interiors, short enough to be parked sideways on and fitted with a little engine offering low consumption — was met enthusiastically. The Smart has proved to be a particular success in Italy where over 200,000 have been sold. Overall, 750,000 Smarts have been sold.

The development of the small car, which in the meantime has been rebaptised ForTwo, has seen the production of a coupé version, a roadster with rear-mounted engine and a four-seater.

(R.J.F.K.)

smart

limited/1

European Design: the 1930s

Isotta Fraschini

Tipo 8 ASS torpedo sport, 1927

• *Make and Model*
Isotta Fraschini Tipo 8 ASS
• *Year of production*
1927
• *Coachwork*
Torpedo sport (Carrozzeria Italiana Cesare Sala)
• *Engine*
Push-rod, in-line 8-cylinders
• *Bore and stroke / Engine displacement*
95 x 130 mm / 7370 cc
• *Maximum power*
160 b.h.p. at 2800 rpm
• *Top speed*
155 kph (96 mph)
• *Dimensions*
Length 5000 mm, width 1800 mm,
height 1800 mm, wheelbase 3400 mm
• *Weight*
2500 Kg
• *Total built*
About 950 (Tipo 8 A, 8 AS, 8 ASS)

Private collection
© Photo Diego Cassetta – Mart

Isotta Fraschini falls within the small number of marques which in the 1920s and 30s produced what are still today considered to be the most exclusive motor cars ever built, together with Rolls-Royce, Hispano-Suiza, Bugatti and Mercedes-Benz in Europe, and Duesenberg and Packard in the United States.
One of the first to introduce hydraulic braking and braking on all four wheels in its standard models, Isotta Fraschini added another world first when, in 1919, it produced an in-line eight-cylinder engine.
The design for the Tipo 8, dating from 1919, was updated and revised in 1924, when the Tipo 8 A was presented, from which derived the models destined for a more 'sporty' use, the 8 AS and the 8 ASS, presented in 1927.
Isotta Fraschini used to produce and sell the car chassis, that is, the chassis coupled with engine and gearbox, radiator, bonnet and dashboard. For everything else, it was necessary to turn to coachbuilders, a task that was up to the customer. Not that these were ordinary customers: Pope Pius XI, heads of state, crowned heads, Indian maharajahs, Italian and European aristocrats, poets such as Gabriele d'Annunzio, great industrialists and Hollywood stars, such as Rudolph Valentino, Douglas Fairbanks and others.
Thanks to the size of the chassis (the Tipo 8 A had a wheelbase of 3710 millimetres) and the large engine displacing no less than 7370 cc, every great coachbuilder of the period, such as Castagna, Pinin Farina, Sala, Stabilimenti Farina and Touring in Italy, or Fleetwood and Le Baron in America, Figoni & Falaschi in France and Hooper and Gurney Nutting in Britain, were able to produce exclusive masterpieces, many of which have happily survived to this day to bear witness to a creativity and manual dexterity that modern computers have, sadly, swept aside.
Carrozzeria Italiana Sala (which traded until 1933) and Carrozzeria Castagna, both Milanese, enjoyed a privileged relationship with Isotta Fraschini and it is they who probably produced the most beautiful coachwork for the prestigious Tipo 8 A chassis and its derivatives.
The torpedo sport (or torpedo-bateau) coachwork, which we can admire in the Tipo 8 ASS pictured, is a typical example of the care taken by Carrozzeria Sala: the simple but at the same time elegant line is highlighted by the the attention taken over details, such as, for instance, the front and rear doors which open in different directions, the mahogany woodwork around the cabin and the soft top which, when folded, is completely hidden. The inclined windscreen was a bold touch for the period.
(H.S.)

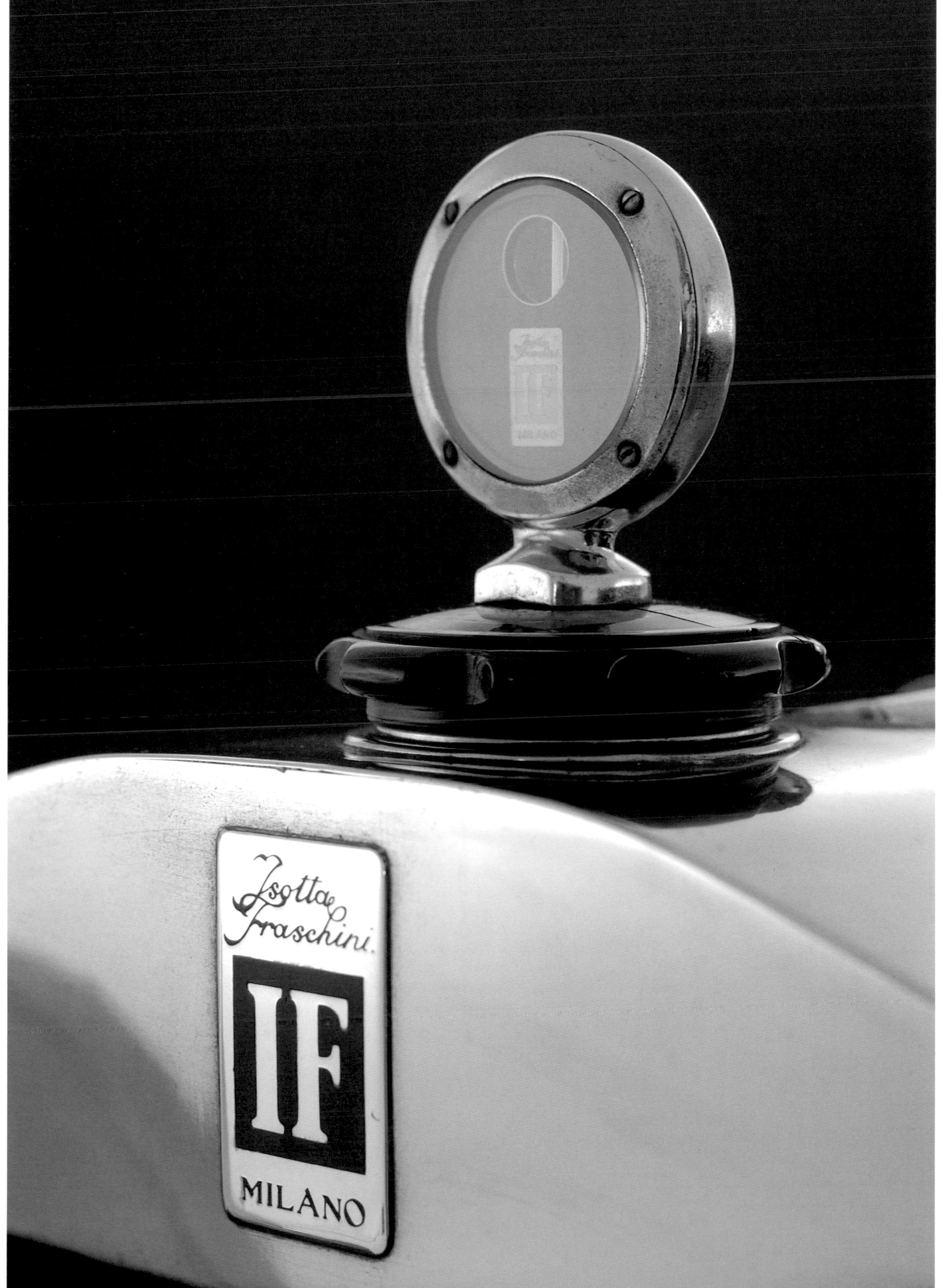
Isotta Fraschini
IF
MILANO

Alfa Romeo

6C 1750 Gran Sport Flying Star, 1930

• *Make and Model*
Alfa Romeo 6C 1750 Gran Sport
• *Year of production*
1930
• *Coachwork*
Flying Star type roadster (Touring coachwork)
• *Engine*
In-line 6-cylinders, 2 overhead camshafts
• *Bore and stroke / Engine displacement*
65 x 88 mm / 1752 cc
• *Maximum power*
85 b.h.p. at 4400 rpm
• *Top speed*
145 kph (90 mph)
• *Dimensions*
Length 4120 mm, width 1380 mm, height 1260 mm, wheelbase 2745 mm
• *Weight*
900 Kg
• *Total built*
257 (modello Gran Sport)

Keller Collection

The model on show dates from 1931

The 6C 1750 was one of the most important cars ever produced by Alfa Romeo and is today one of the most sought-after of classic cars by collectors around the world. The result of a project started in 1925 with the 6C 1500, the 6C 1750 is one of the masterpieces produced by designer Vittorio Jano. It was presented to the public at the Salone dell'Automobile of 1929, the sole year in which this was organized in Rome. This was no casual presentation given that Mussolini was a great enthusiast of Alfa Romeo; the factory, at the time controlled by the Liquidations Office, had an impelling need for the financial support of the state.
Produced until 1933 in various series, the 6C 1750 was fitted with engines of different specifications and power outputs. Moreover, the chassis fitted with the most powerful engines, sporting superchargers, were also equipped with important coachwork, such as the Flying Star, a line the that Touring presented in spring 1931 on some Isotta Fraschini chassis. The Flying Star series cannot simply be defined an exercise in style but nor does it a mark a break with the traditional lines hitherto used by all coachbuilders, including American ones; rather, it declares a new way of seeing the car and, above all, its coachwork. In those years, probably only Touring could allow itself such showy and innovative solutions as it was without doubt more advanced in its research than any of its competitors.
In observing the lines of the Flying Star type, one immediately notes the almost total lack of the air vents on either side of the engine bonnet; these are replaced by mouldings which, like a comet's tail, point downwards, terminating beyond the actual bonnet at the height of the windscreen support. The upper rear part of the door lies not at the same height as the tail but actually drops to follow the sweep of the mouldings, instead of rising towards it (the common solution in many sports cars). The unusual look of the wings front and rear, which do not join to form a running board, does away with its function as a step and looks forward to a future without running boards at all (for many cars produced around the world, these were definitively done away with only in the 1950s). The 6C 1750 Gran Sport won the Coppa d'Oro — Gran Premio Referendum at the *Concours d'Elégance* at Villa d'Este on 12th-13th September 1931.
(H.S.)

Alfa Romeo

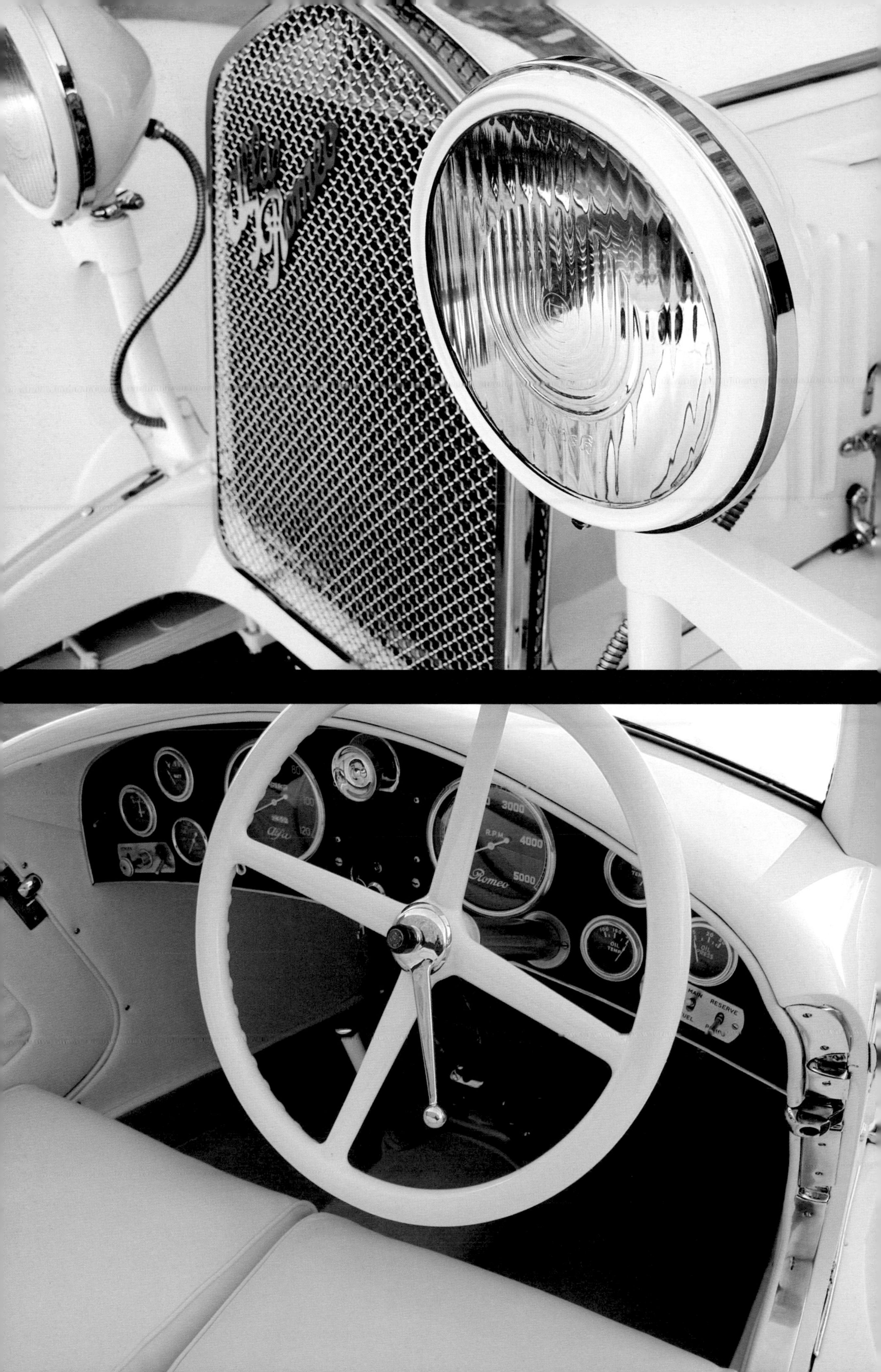
80
100
120
Alfa
3000
R.P.M.
4000
5000
Romeo
OIL TEMP
OIL PRESS
MAIN
RESERVE

Maserati

V4 Sport Spider Zagato, 1932

• *Make and Model*
Maserati V4 Sport
• *Year of production*
1932
• *Coachwork*
Roadster
• *Engine*
V16, twin overhead camshafts
• *Bore and stroke / Engine displacement*
62 x 82 mm / 3961 cc
• *Maximum power*
280 b.h.p. at 5500 rpm
• *Top speed*
250 kph (155 mph)
• *Dimensions*
Length 4216 mm, width 1625 mm, height 1320 mm, wheelbase 2900 mm
• *Weight*
1200 Kg
• *Total built*
1

Lawrence Auriana Collection

The Zagato coachwork dates from 1934

'How many cylinders does it have?' was the question one asked to discover what car one was looking at and how rich the owner was. Over time, the race for maximum power resulted in an increase in the number of cylinders: Benz's Dreirad had just one cylinder, but was soon followed by two-cylinder cars, then 4, 6, 8 and 12. This increase in the number of cylinders was not simply a question of prestige: early engines were inefficient, slow-revving and rough: the more cylinders an engine had, the smoother and more powerful it was. Few manufacturers, however, tackled the complexity of 16 cylinders, the most numerous in the car sector. Some did so for production cars, simply to strive for maximum smoothness, such as Cadillac, Marmon and Peerless in America; others opted for this solution to achieve maximum power, for racing or record-breaking cars. By 1930, these included Duesenberg and Stutz of the United States, Bugatti in France and Maserati in Italy.
In order to limit the cost of racing cars, an H layout was preferred: two 8-cylinder engines mounted in-line in the same cylinder block or in parallel (as in the case of Bugatti and Duesenberg), or with a slight vee (Stutz and Maserati, and precisely at 30° and 22.5° respectively): the two transmission shafts were then linked through a gearbox which transmitted the power to the wheels. The Maserati brothers were the first in the world to race using a 16-cylinder engine, preceding even Bugatti. The team went to Monza on 15th September 1929 and immediately established the fastest lap.
Two weeks later, on the same day as the records at Cremona, Baconin Borzacchini established a world record over 10 kilometres at an average speed of over 246 kph: this, it should be noted, on an unasphalted road! The Grand Prix 16-cylinder (called V4) won at Tripoli in 1930 and in Rome in 1931, showing itself to be the fastest car of its time. It could have won more races if tyres able to cope with the engine's great power had then existed.
The Maserati brothers had to make great sacrifices in order to race: to finance the construction of the more powerful V5 (equipped with a 5-litre engine) in early 1932, they sold the V4 Grand Prix, registered for road use and redubbed 'Sport', to professor Riccardo Galeazzi of Rome. After a couple of years and a few races, the owner, then the pontifical archiater, commissioned Ugo Zagato to build a new body for this car which we may define the first 'supercar' of history. Nowhere else in Rome, or indeed in the world, was there another road vehicle able to offer such great acceleration and high top speed. Nor was it painted in red like all Italian racing cars, but in two-tone green. *Noblesse Oblige!*
(H.S.)

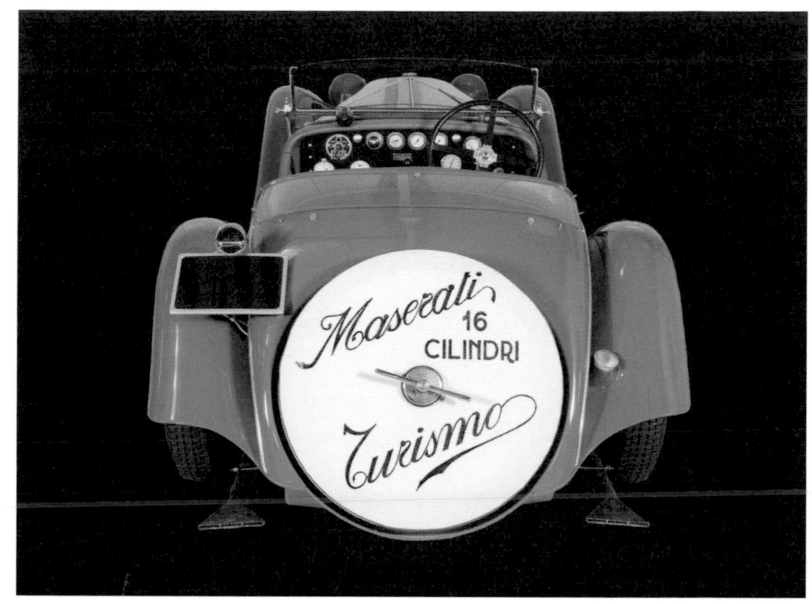
Maserati
16
CILINDRI
Turismo

AUTOMOBILI MASERATI
CHASSIS N
BOLOGNA
PUMP

MASERATI

Bugatti

Type 46 Coach Surprofilé, 1933

• *Make and Model*
Bugatti Type 46
• *Year of production*
1933
• *Coachwork*
Coach surprofilé
• *Engine*
In-line 8 cylinder, 3 valves per cylinder
• *Bore and stroke / Engine displacement*
81 x 130 mm / 5359 cc
• *Maximum power*
150 b.h.p.
• *Top speed*
145 kph (90 mph)
• *Dimensions*
Length 4780 mm, width 1920 mm, wheelbase 3500 mm
• *Weight*
1150 Kg
• *Total built*
About 400

Mulhouse, Cité de l'Automobile – Musée National – Schlumpf Collection
Photo Frederic Hurst

In the second half of the 1920s, Ettore Bugatti was at the peak of his success thanks to his Grand Prix cars, such as the Type 35 and the smaller Type 37, and his touring cars, such as the Type 38 and the Type 44, which brought both racing and commercial success. He decided to return to an old idea he had cherished even before the outbreak of the Great War and never totally abandoned:
the production of a highly prestigious motor car, superior to any other hitherto built anywhere in the world.
The studies began in 1925 and after a long gestation period and numerous road trials, conducted by Ettore himself, the Type 41 'Royale' was ready to be produced and sold to the world's crowned heads by 1927.
Unfortunately for Bugatti, his hopes failed to materialise and orders for the prestigious and immense car, fitted with an in-line 8-cylinder engine of over 12,700 cc mounted on a chassis over 6 metres in length, failed to materialize.
By 1928, Bugatti had already understood that the Royale adventure would not bring the hoped-for commercial acclaim and he thus decided to manufacture a smaller but still superior car, able to compete with Rolls-Royce, Isotta Fraschini and Hispano-Suiza. Thus was born the Type 46 in 1929, also known as the 'Petite Royale,' fitted with a more 'down-market' 8-cylinder, 5-litre engine.
All sorts of coachworks were built atop the robust, reliable chassis: saloons, convertibles and coupés, both by Bugatti and by the most famous coachbuilders of the time.
Among those producing the finest and most exclusive coachworks for Bugatti chassis in the 1920s and 1930s, was Jean Bugatti, Ettore's eldest son and designated heir.
Creator of all the technical innovations brought about in the factory, like all the Bugatti family, Jean had a strong artistic vein which he manifested in the creation of bold, futuristic coachworks. The coach surprofilé of the Type 46 is a unique model to which Jean applied his aerodynamic concepts, highlighted by the steeply sloping windscreen.
Sadly, Jean died in an accident in 1939, several years after Ettore had already stepped down, leaving him in charge of the factory. His premature death effectively sealed the fate of the Bugatti factory itself.
(H.S.)

Peugeot

402 Eclipse cabriolet, 1937

• *Make and Model*
Peugeot 402 Eclipse cabriolet
• *Year of production*
1937
• *Coachwork*
Drophead coupé with folding steel roof
• *Engine*
4-cylinder, overhead valves
• *Bore and stroke / Engine displacement*
83 x 92 mm / 1991 cc
• *Maximum power*
55 b.h.p. at 4000 rpm
• *Top speed*
110 kph (68 mph)
• *Dimensions*
Length 5200 mm, width 1690 mm, height 1540 mm, wheelbase 3300 mm
• *Weight*
1014 Kg
• *Total built*
58,748 (402/402 B)

Sochaux, L'Aventure Peugeot

In 1885, Armand Peugeot's company, Peugeot, which was first set up in 1810 as a foundry, began making bicycles. These were times of great changes: in 1888, Peugeot signed an agreement with Serpollet for the purchase of steam engines to fit to a tricycle; in 1891, it was the turn of quadricycles to be fitted with a Panhard-Levassor internal combustion engine (built under licence from Daimler); in 1897, Peugeot decided to start producing its own 2-cylinder internal-combustion engines, followed later by a single-cylinder and a 4-cylinder engine. In a short time, Peugeot became one of Europe's leading manufacturers, thanks also to successes in racing with Grand Prix cars of new concept: between 1913 and 1919, they won the 500 Miles at Indianapolis no less than three times.
Always attentive to product quality and to the application of technical innovation in a continuously expanding sector, at the end of 1935, Peugeot presented a new model, its response to the Citroën Traction Avant of 1934. This was the 402, fitted with a two-litre engine with overhead valves, independent front wheels and, above all, aerodynamic bodywork clearly influenced by the studies undertaken by Chrysler for the Airflow. It offered innovative curved lines and was characterized by the position of the headlamps behind the radiator grill.
Built with short (3150 mm) and long (3300 mm) wheelbase chassis, the 402 range offered a broad choice of different models: saloon, limousine, goods vehicle, taxi, coupé, drophead coupé and roadster.
Only the long wheelbase version offered a drophead coupé with metal roof which, thanks to a series of levers, could be folded into the boot.
At last, here was a standard model that made use of a patent first presented in 1934 in some drophead coupés of the 301 and 601 series, by Georges Paulin, a dentist whose true passion was for car design, to which he dedicated his spare time. It was he who was responsible for some Delage and Talbot-Lago models, as well as the beautiful Bentley Embiricos, all with coachwork built by Pourtout.
The original design for the Eclipse include an electric powered roof (exactly like the coupé-cabriolets manufactured today), but this was abandoned after the first trials: the capacity of car batteries in the 1930s was insufficient to power this innovative optional.
(H.S.)

Peugeot
402
CHAUSSON

Mémoire de la Nationale 7

Peugeot
402
CHAUSSON

Alfa Romeo

6C 2300 B Mille Miglia berlinetta Touring, 1937

• *Make and Model*
Alfa Romeo 6C 2300 B Mille Miglia
• *Year of production*
1937
• *Coachwork*
Berlinetta (Touring)
• *Engine*
In-line 6-cylinder, 2 overhead camshafts
• *Bore and stroke / Engine displacement*
70 x 100 mm / 2309 cc
• *Maximum power*
95 b.h.p. at 4500 rpm
• *Top speed*
155 kph (96 mph)
• *Dimensions*
Length 4800 mm, width 1700 mm, height 1500 mm, wheelbase 2770 mm
• *Weight*
1380 Kg
• *Total built*
107

Giovanni Sandri Collection
© Photo Diego Cassetta – Mart

The model on show dates from 1939

Alfa Romeo presented its 6C 2300 at the Milan Salone dell'Automobile of 1934; designed by Vittorio Jano, it was the heir of the glorious 6C 1750, the last series of which — the sixth — fitted with a 1900 cc engine, was presented only the year before. The 6C 2300 was a new, modern car, designed for a more demanding public and for those wishing to take up racing. For this reason, the Turismo version (equipped with a 68 b.h.p. engine on a chassis with a wheelbase of 3210 mm) was initially flanked by the Gran Turismo model (with 76 b.h.p. and 2925 mm wheelbase), and then the Pescara model, with a 95 b.h.p. engine. This model was soon updated and 1935 saw the launch of the 6C 2300 B, the top of the range being the Mille Miglia (offering 105 b.h.p.), launched for the 1937 edition of the famous race. Driven by Ercole Boratto, Mussolini's personal chauffeur, and by Giovanni Battista Guidotti, the manufacturer's test driver, the car won its class and finished in fourth place overall.
The car used by Boratto and Guidotti was one of the first berlinettas to be built by Touring using the Superleggera construction method, a system that was to make the Milanese company extremely famous. Aerodynamic research had led to the elaboration of new forms for car bodies, which became rounder and more curved, but this made them harder to build using old-fashioned techniques, as these still foresaw the use of wooden frames and semi-rigid materials such as pegamoid. On the other hand, advances in casting techniques had led to a sharp improvement in the quality of special alloys based on aluminium. Carrozzeria Touring, which at the time was at the cutting edge, and not only in research into new forms, had studied and implemented a new construction method called Superleggera: this consisted of a steel frame made of small-diameter tubing, shaped and welded together. Fixed to the chassis members, this became the support for the hand-shaped aluminium panels.
The result was a light, robust body, one certainly more resistant than those built using the older methods, whether in everyday use or in racing.
(H.S.)

Alfa Romeo
ALFA ROMEO · 6C 2300 B MILLE MIGLIA · ANNO 1939 · ASI 6693
6C
2300B

Superleggera

Alfa Romeo

NORDKAPP

Saloons

Rolls-Royce

Silver Cloud, 1955

• *Make and Model*
Rolls-Royce Silver Cloud
• *Year of production*
1955
• *Coachwork*
Four-door saloon
• *Engine*
In-line 6-cylinder, 2 overhead camshaft
• *Bore and stroke / Engine displacement*
95.2 x 114.3 mm / 4887 cc
• *Maximum power*
Not available
• *Top speed*
Not available
• *Dimensions*
Length 5380 mm, width 1890 mm, height 1600 mm, wheelbase 3120 mm
• *Weight*
2400 Kg
• *Total built*
2238

Davide Bassoli Collection

The model on show dates from 1959

In an exhibition sporting the name *Mitomacchina*, it would be impossible not to include a Rolls-Royce. If there is a marque of legends, then that marque is Rolls-Royce. Unlike other car manufacturers of the 1920s and 1930s, which produced vehicles of the highest quality before sinking without trace (Bugatti, Hispano-Suiza, Isotta Fraschini and Maybach in Europe, Duesenberg and Packard in the United States), Rolls-Royce continued and still continues to make cars for a clientele that wished (and wishes) to own the best of the best. One hundred years have passed since 1906, the year in which Charles Stewart Rolls and Henry Royce decided to combine their names in a new company. That year saw the launch of the 40/50 HP model, the legendary Silver Ghost, an extraordinary vehicle built to exacting standards; some engines covered 300,000 km without needing an overhaul! The typical radiator recalling the tympanum of a Greek temple had already made its appearance, and has since provided the element that distinguishes the company's cars. As for the Spirit of Ecstasy, the equally characteristic mascot in the form of a winged figure, it was modelled by sculptor Charles Sykes on the suggestion of Lord Montagu, and placed atop the radiator as of 1911. The 'Silver Ghost,' defined 'the best car in the world,' laid the basis for the legend, which was spread in part by the servicing provided by the company at the owners' homes, and a driving school for the privileged chauffeurs who would drive them. Change at Rolls-Royce has always been a long-drawn-out and carefully-meditated affair: proof of this lies in the model pictured here, the Silver Cloud, launched in 1955. The chassis is still separate, the engine is still the (glorious) straight-six that made its first appearance in 1906 in the Silver Ghost, although admittedly updated and perfected. Thanks to an elegant line, often highlighted by two-tone paintwork, the Silver Cloud disguised its true size. Construction was, as ever, of the highest standard; reliability was absolute and every possible comfort was provided for the passengers. Not for nothing was it the vehicle of choice for the Beatles at the height of their fame. With the Silver Cloud II and III, a modern V8 engine would be introduced. The presentation in 1965 of the Silver Shadow was revolutionary (for Rolls-Royce, that is): it was the first Rolls-Royce to boast a monocoque chassis and disc brakes.
(H.S.)

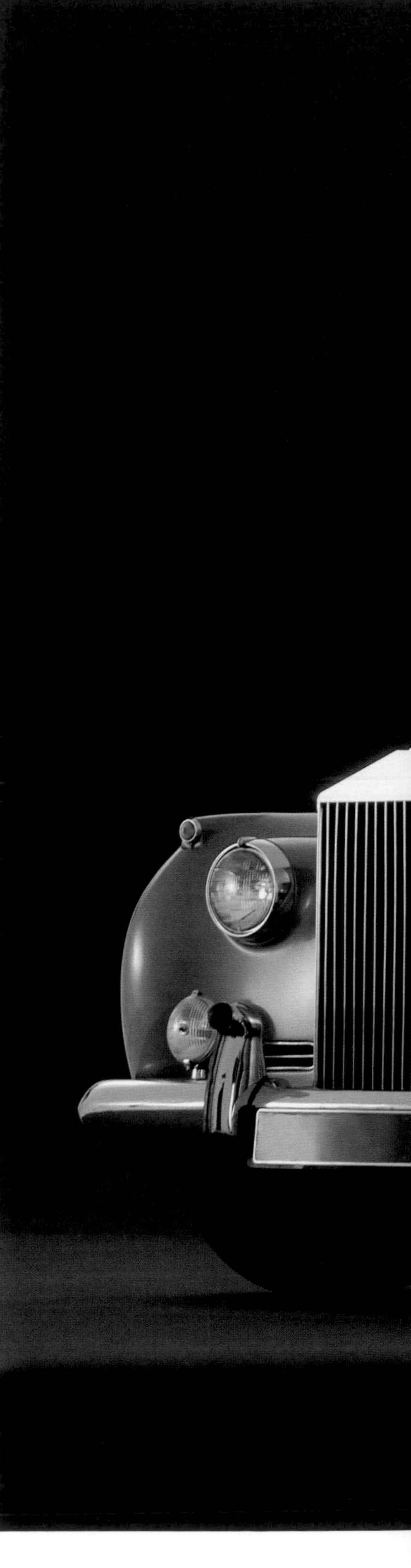

ROLLS
ROYCE

ROLLS
RR
ROYCE

GEN.
OFF
FUEL

Lancia

Flaminia, 1963

• *Make and Model*
Lancia Flaminia
• *Year of production*
1963
• *Coachwork*
Four-door saloon (Pinin Farina)
• *Engine*
Push-rod 60° V6
• *Bore and stroke / Engine displacement*
80 x 81.5 mm / 2458 cc
• *Maximum power*
110 b.h.p. at 5200 rpm
• *Top speed*
167 kph (103 mph)
• *Dimensions*
Length 4855 mm, width 1750 mm, height 1480 mm, wheelbase 2870 mm
• *Weight*
1560 Kg
• *Total built*
3932 (all series)

Turin, Collezione Storica Lancia
© Photo Diego Cassetta – Mart

At the Turin Show of 1955, the attention of both public and manifacturers alike was caught by the research prototype using the Lancia Aurelia platform that Pinin Farina was presenting on its stand: this was the Florida, a two-door saloon now recognized as one of the masterpieces of the Turin-based coachbuilder. At the Paris Salon of the same year, the Florida was presented in the four-door version without central pillar and in almost every detail it now resembled what would become Lancia's new prestige saloon, the Flaminia.
This was presented still in prototype form at the Turin Show of 1956 and then in final form in the Geneva Show of 1957. Compared to the Aurelia which it was to replace, the Flaminia had a new chassis, modified especially at the front, while the engine, although completely redesigned, maintained the classic layout of V6 60°.
The true novelty came from the design of the bodywork, which not only broke with the austere, conservative traditional style, as the Florida itself had done, of Lancia in the postwar years (Aurelia and Appia), but also introduced new canons of design, sharply in contrast with those typical of Italian and European design schools or indeed of the dominant American one.
With the Florida, Pinin Farina treated the vehicle as two overlying but separate volumes, highlighted by a change in colour. Gone were soft, round lines, abandoned in favour of straighter, more angular ones, opening a new styling direction that would be followed by all designers until the 1980s.
For industrial and safety reasons, the door supports without central pillar were unfortunately abandoned for the production vehicle, while the swage line that runs along the whole side of the car and which, with the necessary two-tone paintwork, helps slim the volume, was retained. Being a prestigious car, the Flaminia was equipped with comfortable, well-made interiors, including seats for up to six people, comprehensive instruments and rear quarterlights that could be opened using a sophisticated electro-pneumatic control from the driving position.
Sadly, the four rear windscreen wipers, two inside and two outside — one of the car's most characteristic features — were eliminated in 1960. From the front, the Flaminia is characterized by a high heavily curved windscreen and a fairly low bonnet line which required the sacrifice of the Lancia shield, recalled by the smaller logo placed at the centre of the new grille.
(H.S.)

Maserati

Quattroporte, 1963

• *Make and Model*
Maserati Quattroporte
• *Year of production*
1963
• *Coachwork*
Four-door, five-seater saloon (Frua)
• *Engine*
V8 90°, twin overhead camshafts per bank
• *Bore and stroke / Engine displacement*
88 x 85 mm / 4136 cc
• *Maximum power*
260 b.h.p. at 5200 rpm
• *Top speed*
230 kph (143 mph)
• *Dimensions*
Length 5000 mm, width 1690 mm,
height 1360 mm, wheelbase 2800 mm
• *Weight*
1900 Kg
• *Total built*
773

Adolfo Orsi Collection
© Photo Diego Cassetta – Mart

The model on show dates from 1965

By 1963, the 3500 GT Touring, the 2+2 powered by a straight six engine and which had been the most important car in the Maserati line-up since 1957, was beginning to feel the weight of the years. Italy had changed since 1957: a single 2+2 model was no longer sufficient, even if offered in open or closed version, for people who wanted to travel fast. Various parts of the north-south Autostrada del Sole opened in 1963, there was greater wealth, new cars were coming out (including the Jaguar E-type), and a single 2+2 could only cover a part of the market. Adolfo and Omer Orsi, owners of Maserati, found themselves in the difficult position of having to replace this model, more than 2000 of which had been built; an enormous number for such an exclusive market. The question was: would there be enough space in the market for a fast four-door executive saloon offering four comfortable seats? The attempts made by Facel Vega, with the Excellence, and by Aston Martin, with the Lagonda, suggested the contrary. The mechanical components were already available, in that the V8 created in 1956 for racing had been detuned for the 5000 GT, little more than 30 examples of which were built for the international jet-set. The courageous decision was thus taken to entrust the project for two new models at the same time to the Turinese designer, Pietro Frua: the Quattroporte ('four-door') saloon and the 2 Posti (later rebaptised Mistral), both of which were presented at the Turin Show in 1963. Frua was an old acquaintance of Maserati: since 1950, he had been designing the coachwork for a number of magnificent roadsters and two-litre coupés. In 1962, for Karim Aga Khan, he built a modern, classy 5000 GT. The Quattroporte took its inspiration from this car, characterized by square headlights and a large greenhouse area. Fitted with a 4200 cc V8 delivering 260 b.h.p., it offered a top speed of 230 kph and boasted it was 'the fastest four-door saloon in the world.' At a cruising speed of 200 kph, it provided its passengers pleasant high-speed cruising, comfortably ensconced on Connolly leather seats, with electric windows and air-conditioning. The boot was large and suited to travelling with the family. The gamble was a success: the Quattroporte became the favourite car of such actors as Alberto Sordi, Stewart Granger, Peter Ustinov, Anthony Quinn, Marcello Mastroianni (first owner of the car displayed here), of industrialists such as Raul Gardini, and of heads of state, including Prince Rainier of Monaco and (secretly) Leonid Brezhnev, who used it for flings along Russian roads. Today, the Quattroporte is still the name of Maserati's finest model, carrying the Italian tradition for speed and beauty around the world.
(H.S.)

EU · 101
OFF-ON
MED
HOT
OFF
CITY
COLDER
HI WAY
MASERATI
8 10 12 14 16
2 4 6 8 10

Roadsters

Ferrari

166 MM Barchetta, 1948

• *Make and Model*
Ferrari 166 MM
• *Year of production*
1948
• *Coachwork*
Racing roadster, barchetta (Touring)
• *Engine*
60° V12, 2 overhead camshafts
• *Bore and stroke / Engine displacement*
60 x 58.8 mm / 1995 cc
• *Maximum power*
140 b.h.p. at 6600 rpm
• *Top speed*
220 kph (136 mph)
• *Dimensions*
Length 3960 mm, width 1520 mm, height 1270 mm, wheelbase 2250 mm
• *Weight*
649 Kg
• *Total built*
25

Zaventem, Fondazione Swaters
© Photo pp. 198–99 La Presse / Ferrari Spa

The first Ferrari in history, the 125 Sport, emerged on the race track on 11th May 1947 at Piacenza; it was a 1500 cc engine that would make the Maranello-based builder famous, the V12 designed by Gioachino Colombo. Ferrari was a new manufacturer and Enzo Ferrari, probably in an aim to establish the company's own identity, rather than one deriving from coachbuilders, deliberately avoided the most famous names, such as Touring and Pinin Farina, and entrusted the bodywork for the first chassis to be sold to Carrozzeria Allemano.
Dissatisfied, in 1948 he returned to a collaboration with Carrozzeria Touring, started in the 1930s when many of the Alfa Romeos racing for the Scuderia Ferrari were built by the Milanese company. This continued in 1940, when Touring provided the bodies for the first two cars to be built by Ferrari, the Auto Avio Costruzioni 815 model, with a 1500 cc eight-cylinder engine; these could not be named Ferrari because of agreements signed with Alfa Romeo in 1939 when he left the Milanese firm.
But Felice Bianchi Anderloni, the soul of Carrozzeria Touring, died suddenly on 3rd June 1948 and the responsibility for drawing the new car fell solely to his young son, Carlo Felice, who had started working alongside his father in 1944. On 15th September, the first two Ferraris with Touring bodywork were presented at the Turin Show: they were a four-seater saloon displayed on the Touring stand and a racing convertible displayed on the Ferrari stand. Giovanni Canestrini, the doyen of Italian journalists, defined the coachwork of the latter 'astonishing,' saying that it reminded him not so much of a convertible as a small boat, a 'barchetta.' Thus the nickname for this new type of vehicle. The young Bianchi Anderloni had been bold, risking losing the trust of Enzo Ferrari; he had revolutionized the codified canons for racing cars, which were normally wide low down, narrow at the top and ground-hugging. The new coachwork had its widest point halfway up the flank and it looked high off the ground. But the Barchetta proved popular. It became the forebear of a whole generation of open-top sports cars. Its lines were borrowed by coachbuilders and car manufacturers around the world, starting with the British.
The 166 Barchettas were used in competition, often successfully (such as the win at Le Mans in 1949), but they were also used on roads by the lucky owners of the time, such as the example shown here, built with this elegant two-tone paintwork for a young lawyer by the name of Gianni Agnelli...
(H.S.)

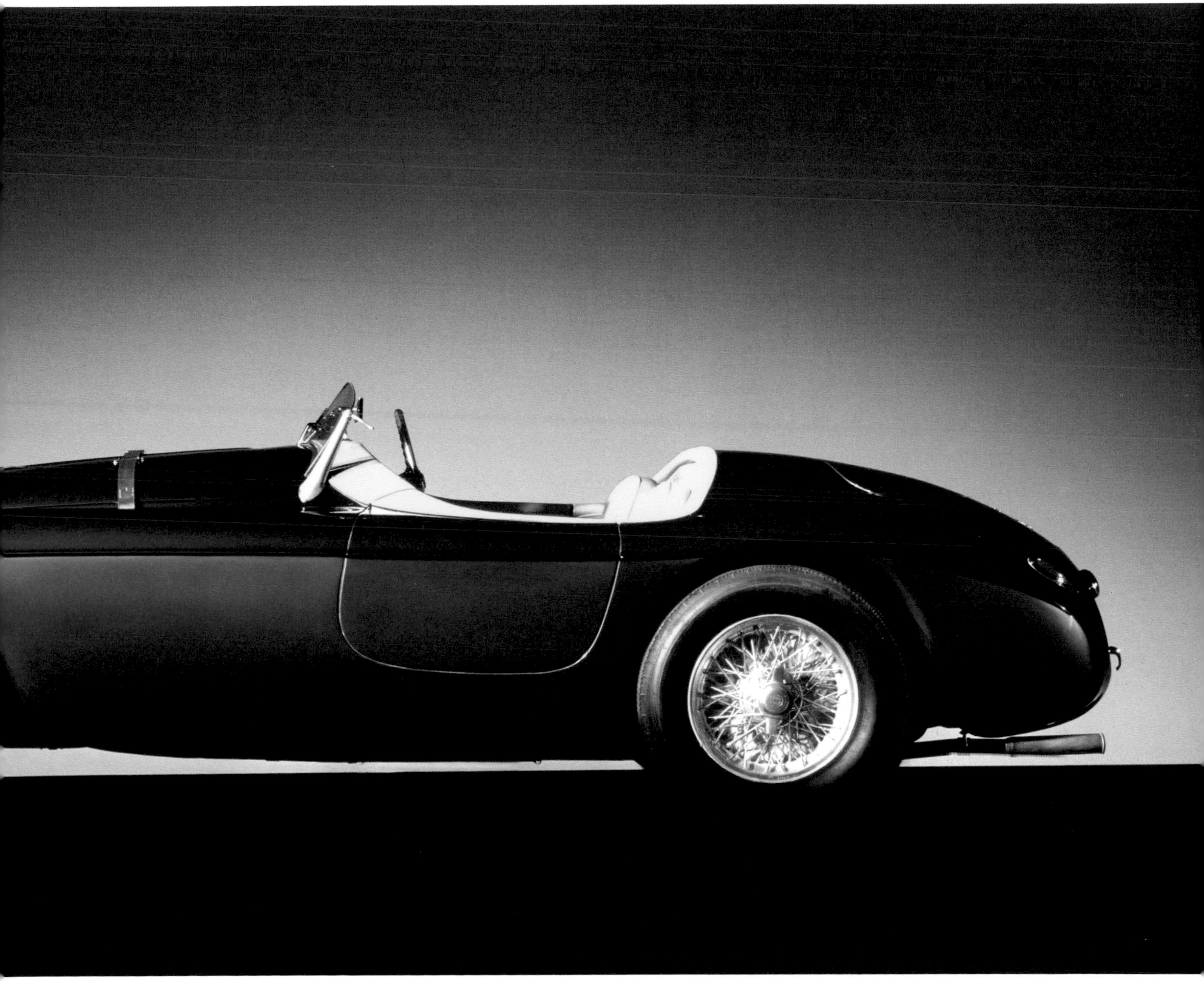

Ecurie
Francorchamps
14

Lancia

Aurelia GT B24 Spider, 1955

• *Make and Model*
Lancia Aurelia GT B24
• *Year of production*
1955
• *Coachwork*
Roadster (Pinin Farina)
• *Engine*
60° V6
• *Bore and stroke / Engine displacement*
78 x 85.5 mm / 2451 cc
• *Maximum power*
118 b.h.p. at 5300 rpm
• *Top speed*
Over 180 kph (112 mph)
• *Dimensions*
Length 4200 mm, width 1555 mm, wheelbase 2450 mm
• *Weight*
1060 Kg
• *Total built*
240

Turin, Collezione Storica Lancia

In 1946, Lancia had just two models to offer, the Aprilia, dating from 1936, and the Ardea, presented in 1939; both were highly advanced for the time but they were beginning to look old-fashioned. In 1948, Adele and Gianni Lancia, respectively Lancia's President and general director as well as wife and son of Vincenzo, founder of the company, who had died in 1937, had already started work on a new car at the end of 1943. At this time, they had undertaken research into a 60° V6 engine with an absolutely original architecture in the tradition of the ever innovative company. The new saloon, the Lancia Aurelia B10, presented in May 1950, immediately met with public favour: longer and wider than the Aprilia, the Aurelia was an elegant car free of ornament. The lines were rounded and modern with enclosed wings; the space available for passengers and baggage satisfied the requirements of the time; finally, the 1750 cc engine delivering 56 b.h.p. offered good performance although clearly not of a sporty nature. This sporty nature became apparent in the following year, 1951, in the first derivation of the Aurelia saloon, the B20 Gran Turismo. Powered by a two-litre engine, this was an elegant coupé originally designed by Felice Mario Boano, at the time interested in Carrozzeria Ghia, while Pinin Farina was commissioned to build almost all the GT B20s, except for a first batch of the first series. The B20 became the favourite car of Italian gentleman drivers, and its commercial and racing success lies at the basis of the creation of the convertible version of the Aurelia, the B24. Considered to be one of the most attractive of Pinin Farina's creations, the B24 Spider (with a 2.5 litre engine) was presented at the Brussels Salon in mid-January 1955 and remained in production until the end of that year, to be replaced in mid-1956 by the more conventional convertible version.

The long bonnet ends with the classic Lancia shield pointing downwards between the two short bumpers; the long, sweeping rear presents a hint of fins at the ends of which are the tail-lights; the cabin is small, the doors without windows (as in the purest British tradition of convertibles) and the three instrument clusters feature the speedometer set highest and protruding. The sporty yet elegant lines of the B24 Spider subsequently inspired other cars from the same Turinese coachbuilder (especially those of the Giulietta Spider) and were also used for the later Convertible version, the unforgettable protagonist of one of the cult films in Italian cinema, *Il Sorpasso*, in which it is driven by the great Vittorio Gassman.
(H.S.)

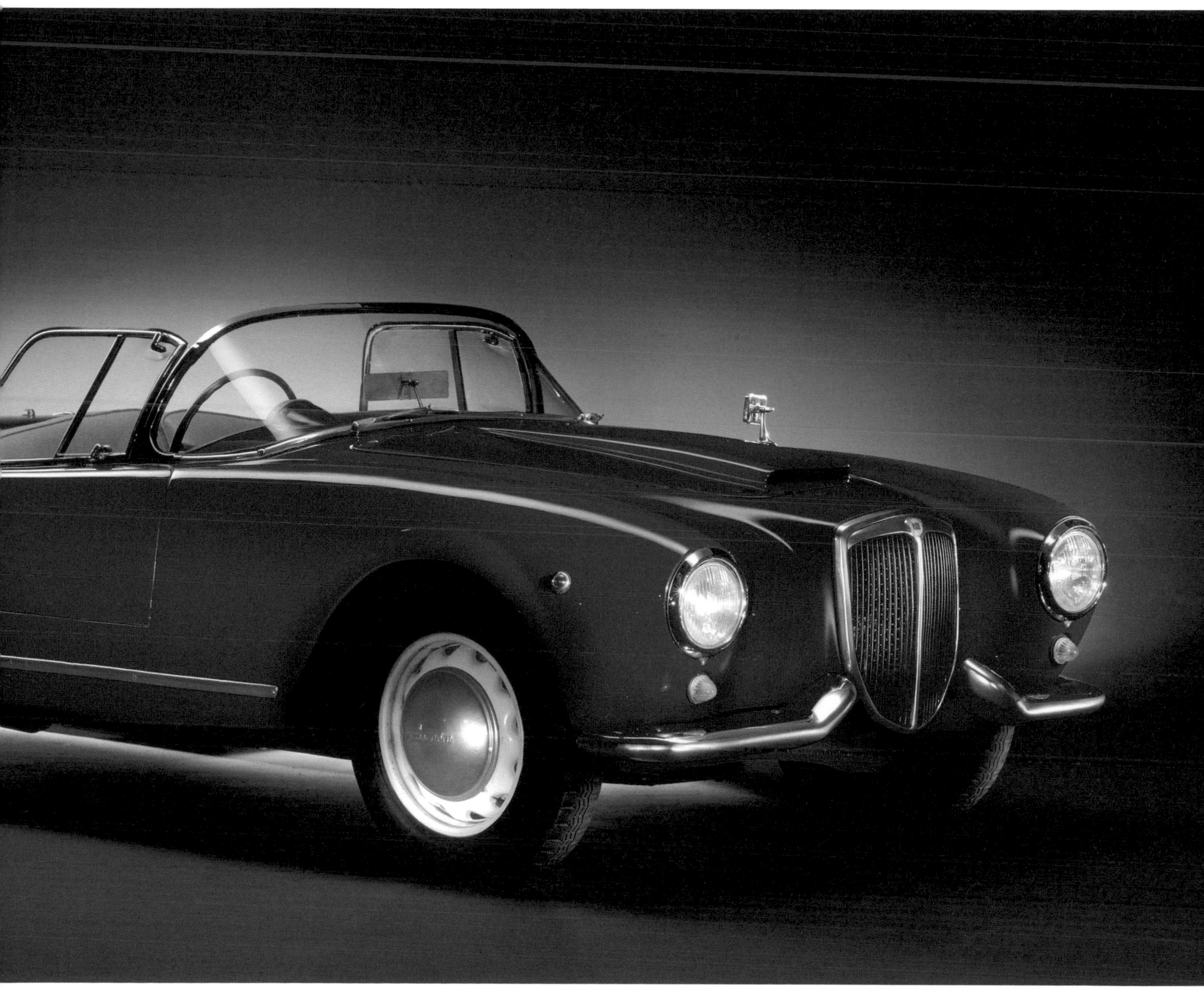

Alfa Romeo

Giulietta Spider, 1955

• *Make and Model*
Alfa Romeo Giulietta
• *Year of production*
1955
• *Coachwork*
Roadster (Pinin Farina)
• *Engine*
Four cylinders, twin overhead camshafts
• *Bore and stroke / Engine displacement*
74 x 75 mm / 1290 cc
• *Maximum power*
65 b.h.p. at 6000 rpm
• *Top speed*
165 kph (102 mph)
• *Dimensions*
Length 3860 mm, width 1580 mm, height 1335 mm, wheelbase 2200 mm
• *Weight*
830 Kg
• *Total built*
17,096 (Spider and Spider Veloce)

Arese (Milan), Automobilismo Storico Alfa Romeo, Museo Storico, Centro di Documentazione Storica
Photo © Automobilismo Storico Alfa Romeo, Centro di Documentazione Storica

The model on show is the 1955 prototype

At the beginning of the 1950s, Alfa Romeo's production was centred on just two models: the 6C 2500, a model that was rapidly becoming dated, and the new 1900, presented in October 1950, a car that fell into a higher segment than usual in the Italian market and hence was set for a limited market penetration. In order to ensure jobs for the entire Alfa Romeo workforce and increase sales of the market, it was necessary to appeal to the emerging class that was building the Italy of the economic 'boom.' It was within this context that the '750' project was born in 1952.
The new car, the Giulietta (this was the first time that Alfa Romeo used a name rather than a number to denominate one of its models), was presented officially at the Turin Show in spring 1954 in its coupé version, the Sprint, built by Carrozzeria Bertone. The four-cylinder 1290 cc engine delivered 65 b.h.p. and provided a top speed of 160 kph. The reception of the Sprint exceeded all expectations and the success was repeated the following year with the presentation of the four-door saloon version.
In America, Alfa Romeo was distributed by Max Hoffman, an Austrian who was deeply involved in the racing scene; he expressly asked the directors of Alfa Romeo to produce a sporty, open-top, two-door model with which to compete — especially in California — with the success of the small British convertibles like MG, Triumph and Morgan.
In order to win over the Italian company, at the same time as his request, he placed an order for 600 of these new cars. The offer could not be turned down and Alfa Romeo asked Pinin Farina and Bertone to build a working prototype of an open-top car using the Giulietta running gear.
This particular challenge was won by Pinin Farina which, exploiting the lines already designed for the Lancia B24, presented a light, elegant convertible with low, sweeping lines that were destined not to age. The Giulietta Spider, presented at the Paris Salon of 1955, immediately won over not only the Americans but also the Italians who, however, had to wait months before being able to buy one of these jewels of design: the first 600 were all destined for Max Hoffman.
The car on display here is one of the pre-production prototypes and presents a few differences with respect to the standard vehicle, including the wraparound windscreen (at the time defined as 'American-style'), the lack of handles on the doors and the dashboard with three separate instrument clusters, which was certainly a stunner to look at but also difficult to make at an industrial level.
(H.S.)

BMW

507, 1955

• *Make and Model*
BMW 507 Touring Sport
• *Year of production*
1955
• *Coachwork*
Roadster with hard top
• *Maximum power*
150 b.h.p. at 5000 rpm
• *Engine*
V8
• *Bore and stroke / Engine displacement*
82 x 75 mm / 3168 cc
• *Top speed*
From 190 to 220 kph (118-136 mph), depending on gearbox ratios
• *Dimensions*
Length 4380 mm, width 1650 mm, height 1300 mm, wheelbase 2480 mm
• *Weight*
1330 Kg
• *Total built*
252

Francesco and Mietta Gandolfi Collection
© Photo Diego Cassetta – Mart

The model on show dates from 1957

The design of the new BMW sports cars was entrusted in January 1955 to Albrecht Goertz, a German who had been working for some time in the United States. Goertz designed an elegant 2+2 coupé, the 503, and an open-top, more sporty car, the 507, both of which were rapidly developed by BMW.
The 507 is characterized by a low-slung, aggressive body, a slender front end with the typical BMW 'kidneys' restyled for the occasion, and a crease line running the whole length of the car from the front wing to the rear one.
Presented in September of that same year at the Frankfurt Show, the 507 was received with great public enthusiasm, although its high price prevented a corresponding commercial success. In the United States, industrial designer Raymond Loewy fitted a new bodywork he had himself designed over the frame of the 507. The wooden models of this 507, built between November 1956 and April 1959, were subsequently preserved by a BMW employee.
During a series of tests using a 507 powered by a 165 b.h.p. engine made for the American market, the 'Schweizerische Automobil-Rundschau' recorded a top speed of 222 kph. A special version, made for Alexander von Falkenhausen, a driver and engine designer, reached a top speed of 240 kph, thanks to special preparation of the engine.
(R.J.F.K.)

180
210
240
50
60

Lotus

Seven, 1958

• *Make and Model*
Lotus Seven
• *Year of production*
1958
• *Coachwork*
Roadster
• *Engine*
BMC in-line 4-cylinder, side valves
•*Bore and stroke / Engine displacement*
62.94 x 76.2 mm / 948 cc
• *Maximum power*
37 b.h.p. at 4800 rpm
• *Top speed*
130 kph (81 mph)
• *Dimensions*
Length 3125 mm, width 1350 mm, height 710 mm, wheelbase 2240 mm
• *Weight*
410 Kg
• *Total built*
2885 (all series)

Spelberg Collection

A former RAF pilot, Colin Chapman built his first car, called the Mark 1, in 1948, for personal use in classic British trial races. The car immediately showed its worth and Chapman had to build a few other cars to satisfy the requests of friends and enthusiasts. Within a few years, he gained a fine reputation as a builder of racing cars and in 1956 decided to go a step further: to build a cheaper road model alongside his racing cars. Chapman's aims were low weight, low cost, ease of maintenance, driving pleasure and performance. In 1957, a prototype of the Mark 7, later known simply as the Seven, participated in its first races and in 1958 the same car, slightly simplified compared to the prototype, was ready for sale. The spaceframe chassis was made of rather slender steel tubing but offered exceptional rigidity; the bodywork was of aluminium; the engine initially chosen was the Ford 100E of 1172 cc which, tuned, could provide up to 50 b.h.p. There was a three-speed gearbox and drum brakes. The front suspension was independent wheels, while the rear de Dion of the prototype was changed in favour of a cheaper live axle. The bodywork echoes that of the Mark 6, with no doors and with separate cycle wings. The cabin was extremely spartan with only two seats, a few instruments on the dashboard. Even windscreen wipers, like a spare tyre, were optional extras. The car could be bought ready-assembled or in kit form at about half price, taking advantage of a UK tax concession. Weighing just 410 kg, the Seven offered such brilliant performance, agility and superb control as to be defined a 'motorcycle on four wheels.' In its first year, about 100 examples were sold. More demanding customers were given the option of a more powerful engine, a Coventry Climax offering 75 b.h.p. in 1098 cc-form. Very light, easy and fun to drive, with performance that can be exciting if a bigger engine is fitted, the Seven, modernized over the years and always offered with a wide range of engines, remained in production with Lotus until the 1970s. When Chapman decided to cease production of this cult model, the company that handled its distribution, Caterham, decided to buy all the rights and continue production, which it still does to this day.
(H.S.)

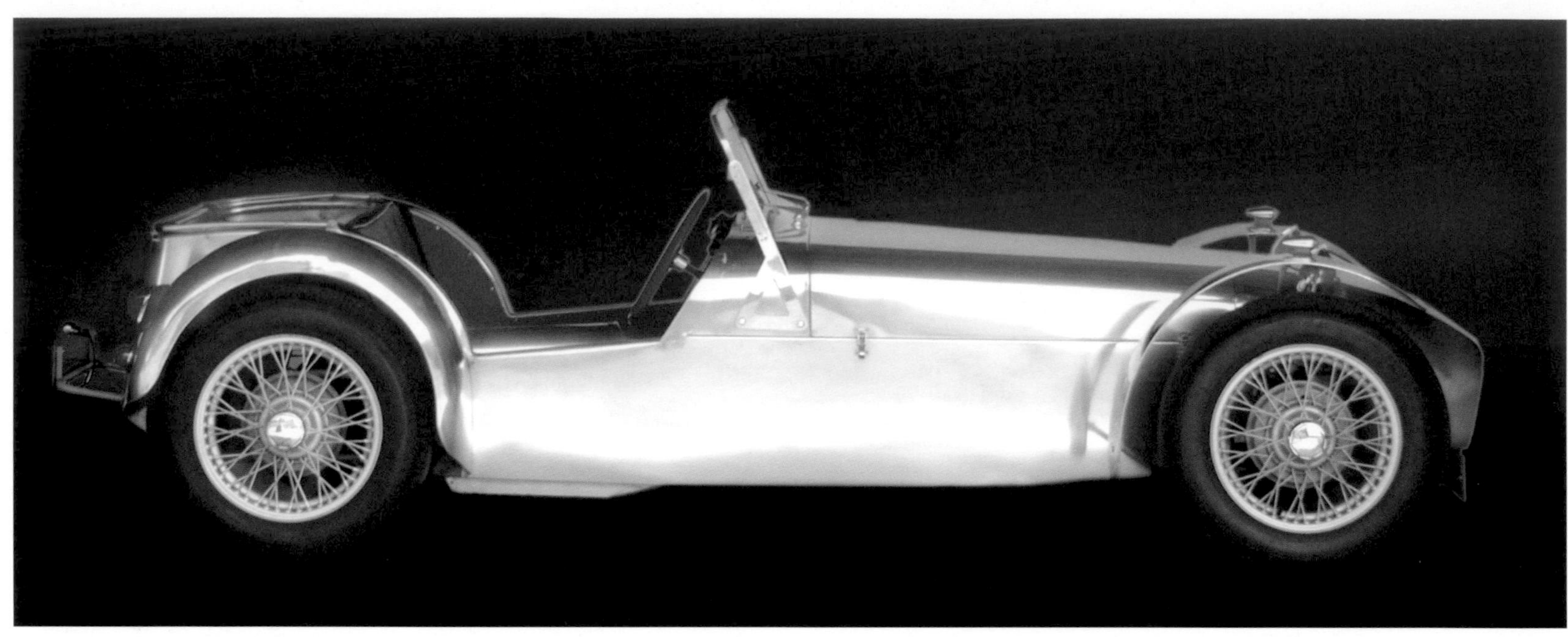

AUSTIN

Chevrolet

Corvette convertible, 1958

• *Make and Model*
Chevrolet Corvette
• *Year of production*
1958
• *Coachwork*
Convertible roadster
• *Engine*
Push-rod V8
• *Bore and stroke / Engine displacement*
98.4 x 76.2 mm / 4600 cc
• *Maximum power*
250 b.h.p. at 4800 rpm
• *Top speed*
210 kph (130 mph)
• *Dimensions*
Length 4495 mm, width 1854 mm,
height 1295 mm, wheelbase 2590 mm
• *Weight*
1320 Kg
• *Total built*
29,099 (1958–60)

Fabrizio Sama Collection
© Photo Diego Cassetta – Mart

The model on show is a third series car dating from 1960

In America, the Corvette is no longer just a car, it is a religion. For the past 53 years, it has been the 'American sports car' and is the sole constant point of reference in car manufacturing; if an American is unable to remember a precise year, he will refer to the time when he, or his brother or his brother's friend had a Corvette.
However, at the outset, things were not easy. Created by Edward Cole and Harley Earl, the manager of the famous General Motors Styling Centre, it was presented at the 1953 Motorama. The public was indeed bowled over by this splendid car, with its curvy lines and fibreglass bodywork (the first time this was used in a mass-produced car), but also disappointed by the poor engine, a 3900 cc six-cylinder with only 150 b.h.p. Indeed, sales were far lower than expected and it was a miracle that a colossus like GM should keep the plants running for just 3640 cars in 1954 and only 700 in 1955. The turn-around came and was facilitated both by the arrival of Zora Arkus-Duntov in GM and by some success of the car in competition. Duntov designed the 1956 model, which was finally equipped with what the Americans wanted: a fine V8 engine with lots of torque and horsepower to spare).
1957 saw the introduction of a fuel injection, 4-speed version and the Corvette won its class in the 12-Hours at Sebring. Production had by now risen to 6339 examples, but the Corvette had above all found its market, and had finally discerned what Americans were looking for. The 1958 model, the third series which remained in production until 1962, was equipped for the first time with four headlights but also appeared heavier as a result of the excessive addition of brightwork. On the other hand, there was more horsepower, from 230 b.h.p. in the 283 engine in 1958 to 360 in the 327 engine of 1962. 1960 also saw a breakthrough in production: for the first time, the barrier of 10,000 units per annum was swept aside. Over the years, the lines of the bodywork were constantly adjusted in accordance with the dictates of the design of the times, and the car became larger and more voluminous to meet the taste of the average American. Despite this, its styling has always ensured the Corvette provided the only adequate response to classic European GTs cars, conquering the right to be defined the 'USA's Ferrari.' Sweeping, low and sexy, the Corvette 'seemed to be racing even when parked.'
(H.S.)

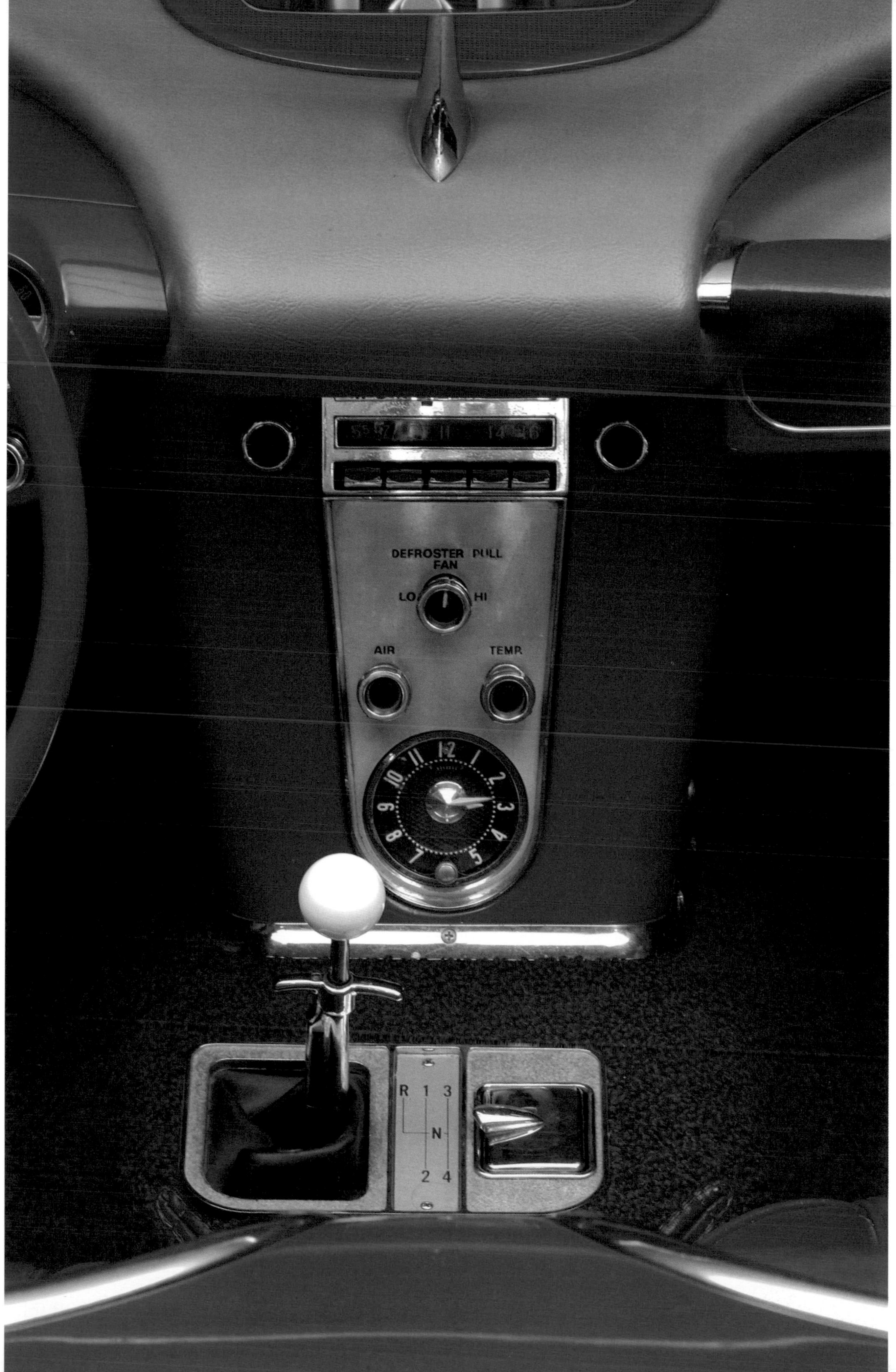
DEFROSTER PULL
FAN
LO
HI
AIR
TEMP
R 1 3
N
2 4

CORVETTE

Maserati

3500, GT Vignale Spyder, 1959

• *Make and Model*
Maserati 3500 GT Spyder
• *Year of production*
1959
• *Coachwork*
Roadster (Vignale)
• *Engine*
In-line six-cylinder, twin overhead camshafts per bank
• *Bore and stroke / Engine displacement*
86 x 1000 mm / 3485 cc
• *Maximum power*
230 b.h.p. at 5500 rpm
• *Top speed*
230 kph (143 mph)
• *Dimensions*
Length 4490 mm, width 1685 mm,
height 1295 mm, wheelbase 2500 mm
• *Weight*
1200 Kg
• *Total built*
250

Adolfo Orsi Collection

The 3500 GT was a fundamental model in the history of Maserati: indeed, not only did it enable the survival of the manufacturer during a difficult period, but it even enabled it to make a first-rate entry into the market for high-performance GT cars. At the end of 1957, after Maserati had won the Formula One Drivers' World Championship with Fangio and the immortal 250F single-seater, and had also dominated races in the Sports category, it was forced to withdraw from competition because of the financial problems besetting the tooling machine sector, which was the Orsi Group's most important industrial activity. Maserati had actually started producing GT cars in 1947, but this had always served as a corollary to the production of racing cars, never exceeding a production of 20 examples a year.
The 3500 GT, presented at the Geneva Show in 1957, was powered by a six-cylinder, 3500 cc engine with double overhead camshafts, derived from the engine used in racing, and it was fundamental for the survival of the marque.
The elegant lines of the Touring model, and the reliability of the mechanical parts, which enabled the car to reach a top speed of 230 kph, were the ingredients for a highly successful cocktail: indeed, between 1957 and 1964, almost 2000 models were built, a record for a car costing nearly lire 5,000,000. But there was also demand from the market for an open-top version: in the wake of a proposal from Touring itself and of another from Frua, Maserati turned to the Turin-based coachbuilder, Alfredo Vignale, who built cars whose lines came from the talented pen of Giovanni Michelotti, and supplied a short-wheelbase version of the chassis for a Spyder version. Michelotti proposed a convertible boasting, a modern, sporty line, but not too showy; in other words, in line with the elegant style of Maserati's usual production. From that proposal, Michelotti sketched out a number of versions: incredible as it might seem today, all of these were built as one-offs. These were times when it was still possible to build prototypes by hand, without spending enormous amounts of money, check the results and offer them to clients who wished to possess unique cars. The car on display here was presented at the Vignale stand at the Turin Show of 1959, to test the market. It bears the signature of the designer on the bonnet and is close to the characteristics of the model that would enter standard production in mid-1960, although differing in numerous details: among the most evident of these is the different treatment of the front end, the characteristic air vent on the side and the more sporty and spartan interior. The model proved a success and about 250 examples were built until 1964, selling primarily to the international jet-set.
(H.S.)

Coupés

Cisitalia

202 Gran Sport, 1948

• *Make and Model*
Cisitalia 202 Gran Sport
• *Year of production*
1948
• *Coachwork*
Coupé (Pinin Farina)
• *Engine*
Push-rod in-line four-cylinder
• *Bore and stroke / Engine displacement*
68 x 75 mm / 1090 cc
• *Maximum power*
60 b.h.p. at 5500 rpm
• *Top speed*
170 kph (105 mph)
• *Dimensions*
Length 3400 mm, width 1450 mm, height 1390 mm, wheelbase 2400 mm
• *Weight*
780 Kg
• *Total built*
About 170 (all series, coupés and convertibles)

Coen Collection
Photo Automobilia srl Milan

'A rolling sculpture' was how the Cisitalia 202 Gran Sport was defined when it was one of the eight cars chosen in 1951 for an exhibition at the Museum of Modern Art in New York (MoMA), dedicated to car design, where it is still on display. Why the Cisitalia 202, precisely? After all, when all is said and done, it is merely a car with a 1100 cc engine and mechanical parts derived from Fiat, in other words mass-production running gear.
Its lines had a strong impact on the aesthetics of car design at the time, breaking with tradition and introducing new concepts in style: according to many car designers, the 202 is the progenitor of all modern sports cars. Underlying it all is, a tubular spaceframe making it possible to locate the engine and all other mechanical parts low down; thanks to this, for the first 202 coupé (dubbed the 'Cassone'), its designer, Giovanni Savonuzzi was able to draw a body that was still rough in parts but lower than normal; this idea was then developed in the second coupé (known as the 'Aerodinamica Savonuzzi' and in the Mille Miglia roadster (subsequently called the 'Nuvolari'). Thanks to the excellent aerodynamics, the Cisitalia could achieve a creditably high top speed for its modest engine; for the rest, it was easy to drive and had good road-holding thanks to a design form towards the end of the war from the fertile mind of engineer Dante Giacosa, on loan to Cisitalia from Fiat.
The Cisitalia (Compagnie Industrie Sportive Italia) had already made a name for itself in racing, but Piero Dusio, the Turinese company's founder, was not yet satisfied and wanted to take advantage of favourable market conditions with a series production sports car.
Savonuzzi's Aerodinamica, built by the skilled hands of Alfredo Vignale, lies at the basis of the project; but when it came to the step from design to production, Dusio turned to Pinin Farina. He decided not to change Savonuzzi's original design radically, but to intervene in a number of details he considered not right for a road car. Besides, the aerodynamic line already constituted an absolute innovation, a world first: the line of the bonnet was lower than the line of the front wings. Pinin Farina retouched the rear end, lowering it and harmonising it with the rear wings; changed the size of the doors, windscreen and rear window; retouched the sweep of the flanks, but left the front, characterized by the imposing and characteristic radiator grille virtually unchanged. And a fine car became a masterpiece.
(H.S.)

Porsche

356, 1948

• *Make and Model*
Porsche Model 356/2
• *Year of production*
1948
• *Coachwork*
Coupé (Kastenhofer, Vienna)
• *Engine*
Air-cooled four-cylinder boxer
• *Bore and stroke / Engine displacement*
75 x 64 mm / 1131 cc
• *Maximum power*
40 b.h.p. at 4000 rpm
• *Top speed*
140 km/h
• *Dimensions*
Length 3870 mm, width 1660 mm,
height 1300 mm, wheelbase 2100 mm
• *Weight*
680 Kg
• *Total built*
43

Private collection – Member of the Registro 356 Porsche Italia
© Photo Diego Cassetta – Mart

For the car marathon from Berlin to Rome, three Porsches were prepared: no. 60 K 10 (or 64), based on the Kraft durch Freude from the Reutter coachworks of Stuttgart.
A body that swept back and down at the rear and offered aerodynamic lines, with a steeply sloping front end — like in the KdF cars — on the bonnet of which is sculpted a sort of channel separating left and right from the headlights integrated into the body.
This basic design was used by Porsche under the direction of Porsche's son, Ferry, as the starting point for a sports car, under project number 356. During the war, Ferry Porsche moved to Stuttgart to Gmünd in Austria, and it was in this new location that the 356 was designed in 1947.
Like for the 1939 model, the 356 was also designed by Erwin Komenda. Between 1948 and 1951, a small number of cabriolets and coupés were built.
This type of car, fitted with an aluminium body like its progenitor, was made to measure for racing. And indeed, because of the length of the cabin, it could seat only two passengers, plus an extra two squeezed into occasional seats behind. In the wake of the difficulty of producing curved windscreens, a flat windscreen was used made of two separate panes joined in the middle. The 40 b.h.p. produced by the Volkswagen engine, made the little sports car quite fast, as it was extremely light and had good aerodynamics.
The variations made to the series models produced after 1951 by the Reutter coachworks in Stuttgart were limited. Among these was the replacement of the Knickscheibe (split windscreen) — as it had been dubbed by the public — on the basic model with a curved screen. From a mechanical point of view, the engine was beefed up.
It remained in production until 1965 with the 356 C and is today considered a classic in the history of car production.
(R.J.F.K.)

PORSCHE

Alfa Romeo

6C 2500 Super Sport Villa d'Este, 1949

• *Make and Model*
Alfa Romeo 6C 2500 Super Sport
• *Year of production*
1949
• *Coachwork*
Coupé Villa d'Este (Touring)
• *Engine*
In-line 6-cylinder, twin overhead camshafts per bank
• *Bore and stroke / Engine displacement*
72 x 100 mm / 2443 cc
• *Maximum power*
105 b.h.p. at 4800 rpm
• *Top speed*
165 kph (102 mph)
• *Dimensions*
Length 4580 mm, width 1780 mm,
height 1500 mm, wheelbase 2700 mm
• *Weight*
1420 Kg
• *Total built*
About 400 (Super Sport chassis from 1947)

Francesco and Mietta Gandolfi Collection

The model on show dates from 1951

Presented at the Berlin Show of 1939, the 6C 2500 was the latest development of a concept dating from the 1920s with the 6C 1500 and continuously updated. Except that in 1939, Vittorio Jano was no longer around as technical director of Alfa Romeo.
The main difference to the 1937 6C 2300 B, from which the new car descended directly as regards both chassis and engine, was the lowering of the chassis itself and driving position, which enabled independent coachwork designers and the manufacturer's own styling centre to draw bodies with more sweeping, more modern forms. Remaining in production until 1953, the Alfa Romeo 6C 2500 was, in the immediate post-war years, the most prestigious Italian car at an international level, able to make up for the dated nature of the mechanical parts, designed years before, thanks to the modernity of the lines of its body. Once again, as often occurred in the 1930s, it was the creations of Carrozzeria Touring that attracted the attention and admiration of both the industry and enthusiasts. The bodywork designed in 1949 for the short wheelbase chassis, 2700 mm, of the 6C 2500 is considered one of the finest creations of the Milanese company and one of the greatest stylistic examples of the entire Italian design school in the immediate post-war period.
The body, stripped of the ornamental excesses of the period and of the redundant chrome decorations of American inspiration, has a clean, sweeping line highlighted by a large glazed area and, seen from the side, by the two crease lines running rearwards from the top of the wheelarches which hint at the separate wings of the 1920s and 1930s. The narrow Alfa shield is in strong relief and gives rise to the sweeping bonnet line that rises between the crests of thge wings. The shield is flanked by extra headlights, which recur as a motif in the low, sweeping tail.
The car acquired the unofficial name of 'Villa d'Este' coupé after winning the the Gran Premio Referendum at the *Concours d'Elégance* at Villa d'Este in 1949; that is, after being voted as the most attractive car in the contest by the spectators of the 102 cars presented, produced by no less than 36 coachbuilders. It is interesting to note that the car was acclaimed as winner by the public but not by the jury, which deemed it a 'facelift' of an earlier model.
(H.S.)

ALFA-ROMEO
MILANO

Superleggera

Mercedes-Benz

300 SL Gullwing, 1954

• *Make and Model*
Mercedes-Benz 300 SL (W 198 I)
• *Year of production*
1954
• *Coachwork*
Coupé (Sindelfingen)
• *Engine*
In-line six cylinder, fuel injection
• *Bore and stroke*
85 x 88 mm
• *Maximum power*
215 b.h.p. at 5800 rpm
• *Top speed*
From 235 to 260 kph (according to gearbox), (146-161 mph)
• *Dimensions*
Length 4250 mm, width 1790 mm, height 1300 mm, wheelbase 2400 mm
• *Weight*
1310 Kg
• *Total built*
About 1400, including 28 examples with aluminium bodywork and one in fibreglass

Quattroruote Collection
© Photo Diego Cassetta – Mart

When Mercedes-Benz decided to re-enter the world of racing in 1951, plans were made for a sports car able to participate in both touring car races and rallying, based on the engine for the 300 saloon the company had just presented. For the first races, the engine was tuned to increase the horsepower from an initial 115 b.h.p. to between 166 and 200 b.h.p. To this end, the car was transformed into a functional sporty coupé called the 300 SL (SL standing for 'Sport Leicht' or 'light sports [vehicle]'), characterized by a short wheelbase, a modern three-box design and completely smooth sides. The low drag coefficient, added to ample power from the engine and the low weight of the vehicle achieved thanks to a tubular spaceframe chassis led to a good weight / power ratio and high top speed. Because of the deep sides of the spaceframe, a solution was adopted for the doors which in the USA was called 'gullwing,' and this soon became the name and symbol of the car. The director of the technical design was Rudolf Uhlenhaut while the design itself was the fruit of years of research by the head of the experimental bodywork department, Karl Wilfert, with the assistance of Friedrich Geiger. Following the preparation of ten models preceding the 300 SL (W 194) and of a prototype, the series car was presented in New York in 1954. The decision to present the car there came about as a result of North American racing successes, such as the victory in the Mexican Carrera Panamericana. After the W 198 I series with the gullwing doors (produced from 1954 to 1957), the model was rebaptised W 198 II (produced from 1957 to 1963) and transformed into a roadster and fitted with hardtop and normal doors.
(R.J.F.K.)

Ferrari

250 GT Berlinetta passo corto, 1959

• *Make and Model*
Ferrari 250 GT Berlinetta passo corto
• *Year of production*
1959
• *Coachwork*
Coupé (Pinin Farina / Scaglietti)
• *Engine*
V12, single camshaft per bank
• *Bore and stroke / Engine displacement*
73 x 58.8 mm / 2953 cc
• *Maximum power*
240 b.h.p. at 7000 rpm
• *Top speed*
About 240 kph (149 mph)
• *Dimensions*
Length 4153 mm, width 1651 mm,
height 1283 mm, wheelbase 2400 mm
• *Weight*
1200 Kg
• *Total built*
90 Lusso (Luxury), 75 Competizione (Competition)

Private collection

The model on show dates from 1961

Designed by Pinin Farina and built at Modena by Carrozzeria Scaglietti, the 250 GT Berlinetta passo corto (short wheelbase) is today considered one of the most beautiful Ferraris ever produced. Presented at the Paris Salon in October 1959, together with the new version of another legend of Ferrari's production, the 250 GT Spider California, the 250 GT Berlinetta is universally known as the SWB today, a contraction of 'short wheelbase' (2400 mm) to distinguish it from the earlier 250 GT Berlinetta 'Tour de France,' built on a longer 2600 mm wheelbase. It was available in two versions: Competizione with an aluminium body and 260/280 b.h.p. engine, and one with a lower output 220/240 b.h.p. engine. This was the first Ferrari GT to be sold with disc brakes. 165 examples of this superb car were produced, and since Ferrari customers could have their car 'made to measure,' it is very difficult if not impossible today to find two completely similar Berlinettas.
The 250 GT Berlinetta was not simply beautiful but also offered brilliant performance. It was fast and easy to drive, and it occupies a special place in the history of Ferrari as it was the last to be built to satisfy customers who wanted a car with a double personality: a sports car to race at weekends, and yet one that could be used in normal day-to-day traffic, perhaps even with a suitcase in the boot.
In its first race, the 12-Hours at Sebring in 1960, three 250 GT Berlinettas dominated their category and finished fourth, fifth and sixth overall. At the later 24-Hours of Le Mans, another 250 GTs finished from fourth to seventh overall. The list of all the victories in the GT class achieved around the world by the SWB Berlinetta is very long. The most prestigious result was the third overall place in the Le Mans 24-Hours in 1961, which assured Ferrari a great return in terms of image, and benefitted sales of the standard models.
(H.S.)

Jaguar

E-type coupé, 1961

• *Make and Model*
Jaguar E-type
• *Year of production*
1961
• *Coachwork*
Coupé
• *Engine*
In-line six cylinder, twin overhead camshafts per bank
• *Bore and stroke / Engine displacement*
87 x 106 mm / 3781 cc
• *Maximum power*
265 b.h.p. at 5500 rpm
• *Top speed*
240 kph (149 mph)
• *Dimensions*
Length 4452 mm, width 1530 mm,
height 1219 mm, wheelbase 2438 mm
• *Weight*
1150 Kg
• *Total built*
Over 70,000 (all series)

San Martino in Rio (Reggio Emilia), Scuderia San Martino Museo dell'Auto

The model on show dates from 1962

The start of the history of the E-type dates back to 1957, when four Jaguar D-types took the first four positions in the 24-Hours at Le Mans. Jaguar had officially retired from racing and the cars were being fielded by Ecurie Ecosse, but such was the effect of that success (the third consecutive win and the fifth since 1951) that it convinced Sir William Lyons to continue with development of the D-type to arrive at production of a road car directly derived from the victorious racing car. The chassis of the D-type was a monocoque from the bulkhead back with a front tubular sub-frame transferred with a few changes to the new model, which was fitted with independent suspension and disc brakes on all four wheels. The E-type's engine was derived from the six-cylinder 3.8 litre of the XK 150 and, thanks to its 265 b.h.p., provided dazzling acceleration and an extremely high top speed.
Geneva, 15th March 1961, the inaugural day of the Salon de l'Automobile: Jaguar presented its new E-type in both coupé and roadster versions. Many cars from manufacturers around the world suddenly looked 'old' and dated. Never had the public and press been so excited as they rushed to the British manufacturer's stand to admire this marvel of marvels from close-to. The long, long bonnet immediately suggested speed and, when opened, revealed everything, from the engine to the suspension, brakes and wheels.
The cabin was compact but spacious, with leather seats and fine instrumentation. The coupé's tailgate had large rear window giving a view of the large boot.
Low, sweeping, sensual: any number of adjectives were used to describe the lines of the car in the press world-wide; some defined it a missile, and others saw it as a sex symbol; it seemed a dream car but was actually a normal production car. And it cost far less than its main competitors, the Italian sports cars, while offering similar performance.
As though the enormous amount of publicity the car gained free of charge in the car magazines of the whole world were not enough, the following April the E-type won with Graham Hill on its debut race, was chosen by Diabolik, a cartoon character, to flee from the clutches of Inspector Ginko, and became the car of choice for stars.
In 1961, the line of the E-type was truly revolutionary and futuristic, and was destined to be one of the most beautiful cars ever made. Perhaps the general rule that applies to all cars is all the more true of the E-type: it is the first version that is the most beautiful; the later, modified versions, made until 1974 lost a little of their original purity. *(H.S.)*

Studebaker

Avanti, 1962

• *Make and Model*
Studebaker Avanti
• *Year of production*
1962
• *Coachwork*
Coupé
• *Engine*
V8
• *Bore and stroke / Engine displacement*
90 x 92 mm / 4736 cc
• *Maximum power*
240 b.h.p.
• *Top speed*
210 kph (130 mph)
• *Dimensions*
Length 4900 mm, width 1800 mm,
height 1371 mm, wheelbase 2768 mm
• *Weight*
1427 Kg
• *Total built*
4643

Munich, Die Neue Sammlung Pinakothek der Moderne

Like many other car manufacturers, Studebaker started business by making carts and carriages: Henry and Clem Studebaker set up their cart factory in Indiana in the mid-19th century, becoming suppliers of the Northern army during the civil war. The first Studebaker cars were electric and date back to 1902, while the production of cars with internal combustion engines started in 1904. Studebaker survived the hard years following the Wall Street Crash in 1929, and in 1935 began collaborating with Raymond Loewy, the French designer born in Paris in 1893, who moved to America in 1919 and is considered the pioneer of American industrial design. Of a highly active nature, he worked for a variety of sectors: from skyscrapers to cigarette makers (Lucky Strike), drinks machines (Coca-Cola), typewriters (IBM) and ceramics (Rosenthal). He also left his mark in naval architecture, and in aircraft design (interiors for Douglas aircraft), as well as in public transport (buses for Greyhound). Loewy's innovative ideas proved successful in the car sector too.
Studebaker entered a period of crisis in the early 1950s, and in 1954 merged with Packard, another noble casualty of the American car industry. The last work Raymond Loewy completed for Studebaker was the design of the futuristic Avanti coupé. Characterized by angular lines that were very different to both American and European GTs, the Avanti was presented in 1962 as a 'model year 1963.' The bodywork was of fibreglass and the cabin, particularly refined and full of accessories, could seat five passengers. The engine was a classic V8, which in the supercharged version, delivered 258 b.h.p. The hopes of Studebaker's management was that the Avanti would compete with the Chevrolet Corvette: offered at $ 4445 as against the $ 4257 of its rival, sales did not take off, however, and production ceased at the end of the same year, 1963, immediately after presentation of the 1964 model, characterized by the setting of the headlamps in a square frame. The Studebaker American factory closed and production of the cars, except for the Avanti, continued for a few years more in Canada. However, this did not mark the death of the Avanti: two courageous concessionaires bought the rights and moulds for the car which is still produced to order to this day, virtually unchanged aesthetically, although with a new engine. Loewy's design was so unusual that it still appears modern today, more than 40 years after its creation.
(H.S.)

Studebaker

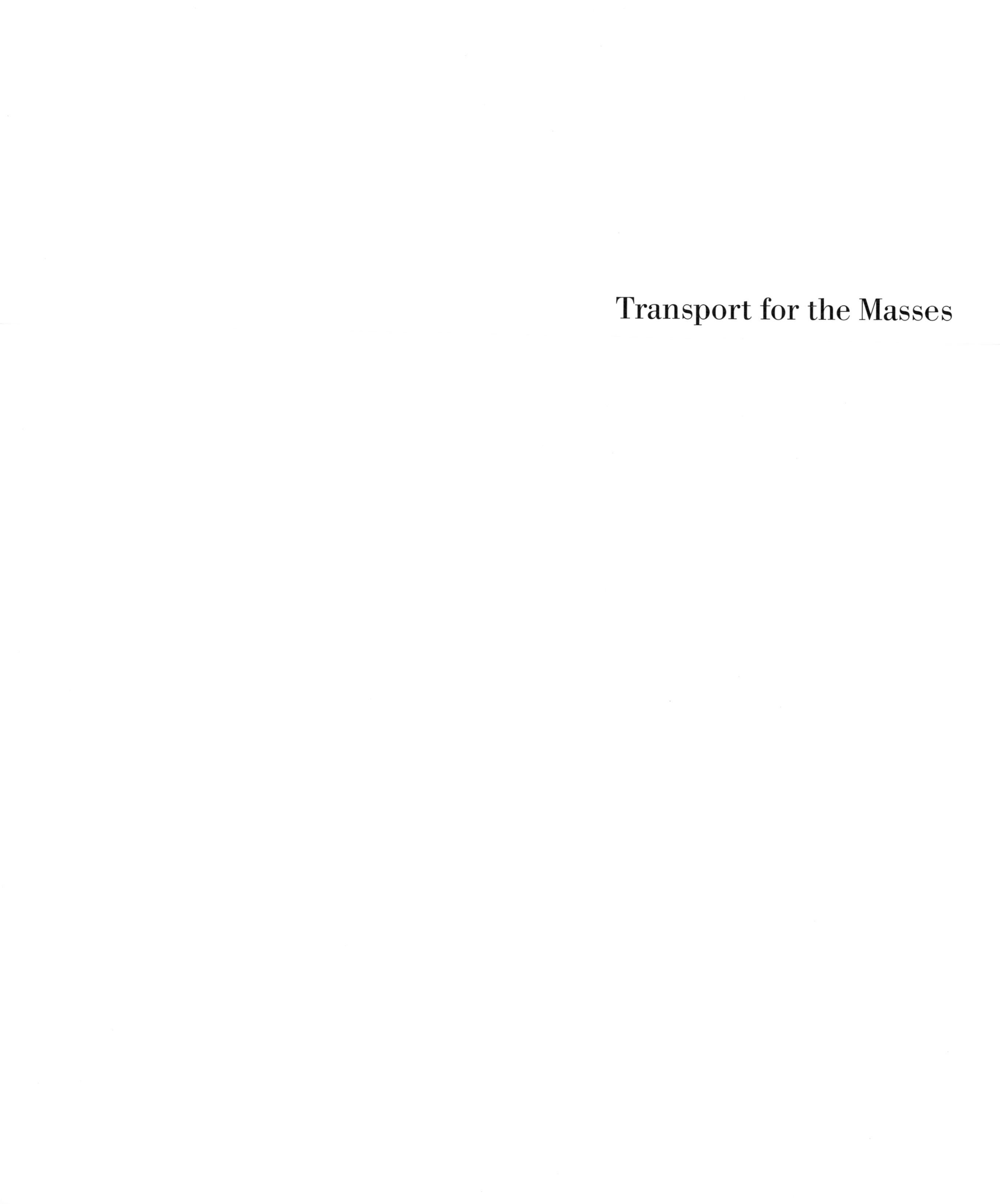

Transport for the Masses

Ford

Model T, 1908

- *Make and Model*
Ford Model T
- *Year of production*
1908
- *Coachwork*
Runabout (two-seater torpedo)
- *Engine*
In-line four-cylinder, side valves
- *Bore and stroke / Engine displacement*
95 x 101.5 mm / 2890 cc
- *Maximum power*
22 b.h.p. at 1600 rpm
- *Top speed*
60 kph (37 mph)
- *Dimensions*
Length 3350 mm, width 1770 mm, height 219 mm, wheelbase 2552 mm
- *Weight*
660 Kg
- *Total built*
15,007,033 (all models)

Villafranca di Verona, Museo Nicolis dell'Auto, della Tecnica, della Meccanica
Photo © Museo Nicolis, Villafranca di Verona

The model on show dates from 1917

'I will build a motor car for the great multitude. It will be large enough for the family but small enough for the individual to run and care for. It will be constructed of the best materials, by the best men to be hired, after the simplest designs that modern engineering can devise. But it will be so low in price that no man making a good salary will be unable to own one, and enjoy with his family the blessing of hours of pleasure in God's great open spaces.' Thus wrote Henry Ford, and this is exactly what he did. After having maddened the population of Detroit in the last years of the 19th century by driving around in a powered quadricycle (the city mayor was obliged to grant him a special permit, effectively making Ford the first person in America to have a driving licence), Henry Ford set up the Ford Motor Company in 1903 with the financial help of about ten partners. With the fixed idea of 'motorising America,' Ford immediately focused production almost exclusively on cheap vehicles: the Model T (popularly known as the 'Tin Lizzie') was presented in America in October 1908, and immediately after in Europe at the London Show. Simple, reliable, robust and light, the Model T had interchangeable bodywork, a four-cylinder engine with epicyclic gearbox with two speeds and reverse, a pedal-operated clutch (serving only to start moving), mechanical brakes on the rear wheels, and worm-gear steering. There was no fuel pump because the tank was placed higher than the carburettor, which it fed simply through gravity. Finally, and for the first time, the steering wheel was placed on the left-hand side both to provide a better view of the road when overtaking and to enable the driver to get out on the clean side of the road.
The quality of the materials was always accompanied by simplicity, and everything was made to agree with the motto 'whatever isn't there can't break.' Not for this was the Model T lacking in comfort; besides, anyone could modify and personalise it: over 5000 different accessories were created for this model in the 19 years of production. But the true revolution, the one that enabled Henry Ford to produce a car such a low price, was the use for the first time in the car industry, of the assembly line. This was 1913 and the time needed to build a single car changed suddenly from around 12 hours to little more than an hour and half. With 15 million examples built between 1908 and 1927, the Ford T is the one car that truly revolutionized the car sector.
(H.S.)

Ford

Volkswagen

Käfer (Beetle), 1938

• *Make and Model*
Volkswagenwerk Kafër type 11 to Export
• *Year of production*
1950
• *Coachwork*
Saloon
• *Engine*
Four-cylinder boxer
• *Bore and stroke / Engine displacement*
75 x 64 mm / 1131 cc
• *Maximum power*
25 b.h.p. at 3300 rpm
• *Top speed*
105 kph (65 mph)
• *Dimensions*
Length 4070 mm, width 1540 mm, height 1550 mm, wheelbase 2400 mm
• *Weight*
720 Kg
• *Total built*
About 21 million

Autostadt GmbH

The model on show dates from 1950

In 1930, Ferdinand Porsche set up a design company in Stuttgart. This produced two designs for small cars, produced for Zündapp and NSU — four-seaters with a rear-mounted engine placed within an aerodynamic form — and paved the way for a mass-produced car for the German people, the project for which the Porsche company became responsible.
The state decided that the project would be carried forward by the German Labour Front via its company dedicated to free time, Kraft durch Freude (Strength through joy), which also provided the model's name.
The outlines of the design had already been finalized by about 1930 by Porsche's own bodywork designer, Erwin Komenda, while he was working for Daimler-Benz.
In that original design, however, no running board existed between the wings. The headlights, no longer adjuncts to the bodywork, were integrated within the wings.
As an aesthetic touch, Komenda included rounded lines on both the bonnet and the boot lid. The split rear windscreen, characterized by the central strut, perhaps foresaw the application of a stabilizing fin.
In the place of a wooden chassis with sheet metal panels, a lightweight bodyshell welded to a floorpanwas envisaged.
The car was fitted with an air-cooled four-cylinder boxer engine, designed to cope with on the new motorways.
The car was equipped with independent torsion bar suspension on all four wheels. After many tests, the 1938 model, now ready for mass-production, with a drag coefficient of 0.385 Cx, was put into production in 1946 by the British occupation forces in Germany. Production of the Käfer (Beetle) finally ceased in the Mexico plant on 30th July 2003, having become a cult object over the years, with a record figure of 21 million examples built.
(R.J.F.K.)

1950
AUTOSTADT

1950

Citroën

T.P.V. (Toute petite voiture), 1939

• *Make and Model*
Citroën 2CV
• *Year of production*
1948
• *Coachwork*
Four-door saloon
• *Engine*
Air-cooled 2-cylinder boxes
• *Bore and stroke / Engine displacement*
62 x 62 mm / 375 cc
• *Maximum power*
9 b.h.p. at 3500 rpm
• *Top speed*
65 kph (40 mph)
• *Dimensions*
Length 3780 mm, width 1480 mm,
height 1600 mm, wheelbase 2400 mm
• *Weight*
495 Kg
•*Total built*
128,685 (type 2CV A)

Citroën

The technical characteristics refer to the model manufactured as of 1948

It has been written that the 2CV, affectionately nicknamed 'Deuche' by the French (from 'deux chevaux' or 'two horses'), is not a car but a way of life: for sure, it represents essentiality and simplicity in its purest state. Anyone who has driven it even once will remember it for the rest of his life.
In 1922, the Michelin brothers, owners of the tyre company, launched the first market investigation in Europe to discover the characteristics required of an economical car. The results were that it had to be large within, with four seats, be able to transport 50 kilos and be cheap. They could not have imagined that a quarter of a century later, they would produce exactly the car to meet these requisites. Having become majority shareholders in Citroën as a result of unpaid credits, it was they who requested a design for a '4 roues sous un parapluie' ('four wheels beneath an umbrella'). Like the 'KdF' car wanted by Hitler for Germany, the project for the 2CV was also started before the Second World War; a first prototype was already tested on the road in 1937 and by May 1939 about 250 pre-production cars were ready for the launch. The outbreak of war stopped everything: very little is left of those 250 cars today, with their even more basic bodywork, single headlight and tail-light, an external starting handle and canvas roof. The water-cooled engine was a two-cylinder unit able to push the car only up to about 50 kph (31 mph). The seats for four passengers were essentially bent metal tubes with canvas stretched over them.
The idea of a light, robust, spartan, economical and cheap car survived the war and the project was picked up again and improved, thanks to the intervention of two Italians who had already worked in France for some time: Walter Becchia, who redesigned the layout of the mechanical components with four independent wheels, a two-cylinder, air-cooled engine and four-speed gearbox, plus an electric starter; and Flaminio Bertoni, who did not overturn the original design but came up with a more harmonious one.
Three examples of the revised 2CV were the main attraction at the Paris Salon of 1948. Like everyone else in Europe, the French aspired to a new life and wanted to forget the dark years of the war; a car was one of their prime desires.
The trade press and industry in general, including the concessionaires, did not seem too keen on the new model but the commercial success was extraordinary: the first deliveries were effected in 1949 and by 1950 the average waiting list for a 2CV had grown to six years! The 2CV remained in production in various series (including the Mehari and Dyane) until 1990, with almost seven million being built in all.
(H.S.)

1939
2 cv T.P.V
1939
2 cv T.P.V

Fiat

600, 1955

• *Make and Model*
Fiat 600
• *Year of production*
1955
• *Coachwork*
Two-door saloon
• *Engine*
Push-rod four-cylinder
• *Bore and stroke / Engine displacement*
60 x 56 mm / 633 cc
• *Maximum power*
21.5 b.h.p. at 4600 rpm
• *Top speed*
Over 95 kph (59 mph)
• *Dimensions*
Length 3215 mm, width 1380 mm, height 1405 mm, wheelbase 2000 mm
• *Weight*
590 Kg
• *Total built*
Over 2.5 million (all series)

Turin, Centro Storico Fiat
Photo Franco Turcati

Pictured is the wooden styling buck

March 1955, Salon de l'Automobile, Geneva: Fiat presents the 600. The project for the 'little four-seater car,' as Fiat itself described the car in its press release at the time, actually began life a long time before, back in 1951, when the engineer, Dante Giacosa, was commissioned to design a utility vehicle to replace the old and glorious 'Topolino.' The instructions were simple and clear: four seats in a car no larger than the 500, light, safe, robust, with low fuel consumption and low operating costs, but offering sprightly performance.

Giacosa was given carte blanche as to the design; he opted for the rear-engined solution (as Ferdinand Porsche had done in the 1930s for the Beetle, and Renault for its 4CV in 1946) and designed the car that put Italy on wheels during the boom years. The chassis was a monocoque and the location of the engine and gearbox at the rear made it possible to do away with the transmission tunnel and so increase the space within. With no rear axle, all four wheels were independent and this helped assure excellent road-holding. The power of the 21.5 b.h.p. engine ensured a top speed of over 95 kph (59 mph) and a consumption of six litres per 100 km. The retail price at the date of launch was fixed at lire 590,000 (less than the 500 C Topolino), although on the road it would actually cost lire 621,000. The only optional extras that were charged for were white-wall tyres and a radio.

Despite the fact that the wheelbase remained the same as the Topolino (2000 mm) and the overall length (3215 mm) even less than that of the Belvedere, there were four comfortable seats, and baggage could in part be placed behind the back seat and in part under the front bonnet, alongside the petrol tank.

The design was characterized by forward opening doors ('suicide doors' as they were dubbed in Britain), by sliding windows (replaced in 1957 with wind-up ones) and by indicators on the wings above the headlights.

The production line at Mirafiori was expanded and production capacity increased to 1300 cars a day (including the 1100, 1400/1900 models). The first series of the two-door 600, built until 1960, boasted a production run of 890,000 examples; the second series, denominated 600 D and fitted with a 767 cc engine, would be built until 1970, with over 1.6 examples made.
(H.S.)

Trabant

P 600 ('P 60 Kombi-Sonderwunsch'), 1958

• *Make and Model*
AutoUnion DKW Trabant P 600
• *Year of production*
1958
• *Coachwork*
Estate (Karrossoriewerk Meerane)
• *Engine*
In-line, air-cooled two-cylinder
• *Bore and stroke / Engine displacement*
72 x 73 mm / 594 cc
• *Maximum power*
23 b.h.p. at 3900 rpm
• *Top speed*
95 kph (59 mph)
• *Dimensions*
Length 3360 mm, width 1493 mm,
height 1460 mm, wheelbase 2020 mm
• *Weight*
660 Kg
• *Total built*
36,244 examples of the Universal/Camping model

Verein Internationales Trabant Register e.V. 'InterTrab'

The model on show dates from 1965

In the German Democratic Republic car industry, the small cars produced by AutoUnion DKW served as a basis for new lower and middle-category vehicles.
A number of projects were started to this end from 1953 onwards to produce a three-box four-seater car. Because of the lack of raw materials, much of the panelling had to be made of plastic, as in the case of the type 70 built in what was then the Audi plant at Zwickau.
The preliminary designs for this car were to be compared with the small vehicles produced by other European makers, so both front and rear-mounted engine versions were taken into consideration.
In 1958, the definitive model of the small car was presented, fitted with a front-mounted two-stroke engine, and called Trabant (satellite). A competition with prizes was held to choose the name which recalls the Soviet idea of the Sputnik.
The indication of the model, P 50, is linked to the cylinder size, totalling 500 cc. As a later development, a model in two colours was offered. From this point of view, the later P 500 and P 600 presented only a number of technical improvements. The P 601 model was the last incarnation of the Trabant and featured a more angular treatment of the roof and tail, and a more modern trapezoidal radiator grille. Between 1964 and 1989, there were many other detail changes.
An open-top version was also designed, called the Phaeton, as well as an estate, later rebaptised Universal by AutoUnion DKW in Ingolstadt. The coupé model never made it to production.
Designs for more modern Trabants were presented from the 1960s onwards by industrial designers such as Claus Dietel, but never saw the light of day. The design for the Trabant remained unchanged until the reunification with Germany in 1989, which transformed this car into a cult object, and the symbol of the German Democratic Republic.
(R.J.F.K.)

Volkswagen

Golf GTI, 1974

• *Make and Model*
Volkswagenwerk Golf GTI
• *Year of production*
1974
• *Coachwork*
Hatchback (Italdesign Giugiaro)
• *Engine*
Transverse, in-line four-cylinder
• *Bore and stroke / Engine displacement*
1600 cc
• *Maximum power*
110 b.h.p. at 6100 rpm
• *Top speed*
About 182 kph (113 mph)
• *Dimensions*
Length 3705 mm, width 1628 mm,
height 1390 mm, wheelbase 2400 mm
• *Weight*
868 Kg
• *Total built*
1

Italdesign Giugiaro
Photo Italdesign Giugiaro archive

The model on show is a 'special' version built for Giugiaro with GTI running gear and four-door bodywork

The Volkswagen planning and design centres had been working for decades on the creation of a model that could prove a worthy replacement for the Beetle.
After many internal designs dating from the 1960s and 1970s, Volkswagen commissioned an Italian designer, Giorgetto Giugiaro, to help. Giugiaro had founded his Italdesign company in 1968, and it was his design for a compact car called the Golf that won the day. This two-box hatchback, with a sharply sloping rear, featured the typically square lines of the 1970s. For the production model, small modifications were made to improve its aerodynamics. The slender front end included bumpers, headlights and air intake for the radiator cooling the transverse, water-cooled engine.
The Volkswagen type 17 was presented in March 1974. Despite its compact dimensions, it offered enough space to carry a family and their luggage. The new model proved a hit with the public, thanks also to its front-wheel-drive and low weight, which ensured excellent performance.
The great success of the Golf following its launch (so great that it soon took over the place of the Beetle) was such that a more sporty version was soon in the pipeline.
The suffix GTI for 'Grand Tourisme Injektion' was added to the Golf name. Performance was so good in part thanks to the improvements made to the chassis and in part to the injection system; top speed was around 182 kph (113 mph), which, for the year the car was presented, 1976, was quite exceptional. This model could be distinguished by the lettering and by the front spoiler which helped reduce lift at speed. The one-off, non-running example displayed here, features an interior like that of the Italdesign Lancia Megagamma and is fitted with a GTI engine.
(R.J.F.K.)

GTI
GIUGIARO Golf GTI

VOLKSWAGEN
GOLF GTI
GIUGIARO Golf GTI

Fiat

Panda 30, 1980

• *Make and Model*
Fiat Panda 30
• *Year of production*
1980
• *Coachwork*
Two-box, three-doorhatchback
• *Engine*
Air-cooled, in-line two-cylinder
• *Bore and stroke / Engine displacement*
77 x 70 mm / 652 cc
• *Maximum power*
30 b.h.p. at 5500 rpm
• *Top speed*
Over 115 kph (71 mph)
• *Dimensions*
Length 3380 mm, width 1460 mm,
height 1445 mm, wheelbase 2160 mm
• *Weight*
650 Kg

Italdesign Giugiaro
Photo Italdesign Giugiaro archive

The model on show is the clay model

After having designed the cars that put Italy on wheels before and after the Second World War — the Balilla, the Topolino, the 600 and the Nuova 500 — Fiat decided to commission the design for the 'Tipo Zero' (the in-house name used to identify the new project) from an external company. Giorgetto Giugaro's Italdesign was given few but precise indications: the now-dated 126 was to be replaced by a more European car which, for the same cost, would offer more comfort and more functionality. The 'Tipo Zero' was to mark the return of Fiat to the top rankings in the sector offering cheap but highly versatile cars.
By the holiday period in the summer of 1976, Giugiaro had defined the outline of the new Fiat utility vehicle: not by concentrating simply, as in the past, on small size, but by seeking to gain the maximum amount of space with the minimum cost.
By September, the first models were ready as was, above all, a schematic dummy of the cabin; the exterior, the bodywork, had become a shell, a mini container, a functional, spartan and essential envelope.
The first working prototype was built by September 1977, Little more than a year after the start of the project and could take a variety of engines, as per Fiat's request. The Panda, the 'large utility vehicle' as it was described in the advertising, was presented at the Geneva Show of 1980. The square lines with the high cabin and flat windscreen, the clam-shell bonnet which provided easy access to the mechanical parts and the protective plastic coverings all round gave the car a new but pleasing line, which gained favour with the public. The bare interior, with accessories reduced to minimum, did not seem that of a car only 3.38 metres long as it offered abundant space both in terms of height and length. Moreover, the simple front seats and rear bench offered a variety of adaptable solutions including the transportation of bulky loads. With the aim of respecting target price, all of this required considerable research, including in terms of construction methods.
As for operating costs, the Panda 30 proved extremely sparing in consumption when compared to all of its European and other competitors. This was another of the targets achieved by Giugiaro and Fiat. The original Panda went out of production recently, and is missed by all those who have used and appreciated it over the years. We believe that in future it will be remembered with the same affection as the 500.
(H.S.)

Fiat Panda

FIAT

Multi-purpose Vehicles

A.L.F.A.

40/60 HP 'Ricotti,' 1914

• *Make and Model*
A.L.F.A. 40/60 HP
• *Year of production*
1914
• *Coachwork*
'Ricotti' aerodynamic drop (Castagna)
• *Engine*
In-line four-cylinder, twin-block, overhead valves
• *Bore and stroke / Engine displacement*
110 x 160 mm / 6082 cc
• *Maximum power*
70 b.h.p. at 2200 rpm
• *Top speed*
139 kph (86 mph)
• *Dimensions*
Length 5500 mm, width 1700 mm, height 2230, wheelbase 3200 mm
• *Weight*
1000 Kg
• *Total built*
1

Arese (Milan), Automobilismo Storico Alfa Romeo, Museo Storico, Centro di Documentazione Storica
Photo © Automobilismo Storico Alfa Romeo, Centro di Documentazione Storica

The A.L.F.A. (Anonima Lombarda Fabbrica Automobili) was founded in Milan in 1910 and began production in the factory at Portello, formerly owned by Darracq Italiana; the first Alfa vehicle was the 24 HP, a four-cylinder 4-litre engine of 42 b.h.p., which stood out for its excellent performance.

1913 saw the presentation of the first 'big' Alfa to offer distinguished sporty performance, the 40/60 HP (the name was derived from its notional horsepower, not the actual power), designed by Giuseppe Merosi, responsible also for the earlier models. The modern engine with overhead valves and two camshafts (one per block of cylinders) delivered 70 b.h.p., enabling the ordinary family torpedoes to achieve a top speed of 125 kph (78 mph); the 'racing' version had a 73 b.h.p. engine and with light roadster bodywork, could achieve 150 kph (93 mph).

Among the sporting customers of the new manufacturer was Conte Marco Ricotti; he had a passion for speed and to satisfy it, he decided to buy one of the new 40/60 HP chassis and have coachwork built by Carrozzeria Castagna, also of Milan.

From the outset, the car industry had sought ways to reduce drag as a car travelled and the first studies in aerodynamics had led to the adoption of symmetrical 'torpedo'-like bodies, like the 'Jamais Contente,' and of drop-shaped ones.

Castagna opted for a drop shape and Conte Ricotti's car was prepared at the beginning of 1914; with the standard 70 b.h.p. engine, the vehicle achieved the noteworthy speed of 139 kph (86 mph), no less than 14 kph (8 mph) more than the standard production car.

Satisfied with having achieved the aim he had set himself, in 1915 Conte Ricotti had the car transformed into a torpedo, simply by removing the roof. Unfortunately, all trace was lost of the car in the years that followed and only at the end of the 1970s did the directors of Alfa decide to build a replica in memory of the original.

The 'Ricotti,' although designed with the shape it has for aerodynamic reasons, is considered the archetype of the 'multi-purpose' vehicles that have borrowed from its basic form to obtain increased space for passengers and their baggage.

(H.S.)

Alfa

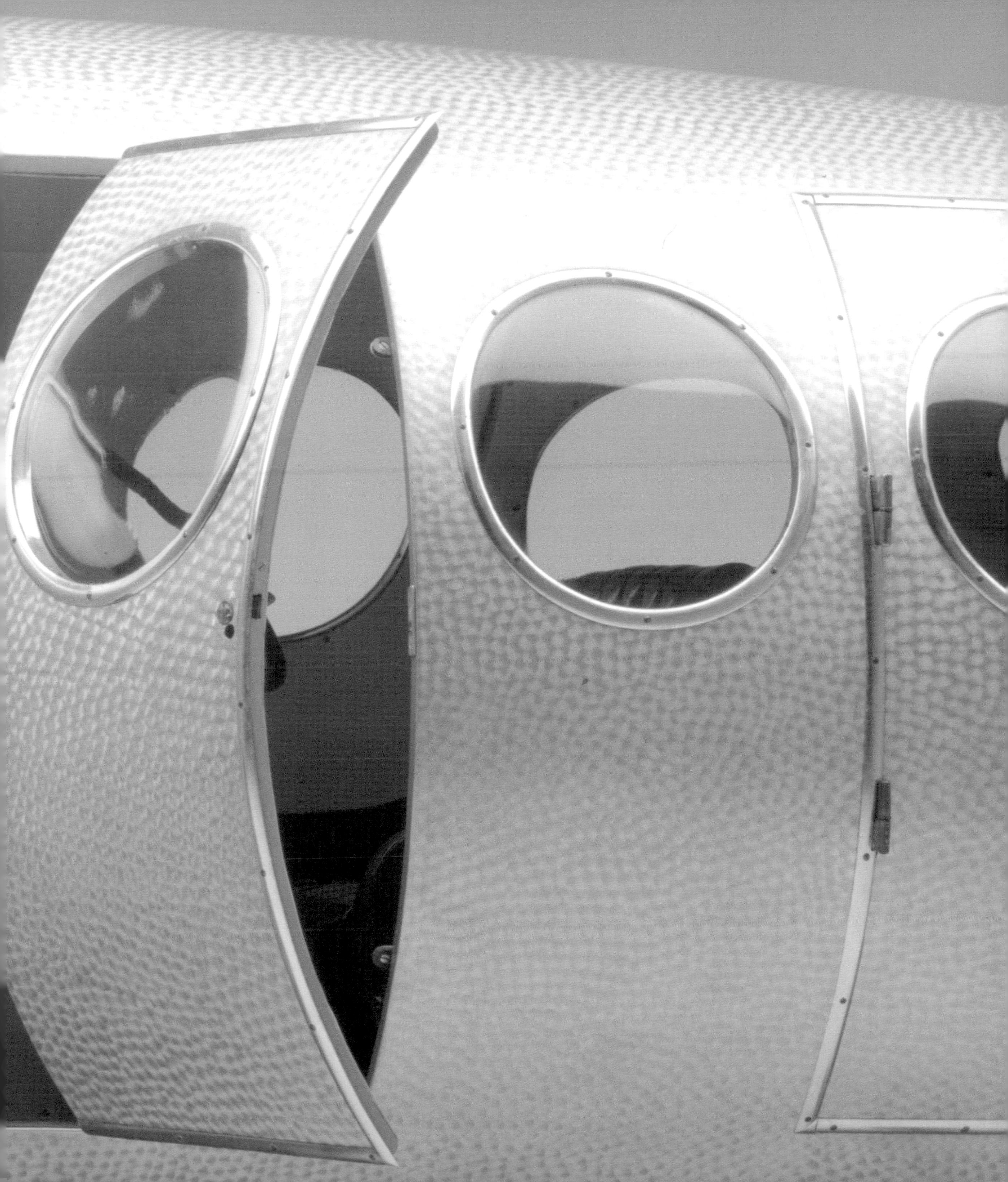

Fiat

600 Multipla, 1956

- *Make and Model*
Fiat 600 Multipla
- *Year of production*
1956
- *Coachwork*
Four-door MPV
- *Engine*
Push-rod four-cylinder
- *Bore and stroke / Engine displacement*
60 x 56 mm / 633 cc
- *Maximum power*
21.5 b.h.p. at 4600 rpm
- *Top speed*
90 kph (56 mph)
- *Dimensions*
Length 3535 mm, width 1450 mm, height 1580 mm, wheelbase 2000 mm
- *Weight*
1150 Kg
- *Total built*
About 243,000 (first and second series)

Turin, Centro Storico Fiat
© Photo Diego Cassetta – Mart

A year after the presentation of the 600, Fiat realized it had hit the bull's-eye, and in the wake of the success of the two-door saloon, presented the first variation on the theme at the Brussels Salon of 1956: the Multipla.
From a mechanical point of view, the sole difference with the saloon lay in the front axle, which with a few modifications made use of that of the 1100/103.
All the real changes were in the bodywork. The car became a four-door; the front boot, which was filled mainly by the fuel tank in the saloon version, was done away with here and the driving position shifted forwards, like in some trucks, with the difference that the driver and the passenger did not dominate the road from above but were sat much lower down: with today's safety regulations, the Multipla would clearly fail any crash test and would not be allowed to take to the road.
Fiat's objective, however, was to increase the space in the cabin to offer various solutions (hence the name), and in this it was successful: the Multipla could be used to carry five passengers plus luggage, could be fitted with three bench seats to seat six, could transport bulky loads by removing the rear seat and, finally, could be used as taxi to carry five passengers plus their luggage in the space alongside the driver. Who can forget the green and black Multipla taxis outside the Stazione Centrale in Milan?
The overall length of the vehicle grew a little, but it remained only 32 cm longer than the two-door saloon, and the wheelbase (2000 mm) remained unchanged.
Because of the increased weight and drag compared to the saloon, the Multipla had a slightly lower top speed and higher consumption.
After 1951, Volkswagen were offering the Typ 2 Samba Bus, but this derived from an earlier commercial vehicle; the Multipla, on the other hand, may be considered the grandmother of modern multi-purpose vehicles, which in the 1980s would spawn a new category of car.
The only earlier attempt at something similar occurred in the 1930s, when an American company, Stout, brought out the Scarab, of which only five were built.
The original exterior appearance may be thought unappealing, but it was certainly functional for the purpose for which it had been designed.
(H.S.)

Multipla
FIAT

ACQUA
0 20 30 40 50 60 70 80 90 100 110
BENZINA

Italdesign Giugiaro

Megagamma, 1978

• *Make and Model*
Lancia Megagamma
• *Year of production*
1978
• *Coachwork*
Four-door MPV
• *Engine*
Four-cylinder boxes
• *Bore and stroke / Engine displacement*
102 x 76 mm / 2484 cc
• *Maximum power*
140 b.h.p. at 6000 rpm
• *Dimensions*
Length 4310 mm, width 1780 mm, height 1617 mm, wheelbase 2670 mm
• *Weight*
1550 Kg
• *Total built*
1

Italdesign Giugiaro
Photo Italdesign Giugiaro archive

In the 1970s, for some users, the car began to lose its lustre as a status symbol and became an everyday tool. In 1972, MoMA in New York exhibited a car with the paradoxical name 'Kar-a-Sutra,' the work of a designer called Mario Bellini, sponsored by Cassina.
It is significant that the first innovative proposal for a multi-purpose vehicle should come not from someone working in the car sector, but from an architect and a company producing padded furniture. Bellini overturned the concept of car design: it was the soft, modular interior that would prevail over the traditional exterior. Bellini proclaimed: 'we need to overturn the parameters of the Car-Man system and bring it back to being a Human Mobile Space destined for human rites rather than car ones: a space in which it is possible to enter, sit down; sit down even more comfortably, lie down, sleep, smile, converse while looking at each other, observe the world outside, breathe it in, enjoy the sun, stand up, film whilst moving, change seat, sit in the opposite direction, or even across, play cards, eat a sandwich and have a drink using a tray, consult a map, pull out and replace anything, carry children, play with them, make non-automotive love, carry luggage and things, lots of things and less people, plus the driver…' This is the manifesto of the multi-purpose vehicle.
In 1976, MoMA asked Giugiaro for a prototype of city taxi to display in an exhibition entitled *The Taxi Project: realistic solutions for today*. With this project, Giugiaro abandoned any aesthetic research in favour of function; the increase in height enabled him to increase comfort within, at the same time making it easier to get in and out of the vehicle, and this in a car that is shorter than the taxis in use (then and now) in the Big Apple. Giorgetto Giugiaro has always been responsive to changes in society: with the Megagamma, presented at the Turin Show of 1978, he developed the concept of the taxi for a car intended for private use. Although starting with a standard chassis, that of the Lancia Gamma, the designer managed to create a flat floor, using the space beneath to house the fuel tank and spare tyre. The height increased from 1370 to 1617 mm, the length dropped from 4600 to 4310 mm, the driving position was moved up and forward for improved visibility. Seats and luggage were on a flat surface, making it easy to embark and disembark passengers and to load any luggage. The lines recall those of the Golf and the Panda. Here was an intelligent proposal offered free of charge to any car manufacturer with the ability to look forward. It would be the Japanese industry, with the Mitsubishi Chariot (1982) and the Nissan Prairie (1983), that would draw inspiration from the proposal by the Turinese designer for the first standard multi-purpose vehicles of the modern era. *(H.S.)*

Renault

Espace, 1984

• *Make and Model*
Renault Espace
• *Year of production*
1984
• *Coachwork*
Four-door MPV
• *Engine*
In-line four-cylinder, single overhead camshaft
• *Bore and stroke / Engine displacement*
88 x 82 mm / 1995 cc
• *Maximum power*
110 b.h.p. at 5500 rpm
• *Top speed*
175 kph (108 mph)
• *Dimensions*
Length 4250 mm, width 1770 mm,
height 1660 mm, wheelbase 2580 mm
• *Weight*
1221 Kg
• *Total built*
Still in production

Renault
Photo Renault communication

Following the presentation of the Megagamma (1978, Lancia components, Giugiaro design), mother of modern multi-purpose vehicles, the first to capitalize on this innovative proposal which opened a new market niche were the Japanese manufacturers. Almost at the same time, two similar vehicles were presented, one in America by the Chrysler group (the Voyager), and the other in Europe by Renault (the Espace). Renault took over a project by Matra, which would subsequent build the car, and in 1984 presented the first mass-produced European multi-purpose vehicle, which enjoyed an immediate success.
The Espace stood out from its Japanese and American counterparts for two reasons, one to do with style and the other with construction. Stylistically, the windscreen and engine bonnet formed a straight line, while in the other models (including the Megagamma) the bonnet still had a different angle, recalling the volumes of a traditional vehicle. The bodyshell of the car was made of a galvanized steel metal skeleton, to which were fixed fibreglass panels with layers of polyester resin; this enabled a considerable reduction in the overall weight of the car. Everything was designed to provide maximum space and comfort within the cabin, from the volume of the actual body itself to the position of the engine and the characteristics of the other mechanical components. The considerable height of the floor pan off the ground made it easier to climb into the cabin and the raised driving position offered improved visibility of the road. The seats were laid out in three rows and seated seven passengers; the two front seats could be spun around 180° to create a sort of welcoming little living room. It was even possible to use the folded central seat of the second row as a small table. By folding over both the second and the third row of seats, one could obtain a long loading bay with a capacity of about 3000 cubic decimetres. The Espace is a car in every way, able to carry a family and luggage, or customers on a promotional tour, or a mass of packages for delivery. It has been more successful than other, similar vehicles because it has maintained performance and comfort similar to those of normal cars, unlike its competitors which suffered from being derivations of commercial vehicles.
The tester for *Quattroruote* magazine wrote the following about the 'road-holding': 'The Espace handles as well, if not better than a true car,' and awarded it five stars, the maximum possible. This was a well-designed, successful model because it took advantage of a change in the way cars are used and perceived. But success only comes when you get a car right, and Renault did.
(H.S.)

The Creative Process

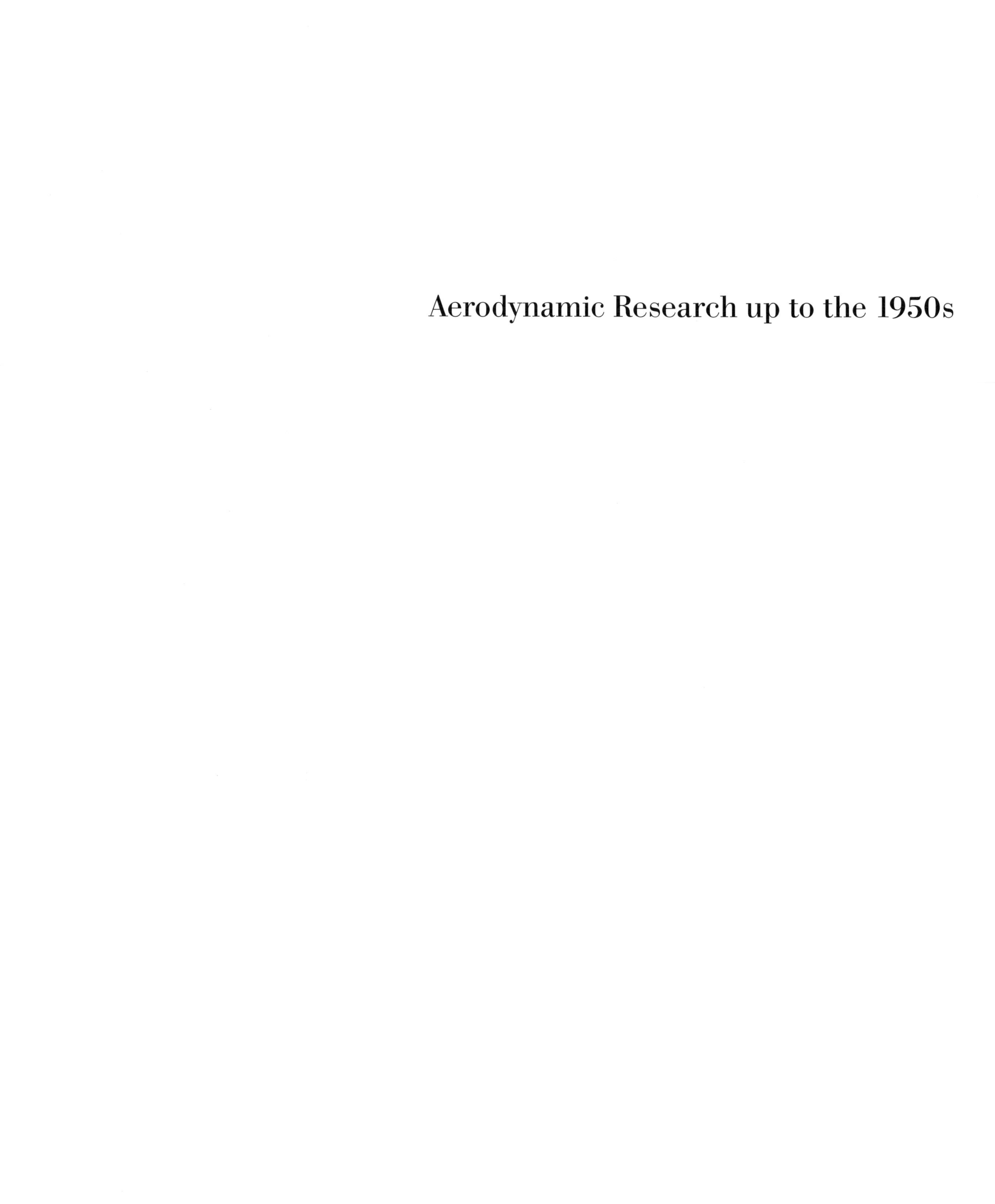

Aerodynamic Research up to the 1950s

Avions Voisin

C6 Laboratoire, 1923

• *Make and Model*
Voisin C6 Laboratoire
• *Year of production*
1923
• *Coachwork*
Grand Prix two-seater
• *Engine*
Sleeve-valve in-line six-cylinder
• *Bore and stroke / Engine displacement*
110 x 62 mm / 1984 cc
• *Maximum power*
80 b.h.p. at 4800 rpm
• *Top speed*
175 kph (108 mph)
• *Dimensions*
Length 4800 mm, width 1450 mm, height 800 mm, wheelbase 2720 mm
• *Weight*
660 Kg
• *Total built*
6

Moch Collection

The model on show is a replica, as no originals survive

At the 1922 Grand Prix organized by the Automobile Club de France, Gabriel Voisin saw the eight-cylinder Bugatti with 'cigar' bodywork in action, and was aware that for 1923 the 'Patron,' Ettore Bugatti, was preparing an aerodynamic car with revolutionary lines. Encouraged by the success achieved in 1922 by his cars in numerous road and circuit races, at the beginning of 1923 Gabriel Voisin decided to build a completely new car to take part in the A.C.F. Grand Prix to be held in July at Tours. The Grand Prix circuit was something completely new for him, a challenge to be faced in order to gain fame and visibility for his factory, founded only in 1919. The engineers commissioned by Voisin, Marius Bernard and André Lefebvre (who would later design the Traction Avant for Citroën), came up with a metal monocoque (inspired by the 1922 Lancia Lambda), with a completely faired-in underbody almost as though to achieve a sort of ground effect years before this became the norm and with the rear track, of 750 mm, much narrower than the front, of 1450 mm.
Thanks to the load-bearing structure, the car was much lower than its competitors and the light aluminium panelling (inspired by the shape of an aircraft's wing) almost touched the ground. The long tail tapers downwards, enclosing the rear axle and wheels. The wedge-shaped front end is characterized by an upright radiator that juts out and features a fan which, turned by the air, actions the water pump.
The engine is a two-litre, straight-six unit with sleeve valves, a feature typical of all Voisin engines (the valve mechanism consisting in a sleeve outside the cylinder). The pistons were magnesium. It was not very powerful (80 b.h.p. as compared to the almost 130 b.h.p. of the Fiats and the 110 b.h.p. of the Sunbeams) but the car, which on the road weighed barely 660 kg (only 10 kg more than the minimum allowable), could achieve a top speed of 175 kph (108 mph).
The C6 Laboratoire was not a beautiful car but it served the purpose for which it was designed. It was fairly easy to drive, unlike Bugatti's new arrival, the 'Tank,' with its wheelbase of only two metres making it unstable at high speeds. However, the Laboratoire had problems with reliability: of the four cars entered, only the one driven by Lefebvre reached the finish line, in fifth place (out of 17 starters).
The unsuccessful participation in the A.C.F. Grand Prix would have two effects on Voisin: on the one hand, it strengthened his conviction of the need to build light and aerodynamic bodies, and on the other convinced him also that racing was of no use when it came to selling standard models.
The Laboratoire remains as an example of an unconventional approach to the construction of a racing car.
(H.S.)

5

Chrysler

Airflow Series CU, 1934

• *Make and Model*
Chrysler Airflow Series CU
• *Year of production*
1934
• *Coachwork*
Four-door saloon
• *Engine*
Push-rod in-line eight-cylinder
• *Bore and stroke / Engine displacement*
82.2 x 114.3 mm / 4900 cc
• *Maximum power*
122 b.h.p. at 3400 rpm
• *Top speed*
120 kph (74 mph)
• *Dimensions*
Length 5150 mm, width 1730 mm, height 1700 mm, wheelbase 3119 mm
• *Weight*
1700 Kg
• *Total built*
7226

Ingolstadt, Museum für Konkrete Kunst

The aerodynamic development carried out to reduce drag as a car moved through the air acquired great importance for manufacturers between the end of the 1920s and the early 1930s. Often, they went hand in hand with those on monocoque chassis, the new road opened by Vincenzo Lancia in 1922 with the Lambda. Two of the companies that dedicated most resources to these studies were Citroën in Europe and Chrysler in America. While Citroën, with the Traction Avant, concentrated more on the realisation of a unitary structure, Chrysler, with the Airflow, paid closer attention to the aerodynamics, building a semi-unitary structure that was cheaper to produce.
In 1927, having observed a squadron of aircraft flying, designer Carl Breer realized that some of the solutions already applied in the aeronautical industry could be exploited to improve the aerodynamic features of a car, and he spoke about this with one of the pioneers of flight, Orville Wright. He was confirmed in his thinking and as a result built a number of scale models, effecting tests in a wind tunnel with positive results. Walter Chrysler personally gave him carte blanche to continue with the design of a new car. The first working prototype was ready by the end of 1932 and the car entered production in 1934: the semi-unitary structure was formed of a sort of cage, fixed to the traditional side members, although lighter in this case, to which the bodywork panels were attached. The engine was mounted far forward, beyond the front axle, which made it possible to put all of the cabin between the axles, improving the distribution of weight between front and rear and increasing the ride comfort for passengers. As a consequence, the radiator had to be moved to the side. The drop-shaped body had a short, curved front, integrated headlights and a split windscreen. There was ritually no tail abd the rear bodywork ended little beyond the rear axle; the boot extended into the cabin towards the rear seat.
One of the advantages of this production system was that the bodywork was in effect made of three pieces: the roof and the two sides. The Airflow was offered both as a Chrysler, with an eight-cylinder engine, and as a DeSoto, with a six-cylinder engine, and the difference between the two models was limited to the bonnet.
The lines, perhaps a little too advanced for American taste of the time, did not prove very popular and the hoped-for commercial success did not appear. By 1938, the Airflow had already vanished from Chrysler's catalogue.
(H.S.)

Tatra

Type 77, 1934

• *Make and Model*
Tatra Type 77
• *Year of production*
1934
• *Coachwork*
Four-door saloon
• *Engine*
Air-cooled V8
• *Bore and stroke / Engine displacement*
75 x 84 mm / 2969 cc
• *Maximum power*
60 b.h.p. at 3500 rpm
• *Top speed*
148 kph (92 mph)
• *Dimensions*
Length 5130 mm, width 1700 mm, height 1500 mm, wheelbase 3150 mm
• *Weight*
1750 Kg
• *Total built*
Between 95 and 101

Lucerna, Verkehrshaus der Schweiz

In 1923 the Tatra factory, opened in 1850 by a carriage-builder, began to concentrate on a highly advanced concept of the car, featuring air-cooled boxer engines, a front without radiator, a backbone chassis and independent suspension. After building a prototype, the model 77 was presented in Berlin, its salient features being its stremlined bodywork, a box-section monocoque chassis, a rear-mounted V8 engine, a rear stabilising fin, central steering and independent suspension front and rear.
The designer was Hans Ledwinka, assisted by some close collaborators, including his son Erich, and the German engineer, Erich Überlacker, and they sought to obtain a licence to use the aerodynamic form from the aircraft manufacturer, Paul Jaray.
The wooden superstructure supported the steel and aluminium panels pressed under licence from Budd, inventor of the pressing process used to shape bodywork panels. The Tatra was equipped with six seats and was rather heavy, but despite a relatively small engine and limited power, the car was able to attain the almost unimaginable speed of about 150 kph (93 mph), thanks to its good air-drag coefficient. Many of the solutions employed by the Tatra were repeated in the 'Kraft durch Freude' ('Strength through joy') car, but had already been anticipated also by Bela Barenyi, who would become chief designer at Daimler-Benz.
There were a number of serious problems with regard to the air-cooling of the engine. Highly visible vents took the place of a single intake over the rear windscreen.
The Type 77 A, modified only in a few details, was replaced by the Type 87, the finest Tatra, presented in 1937. Until 1975, Tatra remained faithful to its original concept, before passing on to its next model, produced until 1998 and featuring a more angular body designed in Italy.
(R.J.F.K.)

TATRA

Avions Voisin

C 28 Clairière, 1935

• *Make and Model*
Voisin C 28 Clairière
• *Year of production*
1935
• *Coachwork*
Four-door saloon
• *Engine*
Sleeve-valve in-line six-cylinder
• *Bore and stroke / Engine displacement*
110 x 80 mm / 3317 cc
• *Maximum power*
115 b.h.p. at 3300 rpm
• *Top speed*
145 kph (90 mph)
• *Dimensions*
Length 5000 mm, width 1750 mm, height 1550 mm, wheelbase 3200 mm
• *Weight*
1200 Kg
• *Total built*
61 (all models)

Moch Collection

Despite the presentation of new models and the efforts made to back the image of the car with prestigious speed records over long distances (500 to 50,000 km), Voisin underwent a crisis from 1930, which showed no sign of letting up.
In 1934, only 92 cars were produced. However, in that same year, Gabriel Voisin once again grasped the attention of public and media like with the C 25 Aérodyne. Presented in autumn at the Paris Salon, the car was the result of considerable aerodynamic research. Many major manufacturers were presenting new models but, as had already happened in the past, Voisin showed himself to be far ahead of the competition with the Aérodyne Voisin. The bodywork of the new saloon, fitted with a 3-litre sleeve-valve straight-six, was very streamlined, with a strong, semi-circular motif shaping the flanks. The fastback tail incorporated the boot, and the roof could be opened thanks to a motor hidden in the boot. The roof featured three round apertures so that, when it moves backwards, these acted as rear windscreens. The many novelties in a single bodyshell (and presented, moreover, in a bold red and white colour) attracted the public but, although admired and appreciated, the Aérodyne did not enjoy great commercial success.
For the Salon, Voisin also launched his manifesto concerning 'la voiture de l'avenir:' a top speed of 200 kph (124 mph), maximum power of 150 b.h.p., consumption of 15 litres per 100 kilometres, a bodyshell weighing 1200 kg, star-shaped engines with five, seven and nine cylinders, monocoque bodyshell. But he was never able to develop all his plans (although a seven-cylinder star-shaped motor was ready for testing in May 1935).
In 1935, he presented a new car: the C 28, in Normal and Aérosport versions. As regards bodywork, the latter was a development of the Aérodyne and was the first car to have integral wings; it has been defined as the last great Voisin. The C 28 range, equipped with the usual sleeve-valve straight-six, now displaced 3.3 litres and developed 115 b.h.p., and was fitted to various two and four-door saloons; the small, formal saloon called the 'Clairière' did not bear any of the extreme stylistic features of the other creations but nevertheless had a design typical of the parentage of the most original French manufacturer of the 1930s, and nor could it be otherwise, given that the car on display here was none other than Gabriel Voisin's own car.
(H.S.)

AVIONS VOISIN

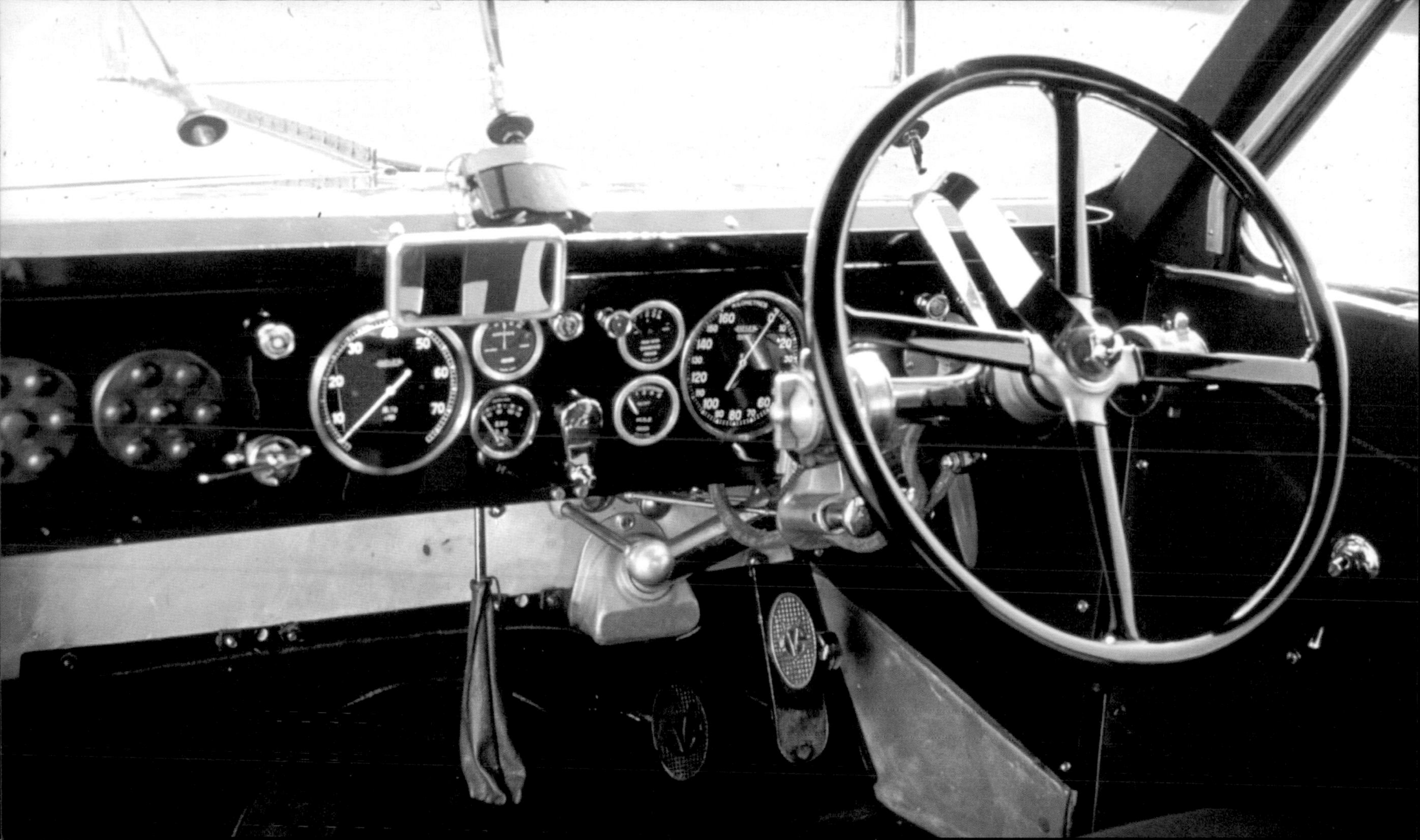

DLY
G-ADLY
DH 87 B
HORNET MOTH
1935

Lancia

Aprilia, 1937

• *Make and Model*
Lancia Aprilia
• *Year of production*
1937
• *Coachwork*
Four-door saloon
• *Engine*
Narrow V4, single overhead camshaft per bank
• *Bore and stroke / Engine displacement*
72 x 83 mm / 1352 cc
• *Maximum power*
47 b.h.p. at 4000 rpm
• *Top speed*
125 kph (77 mph)
• *Dimensions*
Length 3995 mm, width 1470 mm,
height 1455 mm, wheelbase 2750 mm
• *Weight*
850 Kg
• *Total built*
10,354 (first series type 238)

Turin, Collezione Storica Lancia
Photo La Presse Turin

'The technical testament of Vincenzo Lancia' or 'Vincenzo Lancia's last masterpiece' are the most recurrent phrases one hears when speaking of the Lancia Aprilia, presented at the London and Paris Shows of 1936 and launched on the market in the spring of 1937, a few months after the death of the company's founder. It is said that Vincenzo Lancia imposed few but clear constraints upon his designers for a new middle-of-the-range car destined to replace the Augusta: engine not to exceed 1500 cc, a speed of 130 kph (81 mph), the weight not to exceed 900 kg, the length 4 metres, and the interior was to be able to seat five.
The pursuit of these aims (successfully achieved) led the designers to produce a car that has remained a milestone in the history of mid-range cars and has contributed to the consolidation of the fame of Lancia as a company producing high-quality vehicles. The design followed the streamlined solutions of the day, ending in a short, slender tail (in the same manner as Ferdinand Porsche in Germany for Volkswagen), which made it possible to achieve the aimed-for top speed whilst limiting the overall length to less than four metres. Similarly the use of particularly thin panelling and, where possible the use of aluminium (such as the bonnet and bumpers), kept the weight down to the limits imposed.
It is interesting to note that in the 1970s, the Aprilia was tested to check its drag coefficient; the result was a good: 0.47 Cx. The research effected for the car did not limit itself to aerodynamics alone: much care was taken over details in the design of the bodywork, characterized by two doors without central pillar and of exactly the same size and with equally large windows. A crease line runs along the side of the car under the windows, follows the rear wing and joins the line on the other side beneath the boot lid. Another line runs along the roof, divides the rear window in two parts and ends in the frame around the number plate.
Like for the Lambda and Augusta, the engine fitted was a V4, redesigned with hemispherical combustion chambers and aluminium cylinder block and iron wet liners.
The chassis was fitted with independent suspension all-round and inboard rear brakes. It would appear that at the end of the first road test in 1936, Vincenzo Lancia, who had not opened his mouth during the whole experience, exclaimed: 'It's a splendid car. It has just one defect: it's too fast,' and he asked that the top speed be reduced a little, reducing it to 125 kph (77 mph).
(H.S.)

LANCIA

Alfa Romeo

8C 2900 B Berlinetta Aerodinamica Le Mans, 1938

• *Make and Model*
Alfa Romeo 8C 2900 B Berlinetta Le Mans
• *Year of production*
1938
• *Coachwork*
Aerodynamic saloon (Touring)
• *Engine*
Straight-8, with twin supercharger
• *Bore and stroke / Engine displacement*
68 x 100 mm / 2905 cc
• *Maximum power*
220 b.h.p. at 5500 rpm
• *Top speed*
220 b.h.p. at 5500 rpm
• *Dimensions*
Length 4900 mm, width 1770 mm,
height 1500 mm, wheelbase 2800 mm
• *Total built*
1

Arese (Milan), Automobilismo Storico Alfa Romeo, Museo Storico, Centro di Documentazione Storica
Photo © Automobilismo Storico Alfa Romeo, Centro di Documentazione Storica

The 24 Hours of Le Mans is one of the most important races in the history of motor racing. Alfa Romeo won no less than four consecutive races at Le Mans, from 1931 to 1934, with the 8C 2300. In 1938, in an attempt to return to its former glory, termined somewhat over the previous Grand Prix season when it had threatened the invincible 'Silver arrows' of Mercedes and Auto Union (Alfa Romeo prepared an *ad hoc* car for Le Mans, derived from the powerful 8C 2900 B). At Le Mans, it is fundamental that the highest possible speed be gained on the long straight of Hunaudières. To do this, a powerful engine is required, so that of the 8C 2900 was increased to 220 b.h.p. and fitted into a bodyshell with the loest possible drag. Given the close links that had existed for some years with Touring and the studies the coachbuilder had undertaken on aerodynamics, it was natural for Alfa Romeo Corse (whose director was Enzo Ferrari) to commission them to body the car especially as Touring was able to make use of its recently patented 'Superleggera' technology to keep weight to a minimum. The Berlinetta Aerodinamica Le Mans was highly original in form where the modern solution of integrating the front wheelarches into the bodyshell has already been adopted (a concept further developed by Touring in the 'ala spessa' spiders built over the 6C 2500 chassis), while the rear wings are more old-fashioned but elegantly stressed. The extreme bonnet contrasts with the small, narrow cockpit area, almost detached from the rest of the body, and the form of the tail, which made use of the aerodynamic studies of both Wunibald Kamm and Paul Jaray.
At 4 p.m. of 18th June 1938, standing facing their cars parked on the other side of the track, the drivers began run to their charges and the race began. The most feared rivals, as far as Alfa Romeo was concerned, were the French Delahaye and Talbot-Lago, but already by the fifth hour the Italian car, driven by Clemente Biondetti and Raymond Sommer, was one lap ahead of its nearest rival, the Talbot-Lago of the Chinetti-Etancelin pairing. The race seemed destined to be a mere parade, but unfortunately something went wrong: in the last hours of the race, with no less than 14 laps' advantage on its nearest rival, a Delahaye, the Alfa Romeo's front right tyre threw its tread. Sommer avoided a catastrophic accident, and managed to keep the car under control.
The Alfa stopped in the pits, Biondetti leaped in but was soon forced to retire with mechanical problems caused by the blow-out. And so the fifth victory of Alfa Romeo evaporated.
(H.S.)

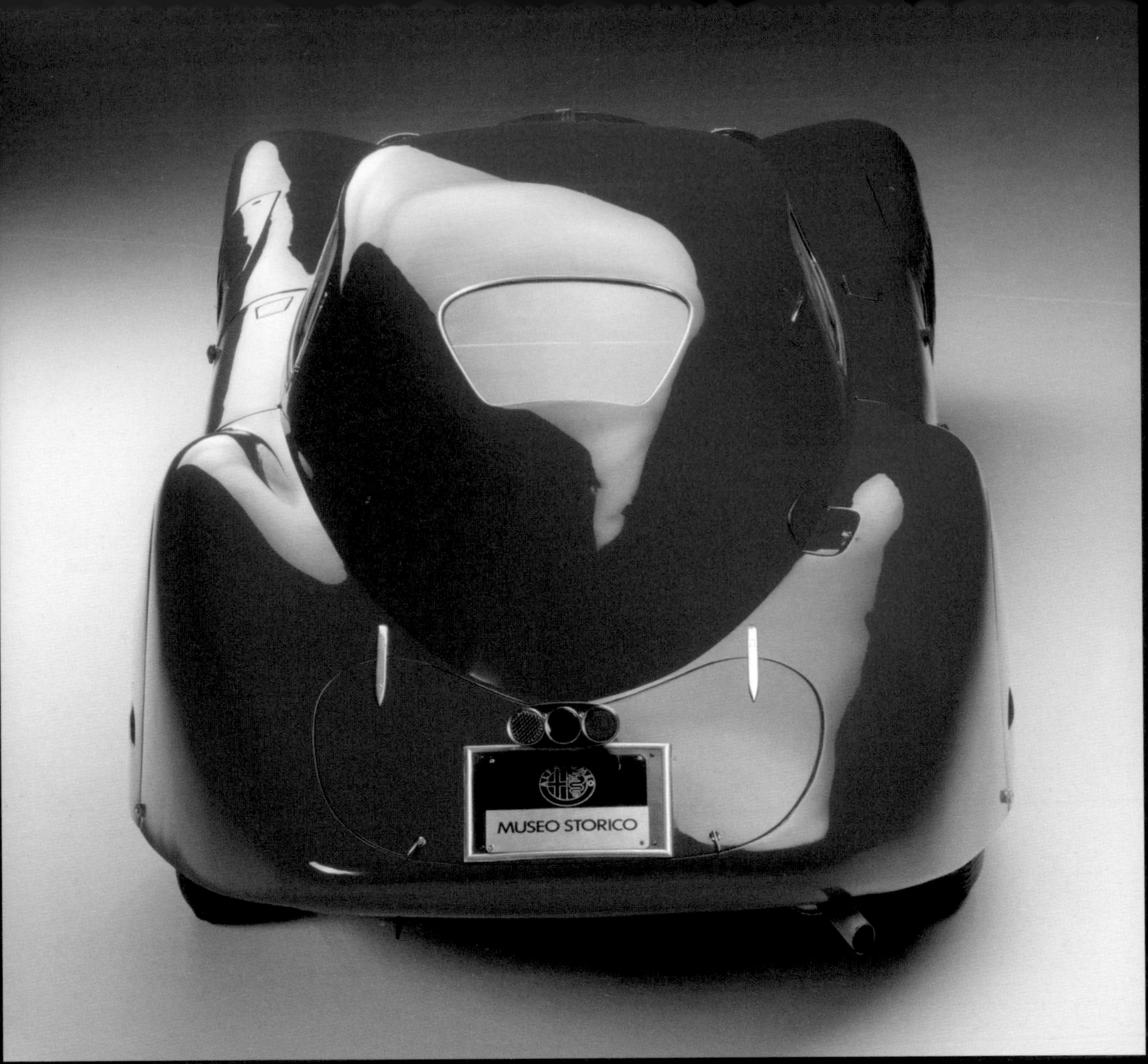

MG

EX.181, 1957

• *Make and Model*
MG EX.181
• *Year of production*
1957
• *Coachwork*
Speed record car
• *Engine*
In-line four, twin overhead camshafts, supercharged
• *Bore and stroke / Engine displacement*
1506 cc
• *Maximum power*
300 b.h.p. at 7000 rpm
• *Top speed*
410 kph (255 mph)
• *Dimensions*
Length 4610 mm, width 1632 mm,
height 972 mm, wheelbase 2438 mm
• *Weight*
866 Kg
• *Total built*
1

Gaydon, British Motor Industry Heritage Trust

Morris Garages Ltd began its activity as distributor for Morris cars and from the outset enabled customers to buy cars with special bodyshells so they could have a unique car. With the arrival of Cecil Kimber as director, work began on tuning engines to give the standard Morris cars better performance and make them sportier. The construction of the first true MG, the Old No. 1, which still exists, dates from 1925. Components derived from Morris were used for the chassis, transmission and gears box, while the engine was a Hotchkiss 1500 cc, which itself used to supply Morris. At the end of the 1920s, various private drivers began using MG for racing in the smallee categories. From 1930, the company decided to participate officially in races for small displacement engines and from 1931 also embarked in the race for speed records in the 750, 1100 and 1500 classes. In 1939, the EX135, with an aerodynamic body designed by Reid Ralton and a 1.1 litre engine exceeded 326 kph (203 mph) on a German motorway with Goldie Gardner behind the wheel.
At the end of the Second World War, MG returned to its normal activities, but also restarted its racing and record bids. In 1957, the EX. 181 was prepared for the speed record. It had an extremely light and low tear-drop shaped body with a forward driving position: the driver had to virtually lie down over the front axle, with the steering wheel in his lap. The clam-shell front was then placed over him and closed from the outside. The engine, a twin cam supercharged four-cylinder 1.5 litre unit, produced 290 b.h.p. at 7700 rpm. It was mounted centrally, right behind the driver's shoulders. There was only one disc brake, operating on the rear wheels, and to be used only to decelerate once the record bid was over.
In August 1957, driven by Stirling Moss on the salt lake of Bonneville, the car achieved a top speed of 395.30 kph (245.64 mph) over a kilometre, establishing a new record for the 1500 class.
'It was more like being inside the cockpit of a fighter plane than like driving a car,' recalled Moss of that day.
Two years later, the same car, fitted with an engine increased to 1506 cc, established the new record for the 2000 class. Driven by Phil Hill, it reached a speed of 410.22 kph (254.91 mph), becoming the fastest MG ever built.
(H.S.)

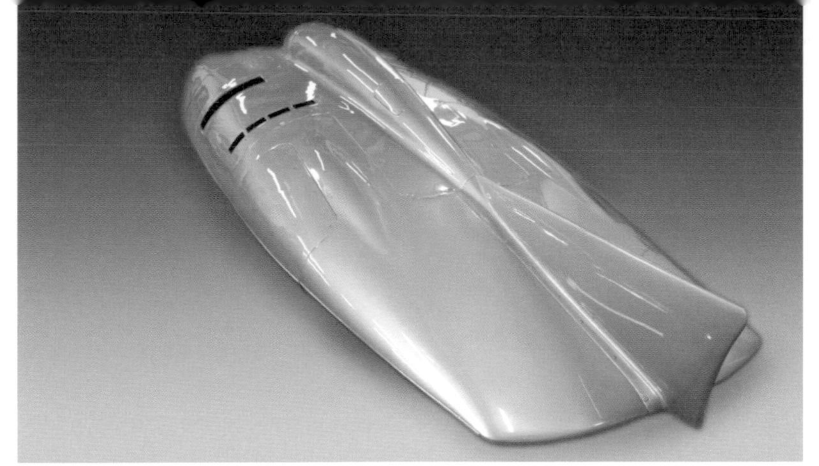

MG

MG

Concept Cars

Bertone

Carabo, 1968

• *Make and Model*
Alfa Romeo 33 Carabo
• *Year of production*
1968
• *Coachwork*
Coupé (Bertone)
• *Engine*
V8, twin overhead camshafts per bank
• *Bore and stroke / Engine displacement*
78 x 52.2 mm / 1995 cc
• *Maximum power*
230 b.h.p. at 8800 rpm
• *Dimensions*
Height 990 mm, wheelbase 2350 mm
• *Total built*
1

Arese (Milan), Automobilismo Storico Alfa Romeo, Museo Storico, Centro di Documentazione Storica
Photo © Automobilismo Storico Alfa Romeo, Centro di Documentazione Storica

On 1st November 1965, an epoch-making event took place at Carrozzeria Bertone: Giorgetto Giugiaro, who had arrived at the end of 1959, left and his position as director of the styling department was taken by a young emerging designer, Marcello Gandini. Gandini was aged just 27 and did not come from the car sector. However, he was full of talent, ideas and impudence, which immediately led him to design new, different, provocative cars.
That same November of 1965 saw the beginning of the long, fruitful relationship between Nuccio Bertone and Ferruccio Lamborghini, which saw its first fruits in the Miura, the result of Gandini's revolutionary thinking. But Bertone also had a historic relationship with Alfa Romeo ever since, in 1954, it was commissioned to design and build the Giulietta Sprint, of which more than 36,000 examples were built. After the Sprint, other series-built cars followed, such as the Giulietta Sprint Speciale, the 2000 and 2600 Sprint and the Giulia Sprint GT, as well as a number of prototypes, including the Canguro of 1964 and the Montreal of 1967 (which later entered production, slightly modified, in 1970).
It was thus natural that when Alfa Romeo should present the 33 Stradale in 1967, Bertone should decide to body one of these prestigious chassis with his own made-to-measure creation.
The creative brilliance of Gandini and the courage of Bertone to push on with bold proposals materialized at the Paris Salon of 1968 with the Carabo, a futuristic prototype still today considered a great example of car styling.
The Carabo has a low wedge-shaped body (it is just 99 centimetres high) with strong, taut lines. The nose ends in a slender point into which are inserted pop-up headlights. The bonnet, featuring three large, horizontal air vents, gives way smoothly to the windscreen. The scissor doors would later be adopted by Bertone for the Lamborghini Countach. The engine bonnet, located at the back, features a set of black vents above the rear window. The tail is high, especially in relation to the rest of the car, and truncated.
The dazzling green colour is the same as a coleopteron, the carabid bombardier beetle (found in some parts of the Alps) from which the Bertone prototype took its name.
(H.S.)

Pininfarina

Modulo, 1970

• *Make and Model*
Pininfarina Modulo
• *Year of production*
1970
• *Coachwork*
Monovolume two-door, two-seater
• *Engine*
V12, four overhead camshafts
• *Bore and stroke / Engine displacement*
81 x 71 mm / 4390 cc
• *Maximum power*
340 b.h.p. at 6600 rpm
• *Dimensions*
Length 4480 mm, width 2040 mm, height 935 mm, wheelbase 2500 mm
• *Weight*
700 Kg
• *Total built*
1

Pininfarina Collection

The end of the 1960s saw the birth of some of the most exceptional stylistic creations by leading Italian designers: able to make best use of the finest chassis and mechanical components (Abarth, Alfa Romeo, Ferrari, Lamborghini, Maserati), each of them gave free rein to their creativity, building prototypes that no longer bore any relation to 'real' cars, but which were exercises in pure form, coincidentally placed on four wheels.
Starting with the form of the prototypes built over Abarth chassis (2000 Coupé Speciale of 1969), Alfa Romeo (P33 Roadster of 1968 and 33 Prototipo Speciale of 1969) and Ferrari (P5 and P6 of 1968 and 512 S of 1969), Pininfarina reached the peak of this research into extreme styling with the Modulo, the star attraction of the Pininfarina stand at the Geneva Show of 1970.
The Modulo was built over a Ferrari 512 S chassis, which proved perfect in terms of size and position of mechanical components.
Lorenzo Ramaciotti, former managing director and director general of Pininfarina Studi e Ricerche, recalls the Modulo with these words: 'The form, absolutely a monovolume, springs from the superimposition of two symmetrical valves, with a line showing at the join. The volume of the shell is marked by two longitudinal dihedrals indicating the shift from the "above"-nose-windscreen-roof to the "flank," and the central section is a taut, continuous but very flat arch. The volume is sharply cut off at the tail to form a perfectly vertical surface. Immediately obvious, two cylindrical surfaces housing the rear tyres break through this simple form. There is no subtle modelling of details; the force of the object lies in its deliberately "geometric" nature. The rest is decoration: colour, the large hexagonal window on the side that combines glazing and air-intake, the gaps above the front and rear wheels [...] The abstraction of the form is as provocative today as then and is still forcefull and appealing. But is it still a car or a service shuttle for some spacecraft from *2001 A space odyssey* departing thanks to some anti-gravitational device rather than prosaically on four wheels driven by an internal combustion engine?'.
This is probably the same question the visitors to Expo '70 at Osaka asked themselves, when the Modulo was sent to represent Italian design.
(H.S.)

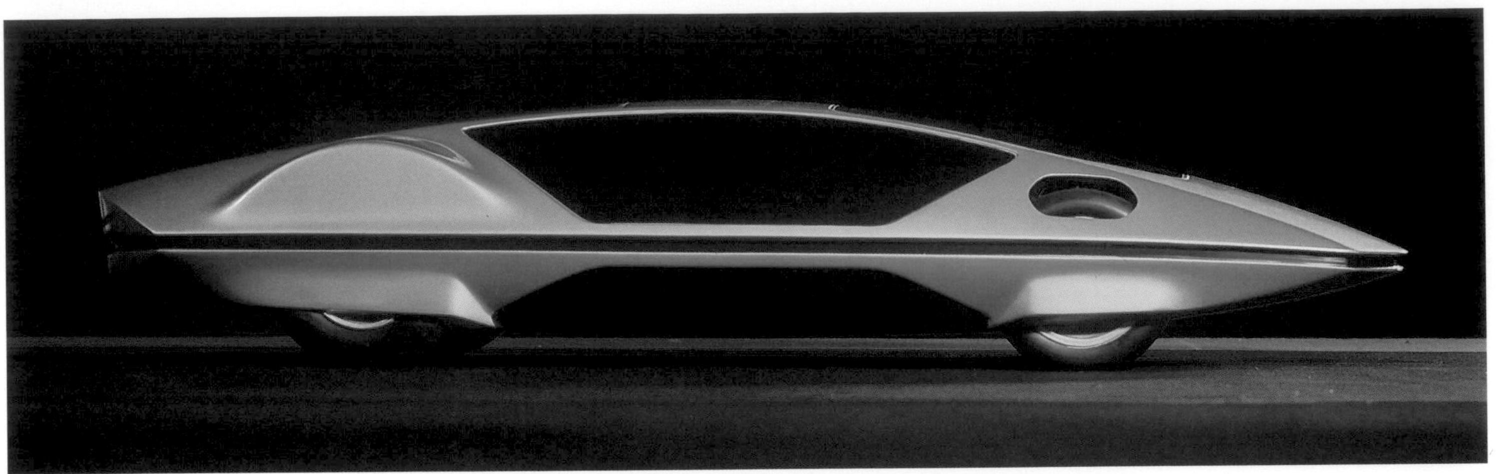

Modulo

Italdesign Giugiaro

Boomerang, 1972

- *Make and Model*
Italdesign Boomerang
- *Year of production*
1972
- *Coachwork*
Coupé two-seater
- *Engine*
V8, four overhead camshafts
- *Bore and stroke / Engine displacement*
93.9 x 85 mm / 4709 cc
- *Maximum power*
310 b.h.p. at 6000 rpm
- *Top speed*
280 kph (174 mph)
- *Dimensions*
Length 4342 mm, width 1860 mm, height 1070 mm, wheelbase 2600 mm
- *Weight*
1400 Kg
- *Total built*
1

Private collection

Giorgetto Giugiaro designed his first Maserati, a 5000 GT, when he was still in charge of styling at Carrozzeria Bertone. Then, when he was at Ghia, he designed the Ghibli, still one of his masterpieces today. When the Modena-based company also decided to join the ranks of rear-engined sports cars, it naturally turned to Italdesign, requesting a modern but sober car, respecting the traditional elegance that has always distinguished Maserati cars. Thus was born the Bora, presented at the Geneva Show of 1971; its lines recalled those of the Ghibli, especially in the handling of the front, despite the profound differences in the mechanical lay-out. The creativity that Giugiaro had to keep reined in for the car to be produced in series, exploded instead in the design of a genuine dream car, the Boomerang, built on the same chassis as the Bora. Presented as a model in epowood at the Turin Show in 1972 and subsequently as a working prototype at the Geneva Show of 1973, it was, according to Giugiaro himself, pure provocation, the irrational taking to extremes of the wedge shape, which made no sense even from an aerodynamic point of view.
The Boomerang marked the arrival point of earlier experiences in styling (the Iguana of 1969, the Tapiro of 1970, the Caimano of 1971), but it also provided inspiration for a number of cars that were later to be designed and produced in the 1970s (Lotus Esprit of 1972, Volkswagen Golf of 1974, Lancia Delta of 1979). All the lines of the bodywork are taut; the perfectly horizontal midway line cuts the side window in two, the upper part of which is fixed. The front bonnet and windscreen (which has an incredible angle of just 13°) lie on a straight line leading to the roof, which it itself perfectly flat and horizontal. This slopes away at the tail at the same angle as the front. In its succession of taut, sharp lines, the interior fits perfectly and is itself dominated by rounded forms, thanks not to the steering wheel but to the unusual arrangement of instrumentation within a circular panel around the steering column. This column, designed with safety in mind, is in two parts linked by chain; in the case of a frontal crash, the backward thrust of the entire wheel block is limited. Could a set of standard wheels be put on a 'sculpture' car? Of course not. Look carefully: they too are a work of art.
(H.S.)

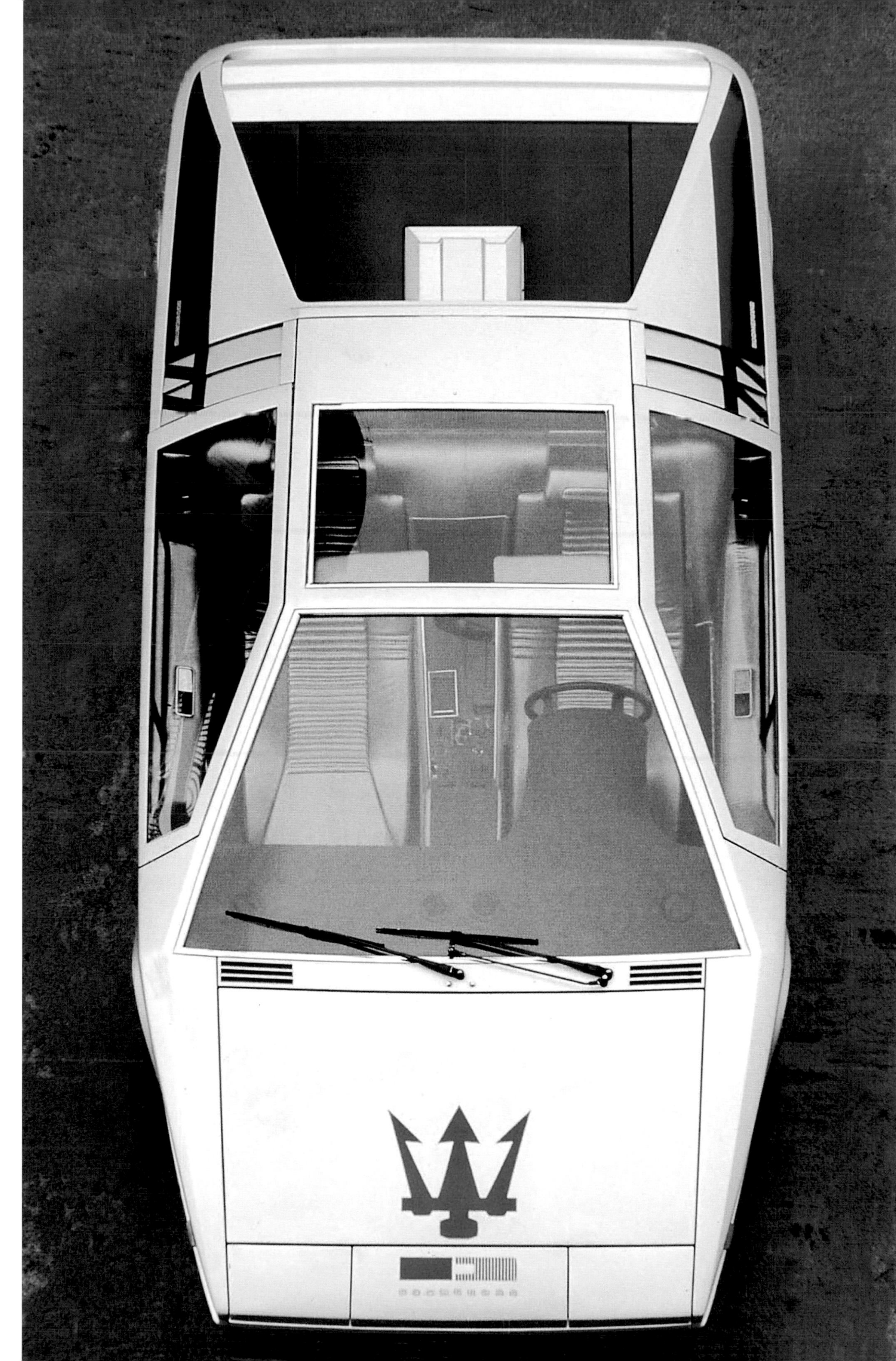

Italdesign Giugiaro

Medusa, 1980

• *Make and Model*
Italdesign Medusa
• *Year of production*
1980
• *Coachwork*
Two-volume, four-door saloon
• *Engine*
In-line four, double overhead camshaft
• *Bore and stroke / Engine displacement*
84 x 90 mm / 1995 cc
• *Maximum power*
120 b.h.p. at 6000 rpm
• *Dimensions*
Length 4405 mm, width 1813 mm,
height 1263 mm, wheelbase 2850 mm
• *Weight*
1215 Kg
• *Total built*
1

Italdesign Giugiaro
Photo Italdesign Giugiaro archive

With the Medusa, Giugiaro faced a new challenge: applying aerodynamics to an everyday car, but without overlooking comfort. He intended to demonstrate that it was possible to obtain a low drag coefficient (Cd) without penalising passenger comfort and space.
The choice of the mechanical components, from a Lancia Beta Montecarlo, has a reason: the mid-rear mounted, engine made it possible to make best use of the interior space and design a much lower, shaped front, to the advantage of the aerodynamic profile. Since the Medusa was a study for a comfortable family saloon car, the wheelbase was increased by 550 mm. The sharp lines more typical of sports cars were here abandoned; the Medusa has a rounded form without anything jutting out, except for the rear spoiler and wing mirror whose position, right next to the front line of the door, was itself carefully tested in the wind tunnel. The bumpers were integrated into the bodywork and the wheels were perfectly aligned with the wheelarches.
A view from the side reveals the three windows on the side (of use for increasing visibility and to lighten the volumes), the cut of the front doors which overlays the A-pillar, while the rear hatch incorporates the D-pillar. The handles are flush-fitting and there are no gutters. The windows of the doors, fixed and flush-fitting, were designed to avoid any turbulence; fresh air came in via the electric sliding rear quarterlights. In this way, there being no window-winding mechanism, it was possible to make use of the space beneath within the door, increasing the roominess.
The interior was characterized by the steering wheel, at the centre of which were placed the main buttons and controls, all within reach without removing the hands from the wheel and transmitted using ultrasound.
The Medusa was presented at the Turin Salon in 1980 after the wind tunnel gave its final results: with a Cd of 0.263, the Medusa was the most aerodynamic car in the vehicle in the world, of those using standard running gears.
Even today, more than 25 years since its presentation at the Turin Show in 1980, it is extremely modern and pleasing to the eye.
(H.S.)

Page 362, below
Styling buck for the Gabbiano, 1983
Italdesign Giugiaro
Photo Italdesign Giugiaro archive
(Work on display in the exhibition)

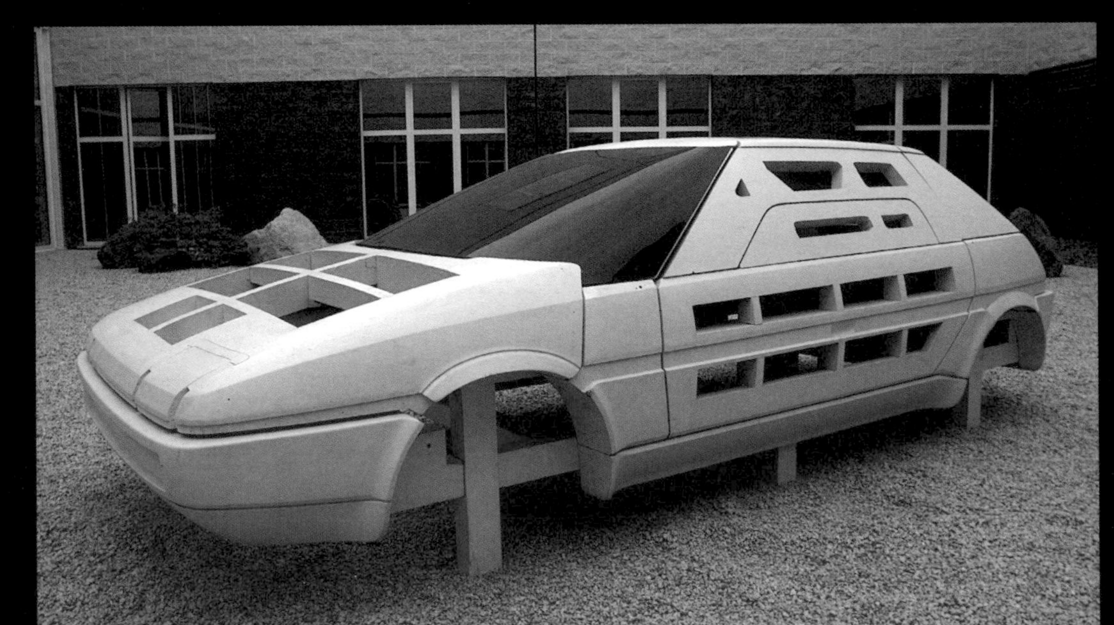

ITAL DESIGN
MEDUSA

Fioravanti

LF, 2001

• *Make and Model*
Fioravanti LF
• *Year of production*
2001
• *Coachwork*
Roadster-coupé
• *Engine*
V6, twin overhead camshafts, 4 valves per cylinder
• *Bore and stroke / Engine displacement*
88 x 68.30 mm / 2492 cc
• *Maximum power*
190 b.h.p. at 6200 rpm
• *Dimensions*
Length 4160 mm, width 1810 mm,
height 1280 mm, wheelbase 2540 mm
• *Weight*
1500 Kg
• *Total built*
1

Fioravanti srl

Before founding his company in 1987, Leonardo Fioravanti worked for many years for Pininfarina, where he was managing director and director general of Pininfarina Studies and Research, and for Ferrari as vice director general, and finally, at Fiat, where he was in charge of the Styling centre. A flexible designer with interests in highly varied fields (for example, he has a patent for a mooring structure for vessels in harbour), since the 1990s Leonardo Fioravanti has dedicated particular attention to the development of innovative cars, such as the 1994 'Sensiva,' a hybrid sports car with patented sensitive tyres, and the two prototypes of 1996: a coupé called Flair, based on Fiat Bravo components, which thanks to a low drag coefficient of 0.18 Cd offered extremely parsimonious consumption; and the Nyce, a cheap car for leisure time, characterized by a considerable reduction of the number of panels. At the Geneva Show of 2001, instead, he presented the LF, based on Alfa Romeo running gear. This was a traditional car as regards the engine but strongly characterized from an aesthetic point of view by the system to open the hard top, designed and patented by Fioravanti. The coupé-cabriolet sector, that is of cars that can be converted from hardtop to soft-top in a few seconds using an electrically-controlled mechanism, is one already explored in the past by Peugeot with the Eclipse, and newly topical in recent years thanks to the offerings of a number of major manufacturers, including Mercedes-Benz with the SLK and Peugeot with the 206 cc. Nevertheless, Fioravanti presented something new, something midway between this solution and that of the Targa, a simplified opening system (and lighter) which makes it possible to eliminate the greatest problem of other coupé-cabriolets: the almost total loss of space for luggage in the boot and a considerable increase in weight resulting from the extra hydraulics. Fioravanti's mechanism, designed for a roof in a single piece and not separated into several structures, makes the roof itself (of transparent plastic) rotate backwards and places it on top of the boot. In this way, the roof does not take any space from the boot and also serves as a windbreak, protecting the passengers from draughts. Unlike many solutions presented in concept cars which, for objective difficulties, remain on paper only and are never given a practical application, this solution by Fioravanti was used almost immediately by Ferrari for its Spider Superamerica, the exclusive car launched in 2005, of which only 559 examples were built. Also interesting in this concept car is the treatment of the front lights, pleasingly integrated into the clean lines of the front, sporting an Alfa Romeo shield.
(H.S.)

Extreme Sports Cars

Lamborghini

Miura P 400, 1966

• *Make and Model*
Lamborghini Miura P 400
• *Year of production*
1966
• *Coachwork*
Coupé (Bertone)
• *Engine*
V12 60°, four overhead camshafts
• *Bore and stroke / Engine displacement*
82 x 62 mm / 3929 cc
• *Maximum power*
350 b.h.p. at 7000 rpm
• *Top speed*
From 256 to 293 kph (159-182 mph)
according to gearbox
• *Dimensions*
Length 4360 mm, width 1760 mm,
height 1055 mm, wheelbase 2500 mm
• *Weight*
980 Kg
• *Total built*
765 (all series)

Automobili Lamborghini

The model on show is an SV model from 1973

The most sensational car presented at the Turin Show in 1965 was a chassis: of a new, box-section concept with large and highly visible holes to lighten it, it had the motor mounted to the rear in a transverse position and was called the 400 TP. The stand on which it was displayed was that of the new Emilian marque created by Ferruccio Lamborghini in 1963.
Here was the new challenge by the former tractor-builder turned car maker to show Enzo Ferrari (whose customer he had been), that he was able to produce high-performance cars in direct competition with him. The 12-cylinder engine, set transversally in front of the rear axle of the chassis (which weighs just 75 kg), was derived from that of the 350 GT but was increased in size to 4 litres and was in unit with the gearbox and differential; the declared power was 350 b.h.p.
The central/rear position of the engine became standard only after 1959 (apart from AutoUnion in the Grand Prix cars of the 1930s) in Formula 1 races in sposrts-prototypes; in the series-production field, there had only been more or less failed attempts at this, as in the case of the ATS 2500 in 1963, or partial successes, such as the René Bonnet Djet, a vehicle with an engine of just 1100 cc presented in 1962 and then produced until 1968 by Matra. But 1964 had already seen the presentation of the Ford GT 40, of which a road version was also planned.
The innovative features of the chassis and mechanics, designed by a young engineer, Giampaolo Dallara, assisted by Paolo Stanzani, required an equally unique bodyshell: to body this chassis, Ferruccio Lamborghini abandoned Carrozzeria Touring and turned to Nuccio Bertone, with whom an immensely talented young designer had just started work, Marcello Gandini. The new Lamborghini chassis became the testbed for his skill; Gandini managed to express himself fully, designing what is still today seen as one of the most beautiful sports cars of all time, an icon of automotive beauty: the Miura. The name is that of a race of fighting bulls and the Miura is indeed a road beast that takes some taming. On the day of its presentation at the Geneva Show of 1966, the Miura left the public dumbstruck. Low, sleek, full of seductive curves, it seemed more of a dream car, a perhaps unrealisable view of the future rather than a car that would enter production within a few months.
Ferruccio Lamborghini understood he had won his bet, but perhaps he never imagined that with the Miura he would enter the history books.
(H.S.)

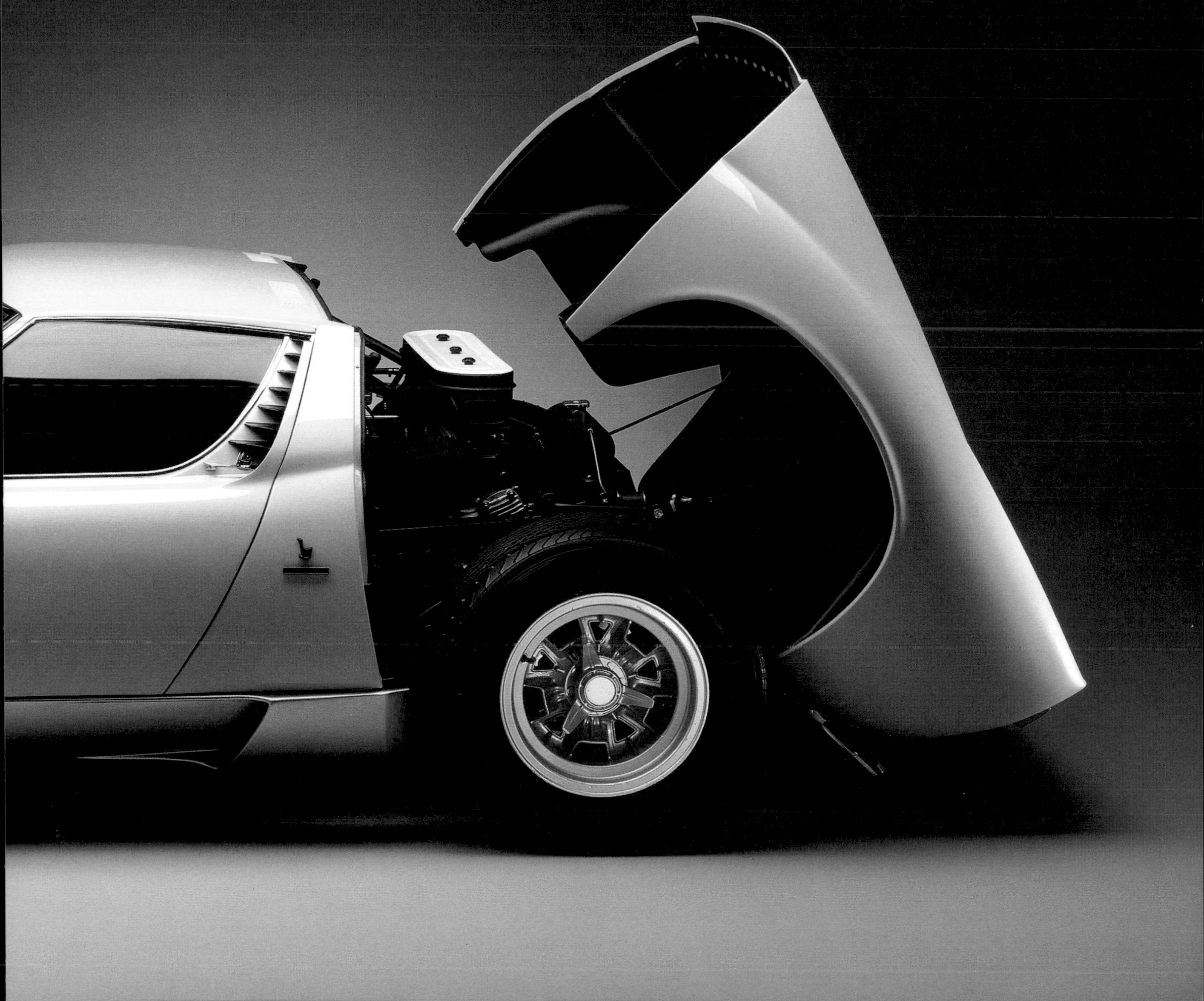

Lamborghini
Miura
SV

Alfa Romeo

33 Stradale, 1967

• *Make and Model*
Alfa Romeo 33 Stradale
• *Year of production*
1967
• *Coachwork*
Coupé (Scaglione/Marazzi)
• *Engine*
V8, four overhead camshafts
• *Bore and stroke / Engine displacement*
78 x 52.2 mm / 1995 cc
• *Maximum power*
230 b.h.p. at 8800 rpm
• *Top speed*
260 kph (162 mph)
• *Dimensions*
Length 3970 mm, width 1710 mm, height 990 mm, wheelbase 2350 mm
• *Weight*
700 Kg
• *Total built*
18

Lawrence Auriana Collection

The model on show dates from 1969

The official return of Alfa Romeo to racing took place in 1966 when the company bought Autodelta (a company founded in 1963 at Tavagnacco by Lodovico Chizzola, former Alfa Romeo and Ferrari designer and subsequent concessionaire for the marque in Udine, and by Carlo Chiti, former Alfa Romeo designer who then moved to Ferrari and ATS for the production and race preparation of the Giulia TZ), naming Chiti as the general director. It started racing in 1967 in the Sport-Prototype class with the Alfa Romeo 33 equipped with a two-litre, eight-cylinder engine. Developed and evolved over the years, the 33 would win the World Constructors' Championship in 1975, with a 12-cylinder three-litre engine.

In order to exploit the decision to come back to racing commercially, Alfa Romeo decided to put a road car into production that recalled the image and features of the racing car. Autodelta was given the task of building this limited production.

The characteristic chassis, featuring cast-magnesium chassis members, had its wheelbase increased by ten centimetres to provide better comfort. The two-litre V8 engine was slightly detuned to 230 b.h.p., reached almost 9000 rpm. Designer Franco Scaglione was commissioned to design the body and oversee its construction (which would be handled by Carrozzeria Marazzi of Caronno Pertusella). The 33 Stradale is another characteristic work by the Tuscan designer: the penetrating aerodynamic curves and minimal height (less than a metre) of the car, the large glazed areas of the windscreen, front and rear, the scissor doors, with the windows extending into the roof giving the appearance of a coupé-targa but also facilitate access to the interior; all of these features have given the 33 Stradale a timeless look. Although remaining in production until 1969, only 18 examples of this exclusive jewel of Italian technology and design were built, some of which were used by Pininfarina, Giugiaro and Bertone for the creation of spectacular specials exhibited and admired in the most important car shows of the period.

The marvellous timeless lines of the 33 Stradale served as inspiration for the Alfa Romeo designers working on the new 8C.

(H.S.)

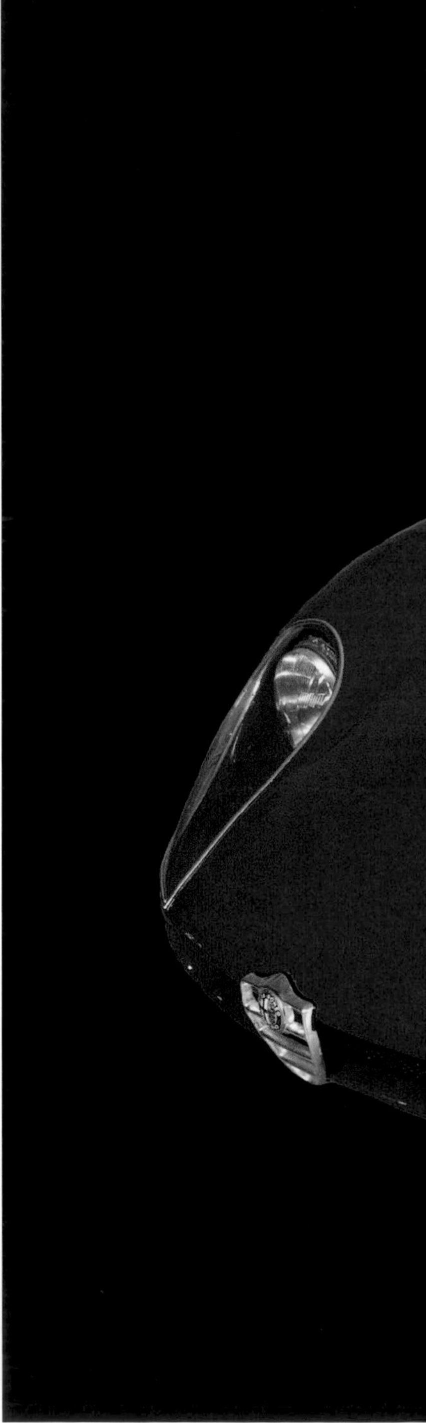

Ferrari

F40, 1987

• *Make and Model*
Ferrari F40
• *Year of production*
1987
• *Coachwork*
Coupé (Pininfarina)
• *Engine*
90° V8, four overhead camshafts
• *Bore and stroke / Engine displacement*
82 x 69.5 mm / 2936 cc
• *Maximum power*
478 b.h.p. at 7000 rpm
• *Top speed*
324 kph (201 mph)
• *Dimensions*
Length 4436 mm, width 1970 mm, height 1125 mm, wheelbase 2450 mm
• *Weight*
1235 Kg
• *Total built*
1315

Maranello (Modena), Galleria Ferrari
Photo La Presse / Ferrari spa

We can be quite sure of being right in saying that it was Ferrari that opened the modern 'supercar' season, when it presented the GTO at the 1984 Show in Geneva.
This was the first of a series of limited-production cars offering exceptional performance. The lines of the car echoed those of the 308 GTB, the Gran Turismo, designed by Pininfarina which had already been on the market for a few years, but everything else changed. There was a tubular steelspaceframe chassis bodywork in composite materials, Formula One technology, a twin-turbocharged engine giving 400 b.h.p. and a top speed of 305 kph (190 mph). With only 272 examples built, the GTO reawakened the desire of sporting clients for a car that could be used on the track as well, and led to Maranello planning a return to the racing circuit in other than Formula One. From the development of the GTO Evoluzione, destined for racing but never built because of a change in regulations implemented by the International Federation, to the launch of a new supercar was but a short step, and the F40 was duly presented at the Frankfurt Show of 1987, almost as a birthday present to Enzo Ferrari for the forty years since the company's foundation.
Once again, There was a tubular steel spaceframe chassis to which was fixed the carbon-fibre and Kevlar bodyshell. The engine was the same V8, with two turbos. However, power was greater than in the GTO, having been increased to 478 b.h.p. and the top speed to 324 kph (201 mph); it now took just 4.6 seconds to get from 0 to 100 kph. The bodywork designed by Pininfarina was particularly appealing: the wedge-shaped line, the low height off the ground, the numerous aeronautical-type air-scoops on the bonnet, sides, tail, and the large rear spoiler all contributed to rendering it unique. Designed to be light, fast and hug the road, the F40 did not offer its passengers much in the way of comfort. The interior was incredibly spartan for a car intended primarily for road use: the seats were a carbon-fibre shell with fabric trim and there was no power steering. Nor were there any of the electronic control systems present on even extreme cars today: traction and stability control, ABS and so on. Here was a beast of the road to tame and respect; it offered exceptional performance but required sensible drivers with a certain amount of experience in order to be able to make full use of it. Initially intended for a production run of 400 examples, Ferrari was obliged to build 1315 in order to satisfy the pressing requests from customers. This was the last Ferrari to be resigned and presented personally by the Commendatore before his death; no model could better represent his thinking as to how a true Ferrari should be.
(H.S.)

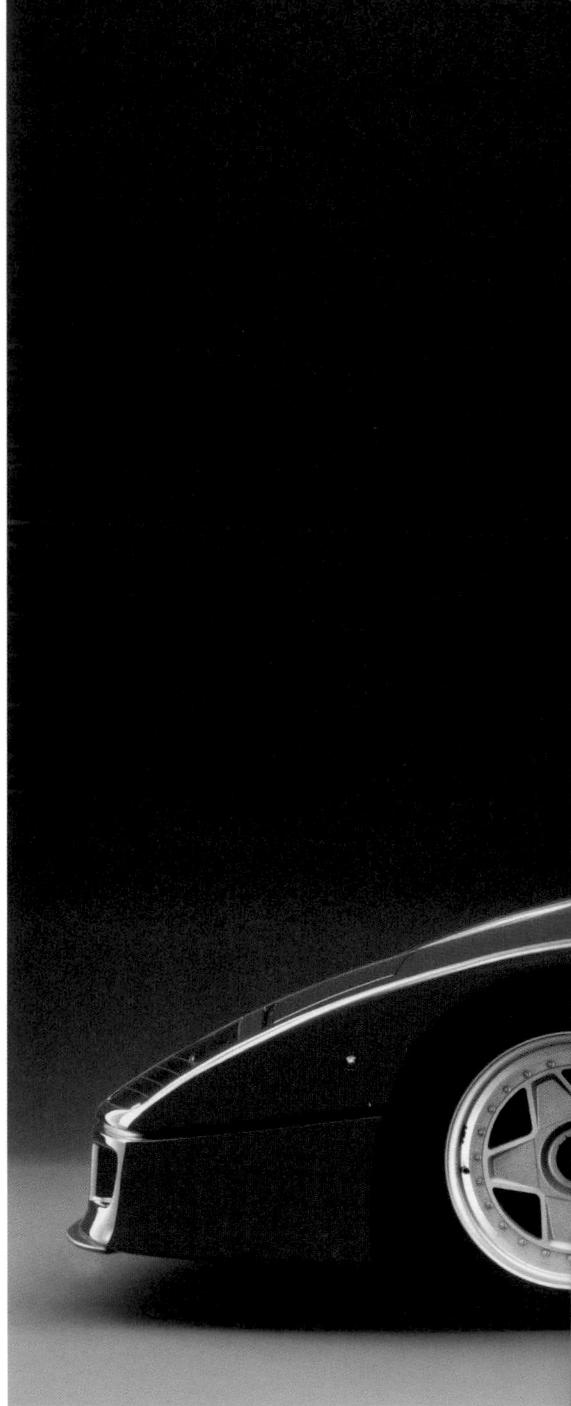

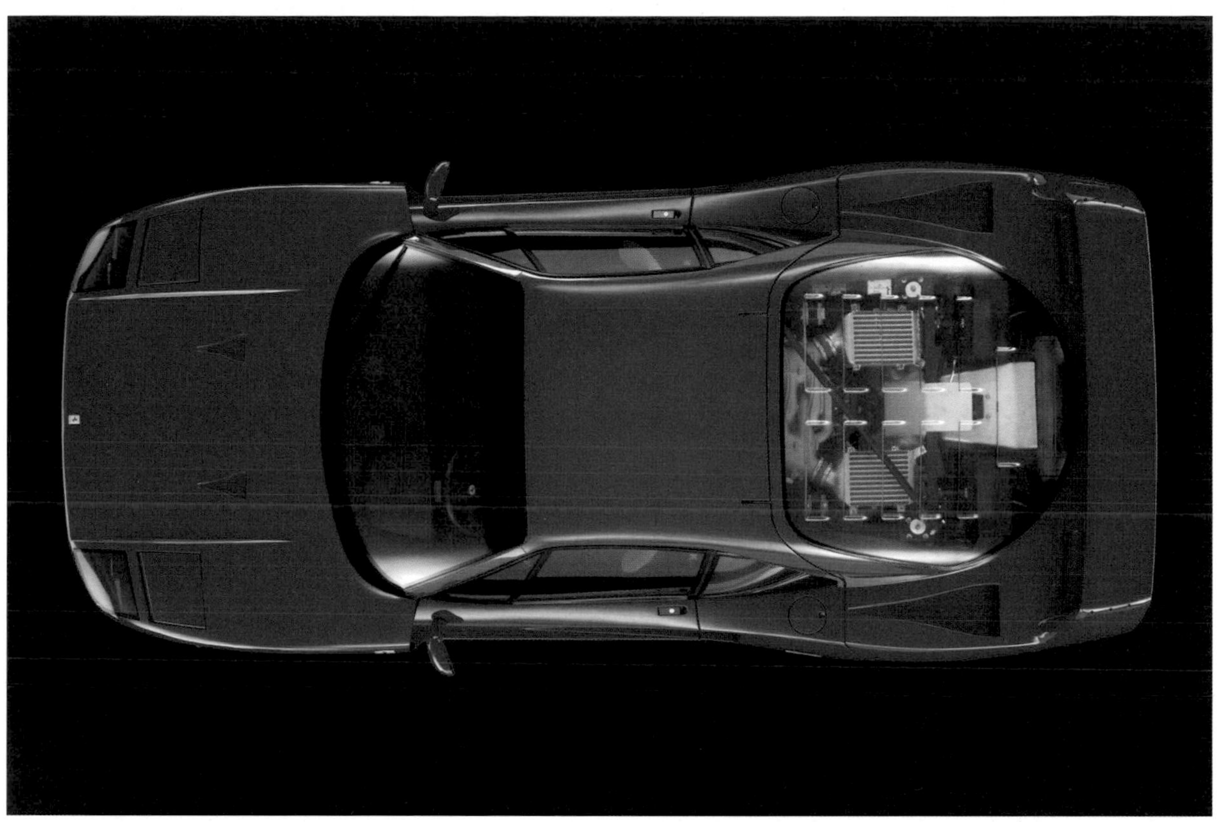

Ferrari

Pagani

Zonda C12, 2002

• *Make and Model*
Pagani Zonda
• *Year of production*
2002
• *Coachwork*
Coupé
• *Engine*
60° V12, four overhead camshafts
• *Bore and stroke / Engine displacement*
91.5 x 92.4 mm / 7291 cc
• *Maximum power*
585 b.h.p. at 7000 rpm
• *Top speed*
320 kph (199 mph)
• *Dimensions*
Length 4395 mm, width 2055 mm,
height 1151 mm, wheelbase 2730 mm
• *Weight*
1280 Kg
• *Total built*
Still in production

Pagani Automobili Spa
Photo Pagani Automobili communication / Roberto Morelli

This car represents the realisation of a child's dream. The child in question, Horacio Pagani, Argentinian, used to build beautiful models of supercars using balsawood and clay when he was just 12. He would read car magazines, follow everything that was happening in Italy with interest, especially in the Modena region, home to Ferrari, Lamborghini and Maserati, where he dreamed he would one day be able to build his own car.
At the age of 20, he built a single-seater for the Argentine Formula Three and met Juan Manuel Fangio. His fellow Argentinian, one of the living legends of car racing, helped him take the first step: Pagani began working for Lamborghini and moved to Modena. He specialized in composite materials and in building with carbon-fibre, which marked the new frontier for racing cars at the time. After a few years, he set up his own company, Modena Design, which collaborated in this avant-garde sector with manufacturing companies, and not only in Italy. Only then did Pagani pull his dream from the closet and start designing his supercar, using the most advanced technology available. He called the project Fangio F1, as a homage to and in admiration of the five times world champion. All he lacked was an engine; in 1988, he showed his plans to Fangio, and it was he who introduced him to Mercedes which, incredibly and for the first time, agreed to supply its own engines to a small independent constructor. Soon after, Fangio died.
In 1999 Pagani presented his car at the Geneva Show; for reasons of modesty and respect for his idol, he changed the name of the car from Fangio to Zonda, the name of the wind that blows over the Andes.
The car has stunning lines and breathtaking performance. The chassis is of carbon-fibre, a cold material, but it can be sensed that, here, it has been worked with passion, with love. Everything has been designed to reduce weight, but the result is harmonious and beautiful. Fifty years later, Pagani is following the same history as the other Modena-based companies. Ferrari and Maserati in the 1950s were boutiques in which masterpieces were created in accordance with customers' wishes. Today, they are companies that produce exceptional cars but in series, however small, but still in series. At Pagani, they are still willing to meet the requests of a customer and build him a made-to-measure car. Not many people are lucky enough to have realized their childhood dreams: Horacio Pagani is certainly one of these.
(H.S.)

Ferrari

599 GTB Fiorano, 2006

• *Make and Model*
Ferrari 599 GTB Fiorano
• *Year of production*
2006
• *Coachwork*
Berlinetta two-seater (Pininfarina)
• *Engine*
V12, four overhead camshafts
• *Bore and stroke / Engine displacement*
5999 cc
• *Maximum power*
620 b.h.p. at 7600 rpm
• *Top speed*
Over 330 kph (205 mph)
• *Dimensions*
Length 4665 mm, width 1962 mm, height 1336 mm, wheelbase 2750 mm
• *Weight*
1690 Kg
• *Total built*
Still in production

Maranello (Modena), Galleria Ferrari
Photo La Presse / Ferrari Spa

The latest offspring resulting from the collaboration between Ferrari at Maranello and Pininfarina, the new Ferrari berlinetta with front-mounted engine was presented at the 2006 Geneva Show and, with its name, continues the homage to its great cars of the past and places of origin: GTB, like the legendary berlinetta 275 of 1964, and Fiorano, the name of the village (now swallowed up by Maranello) in which Enzo Ferrari built his private test circuit.
A paean to power and speed, dressed in a stylistically aggressive bodywork in which careful aerodynamic research perfectly marries the stylistic references to the past, the 599 GTB Fiorano imparts powerful emotions even when parked.
In order to keep the overall weight of the car down to a minimum, the chassis and body are made entirely of aluminium, and the six-litre V12 engine has been mounted in the front but pushed back further than in the past in order to distribute the weight better.
The view from the front highlights the large radiator grille opening with the Prancing Horse at its centre, and two smaller intakes supplying cooling air to the brakes and towards the air-intake ducts of the engine.
The long, bulging engine bonnet is embraced by the front wings, ending in the modern jaired-in headlights.
By contrast, the rear is short and muscular, ending in a curved tail on which stand out the lights, round as in the past.
The separate C-pillars act as buttresses and have a precise aerodynamic function, as they increase the stability and roadholding of the car. However, they are also a reference to the past and a homage to the style of Pinin Farina of the 1950s. Indeed, it was the design company that first presented the rear buttresses which, starting at the rear windscreen stretched down to the tail. This on a 375 Mille Miglia ordered by Roberto Rossellini for Ingrid Bergman and defined a 'special aerodynamic berlinetta.' It was presented for the first time in 1954. This motif, which is both ornamental and aerodynamic at the same time, was used again by Pinin Farina (consider, for example, the Dino 206 of 1966 or the 365 GT4 BB of 1971); it also recurred in the cars of many other manufacturers and coachbuilders.
A detail worth remembering: the Ferrari 599 GTB Fiorano accelerates from 0 to 100 kph in just 3.7 seconds.
(H.S.)

Innovation and Engineering

Lancia

Lambda, 1922

- *Make and Model*
Lancia Lambda
- *Year of production*
1923
- *Coachwork*
Torpedo
- *Engine*
13° V4
- *Bore and stroke / Engine displacement*
75 x 120 mm / 2120 cc
- *Maximum power*
50 b.h.p. at 3250 rpm
- *Top speed*
115 kph (71 mph)
- *Dimensions*
Length 4400 mm, width 1640 mm, wheelbase 3100 mm
- *Weight*
1200 Kg
- *Total built*
About 12,000

Quattoruote Collection
© Photo Diego Cassetta – Mart

The model on show dates from 1923

On 7th December 1918, Lancia e C., registered a patent having as its 'object a type of motor car in which the separate chassis has been done away with and the connection between the rear and front axles is assured by a rigid shell serving the same function as the bodywork in ordinary motor cars.'
Vincenzo Lancia's brilliant intuition remained at a purely theoretical level for more than two more years, but then, in the spring of 1921, the Turinese manufacturer gave instructions for the design of the new car: this was not to have a chassis as used hitherto, was to have independent suspension on the front wheels in order to improve road-holding and hence passenger safety.
Despite the many new features included in the project, everything moved forward rapidly and the 'rigid shell' of the original patent took form; various solutions were studied for the suspension and shock absorbers. A completely new feature was planned for the engine too: this was a narrow V4 with an angle of just 13°. The engine was thus extremely compact, shorter than a straight four and narrower than a 90° V4. Moreover, Lancia was able to use a single overhead camshaft. It ran at over 3500 rpm at a time when all other production engines were unable to exceed 2500 rpm.
At the start of September of the same year, Vincenzo Lancia was able to try the working prototype of the Lambda: he appreciated its stability, the road-holding, the performance, improved by the lightness of the vehicle (just 1200 kg), but decided that brakes were also needed on the front wheels (at the time, only the most luxurious or high-performance cars had these).
The step from prototype to definitive car was quickly taken and the Lambda was presented to the public at the Paris and London Shows.
The model had a square but rakish, low line (thanks to the lowering of the floor along which a transmission tunnel was placed for the first time to deliver power to the rear wheels); its 'revolutionary' modernity anticipated the future and appealed to the fantasy of those who saw it.
Thus was born Vincenzo Lancia's 'masterpiece,' but also — and above all — the modern motor car, with its monocoque chassis. This feature was again used by Lancia for his 1932 Augusta, a closed car. Only in 1934 would another major manufacturer, Citroën, succeed in designing and building a series production car with a monocoque: that car was the Traction Avant.
(H.S.)

LANCIA

MICHELIN CABLE

Citroën

7CV Traction Avant, 1934

• *Make and Model*
Citroën 7CV Traction Avant
• *Year of production*
1934
• *Coachwork*
Four-door saloon
• *Engine*
Four cylinder, single overhead camshaft
• *Bore and stroke / Engine displacement*
72 x 80 mm / 1303 cc (or 78 x 80 mm / 1529 cc)
• *Maximum power*
32 b.h.p. at 3500 rpm (or 35 b.h.p. at 3500 rpm)
• *Top speed*
95 kph (59 mph)
• *Dimensions*
Length 4450 mm, width 1620 mm,
height 1520 mm, wheelbase 2910 mm
• *Weight*
1025 Kg
• *Total built*
81,295 (7 A-B-C-S)

Citroën
© Citroën Communication

The model on show dates from 1939

The Traction Avant was the result of a meeting between two major innovative spirits: André Citroën, a visionary and avant-garde industrialist who loved originality and risk, and André Lefebvre, who took his first professional steps in the aviation division of Voisin, and was the designer of the Voisin Laboratoire of 1923 and of the new car. One need only compare it to other cars of the same year — 1934 — to understand that the Traction Avant was absolutely innovative: much lower than all the other cars in its category, and its aerodynamic lines, modelled by Flaminio Bertoni, offered a soft, highly appealing form expressing speed. Lefebvre abandoned the use of a separate chassis to build a monocoque, for the first time in steel. None of the technical solutions adopted for the Traction Avant were innovative if taken singularly, but this was the first time they were offered all together in a car destined for mass production: front-wheel drive, independent torsion-bar suspension, the engine mounted on rubber mountings, hydraulic brakes with servo. Two models were offered initially: the 7CV with 1303 cc engine delivering 32 b.h.p., and the 11CV with 1911 cc engine delivering 46 b.h.p. The car had also been designed with the standard fitting of an automatic gearbox in mind, but this new solution, strongly promoted by Citroën, had insurmountable problems. 15 days before the launch, the company had to surrender and modify the gearbox, installing a manual one in its place. The company was undergoing a major financial crisis because of the huge investment Citroën had made to build its factory *ex novo*: to save the company, therefore, the car had to be launched even though it had not been tested as much as Citroën would have liked. The official presentation was also in typical Citroën style: not to the public in one of the many motor shows, but to the 350 specialized journalists, each of whom left the conference room at the wheel of one of the new cars in order to be able to test it immediately on the road.
The innumerable teething problems of the Traction Avant drove the factory into receivership, and only the intervention of the Michelin family, already a creditor through their supply of tyres, enabled the company to keep trading. Continuously developed and updated, the Traction Avant was subsequently fitted with more powerful engines, including a six-cylinder, and it remained in production until 1957, for a total of over 760,000 models built of all the series. The front-wheel drive gave the car excellent road-holding further improved by the forward position of the engine and its low centre of gravity. Moreover, its nimble, stable, road-holding and speed resulted it in its being used as a police car and, for the same reasons, the car of choice for France's criminals.
(H.S.)

40
60
80
100
120
0000
13579

MICHELIN
165 - 400
PILOTE

Panhard

Dynavia, 1948

• *Make and Model*
Panhard et Levassor Dynavia
• *Year of production*
1948
• *Coachwork*
Two-door aerodynamic saloon
• *Engine*
Two-boxes cylinder
• *Bore and stroke / Engine displacement*
72.50 x 75 mm / 610 cc
• *Maximum power*
28 b.h.p. at 4000 rpm
• *Top speed*
130 kph (81 mph)
• *Total built*
2

Mulhouse, Cité de l'Automobile – Musée National – Schlumpf Collection

Panhard et Levassor was, together with Peugeot, the oldest French car manufacturer: both began showing an interest in cars in 1889. Today, Peugeot is still trading, while Panhard, absorbed by Citroën in 1965, ceased production in 1967. Panhard opted for the racing circuit to publicize its cars; already by 1894, four Panhards were lined up at the start of the Paris-Rouen, the first motor race ever organized, and in 1904 the company won the first edition of the Vanderbilt Cup. Later, the advertising strategy changed and the company gambled more on the quality of its cars than on their performance. Until the outbreak of the Second World War, the Panhard et Levassor production was geared mainly to the production of high-class cars, with six and eight-cylinder sleeve-valve engines, and the 1930s saw many resources dedicated to aerodynamic research. In 1936, the Dynamic was presented, a saloon with unusual curved lines, flush-fitting headlights, faired-in wheels, an interior with six seats (three in front and three behind) and a central driving position. During the war, the company's designer, Louis Bionier, continued his aerodynamic studies; at the end of the war, however, the social and economic scenario had changed dramatically and Panhard followed the indications of the market, which sought simpler vehicles with low running costs. It thus bought the design of the AFG, a light car designed by Gregoire. Thus was born the Dyna, a cheap car with twin-cylinder 610 cc engine, presented at the Paris Salon in 1946. Based on the standard Dyna mechanics and drawing on what he had himself designed before and during the war, Bionier presented the Dynavia at the 1948 Paris Show. This was an aerodynamic prototype with bold, revolutionary lines, able to reach a top speed of 140 kph (87 mph) pushed merely by the little 28 b.h.p. Dyna engine, and to cruise at 80 kph (50 mph) consuming just 3.5 litres of petrol per 100 Km. Extremely light and with drag coefficient (Cd) of just 0.17, the Dynavia, which could accommodate four passengers, presented a tear-drop shape with pointed tail, only two doors, a large and steeply sloping front and rear windscreen, and an elaborate bumper and radiator grille unit enclosing the single headlight. Anything that could disturb the airflow on the exterior of the car was removed: from door handles and wing mirrors to guttering. The Dynavia represents the state of the art in aerodynamic research of the time. It is also the demonstration of the fact that aerodynamics and style do not always go hand in hand. However, a number of features designed for the Dynavia were later used in the new Dyna series, the Z, presented in 1954. *(H.S.)*

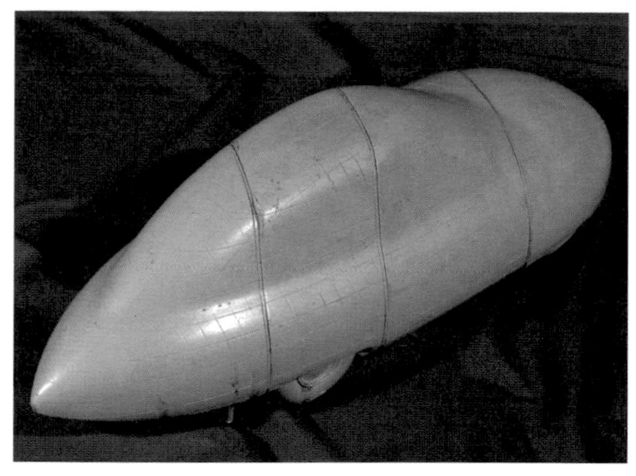

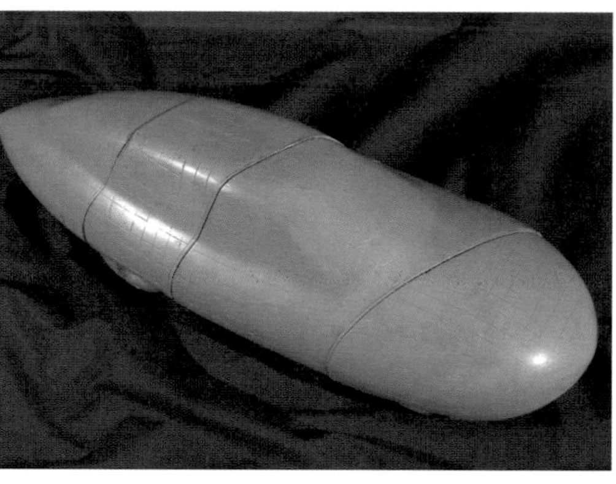

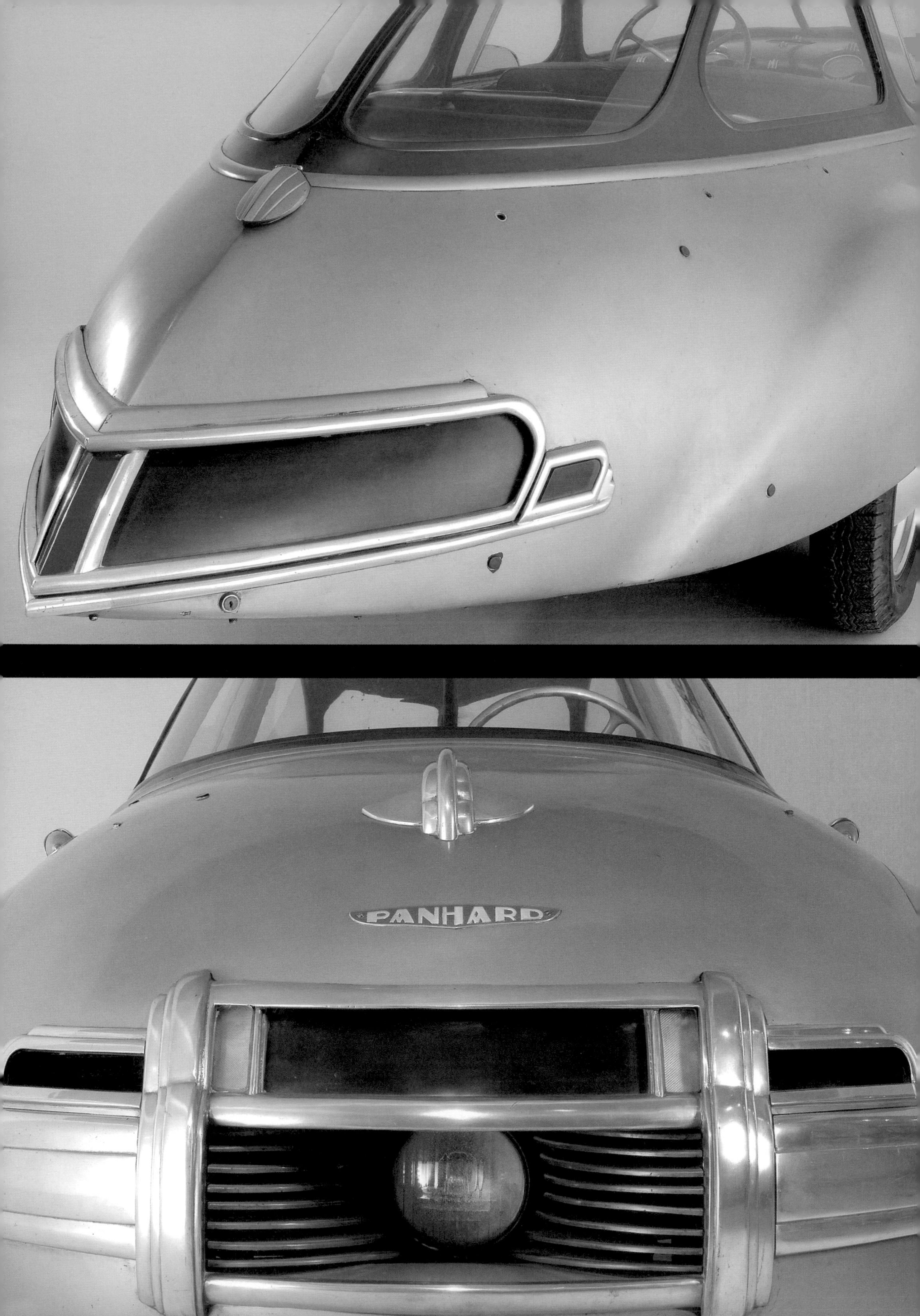
PANHARD

ESSENCE
HUILE

Citroën

DS 19, 1955

• *Make and Model*
Citroën DS 19
• *Year of production*
1955
• *Coachwork*
Four-door saloon
• *Engine*
Four-cylinder, overhead valves
• *Bore and stroke / Engine displacement*
78 x 100 mm / 1911 cc
• *Maximum power*
75 b.h.p. at 4500 rpm
• *Top speed*
140 kph (87 mph)
• *Dimensions*
Length 4800 mm, width 1790 mm, height 1470 mm, wheelbase 3120 mm
• *Weight*
1215 Kg
• *Total built*
1,445,746 (all series)

Citroën
© Citroën Communication

The model on show dates from 1957

Revolutionary! The term has been used and abused, but it is the only word able accurately to define the Citroën DS (the *Déesse*, or 'Goddess' for the French), launched at the Paris Salon de l'Automobile in 1955. The DS resembled no other car then in production, and even in the following years, no other manufacturer dared present anything similar and follow Citroën down such an innovative road. In a single car, made for mass production and not designed as a dream car, Citroën had included every solution that suddenly made any other car manufactured in Europe or America old and obsolete. The Traction Avant had bequeathed its front-wheel drive and engine, itself deriving from that of the 11 D, beefed up to 75 b.h.p. Everything else was new and different, from the semi-automatic gearbox to the front servo-assisted disc brakes, and from the power steering to the constant-height hydro-pneumatic suspension. This system consisted in four spheres, one for each of the four independent wheels, filled with nitrogen gas under pressure and placed over a cylinder containing oil. At every bump, a certain quantity of oil would be pushed into the sphere, where it was unable to mix with the gas, and the effective lwheel travel was thus conditioned by the amount of oil the cylinder contained, which itself determined how high the car stood off the ground. The system assured a comfort never before available on rough roads and at high speed, and at the same time provided better road-holding. This, in synthesis, was the technical innovation, strongly backed or even bettered, by the visual impact of the equally innovative bodywork, designed by Flaminio Bertoni, as usual. Free of any design constraints, Bertoni was able to create an absolute masterpiece, an aerodynamic line that put the DS 20 years ahead of any other car then being produced around the world. The long front end compared to the short, fleeting rear, the large and curved front and rear windscreens, the doors free of any frame around the windows, the front half that was much wider than the rear all contributed to the creation of an eternal line that broke with tradition and opened the way to new stylistic concepts. The interior was also different, with its single-spoke steering wheel and extraordinarily soft seats. Likewise, the construction of the bodywork broke with custom: the roof was made of layered polyester, hot-pressed and reinforced with fibreglass; the enormous front bonnet and boot lid were of aluminium, and the wings were bolted on to make them easier to replace, if necessary. The *Déesse* remained in production in various versions until 1975.
(H.S.)

100 120 140 160
2 3 4

NSU

RO 80, 1967

• *Make and Model*
NSU RO 80
• *Year of production*
1967
• *Coachwork*
Saloon
• *Engine*
Twin-rotor NSU Wankel
• *Engine displacement*
Combustion chamber of 497.5 cc
• *Maximum power*
115 b.h.p. at 5500 rpm
• *Top speed*
181 kph (112 mph; models produced from 1971:
176 kph-109 mph)
• *Dimensions*
Length 4780 mm, width 1760 mm,
height 1410 mm, wheelbase 2860 mm
• *Weight*
1250 Kg (models produced from August, 1969: 1280 Kg;
models produced from May, 1975: 1290 Kg)
• *Total built*
37,406

Auto Union GmbH
© Photo Diego Cassetta – Mart

The NSU company, manufacturers of motorcycles and cars, based in Neckarsulm, decided early on to undertake research into rotary engines, a field of study in which the noted specialist in seals, engineer Felix Wankel, had concentrated for decades. Wankel believed that this type of propulsion represented the engine of the future and that its use was sure to develop widely. Development started on a three-box, four-door saloon with front-wheel drive and a host of design innovations. The small styling department headed by Claus Luthe produced a made-to-measure shape for this collection of designs; one that would adequately reflect the novelty of the propulsion unit. The design of the RO 80 was patented in 1963. The nose of the car was extremely aerodynamic and modern-looking, as was the sloping surface of the boot.
The RO 80 marked the advent of that wedge shape — today used as a standard — as the new basic form for the lines of the bodywork. Wholly innovative too was the instrument panel which, however, never saw production. In line with the typical taste of the 1960s, the chrome trim around the body provided the only adornment.
In 1967, the car was presented to enthusiast journalists from the sector. However, the lack of reliability associated with the engine, and the high design costs ruined the small car company, which in the end was sold to Volkswagen. Nevertheless, the RO 80 continued to be made until 1977 without any changes to the bodywork, but with a new Twin-rotor Wankel engine delivering 170 b.h.p., able to push the car to 210 kph (130 mph).
The NSU RO 80 is today considered a milestone in car design.
(R.J.F.K.)

RO 80

NSU

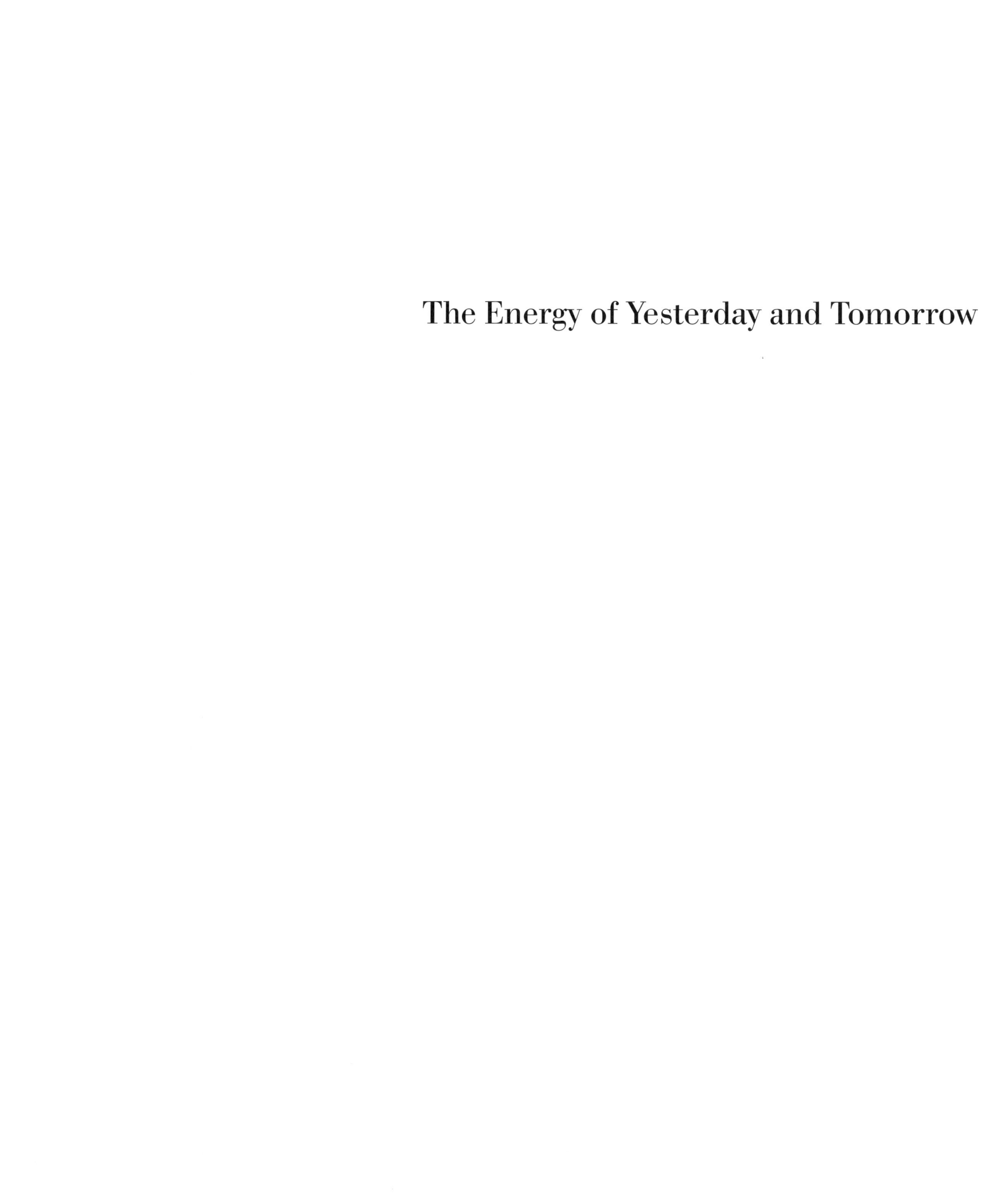

The Energy of Yesterday and Tomorrow

La Jamais Contente

La Jamais Contente, 1899

• *Make and Model*
La Jamais Contente
• *Year of production*
1899
• *Coachwork*
Torpedo
• *Engine*
Two electric motors
• *Maximum power*
68 b.h.p.
• *Top speed*
105.850 kph (65.60 mph)
• *Dimensions*
Length 3600 mm, width 1560 mm,
height 1500 mm, wheelbase 1840 mm
• *Weight*
1350 Kg
• *Total built*
1

Lions Club International Le Bourget – Christian Wannyn

The model on show is a replica

In 1898, *La France Automobile* magazine posed a question that was also a challenge for all car enthusiasts: 'Can mechanical traction beat human traction?' It seems incredible, but in 1897, the speed achieved cycling on a racing track — 64.2 kph (39.89 mph) — was higher than that achieved by motor cars. On 18th December 1898, the challenge was accepted by 21 competitors who met at the Parc d'Achères, near Paris. The fastest along the 1800 m straight, covered in one direction alone, was Comte Gaston de Chasseloup-Laubat who, at the wheel of an electric Jeantaud vehicle, achieved a top average speed of 63.137 kph (39.232 mph) along a flying kilometre. Thus, the first speed record for a car to be officially timed was still lower than that established a year before by a man on his bicycle!
That day did not see a Belgian engineer, Camille Jenatzy, participate. He had already won the first hill-climb in history at Chanteloup, with an electric vehicle from the Compagnie générale des transports automobiles, the company he had founded in Paris. It was Jenatzy who challenged de Chasseloup-Laubat and then beat his record, establishing a new one of 66.5 kph (41.3 mph). That day, 17th January 1899, finally saw the cycling record beaten at last. The Comte soon responded and on 22nd January himself beat the record again, achieving a speed of 70.297 kph (43.68 mph). However, on 27th January, the 'Red Devil,' as his Belgian rival was nicknamed, trumped him again, achieving a speed of 80.321 kph (49.91 mph). De Chasseloup-Laubat knew he could not increase the power of his motor any further, since it had already broken at the end of the previous trial, but he had the right intuition: he reduced the drag resisting the forward motion of the vehicle. Using canvas, he constructed a sort of pointed windbreak for the front end and faired in the underbody. These early, rather rudimentary aerodynamic solutions enabled him on 12th March to arrive at a speed of 93.724 kph (58.239 mph). The ball was back in Jenatzy's court. He responded by building the first purpose-made vehicle built for a speed record; he called it 'La Jamais Contente' — 'The never satisfied' — as an ironic reference, so rumour had it, to his wife's character.
In order to improve its air penetration, he designed a sort of torpedo; to reduce its weight, he mounted two small 68 b.h.p. motors on the rear wheels in order also to eliminate the differential and transmission chain. Moreover, he obtained special tyres from Michelin.
On 1st May 1899, Jenatzy and La Jamais Contente covered the flying kilometre at the Achères track at a speed of 105.850 kph (65.60 mph); the speed record was once again his. The crowd applauded him after having feared for his fate: it was thought that the human body would not be able to support a speed of over 100 kph (62.1 mph)!
The 'Red Devil's' record was to stand until 1902 when a steam-powered Serpollet reached 120.876 kph (75.111 mph), a record itself soon beaten by the American millionaire, Vanderbilt, driving a Mors powered by an internal combustion engine.
(H.S.)

LA JAMAIS CONTENTE
DE CAMILLE JENATZY
RECORD DU MONDE 1899 PAR 105 KM A L'HEURE
AVEC ACCUMULATEURS FULMEN
1899

SECURITE
BOUTON DEVANT
DU VEHICULE
IMPERATIVEMENT
POUSSE A FOND

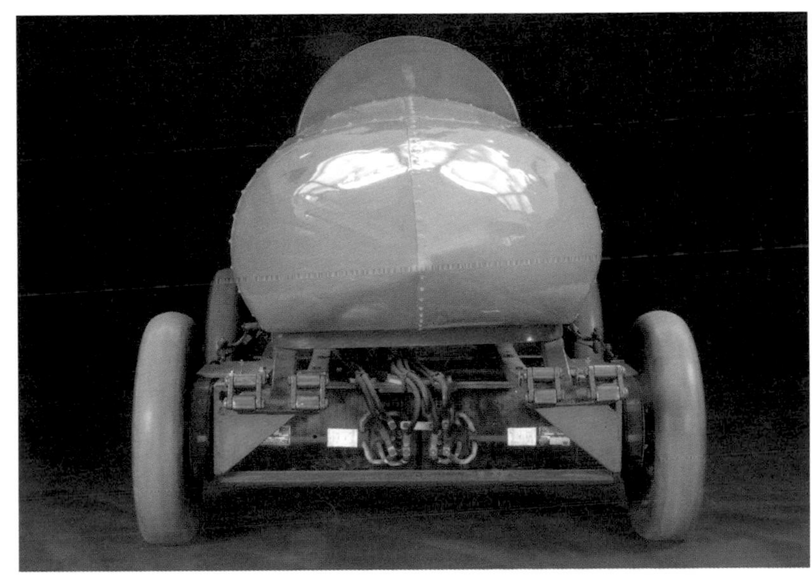

Fiat

Turbina, 1954

• *Make and Model*
Fiat Turbina
• *Year of production*
1954
• *Coachwork*
Coupé
• *Engine*
Gas turbine with two-stage supercharger
• *Maximum power*
300 b.h.p. at 22,000 rpm
• *Top speed*
250 kph (155 mph)
• *Dimensions*
Length 4370 mm, width 1610 mm, height 1255 mm, wheelbase 2400 mm
• *Weight*
About 1000 Kg
• *Total built*
1

Turin, Centro Storico Fiat
Photo Franco Turcati

The car on show is a 1:4 scale model

The initial studies for the construction of a gas turbine date back to 1872, but the first functioning model was built in France only in 1905. At that time, the technology and materials available were insufficient to develop a complete project and only became available in the closing years of the Second World War, which saw the realisation of turbo-jet engines for the aeronautical sector, leading to the construction of the first jet aircraft. Further studies effected on turbine engines for use on land came to nothing. Among the many car manufacturers in Europe and America seeking to exploit the experience matured during the war to develop prototypes of gas-turbine vehicles, there was also Fiat, which in 1948 gave engineer Dante Giacosa and his team the task of exploring the possibility of building an internal-combustion turbine engine.
Built on a chassis derived from that of the 8V, the Fiat Turbina featured an aerodynamic bodyshell designed by Fabio Luigi Rapi, with two directional fins over the rear wheels. Considerable testing was undertaken in a wind tunnel using 1:5 scale models and the Turbina had an aerodynamic coefficient (Cd) of just 0.14.
The engine was located in the rear with power being transmitted direct from the turbine to the rear wheels via a series of reduction gears. Used in some tests on the runway at the Turin airport, the Turbina was an effective advertising vehicle for the Turinese company, which was then seeking to re-establish a position of prestige in the international market. The experiments effected using it were then exploited for the design of engines made to be fitted in heavy vehicles. 'For Fiat, this was an important lesson. And namely that the turbine is not yet, and perhaps will not even in the future be, an engine suited for use in a private car,' wrote Giacosa in his memoires. And indeed, the practical use of turbine-powered cars is limited to just a few examples: in the racing field, there were some attempts made at the 500 Miles at Indianapolis with the STP and Lotus 56; a Rover-BRM took part, unclassified, in the 24-Hours of Le Mans in 1963, and another American car, the Howmet, participated in some races for the World Manufacturers' Championship between 1967 and 1969. At an industrial level, only Chrysler in the early 1960s built a run of 50 cars with turbine engines, which were lent to a selected group of customers for three months' trial, but the project was subsequently and definitively abandoned.
(H.S.)

FIAT

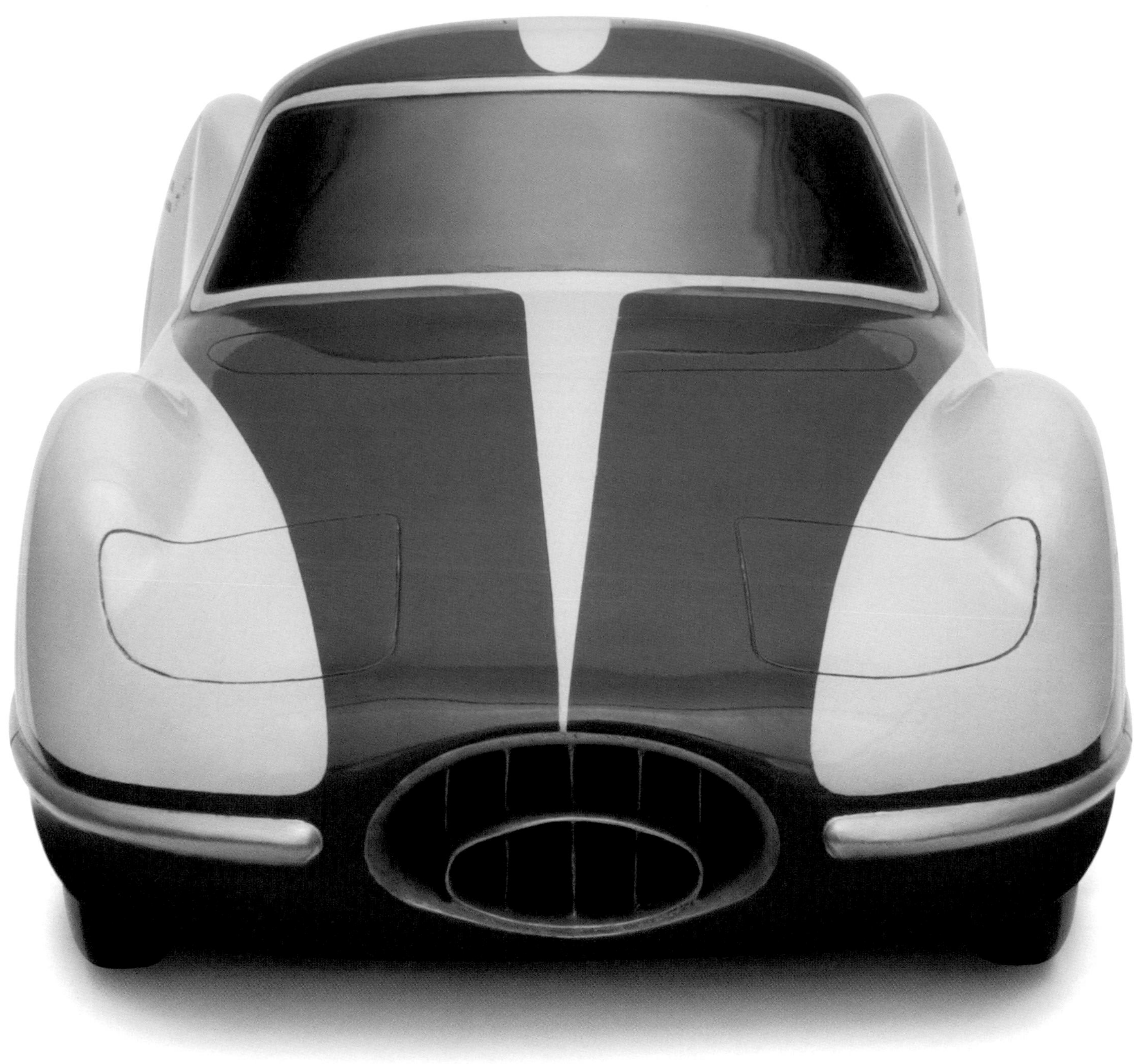

Italdesign Giugiaro

Biga, 1992

• *Make and Model*
Italdesign Biga
• *Year of production*
1992
• *Coachwork*
MPV one door, four/five seats
• *Engine*
Electric with diesel auxiliary
• *Top speed*
60 kph (37 mph)
• *Dimensions*
Length 2030 mm, width 1500 mm, height 1861 mm, wheelbase 1540 mm
• *Weight*
810 Kg
• *Total built*
1

Italdesign Giugiaro
Photo Italdesign Giugiaro archive

In 1989, participating in an international conference on the theme *What car for the year 2000?*, Giorgetto Giugiaro illustrated a theoretical vehicle for city use. At the 1992 Turin Salon, he presented the practical proposal, the Biga. It was not futuristic, but it could be made immediately: it was an ecological vehicle with electric drive providing a response to the problems of pollution in cities, but not only: it was also an absolutely new proposal as regards city transport policy which could resolve the problem of congestion in city centres. Instead of demonizinig the car, it resolved the problem of cohabitation of cars and town centres with a different vision. In practice, Giugiaro suggested that the public authorities create a fleet of ecological vehicles to be hired by anyone needing to enter the city centre. With the creation of special 'park and drive' car parks in the outskirts, it would be possible for a visitor to leave his traditional, 'polluting' car and use the Biga for however long required.
A special electronic card would record the length of time the car was hired and transmit the details for debiting the customer. Everything in the Biga was designed for city use: despite the wheelbase of just 1540 mm and overall length of 2030 mm, the car can seat up to four passengers plus the driver, thanks to two small facing benches set each other longitudinally, one behind the driving position and one on the right-hand side. The height of the car and the single large door at the rear (like the 'biga' or two-horse chariot of Roman times) facilitate access into and, above all, egress from the car, which can be parked both traditionally and perpendicularly into the pavement, offering greater safety for passengers and easier access for children's buggies and for the disabled, thanks to the low floor.
The stainless steel bodyshell is easily recycled and combines the virtues of lightness and ease of repair and maintenance, as well as resistance to corrosion. The almost square form of the bodyshell and the spartan simplicity of the standard fittings make it possible to exploit the interior space to the full, thanks also to the position of the wheels, which are small and located right in the corners of the vehicle. To overcome the problem of the reduced autonomy, the Achilles' heel of all electric cars, the Biga is equipped with a hybrid propulsion unit using the electricity produced by a small diesel engine coupled to an alternator and accumulated in batteries that are charged in the passive phases (such as when stopped and slowing down) so common in city driving.
(H.S.)

TORINO 2006
biga

TORINO 2006
guidami e... lasciami
biga
TORINO 2006
GIUGIARO
biga
biga
biga

TORINO 2006

Fiat

Vanzic, 1995

• *Make and Model*
Fiat Vanzic
• *Year of production*
1995
• *Coachwork*
Two-door, four-seater MPV
• *Engine*
Electric with auxiliary power unit
• *Maximum power*
30 Kw at 9000 rpm
• *Top speed*
105 kph (65 mph)
• *Dimensions*
Length 3350 mm, width 1670 mm, height 1550 mm
• *Weight*
1215 Kg
• *Total built*
1

Centro Ricerche Fiat S.C.p.A.

Electric propulsion was tried out in cars at the turn of the 19th century, even becoming reasonably widespread, especially in the United States, and establishing some speed records. But both the development of the internal combustion engine and the impossibility of resolving the major problem of the reduced range of electric cars, forced their gradual decline at first and their almost total disappearance subsequently, except for a limited commercial application.
But in recent years there has been a rise in studies, research and trials of new electric motors by all car manufacturers around the world; unfortunately, this rise in interest has been stimulated solely by negative events: the continued increase in atmospheric pollution suffocating city centres and the planet more generally, and the forecasts as to the depletion of world-wide oil stocks in the not-so-distant future.
But the underlying problem, the one single factor that had wiped out electric propulsion seems just as hard to resolve today, and thus restricts the distribution of electric cars on a wide scale: autonomy. The low energetic density of batteries present on the market does not yet make it possible to exceed 60-90 km (37-56 miles) and a recharge requires 6-8 hours, limiting the use of the car.
This is why the greatest efforts made by car manufacturers have been geared to the study of so-called hybrid cars: vehicles fitted with small internal combustion engines providing a constant charge to the batteries while the vehicle is in use.
Among the manufacturers active in this field is Fiat, which in 1995 presented a car fitted with hybrid electric propulsion, developed on the basis of a prototype called Zic, presented in October 1994 by the CNR and CRF and made using innovative components (ultralight alloys, polymeric composite materials) and technological processes (low-pressure mouldings, welding processes, gluing methods). An evolution of the Zic was the Vanzic, a second-generation electric vehicle; an MPV for prevalently urban use, powered by an electric motor backed up by an auxiliary power unit (a four-stroke 350 cc internal combustion engine) able to produce the electric energy needed to power the car, in addition to that stored in the batteries. The range of the vehicle is thus increased to 200 kilometres with an average consumption of 4.3 litres per 100 kilometres.
(H.S.)

VANZIC
RICERCHE
FIAT

GM

Hy-wire, 2002

• *Make and Model*
General Motors Hy-wire
• *Year of production*
2002
• *Coachwork*
Four-door saloon
• *Engine*
Fuel cell
• *Maximum power*
60 kw
• *Top speed*
160 kph (99 mph)
• *Dimensions*
Length 5000 mm
• *Weight*
1900 Kg
• *Total built*
1

General Motors

With the Hy-wire, General Motors Corp presented a project that is very close to the re-invention of the car. Beneath the skin, there is a combination of avant-garde technologies, and it is the first vehicle in the world to combine a hydrogen fuel cell and drive-by-wire technology. This is the result of 360° research undertaken by General Motors' engineers in the United States, who have developed the chassis, engineering and integration of the electrical system.

The fuel cell propulsion system was added by GM's research structure in Germany. The Swedish SKF group developed the drive-by-wire technology while the American stylists collaborated with Bertone in Turin. All the car's control and propulsion systems are contained within the chassis, which is just 28 cm high and is shaped like a skateboard. This makes it possible to maximize the space within for passengers and luggage.

Thanks to this solution, the cabin gains in space and visibility, as the engine is invisible; even the pedals are gone. To control the car, there is a control pod, used to accelerate, brake and steer. The whole pod can be simply shifted for driving on the left or the right. The fuel cells are housed at the rear of the chassis. The electric motor powering the front wheels is located transversely between them, while the fuel tanks are located in the central part of the chassis. This revolutionary project was officially presented at the Paris Salon de l'Automobile in 2002 with the aim of demonstrating a significant step forward towards a more environmentally-friendly car, with a car able also to provide additional benefits as regards the dynamics of driving, safety and freedom of expression.
(P.C.D.)

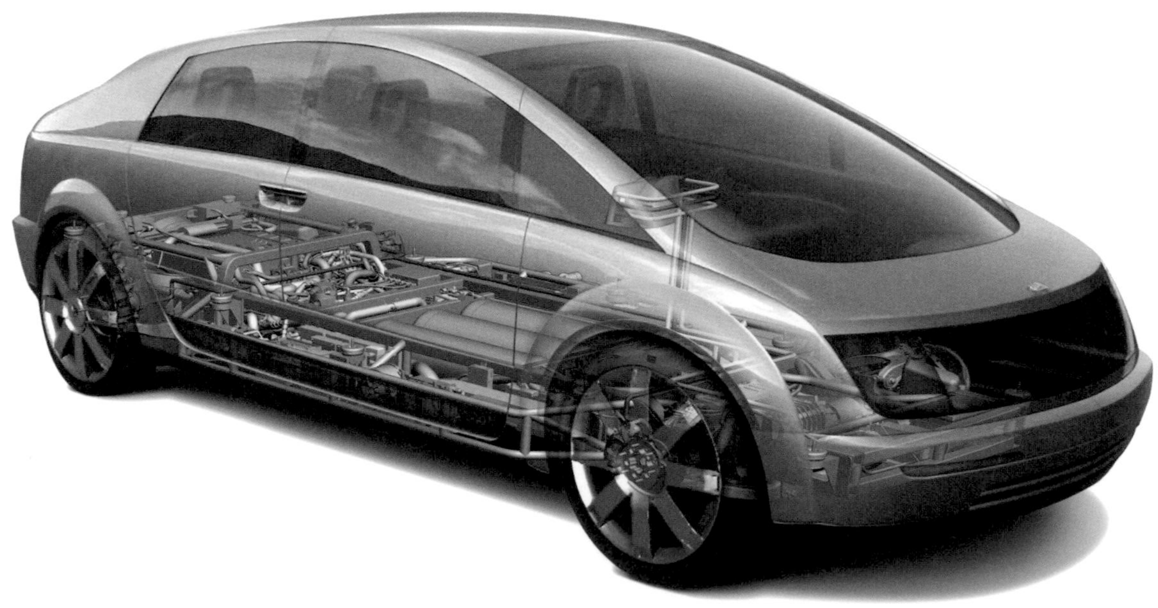

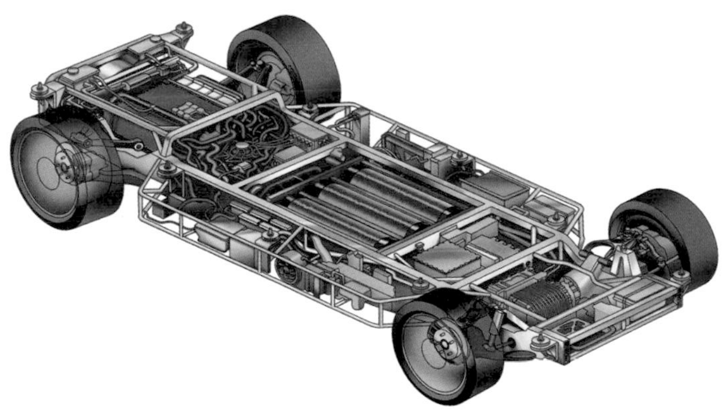

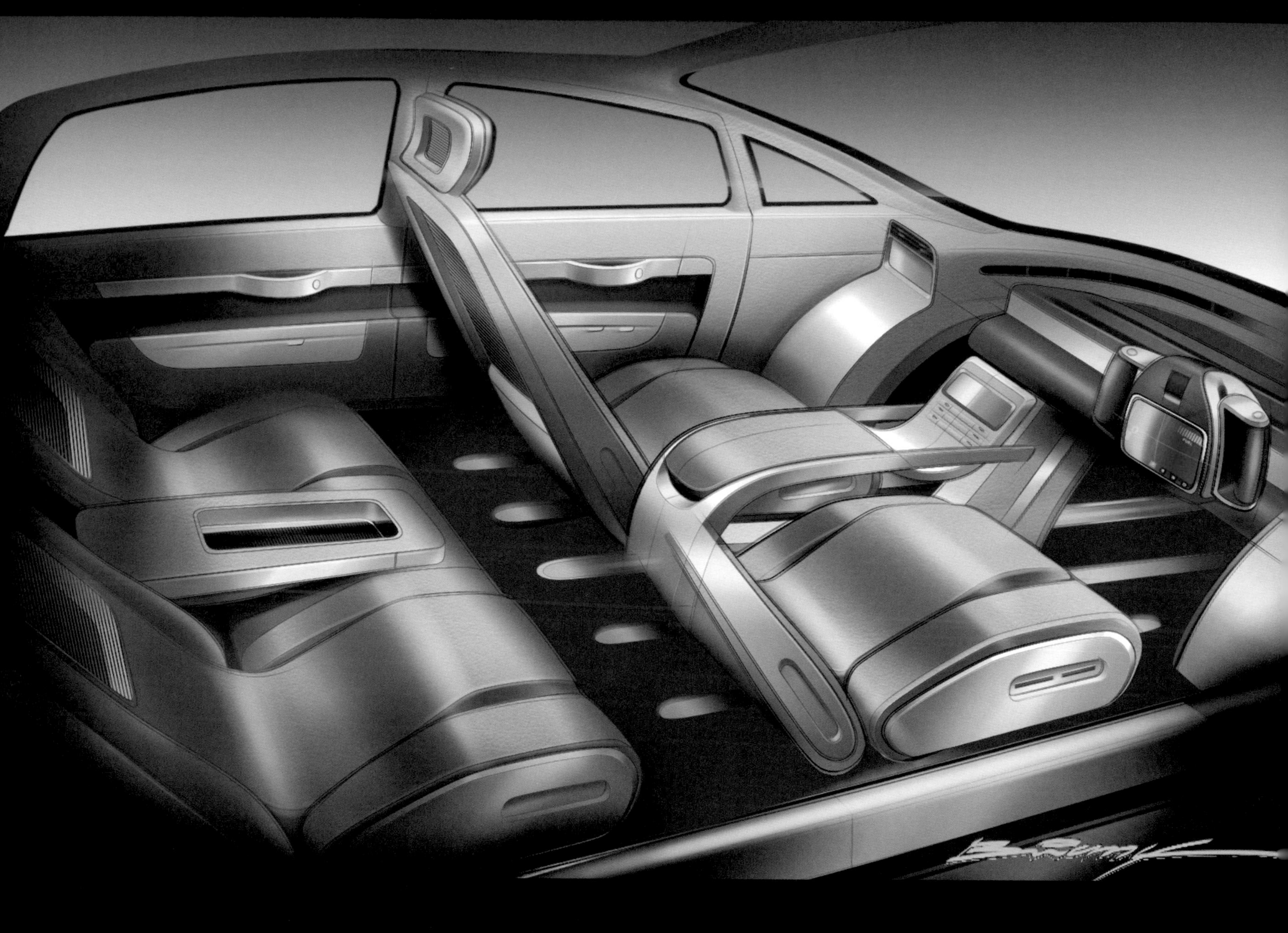

GM
POWER

Pininfarina

Nido, 2004

• *Make and Model*
Pininfarina Nido
• *Year of production*
2004
• *Coachwork*
Two-door, two-seat MPV
• *Dimensions*
Length 2890 mm, width 1674 mm, height 1534 mm, wheelbase 2068 mm
• *Total built*
1

Pininfarina Collection

One of the problems with micro-cars, or city cars, has always been that of passive safety. This is a problem that is all the more important today, with cars tending to become bigger and heavier, both to offer more space within and to satisfy increasingly stringent safety regulations.
With the Nido project presented in 2004, Pininfarina rethought the present design methods underlying the production of cars to arrive at an innovative concept that re-examines the safety of small cars, considering not only the effects of a crash on the single car, but also the problems of compatibility between cars of different masses. This is why the Nido project concentrates essentially on the study of new solutions involving both the structural and design aspects of a small two-seater car, the aim being to increase the safety both of the occupants within and to limit injury to any pedestrians involved in an accident.
Nido is formed of three principal elements: the chassis, whose mass accounts for about two thirds of the total mass of the car and contains all the technical components (comprising a frontal crumple zone and a rigid cell around the passengers), the bodyshell, which totals about a third of the total mass and encloses the driver and passenger (comprising a sort of 'sledge' able to slide horizontally on a central runner within the rigid cell), and a third element comprising two honeycomb impact absorbers acting as energy dissipators and linking the sledge and rigid cell.
In case of a head-on crash, the car absorbs part of the energy in the front crumple zone of the chassis, while the remaining energy causes the sledge to slide forwards, compressing the two honeycomb absorbers positioned between the rigid cell and the sledge below the console area, thus enabling a gradual deceleration. The sledge can be fitted with further, smaller absorbers mounted at the rear between rigid cell and sledge, in order to protect the passengers in the case of being hit behind.
The front scuttle at the base of the windscreen is lined with an energy-absorbing cushion able to minimize physical injury in the case of an impact with a pedestrian. To this end, the same material has also been used for the collapsible A-pillar. Just 2890 mm long, 1674 mm wide and 1534 mm high, the Nido has a rear-mounted engine, rear-wheel drive and automatic gearbox.
(H.S.)

nido

air
nido
safety research prototype
air
airbag

20.5 C°

Mercedes-Benz

F 600 HY, 2005

• *Make and Model*
DaimlerChrysler F600 Hygenius
• *Year of production*
2005
• *Coachwork*
Saloon
• *Engine*
Fuel cells
• *Maximum power*
115 b.h.p., 82 b.h.p. continuous
• *Dimensions*
Length 4348 mm, width 1950 mm, height 1700 mm, wheelbase 2900 mm
• *Total built*
1

DaimlerChrysler Advanced Design Italia
Photo DaimlerChrysler Advanced Design Italia

Experimental cars can boast a long tradition in today's DaimlerChrysler AG.
In recent years, under the F series label, a whole range of prototypes have been built, from the F 100 and F 300 to the F 400 Carving, the F 500 Mind and the exceptional bionic, fish-shaped prototype.
In 2005, DaimlerChrysler presented the F 600 Hygenius, fitted with a hydrogen engine. This compact family car stands out not only for its hydrogen engine, which respects the environment and paves the way for the car industry of the future, but also for a series of innovations aimed at passenger safety and versatility.
The possible autonomy of fuel cell cars could be more than doubled and the good cold start-up characteristics ensures the car can be used even in sub-zero temperatures.
If required, the fuel cells can be used an electricity-generating unit.
The noted PRE-SAFE system has been endowed with further functions to protect the front-seat passenger and an optical system helps in preventing lateral collisions.
The F 600 offers a series of important innovations within the cabin. For instance, the completely variable use of the seats, made possible through the use of a totally flat sandwich structure floor containing the fuel cells, high-yield battery and starter.
The seat next to the driver, as well as the rear seats, are perfectly adaptable for children and make visual contact between adults and them possible at all times. The central console with the bottle-holder, the warming or cooling cupholder, the extractable cushions and many other well-designed details complete this made-to-measure car for the family.
The look of the bodyshell is uncompromisingly wedge-shaped, with large glazed surfaces which express the dynamic nature of the car, despite its small size, and gives a sense of the space within, with a comfortable interior typical of a luxury saloon designed by the Advanced Design Studio of Como, founded in 1998.
(R.J.F.K.)

ENGINE
START
STOP
D
P
N
R
MODE
TEMP
DISC
RADIO
A/C

Zaha Hadid

Z.CAR, 2005

• *Make and Model*
Z.CAR – prototype
• *Year of production*
2005
• *Coachwork*
Three-wheel city car, two wheels at the front; design team: Zaha Hadid, Patrik Schumacher, Jens Borstelmann; commissioned by Kenny Schachter/ROVE; prototype produced in collaboration with GTM, Coventry (United Kingdom)
• *Engine*
Hydrogen with drive-by-wire technology (rear-mounted engine)
• *Dimensions*
Length 3790 mm, width 1850 mm, height variable using hydraulic system (low speeds: high position; high speeds: vehicle lowered 10°)
• *Weight*
About 700 Kg
• *Total built*
1 prototype

Kenny Schachter/ROVE Collection

Zaha Hadid, one of the most important architects of our time, designed the Z.CAR prototype in 2005, under commission from Kenny Schachter/ROVE. Although the first car ever to be designed by Zaha Hadid, this is not her first project in the car sector. In 2002, she designed the new BMW plant at Leipzig in Germany, and in 2005 a car park in Strasbourg, France.

The Z.CAR is a three-wheel city car, its aerodynamic form reflecting the aesthetics of Hadid's studio. The project for this car follows a line of design coinciding with the requirements of potential buyers: the vehicle is extremely simple to park, is very quiet and offers excellent visibility thanks to its ample glazed area. The hydrogen engine has a low environmental impact thanks to the use of renewable energy.

The design of the Z.CAR includes two unusual features: the passenger capsule varies in height according to the speed. At low speeds, the position of the capsule is high and offers a good view of the road; as the speed increases, the body lowers by 10° thanks to a hydraulic system and assures greater stability.

The second unusual feature is an external boot fitted between the passenger cabin and the suspension of the wheels.

In town, the car is used without boot and the driver can thus benefit from a compact vehicle that is easy to manoeuvre and park. When used for a journey, the supplementary boot is attached to the car, providing extra luggage space.

(J.T.)

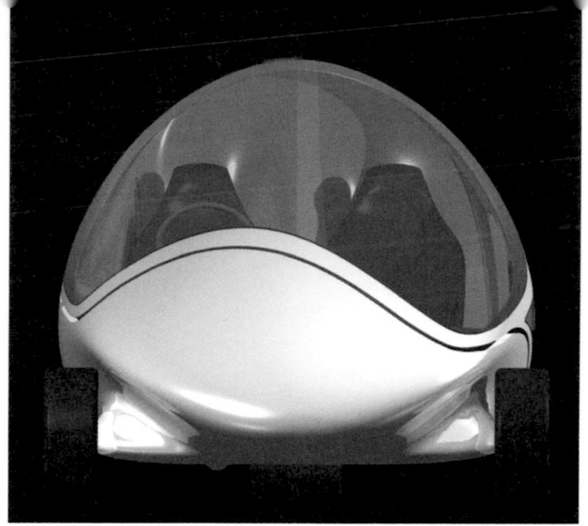

Nissan

Pivo, 2005

• *Make and Model*
Nissan Pivo
• *Dimensions*
Length 2700 mm, width 1600 mm, height 1660 mm, wheelbase 2000 mm
• *Total built*
Still in production

Nissan Motor Company LTD

Nissan presented its vision of the city car of the future with the Pivo project, produced by the Nissan design team in Japan and presented in September 2005 during a special event at the Nissan Gallery in the heart of Tokyo. On that occasion, artist Takashi Murakami created an evocative view of a garden of the future, rendered more cheery by the presence of large balloons and illustrations featuring 'Pivo-chan,' a character created by the artist and inspired by the Pivo design.
The futuristic Nissan concept car features advanced design solutions and technological content, and is a study of the potential future of electric cars in towns.
Just 2700 mm long, the Pivo can comfortably seat three: the driver, in front in a central position, and the two passengers behind, one next to the other. Thanks to the reduced width, only 1600 mm, the Pivo is easy to manoeuvre in traffic and can be parked almost anywhere.
The Pivo has an egg-shaped cabin which can pivot (hence the concept car's name) over the chassis and rotate 360° to facilitate parking and manoeuvres and doing away with a reverse gear. This solution has been made possible through the use of drive-by-wire controls, which do away with all mechanical controls in favour of electronics. The cabin is fitted with an 'Around View' system comprising a series of cameras providing a 360° view outside, synthesized on a monitor within. Avant-garde electronics systems provide further information for the driver.
An infrared (Ir) control system on the dashboard enables the driver to activate the navigator and stereo system without removing his eyes from the road or fiddling with manual controls. Information concerning routes run along the base of the windscreen, like subtitles in a film. And if one wants to raise the volume of the music? Just raise your hand.
Entering and leaving the car is easy, thanks to two electronically-controlled doors. The Pivo is powered by a compact, high-performance, lithium ion battery and a super-electric motor, both developed by Nissan. Being flat, the lithium ion battery takes up much less space and is lighter than a conventional cylindrical cell. Also with an eye to reducing weight, the Pivo uses two compact super-motors, one on each axle, rather than one on each wheel. Each super-motor delivers the driving force to two drive-shafts, each of which can be independently controlled for efficient distribution of torque to the four wheels.
(E.B.)

NISSAN
PIVO

12
FL
FR
RL
RR
P
5523
123
NISSAN
AUTO

Young Designers: Proposals for the Future

Turin, IED

X 1/99, 2005

The X 1/99 project was realized as part of the Master RSP in Transportation Design 2003–04 by Fabio Bisson, Christian Cudly, Tony Gatta, Luis Huertas, Cristiano Nishimura, Michele Salvatore and José Hernandez Wong
• *Idea*
Tony Gatta
• *In collaboration with*
Fiat, Webasto, Cecomp
• *Restyling by*
IED Automotive

Presented in its original version, as produced as part of the Master RSP in Transportation Design (academic year 2003–04), at the Geneva International Motor Show in March 2005, the X 1/99 explored an innovative concept of car transformability, proposing a multi-functional opening roof, made thanks to the contribution of Webasto. A coupé-cabrio, 2+2, sports, versatile, multi-functional car combining features of a city car and of a cabriolet, including practicality, accessible price, particular appeal, fun, playfulness. The advanced model of the X 1/99, the result of a restyling by IED Automotive, presents a roof and interior with a series of innovative and interesting solutions, and highlighting their actual construction in line with Webasto's objectives. The roof (which is transformed into seats when the car is open), has been redesigned to ensure the driver has full visibility through the rear windscreen when open. Moreover, a wind deflector has been installed to regulate the airflow within and, finally, the rear seats have been revised to make them safer and more comfortable for passengers. The colours also express the maturity of the project.

Turin, IED

Ascari, Millechili, 2005

The Ascari project on p. 461 was realized as part of the three-year post-diploma course in Transportation Design – car design at the IED in Turin (academic year 2004–05) by Manuele Amprimo, Werner Gruber and Yu Jae Cheul

A link between history and future.
An idea inspired by the fantastic forms and immortal history of the 'Testarossa,' which is brought up-to-date with raked volumes that interweave as though mechanical components, engine and man were one. A car with sensual, aggressive lines recalling the racing circuit, always a part of Ferrari, but without overlooking comfort and technology to render the drive and comfort of the vehicle more pleasing.
A name and a marque which through the world bring to mind a single word: 'legend.'

The Millechili project illustrated on p. 462–63 was realized as part of the three-year post-diploma course in Transportation Design – car design at the IED in Turin (academic year 2004–05) by Felix Hiller and Luis Agullo Spottomo

The line, the performance and the sensations one feels driving the Millechili transmit everything a Ferrari should be to the driver.
The Millechili represents the desire to exploit the potential to the full and to enjoy the most precise technology in the world to the maximum. Controlling the uncontrollable with a Ferrari as light as the wind.
Equipped with the latest Formula 1 technology, adapted for the Millechili to achieve maximum effectiveness on both racing track and road, the car is visibly light and features carbon-fibre chassis. It weights just 1000 Kg ('mille chili' in Italian) and sports a 400 b.h.p. engine, assuring breathtaking performance without the need for extra power.
Designed for a highly expert driver, able to enjoy a highly precise vehicle on the race track.
Speed in its purest state, always at the service of engineering, able to convey the true excitement and deepest pleasure of driving.
Its characteristics render it unique, just as the driver must be unique in order to be able to tame such a car full of heart and verve.
Its size can be deceptive: 'small' certainly does not mean 'available to all.'
One has to be special to possess this great sports car and exploit to the full the exclusive technology under its skin.

Millechili and Ascari are two of the four winning models in the Ferrari competition: the new concepts of the 'legendary' marque that attracted four of the most famous international car design schools: the Center for Creative Studies of Detroit, the Coventry School of Art and Design, the Istituto Europeo di Design of Turin and Tokyo Communication Arts.

CECOMP
vodafone
CECOMP
MILLECHILI CUP
PIRELLI
69
PIRELLI
PIRELLI
Shell

69

Pforzheim, Fachhochschule

Projects, 2004–06

The project on p. 465 was realized as part of the course in Transportation Design – car design at the Pforzheim Fachhochschule (academic year 2003–04) by Patrick Faulwetter

The project on p. 466 was realized as part of the course in Transportation Design – car design at the Pforzheim Fachhochschule (academic year 2003–04) by Jakob Hirzel

The project on p. 467 was realized as part of the course in Transportation Design – car design at the Pforzheim Fachhochschule (academic year 2005–06) by Gregory John Paul

In 2002 the Pforzheim upper school celebrated its 125th anniversary. The institute has changed from being a school dedicated to crafts to the status of higher institute with three sites in the Pforzheim area. The upper school of economics and engineering is annexed to the Pforzheim institute.
The faculty is divided into different study courses — dedicated to the creation of industrial design, fashion, jewellery and articles of mass culture, visual communications and transportation design — which conclude in a bachelor's degree and are completed with interdisciplinary studies through which it is possible to arrive at a master's degree in Art of Transportation Design and in Creative Direction.
The studies in Transportation Design of the Pforzheim school was founded in 1984 under the name of Kfz-Design ('Car Design') and changed to Transportation Design in 1992. From the winter semester of 2005–06, the principal field of study for this course — which concludes with a bachelor's degree — is industrial design. As a complementary completion of the basic study course, the possibility of arriving at a master's in Transportation Design has been offered since the summer semester of 2001.
The designers of the future are trained in this school for this specific sector, that of the design of means of transport. The content of the single courses are basic subjects and sectorial disciplines providing the designers with the means to draw up formal projects for both private cars and public transportation.

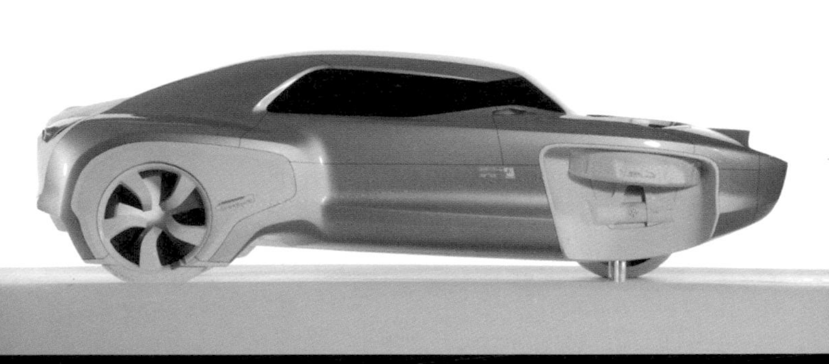

London, Royal College of Arts

Fiat Scratch, Post-consumption, Daedalus Concept, 2006

The Fiat Scratch project on p. 469 was realized as part of the 2005–06 course in Transportation Design at the Royal College of Arts in London by Uros Pavasovic

The Post-consumption project on p. 470 was realized as part of the 2005–06 course in Transportation Design at the Royal College of Arts in London by Johan Jonsson

The Daedalus Concept project on p. 471 was realized as part of the 2005–06 course in Transportation Design at the Royal College of Arts in Londonby Jonathan Punter

Three young graduates from a unique university of art and design present their work in this exhibition: Johann Jonsson, Jonathan Punter and Uros Pavasovic.
They represent the best of a new generation of vehicle designers at an international level.
The Royal College of Arts in London is unique.
It is attended by about 800 students a year, 40 of whom form the vehicle design department. By the turn of the century, this department had produced about 80% of the finest designers at a world-wide level. Directed by Professor Dale Harrow, the Royal College of Arts accepts about 10% of those seeking admission and students come from every continent.
The teaching is characterized by three fundamental branches: Automark, Inside Out and Urban Flow, associated with marque and identity, systems and materials, and transport volumes. The College stresses travel, social imperatives and innovation within the context of commercial situations.
A salient feature of the department is the diversity of races, country of origin and experience of the graduates selected for the course, who work together with MPhil and PhD research students and qualified designers sent by their companies to learn new prospects. A staff of guest specialists and experts within the College's structure work in collaboration with leading designers, with the most important operators and instructors, in order to create the ideal learning environment within a modern structure.
The department aims to guarantee the future professionals the required technical, intellectual, creative and communicative skills to improve mobility in the 21st century, encouraging them to explore new avenues in the design of vehicles and other. The department works in close contact with the College's architecture school and interactive design, textiles and products department, as well as with members and researchers of the transport sector. The department also integrates specific research and design projects with commercial partners, design studios and other partners with philanthropic aims.

The current approach goes beyond the engineering side of things, product development or the simple realisation of brands in order to meet the requirements of consumers in different cultures and evolving society. Innovative solutions are sought based on in-depth research, constructive experimentation, including mobility and sustainable transport.
The post-graduate projects reflect both commercial needs and innovation in design. The students are involved in resolving complex problems concerning the mobility of tomorrow.
The individual portfolio reflects commitment, creativity and fundamental skills in a different setting of applied innovation of absolute intellectual rigour.
The three designers exhibiting their work reflect the diversity of talent and of origins within the department. Johan Jonsson is Swedish and has a degree in industrial planning from Konstfack, Stockholm. He has won awards from BMW and from the Royal Swedish Academy for Science and Engineering. Uros Pavasovic is Slovene. He is a graduate of architecture from the University of Ljubljana. He has received awards from Michelin, Piranesi, Anfia and Ford.
He also won the City of London international design award in 2006, assigned by the Carmen Company. Jonathan Punter is British and a graduate in transport design from Coventry University. He has received awards from the Royal Society of Arts and the Coachmakers company of London.
Jonathan draws his inspiration from nature and from a user's behaviour. His concept of a car of the future from the Daedalus family reflects the trends in family life in 2020 and the needs of families, creating a landscape encouraging social interaction but at the same time favouring private space and stimulating play. Uros dedicates himself to the solution of problems and aspects that go beyond the superficial function and aesthetics, exploring the meaning of an object and the projection of its owner. His 'Scratch-happy' Fiat transforms stress into satisfaction, to the point that everything that causes 'wear and tear' becomes 'habitable' design for a unique form of mobility. Johan seeks to adapt natural forms and materials in an artistic manner to his own design.
His post-consumer car responds the the needs for alternative solutions in terms of energy, production and aesthetic appearance; he makes use of hemp, cereals, rubbish and soya, making use of natural processes for his vehicles, creating a symbiosis between man and machine.
Uros, Johan and Jonathan are the symbol of talent, of refinement and of innovation distinguishing the post-graduate students from the Royal College of Art and its vehicle design department.

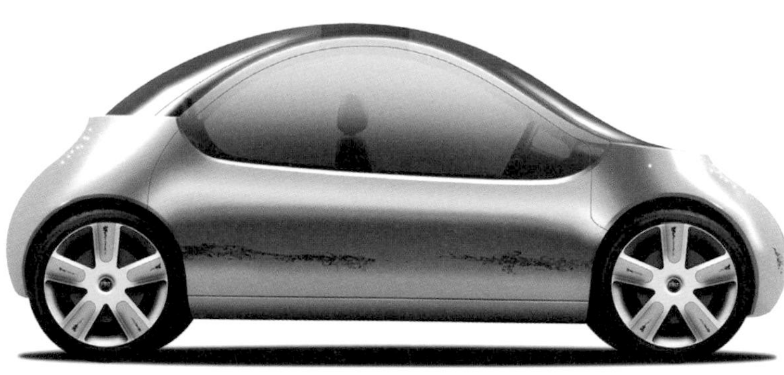

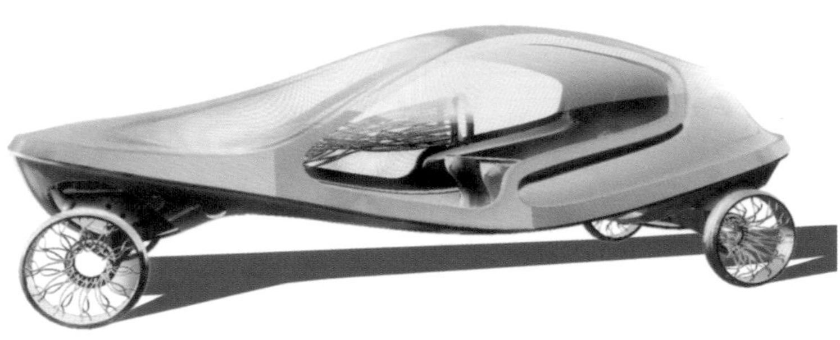

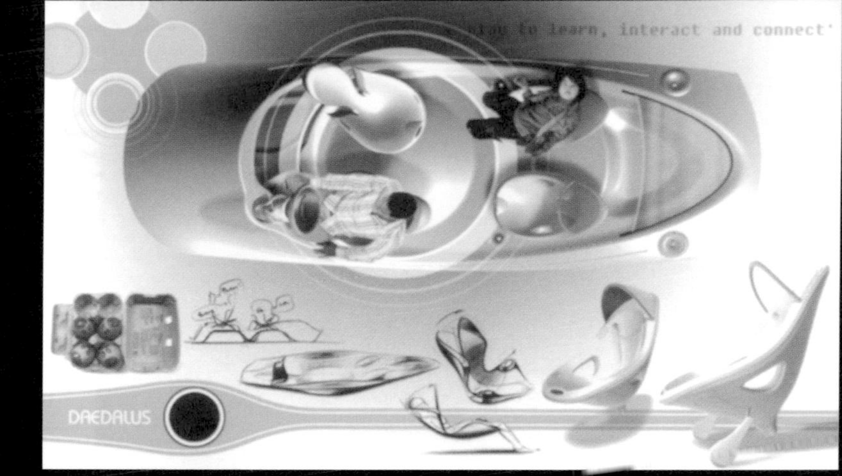
learn, interact and connect'
DAEDALUS

AUTOMARK 1
JONATHAN PUNTER
John Hartnell Award

Summary of Items

Benz Patent Motorwagen, 1886

p. 108

R1-1
Benz Patent Motorwagen (1886)
DaimlerChrysler Classic Archive
© DaimlerChrysler AG
R1-2
Reverse side of patent for the Benz Patent Motorwagen
(1886)
DaimlerChrysler Classic Archive
© DaimlerChrysler AG
R1-3
Period advertisement for the Benz Patent Motorwagen (1888)
DaimlerChrysler Classic Archive
© DaimlerChrysler AG
R1-4
Illustration of Benz Patent Motorwagen (1886)
Period photograph
DaimlerChrysler Classic Archive
© DaimlerChrysler AG
R1-5
Benz Patent Motorwagen model 1, 0.75 b.h.p. (1886)
Period photograph
DaimlerChrysler Classic Archive
© DaimlerChrysler AG
R1-6
Benz Patent Motorwagen model 1, 0.75 b.h.p. (1886)
Period photograph
DaimlerChrysler Classic Archive
© DaimlerChrysler AG

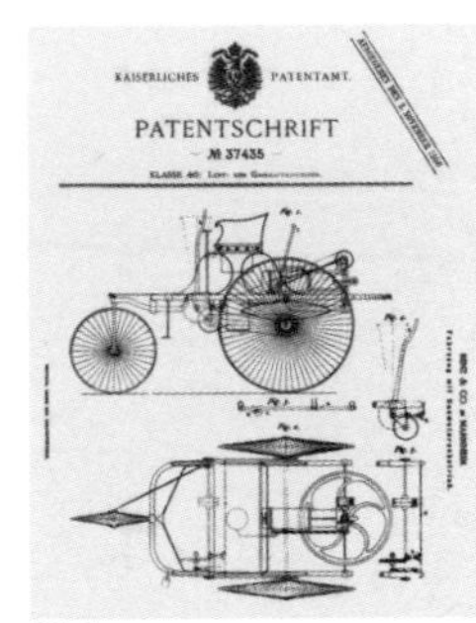

KAISERLICHES PATENTAMT

PATENTSCHRIFT

№ 37435

R1-1

R1-4

KAISERLICHES PATENTAMT

PATENTSCHRIFT

№ 37435

BENZ & CO. in MANNHEIM.

R1-2

R1-5

Neuer Patent-Motorwagen
mit Gasbetrieb durch Benzin.
Benz & Cie., Rheinische Gasmotorenfabrik
Mannheim.

R1-3

R1-6

Alfa Romeo, 8C 2900 B Berlinetta Touring, 1938

p. 112

R2-1
Illustration of 8C 2900 B Berlinetta Touring
Gouache and pencil on paper, 20 x 57 cm
Bianchi Anderloni Collection
R2-2
Study for the 8C 2900 B Berlinetta Touring, internal driving position aerodynamic two-seater, side view (signed Bianchi Anderloni)
Pencil on tracing paper, 30 x 67.5 cm
Bianchi Anderloni Collection
R2-3
Drawing for the 8C 2900 B Berlinetta Touring
Lost drawing, document on file
Bianchi Anderloni Collection

R2-1

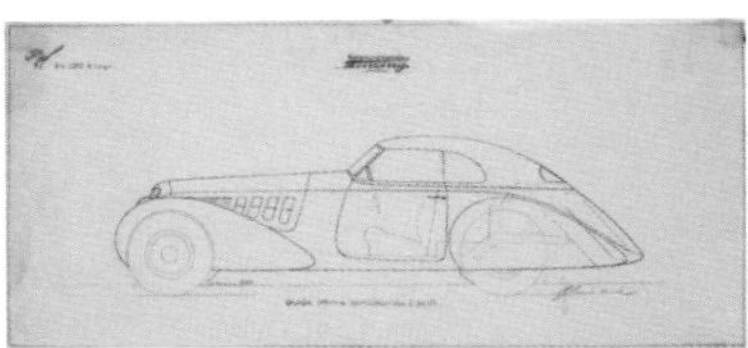

R2-2

R2-3

R2-4
Advertising leaflet by Touring of its coachwork: 'La Carrozzeria Touring alla 1000 Mlglia,' 1938
29.7 x 21 cm
Bianchi Anderloni Collection

R2-4

Hanomag, Kommissbrot, 1925

p. 122

R3-1
Technical drawing of the coachwork for Kommissbrot, with two views, 1925
Ralf J.F. Kieselbach Collection
Christian Jäger
R3-2
Technical drawing of the chassis for the Kommissbrot, 1925
Ralf J.F. Kieselbach Collection
Familie Böhler
R3-3
Open two-seater Kommissbrot (1925)
Period illustration 'Waldorf-Zuban,'
5.9 x 9 cm
Ralf J.F. Kieselbach Collection
R3-4
Two-seater saloon Kommissbrot (1925)
Period illustration 'Waldorf-Zuban,'
5.9 x 9 cm
Ralf J.F. Kieselbach Collection
R3-5
Convertible Kommissbrot (1925)
Period illustration 'Waldorf-Zuban,'
5.9 x 9 cm
Ralf J.F. Kieselbach Collection
R3-6
Electric welding of the coachwork for the Kommissbrot, 1925
Period photograph
Ralf J.F. Kieselbach Collection
Familie Knotter-Meer
R3-7
Assembly line of the Kommissbrot, 1925
Period photograph
Ralf J.F. Kieselbach Collection
Michael Mende

R3-2

R3-5

R3-3

R3-6

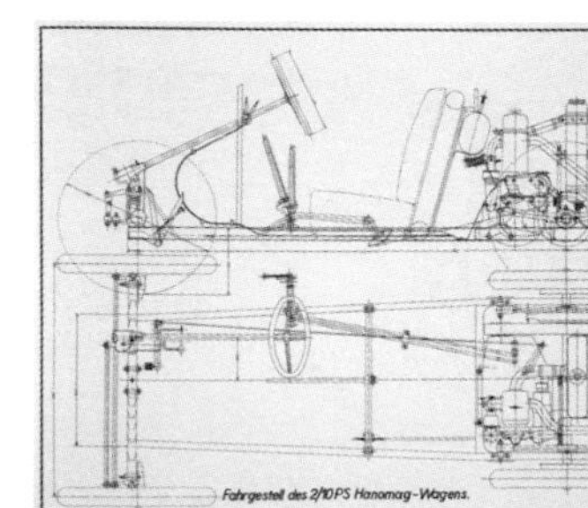

R3-1

R3-4

R3-7

Fiat, 500 Topolino, 1936

p. 126

R3-8
Daily production of the Kommissbrot in storage, 1925
Period photograph
Ralf J.F. Kieselbach Collection
Familie Knotter-Meer

R3-8

R4-1
Technical drawing for the Bn 500, with folding roof, all vehicle views (designer Bianco), 1936
Copy on tracing paper, 56.5 x 88 cm
Turin, Archivio Storico Fiat
Photo Franco Turcati

R4-2
Technical drawing for the Bn 500, all views of the car (designer Bianco), 1934
Copy on tracing paper, 56.5 x 88 cm
Turin, Archivio Storico Fiat
Photo Franco Turcati

R4-3
Technical drawing for the Bn 500, all views of the car (designer Bianco), 1934
Pencil on tracing paper, 56.5 x 84 cm
Turin, Archivio Storico Fiat
Photo Franco Turcati

R4-4
Longitudinal cross-section of the Topolino A
Turin, Archivio Storico Fiat

R4-5
Group of Fiat 500 Topolino As at Lingotto
Period photograph
Turin, Archivio Storico Fiat

R4-1

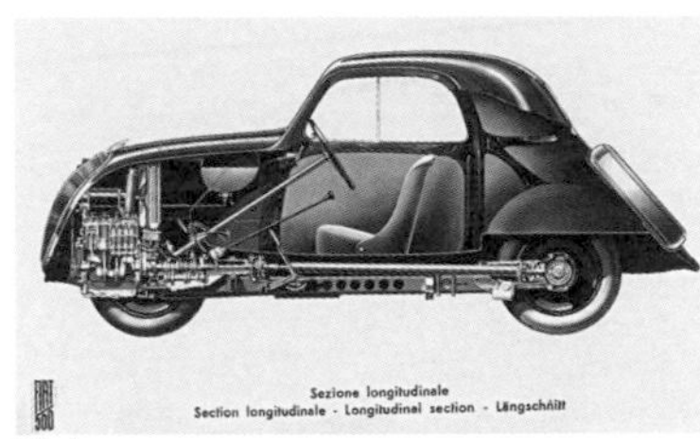

R4-4

R4-2

R4-5

R4-3

Iso, Isetta, 1953
p. 132

R5-1
Technical drawing for the Isetta, sticker for the rear transparent cupola (18.10.53), 1953
Copy of the original
Bonomelli Collection
R5-2
Technical drawing for the Isetta, design of chassis with cabin (6.5.54), 1954
Copy of the original
Bonomelli Collection
R5-3
Technical drawing for the Isetta, overall view of the door lock (27.6.53), 1953
Copy of the original
Bonomelli Collection
R5-4
Technical drawing for the Isetta, coachwork (3.7.53), 1953
Copy of the original
Bonomelli Collection
R5-5
Technical drawing for the Isetta, side window design (2.7.53), 1953
Copy of the original
Bonomelli Collection
R5-6
Technical drawing for the Isetta, three-view drawing, 1953
Copy of the original
Bonomelli Collection
R5-7
Technical drawing for the Isetta, coachwork, detail of the headlight (6.7.53), 1953
Copy of the original
Bonomelli Collection
R5-8
Technical drawing for the Isetta, door handle (7.9.53), 1953
Copy of the original
Bonomelli Collection
R5-9
Technical drawing for the Isetta, detail of the lock and hinge, 1953
Copy of the original
Bonomelli Collection

R5-1

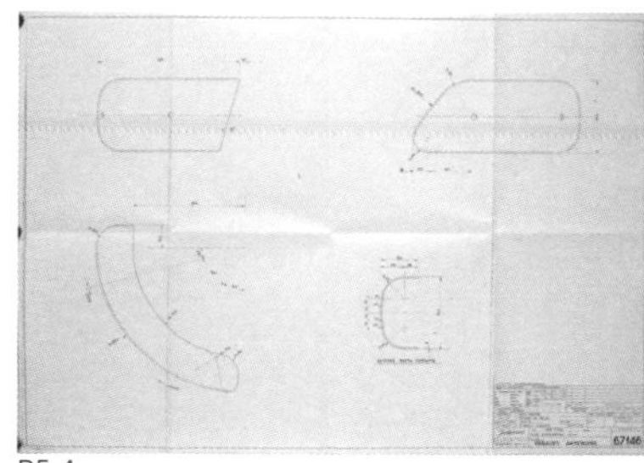
R5-4

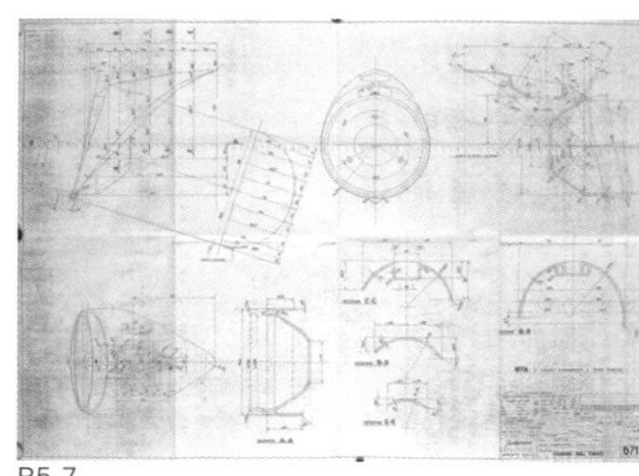
R5-7

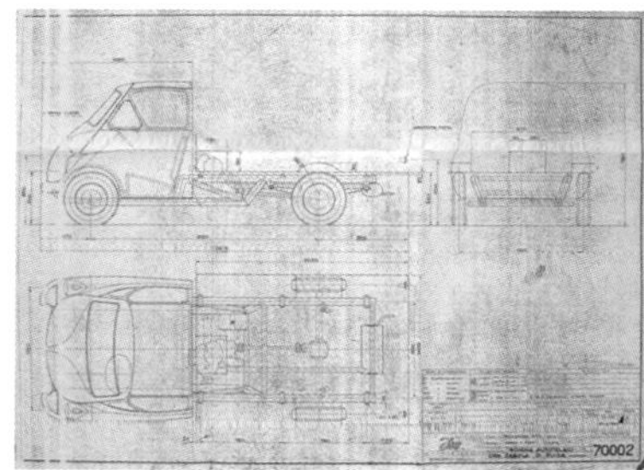

R5-2

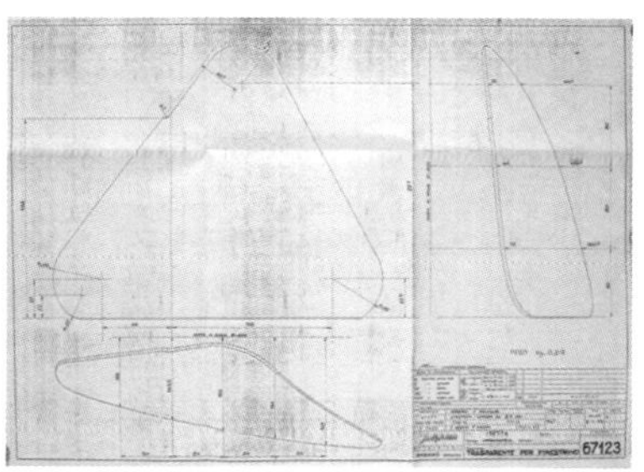

R5-5

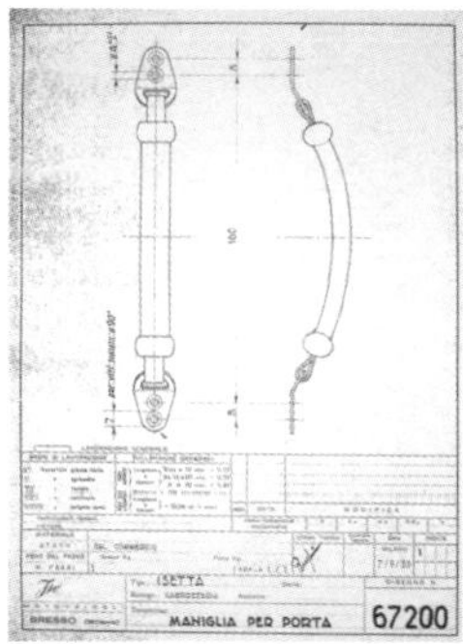

R5-8

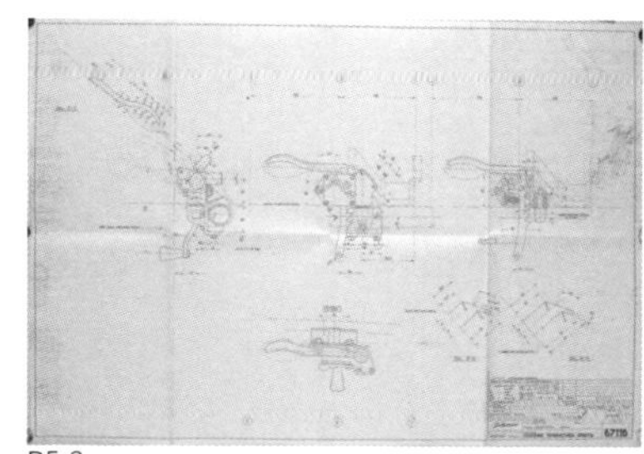
R5-3

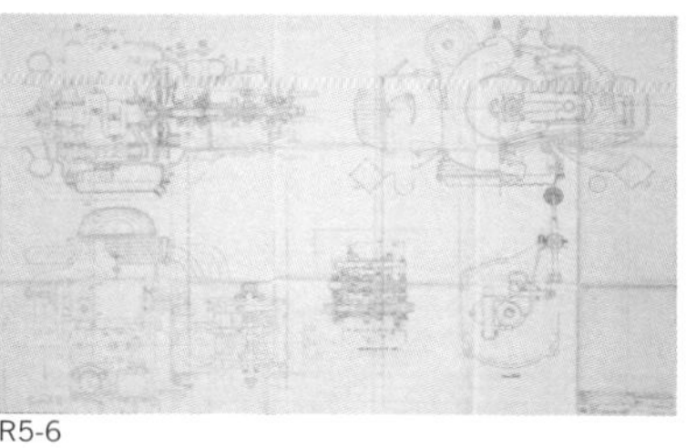
R5-6

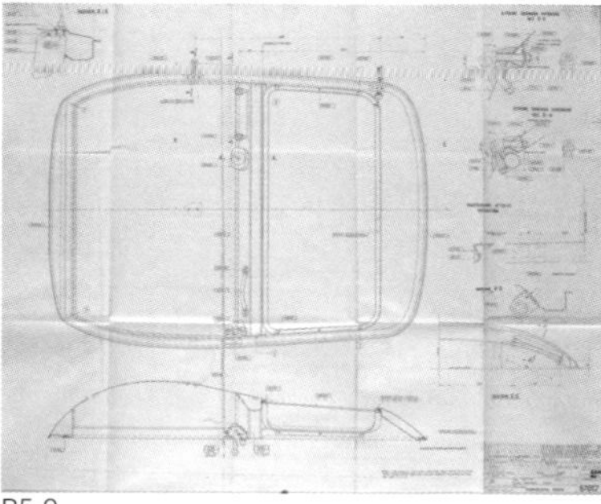
R5-9

R5-10
Cut-away of the Isetta, long wheelbase version, 1953
Copy of the original
Ralf J.F. Kieselbach Collection
R5-11
Isetta BMW, 1953
Period photograph, 12.5 x 17.5 cm
Ralf J.F. Kieselbach Collection
R5-12
Isetta, 1953
Period photograph, 12.5 x 17 cm
Ralf J.F. Kieselbach Collection
R5-13
Isetta, 1953
Period photograph, 12.5 x 17.5 cm
Ralf J.F. Kieselbach Collection
R5-14
Drawing for the Isetta BMW used by the German post office (22.7.1955), 1955
Period photograph
Ralf J.F. Kieselbach Collection
R5-15
Isetta BMW, 1953
Original postcard, 10 x 14.5 cm
Ralf J.F. Kieselbach Collection

R5-11

R5-14

R5-12

R5-15

R5-10

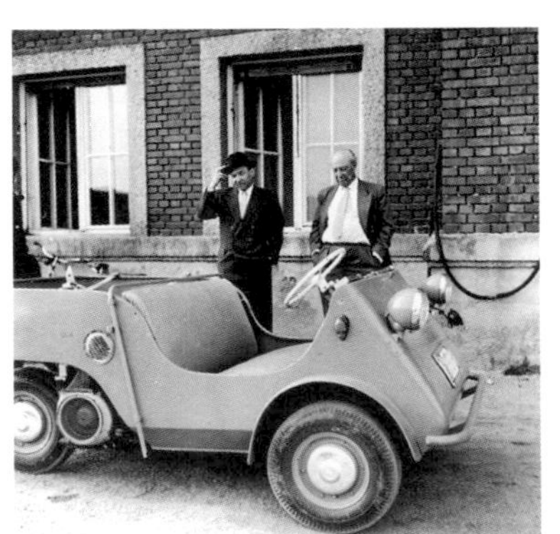
R5-13

Messerschmitt, Kabinenroller KR 200, 1953

p. 136

R6-1
Drawing for the Kabinenroller, side view (1955)
Copy of the original, 30 x 21 cm
Munich, Deutsches Museum
Photo Deutsches Museum
R6-2
Drawing for the Kabinenroller, front and rear view (1955)
Copy of the original, 30 x 21 cm
Munich, Deutsches Museum
Photo Deutsches Museum
R6-3
Study for the Kabinenroller (1955)
Pencil on paper, 21 x 30 cm
Munich, Deutsches Museum
Photo Deutsches Museum
R6-4
Study for the Kabinenroller (1955)
Pencil on paper, 21 x 30 cm
Munich, Deutsches Museum
Photo Deutsches Museum
R6-5
Study for the Kabinenroller (1955)
Pencil on paper, 21 x 30 cm
Munich, Deutsches Museum
Photo Deutsches Museum
R6-6
Study for the Kabinenroller (1955)
Pencil on paper, 21 x 30 cm
Munich, Deutsches Museum
Photo Deutsches Museum
R6-7
Study for the Kabinenroller (1955)
Pencil and coloured pencil on paper, 21 x 30 cm
Munich, Deutsches Museum
Photo Deutsches Museum
R6-8
Study for the Kabinenroller (1955)
Pencil and ink on paper, 21 x 30 cm
Munich, Deutsches Museum
Photo Deutsches Museum
R6-9
Study for the Kabinenroller (1955)
Pencil and ink on paper, 21 x 30 cm
Munich, Deutsches Museum
Photo Deutsches Museum
R6-10
Study for the Kabinenroller (1955)
Pencil and ink on paper, 21 x 30 cm
Munich, Deutsches Museum
Photo Deutsches Museum

R6-11
Letter with sketch and notes for the Kabinenroller (1955)
Pencil and ink on paper, 30 x 21 cm
Munich, Deutsches Museum
Photo Deutsches Museum

R6-3

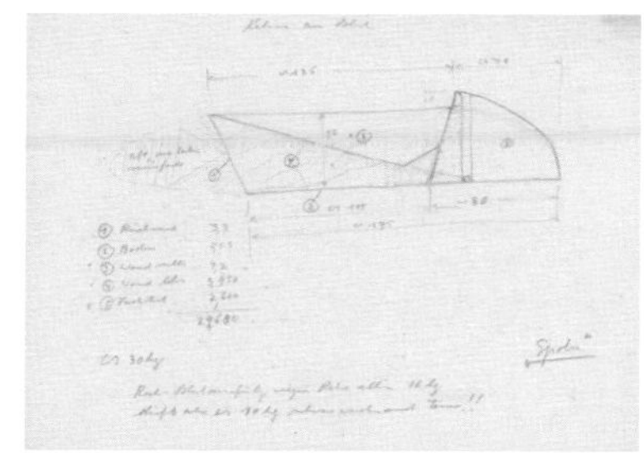
R6-6

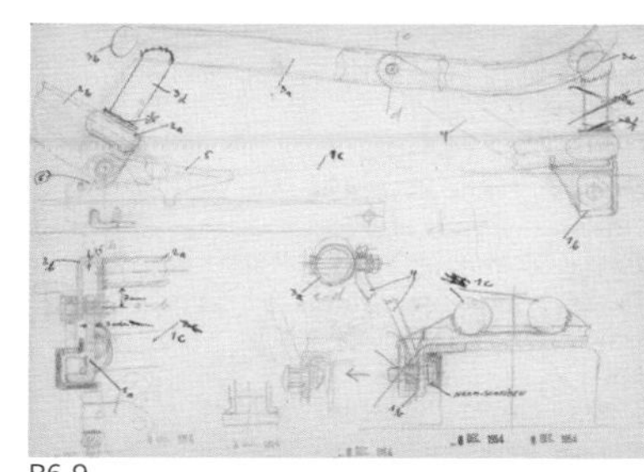
R6-9

R6-1

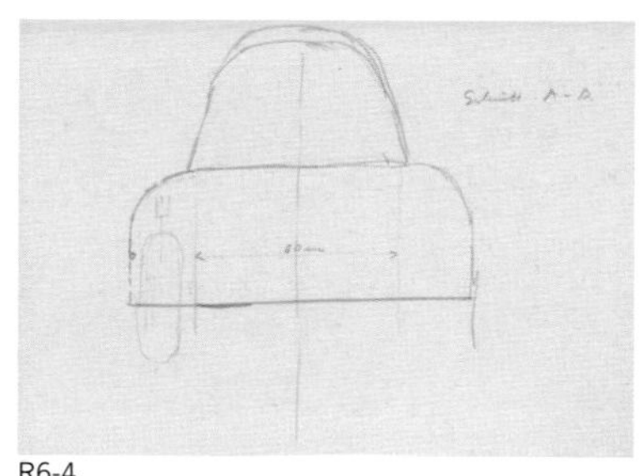
R6-4

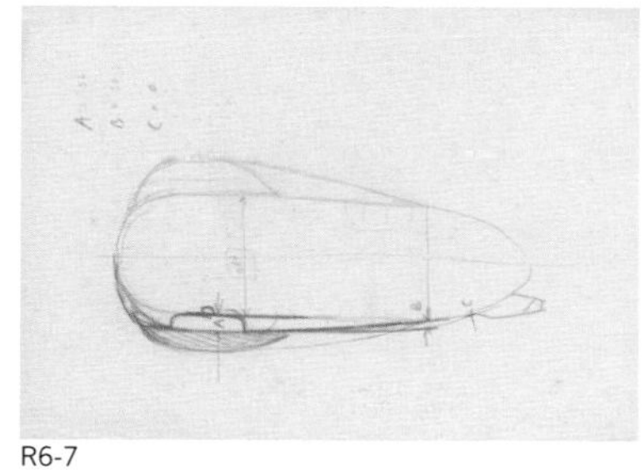
R6-7

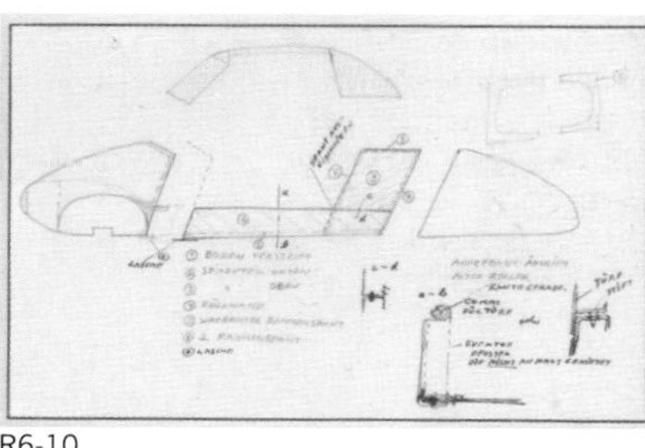
R6-10

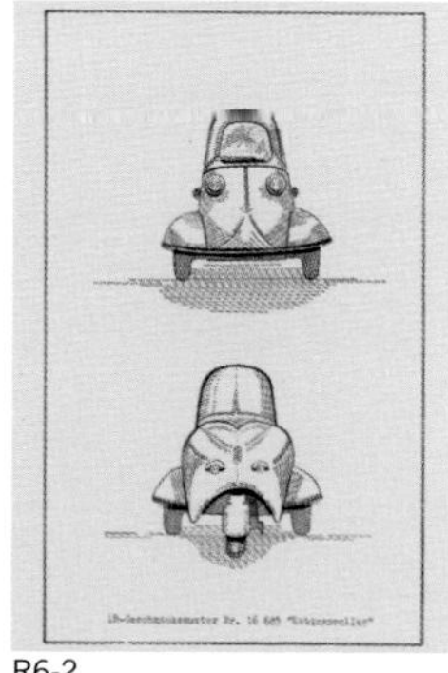
R6-2

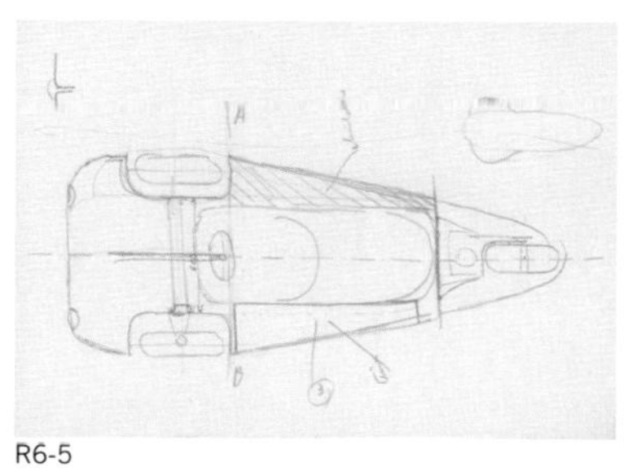
R6-5

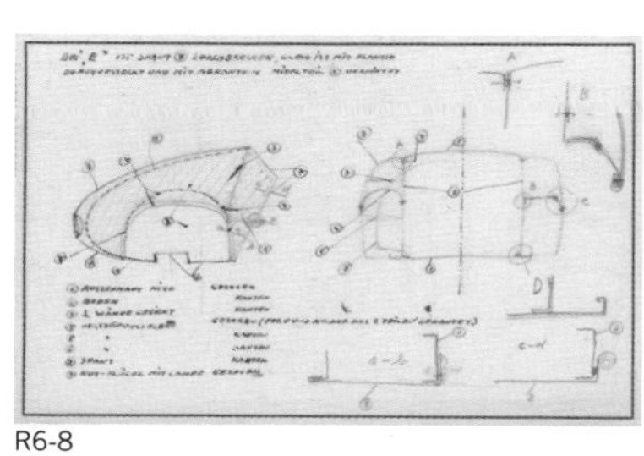
R6-8

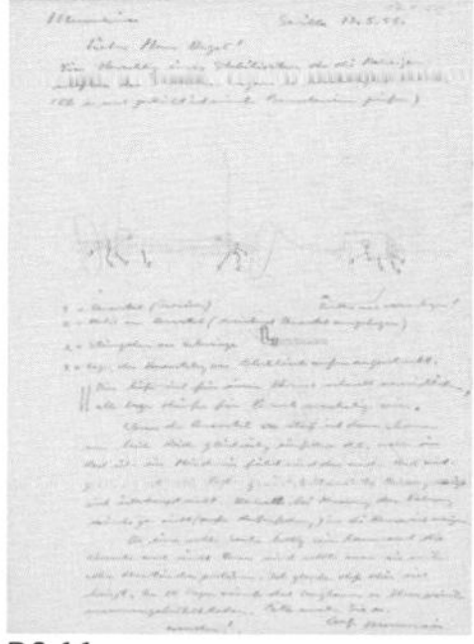
R6-11

R6-12
Cover of the advertising leaflet 'Besser mit Messerschmitt' (Better with the Messerschmitt) (1955)
Munich, Deutsches Museum
Photo Deutsches Museum

R6-13
Advertising leaflet 'Besser mit Messerschmitt' (Better with the Messerschmitt) (1955)
Munich, Deutsches Museum
Photo Deutsches Museum

R6-14
Advertising leaflet 'Besser mit Messerschmitt' (Better with the Messerschmitt) (1955)
Munich, Deutsches Museum
Photo Deutsches Museum

R6-15
Advertising leaflet 'Besser mit Messerschmitt' (Better with the Messerschmitt) (1955)
Munich, Deutsches Museum
Photo Deutsches Museum

R6-12

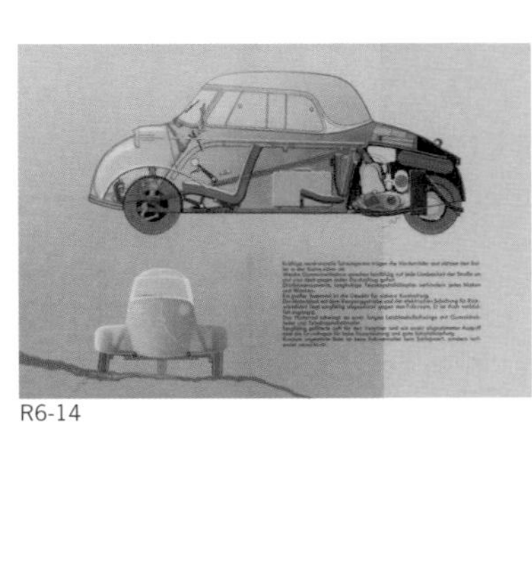

R6-14

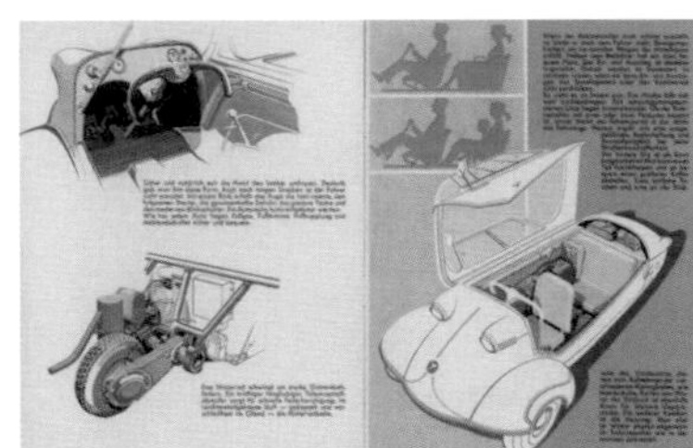

R6-15

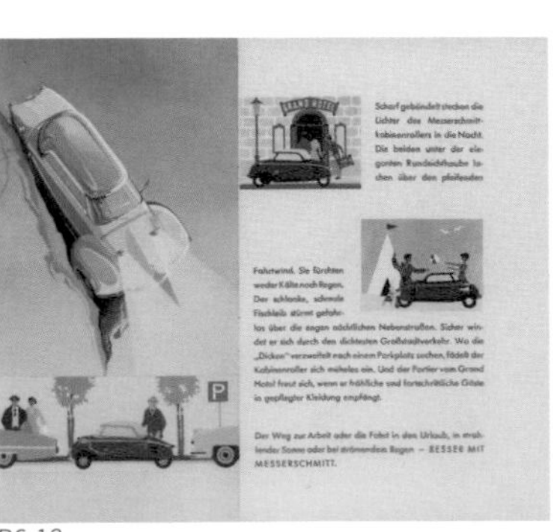

R6-13

Fiat, Nuova 500, 1957
p. 140

R7-1
Study for the design of the Nuova 500, exploded diagram of the body panels, bare chassis and pressed panels, coachwork design by Weinsberg (designer Bauer), 1953
Ozalid, 63 x 88.5 cm
Turin, Archivio Storico Fiat, Fondo Giacosa
Photo Franco Turcati

R7-2
Study for the design of the Nuova 500 (designer Bauer), Four-view drawing for the 'Kleinwagen,' 1953
Ozalid, 59 x 83.5 cm
Turin, Archivio Storico Fiat, Fondo Giacosa
Photo Franco Turcati

R7-3
Four-view drawing of the Nuova 500 (15-6-57, version D), 1957
Ozalid on plastic-coated paper , 60 x 84 cm
Turin, Archivio Storico Fiat, Fondo Giacosa
Photo Franco Turcati

R7-4
Four-view drawing of the car (15-6-68, version F, designer Prato), 1968
Ozalid on tracing paper and pencil, 59.7 x 84.5 cm
Turin, Archivio Storico Fiat
Photo Franco Turcati

R7-5
Study for the design of the Nuova 500, two-view drawing, 1957
Ozalid, 57 x 43.5 cm
Turin, Archivio Storico Fiat, Fondo Giacosa
Photo Franco Turcati

R7-6
Cut-away drawing of the Nuova 500, 1958
Turin, Archivio Storico Fiat

R7-7
Fiat: the Nuova 500, 1957
Poster
Turin, Archivio Storico Fiat

R7-8
Parade of the Nuova 500 in the streets of Turin for the launch of 4 July, 1957
Period photograph
Turin, Archivio Storico Fiat

R7-9
Parade of the Nuova 500 in the streets of Turin for the launch of 14 July, 1957
Period photograph
Turin, Archivio Storico Fiat
R7-10
Parade of the Nuova 500 in the streets of Turin for the launch of 14 July, 1957
Period photograph
Turin, Archivio Storico Fiat
R7-11
Parade of the Nuova 500 in the streets of Turin for the launch of 14 July, 1957
Period photograph
Turin, Archivio Storico Fiat
R7-12
Advertising set for the Nuova 500 (Avigliana), 1957
Period photograph
Turin, Archivio Storico Fiat

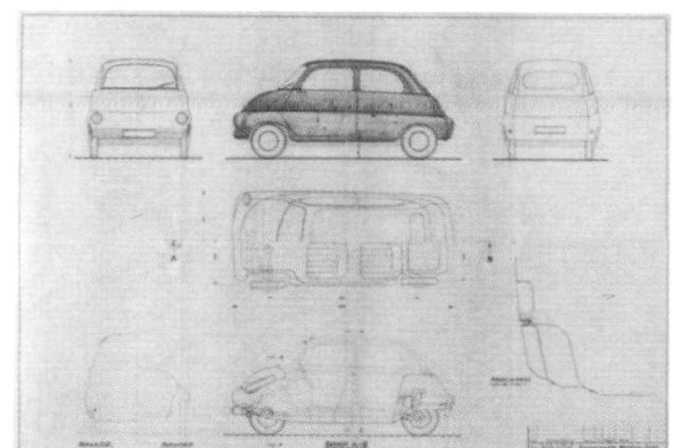
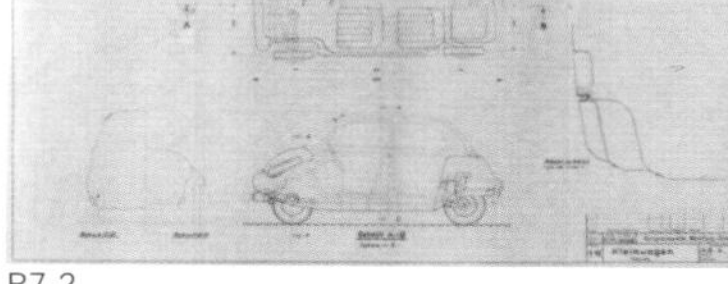
R7-2

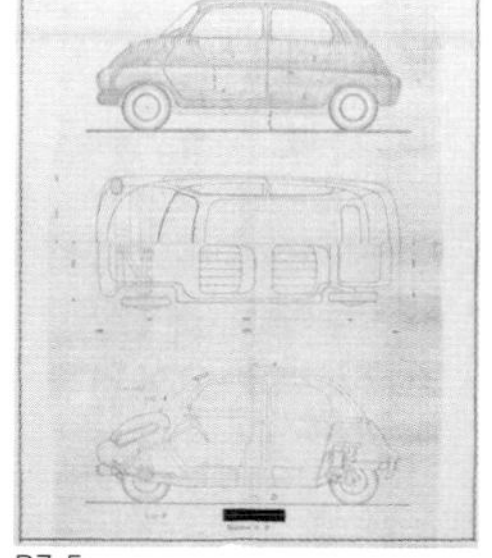

R7-5

R7-8

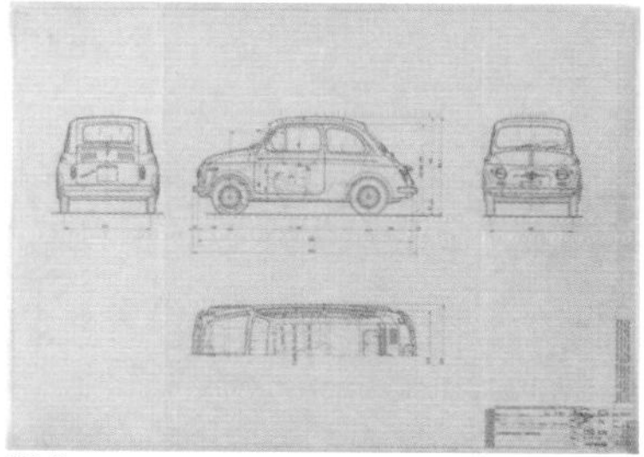

R7-3

R7-6

R7-9

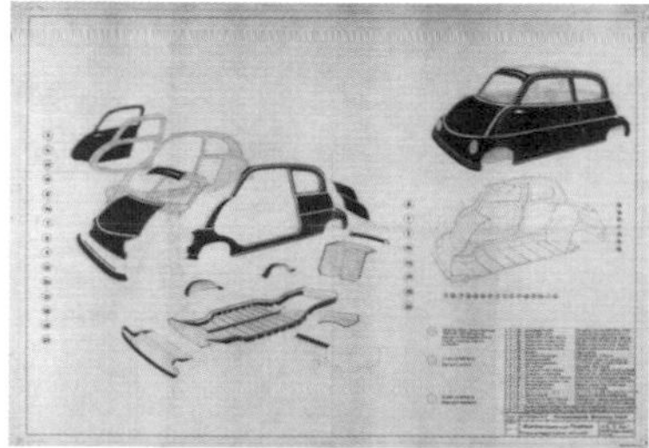
R7-1

R7-4

R7-7

R7-10

R7-11

R7-12

Morris, Mini Minor, 1959

p. 144

R8-1
Study for the Mini Minor with notes by Issigonis
Ink on paper
British Motor Industry Heritage Trust
© BMIHT – British Motor Industry Heritage Trust Film and Picture Library

R8-2
Study of the interior for the Mini Minor with notes by Issigonis
Ink on paper
British Motor Industry Heritage Trust
© BMIHT – British Motor Industry Heritage Trust Film and Picture Library

R8-3
Study by Issigonis for the Mini Minor on an envelope
Ink and pencil on paper
British Motor Industry Heritage Trust
© BMIHT – British Motor Industry Heritage Trust Film and Picture Library

R8-4
Study by Issigonis for the Mini Minor, plan view
Ink on paper
British Motor Industry Heritage Trust
© BMIHT – British Motor Industry Heritage Trust Film and Picture Library

R8-5
Technical drawing, exploded diagram for the 'Austin saloon,' 1959
Ink on paper
British Motor Industry Heritage Trust
© BMIHT – British Motor Industry Heritage Trust Film and Picture Library

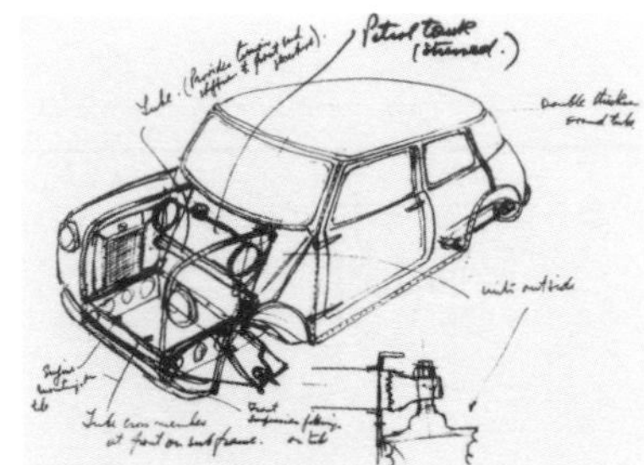

R8-1

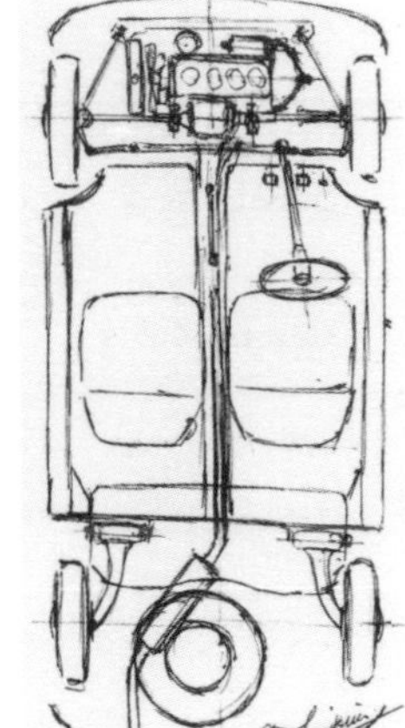

R8-4

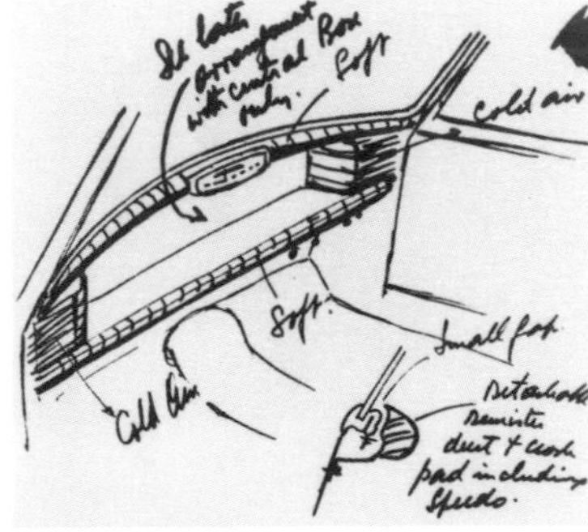

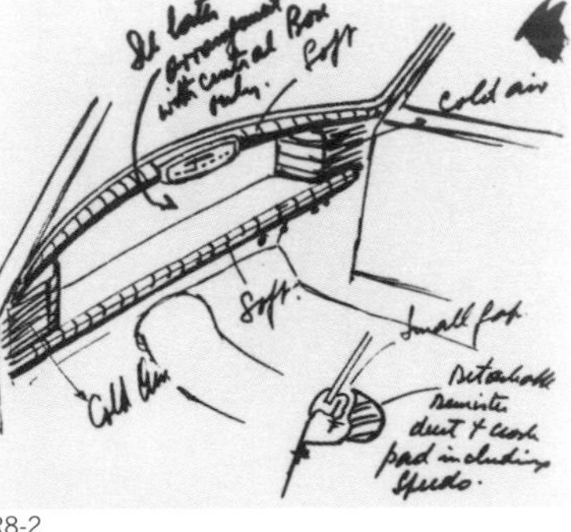

R8-2

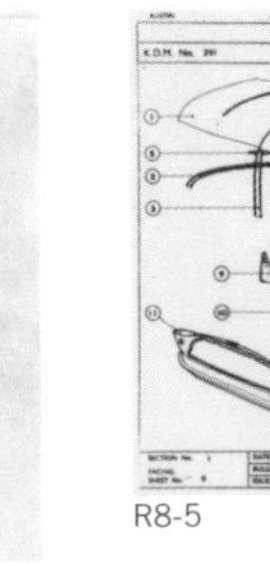

R8-3

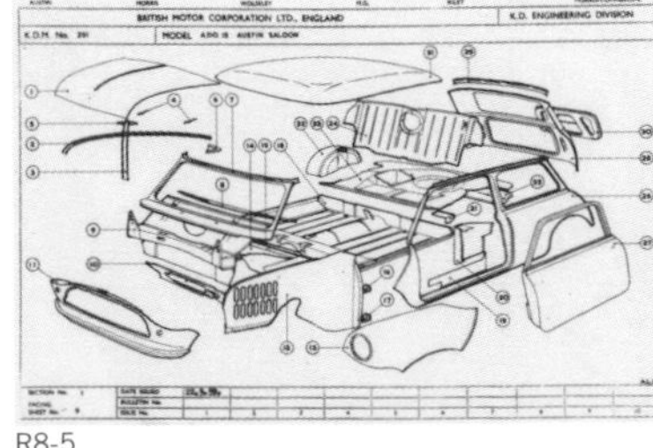

R8-5

Smart, 1997

p. 118

R9-1
Sketch for the Smart (1995)
Smart
Photo Smart
R9-2
Sketch for the Smart
(signed Leutz 95), 1995
Smart
Photo Smart
R9-3
Sketch for the Smart
(signed Leutz 01/95), 1995
Smart
Photo Smart
R9-4
Sketch for the Smart scuba
(signed Leutz 09/94), 1994
Smart
Photo Smart
R9-5
Sketches for the Smart (1995)
Smart
Photo Smart
R9-6
Sketch for the interior of the Smart (1995)
Smart
Photo Smart
R9-7
Sketch for the interior of the Smart (1995)
Smart
Photo Smart
R9-8
Sketches for the dashboard of the Smart
(signed A. Pruhl) (1995)
Smart
Photo Smart

R9-1

R9-4

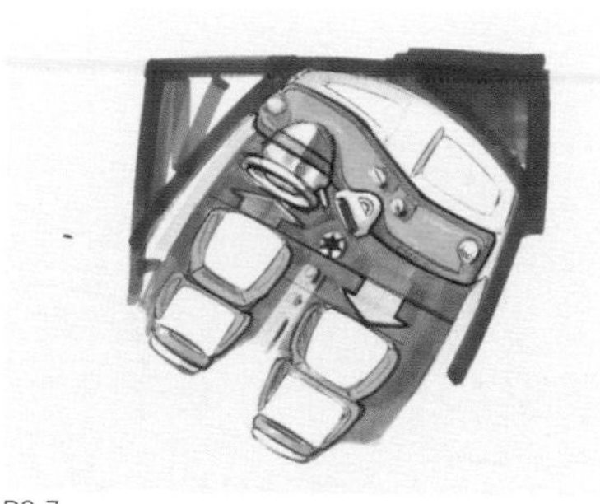

R9-7

R9-2

R9-5

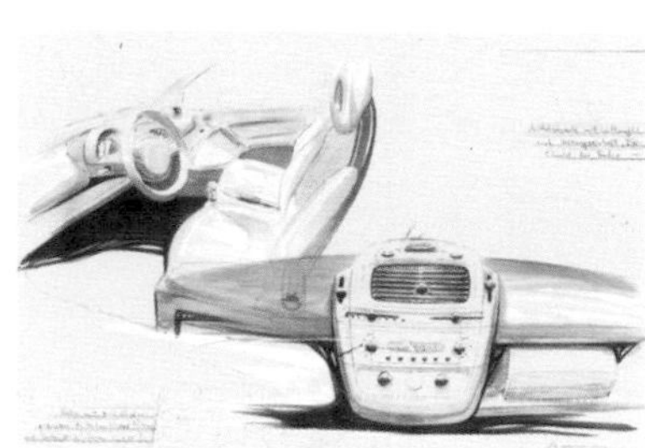

R9-8

R9-3

R9-6

Isotta Fraschini, Tipo 8 ASS torpedo sport, 1927
p. 154

R10-1
Benito Mussolini and some Milanese notables visit the stand of Carrozzeria Italiana & Cesare Sala, Salone dell'Automobile di Milano (12-27 April 1927)
Period photograph
Anselmi Archive

R10-1

Alfa Romeo, 6C 1750 Gran Sport Flying Star, 1930
p. 158

Maserati, V4 Sport Spider Zagato, 1932
p. 162

Bugatti, Type 46 Coach Surprofilé, 1933
p. 166

Peugeot, 402 Eclipse cabriolet, 1937
p. 170

Alfa Romeo, 6C 2300 B Mille Miglia berlinetta Touring, 1937
p. 174

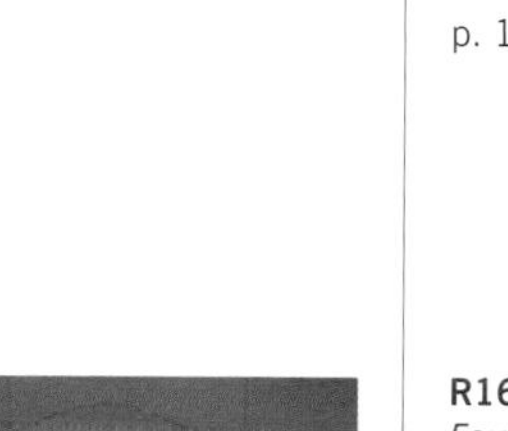

R15-1
Master model of the mould for the front panel
of the 1500 Super Sport, 1928
Painted wood, 60 x 50 x 50 cm
Arese (Milan), Automobilismo Storico
Alfa Romeo, Museo Storico, Centro
di Documentazione Storica
Photo © Automobilismo Storico Alfa Romeo, Centro di Documentazione Storica
R15-2
Master model of the mould for the front panel
of the 8C 2300 Monza, 1931
Painted wood, 60 x 50 x 50 cm
Arese (Milan), Automobilismo Storico
Alfa Romeo, Museo Storico, Centro
di Documentazione Storica
Photo © Automobilismo Storico Alfa Romeo, Centro di Documentazione Storica
R15-3
Master model of the mould for the front panel
of the 8C 2900 B, 1938
Painted wood, 60 x 50 x 50 cm
Arese (Milan), Automobilismo Storico
Alfa Romeo, Museo Storico, Centro
di Documentazione Storica
Photo © Automobilismo Storico Alfa Romeo, Centro di Documentazione Storica

R15-1

R15-2

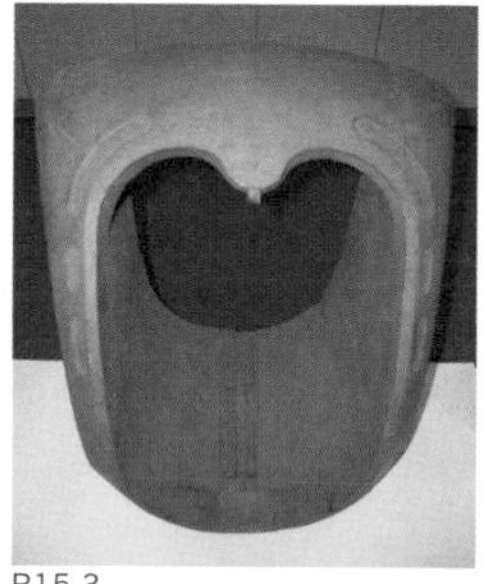

R15-3

Rolls-Royce, Silver Cloud, 1955
p. 182

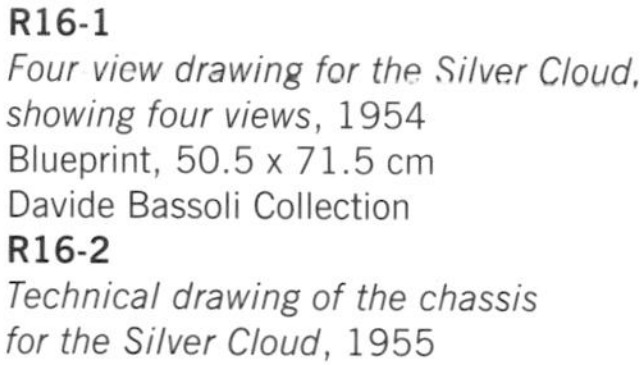

R16-1
Four view drawing for the Silver Cloud, showing four views, 1954
Blueprint, 50.5 x 71.5 cm
Davide Bassoli Collection
R16-2
Technical drawing of the chassis for the Silver Cloud, 1955
Original photograph, 10 x 20 cm
Davide Bassoli Collection

R16-1

R16-2

R16-3
Drawing of the Silver Cloud convertible
Marco Makaus Collection
R16-4
Four-view drawing for the Silver Cloud (31.3.55), 1955
Marco Makaus Collection

R16-3

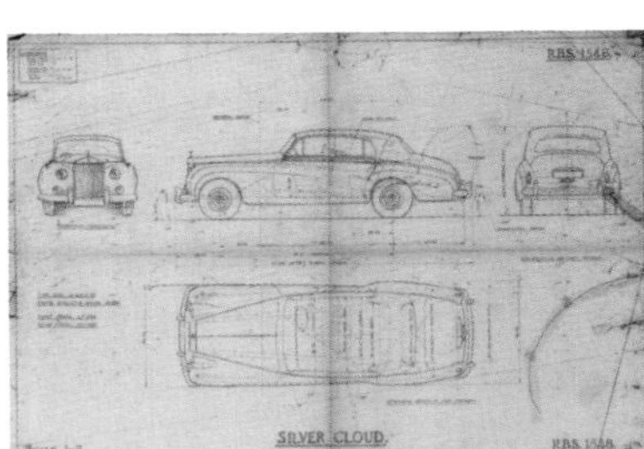

R16-4

Lancia, Flaminia, 1963

p. 188

Maserati, Quattroporte, 1963

p. 192

R18-1
Side elevation sketch for the Quattroporte, scale 1:1 (1963)
White chalk on black card, 140 x 580 cm
Turin, Rigoli Collection
R18-2
Masterplan for the Quattroporte, scale 1:1
Pencil, chalk, pen and indian ink on paper, 121 x 562 cm
Turin, Rigoli Collection
R18-3
Masterplan for the Quattroporte, front view
Pencil, chalk, pen and indian ink on paper, 132 x 121 cm
Turin, Rigoli Collection
R18-4
Sketch for Quattroporte
Pencil on tracing paper, 36 x 79.5 cm
Turin, Rigoli Collection
R18-5
Sketch for the Quattroporte with notes by Pietro Frua
Pencil and ink on onionskin paper, 39 x 76.5 cm
Turin, Rigoli Collection
R18-6
Side elevation sketch for the Quattroporte, 1971
Pencil on tracing paper, 30.5 x 75.2 cm
Turin, Rigoli Collection
R18-7
Side elevation sketch for the Quattroporte, the four-door saloon on 121 chassis, 1971
Pencil and brush on tracing paper, 40 x 84.2 cm
Turin, Collection Rigoli
R18-8
Side elevation sketch for the Quattroporte, the four-door saloon on 121 chassis, 1971
Pencil, white chalk, brush and indian ink on paper, 30.5 x 79.5 cm
Turin, Collection Rigoli
R18-9
Original model of the Quattroporte saloon, first series, 1963
Plaster model, 20 x 63 x 27 cm
Modena, Maserati srl

R18-1

R18-2

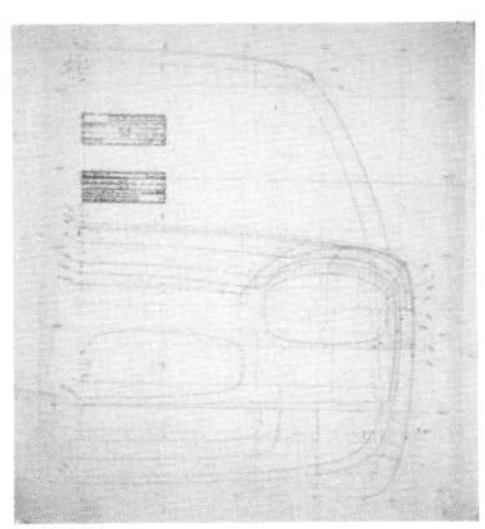
R18-3

R18-4

Ferrari, 166 MM Barchetta, 1948

p. 198

R18-5

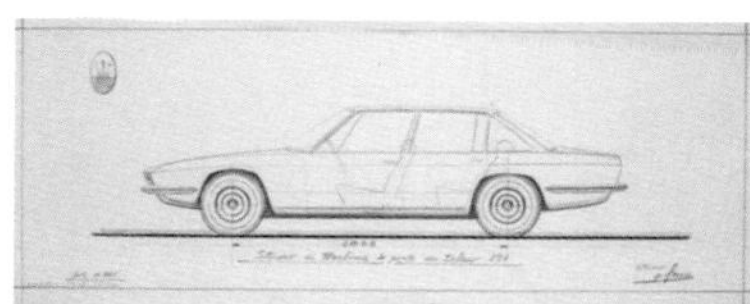

R18-8

R18-6

R18-9

R18-7

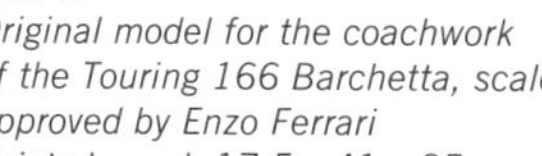

R19-1
Three drawings of the three versions of the Ferrari 166/212: Barchetta, Berlinetta Mille Miglia and Berlinetta Gran Turismo Quattroposti (signed F. Formenti)
Gouache on paper, 61 x 51 cm
Bianchi Anderloni Collection
R19-2
Original model for the coachwork of the Touring 166 Barchetta, scale 1:10, approved by Enzo Ferrari
Painted wood, 17.5 x 41 x 25 cm
Bianchi Anderloni Collection
R19-3
Four-view drawing for a 2/3 seater coupé on the second series of the Ferrari 166, (dwg. no. 1289, 17.11.1949, designer A. Gilardi), 1950
Blueprint, 45.5 x 74.5 cm
Bianchi Anderloni Collection
R19-4
Illustration of 166 MM, berlinetta version (signed F. Formenti)
Gouache and pencil on paper, 29.5 x 64 cm
Bianchi Anderloni Collection

R19-2

R19-3

R19-1

R19-4

R19-5
Four-view drawing for the Ferrari racing Spider, 1949 1000 Miglia project, scale 1:10 (dwg. no. 1275, 6.7.1948), 1948
Blueprint, 47.5 x 76.5 cm
Bianchi Anderloni Collection

R19-5

Lancia, Aurelia GT B24 Spider, 1955

p. 202

R20-1
Four-view drawing for the coachwork of the Aurelia trasformabile B24 Spider (20.1.1955), 1955
Pencil on tracing paper, 59 x 104.5 cm
Turin, Archivio Storico Fiat
Photo Franco Turcati

R20-2
Four view cut-away drawing for the coachwork of the Aurelia B24 Spider (9.9.57), 1957
Pencil on tracing paper, 57.5 x 103.5 cm
Turin, Archivio Storico Fiat
Photo Franco Turcati

R20-3
Technical drawing for the radiator surround of the Aurelia B20, stone guard for the radiator frame (2.6.52), 1952
Pencil on tracing paper, 93 x 78 cm
Turin, Archivio Storico Fiat
Photo Franco Turcati

R20-4
Technical drawing for the radiator surround of the Aurelia B20 (8.5.52), 1952
Pencil on tracing paper, 98 x 82 cm
Turin, Archivio Storico Fiat
Photo Franco Turcati

R20-5
Technical drawing of the steering wheel of the Aurelia B24 (12.10.54), 1954
Pencil on tracing paper, 68 x 94.5 cm
Turin, Archivio Storico Fiat
Photo Franco Turcati

R20-1

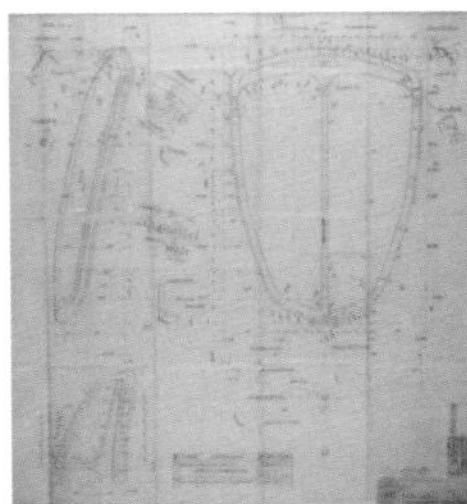

R20-4

R20-2

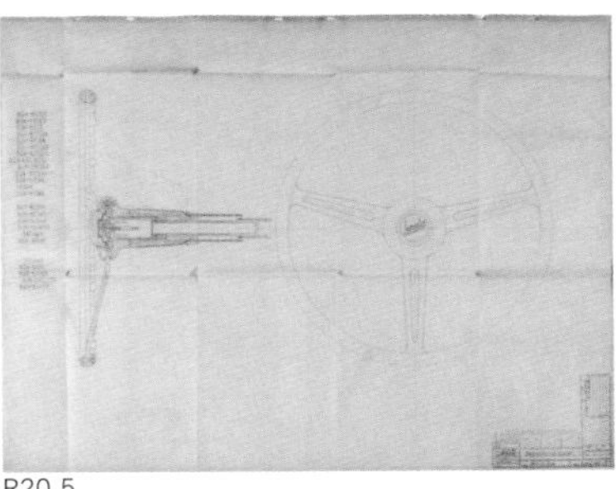

R20-5

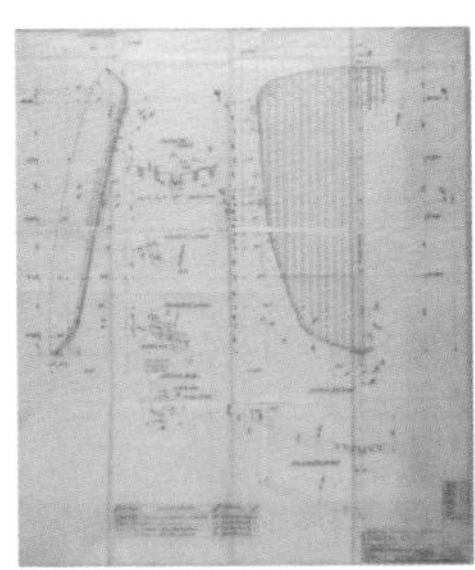

R20-3

Alfa Romeo, Giulietta Spider, 1955
p. 206

R21-1
Four-view drawing for the Giulietta Spider (15.7.55), 1955
Copy of the original, 39 x 84 cm
Pininfarina SpA
R21-2
Four-view drawing for the Giulietta Spider (20.2.56), 1956
Copy of the original
Arese (Milan), Automobilismo Storico Alfa Romeo, Museo Storico, Centro di Documentazione Storica
Photo © Automobilismo Storico Alfa Romeo, Centro di Documentazione Storica

R21-1

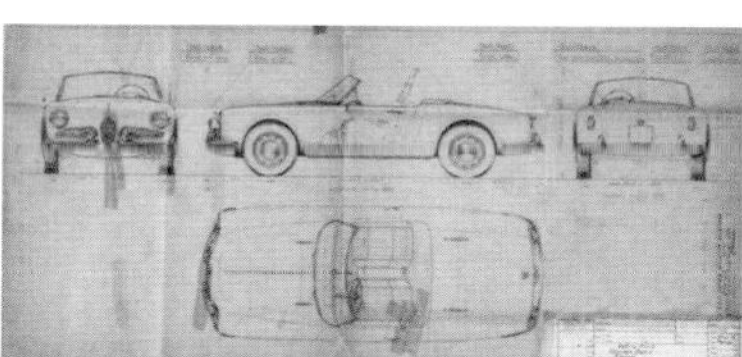
R21-2

BMW, 507, 1955
p. 212

R22-1
Sketch for 507 by Goertz (1955)
Pencil on paper
BMW AG Konzernarchiv / BMW AG Konzernarchiv
R22-2
Sketch for 507 by Goertz (1955)
Mixed media on paper
BMW AG Konzernarchiv / BMW AG Konzernarchiv
R22-3
Sketch for 507 by Goertz (1955)
Pencil on paper
BMW AG Konzernarchiv / BMW AG Konzernarchiv
R22-4
Sketch for 507 by Goertz (1955)
Pencil on paper
BMW AG Konzernarchiv / BMW AG Konzernarchiv

R22-2

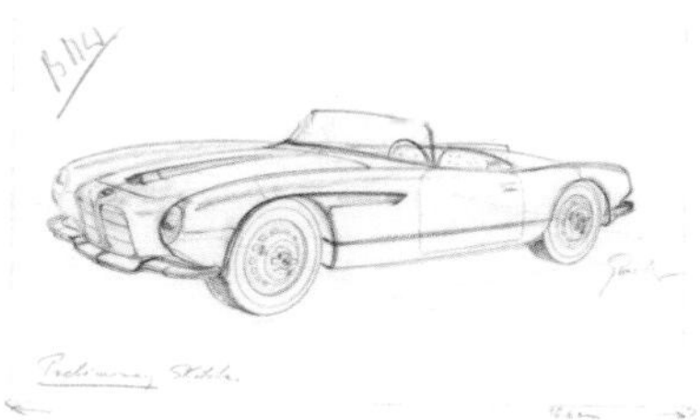
R22-3

R22-1

R22-4

R22-5
Side elevation drawing for the two-seater coupé on 507 base (signed Studio G. Michelotti, 25.7.57), 1957
Pencil on acetate
BMW AG Konzernarchiv / BMW AG Konzernarchiv
R22-6
Sketch for the first version of the 507 by Goertz, 1955
Pencil on paper
BMW AG Konzernarchiv / BMW AG Konzernarchiv
R22-7
Four-view drawing for the 507, 1957
Ink on acetate
BMW AG Konzernarchiv / BMW AG Konzernarchiv
R22-8
Side elevation drawing for the 507 (signed E. Palm), 1957
Watercolour and ink on card
BMW AG Konzernarchiv / BMW AG Konzernarchiv
R22-9
Side elevation drawing for the 507 roadster with hardtop (signed Bertram) (1957)
Airbrush and ink on card
BMW AG Konzernarchiv / BMW AG Konzernarchiv
R22-10
Rendering of the 507 (1955)
Pencil on paper
BMW AG Konzernarchiv / BMW AG Konzernarchiv
R22-11
Rendering for the prototype of the 507 (1955)
Mixed media on paper
BMW AG Konzernarchiv / BMW AG Konzernarchiv
R22-12
Photograph of Jobann König with the clay model of the 507, scale 1:1, 1954/1955
Period photograph
BMW AG Konzernarchiv / BMW AG Konzernarchiv

R22-5

R22-8

R22-11

R22-6

R22-9

R22-12

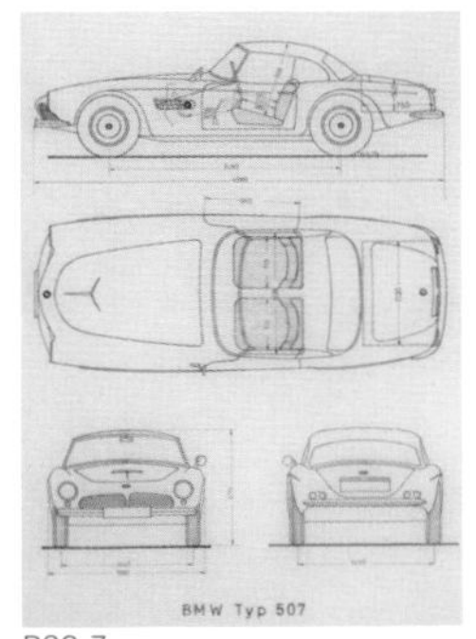

R22-7

R22-10

Lotus, Seven, 1958

p. 218

Chevrolet, Corvette convertible, 1958

p. 224

Maserati, 3500, GT Vignale Spyder, 1959

p. 230

R25-1/7
Sketches for the 3500 GT Spyder concerning the Vignale coachwork (designer G. Michelotti), 1959
Edgardo Michelotti Archive
Adolfo Orsi Collection

R25-1

R25-2

R25-3

R25-4

R25-5

R25-6

R25-7

Cisitalia, 202 Gran Sport, 1948

p. 236

R26-1
Master plan for the 202, 1946
Copy of the original, 40.3 x 137 cm
Pininfarina SpA

R26-1

Porsche, 356, 1948

p. 240

R27-1
Cross-section of the 356 B coupé, 1962
Mixed media
© Dr. Ing. h.c.F. Porsche AG
R27-2
Technical drawing of the dashboard for the 356 ('Schautafel'), 1957
Blueprint, coloured pencil, ink
Ralf J.F. Kieselbach Collection
R27-3
Technical drawing for the 356 ('Rücklehnen-Rahmen vollst'), 1957
Blueprint, pencil, coloured pencil, ink
Ralf J.F. Kieselbach Collection
R27-4
Technical drawing for the 356 ('Dachrahmen vorn quer'), 1957
Blueprint, coloured pencil, ink
Ralf J.F. Kieselbach Collection
R27-5
Technical drawing for the 356 ('Fenstersäule vollst'), 1957
Blueprint, pencil, coloured pencil, pen and ink
Ralf J.F. Kieselbach Collection
R27-6
Technical drawing for the 356 ('Radkasten-Innenverteilung'), 1957
Blueprint, coloured penci, ink
Ralf J.F. Kieselbach Collection
R27-7
Technical drawings for the 356, 1957
Blueprint, pencil, coloured pencil, pen and ink
Ralf J.F. Kieselbach Collection
R27-8
Erwin Komenda
Period photograph
Ralf J.F. Kieselbach Collection
R27-9
Erwin Komenda
Period photograph
Ralf J.F. Kieselbach Collection

R27-1

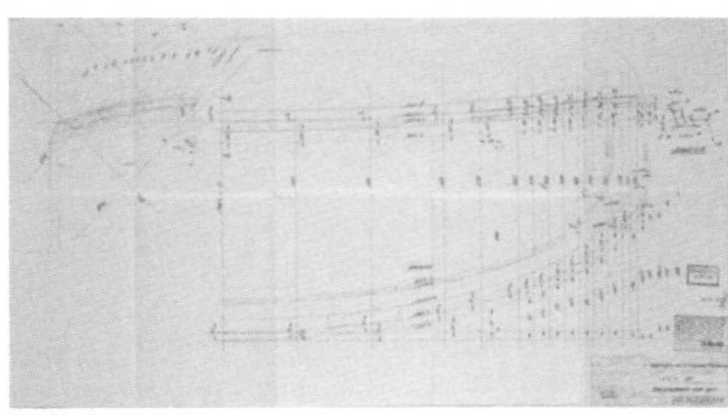

R27-4

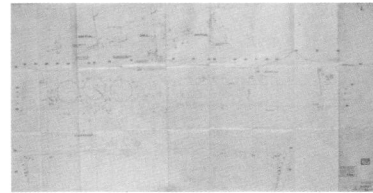

R27-2

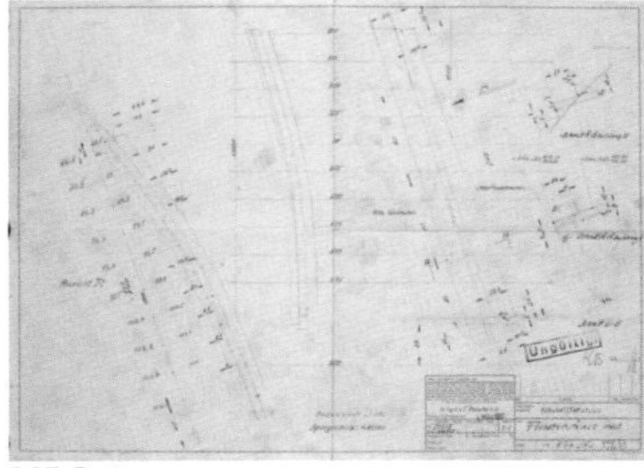

R27-5

R27-3

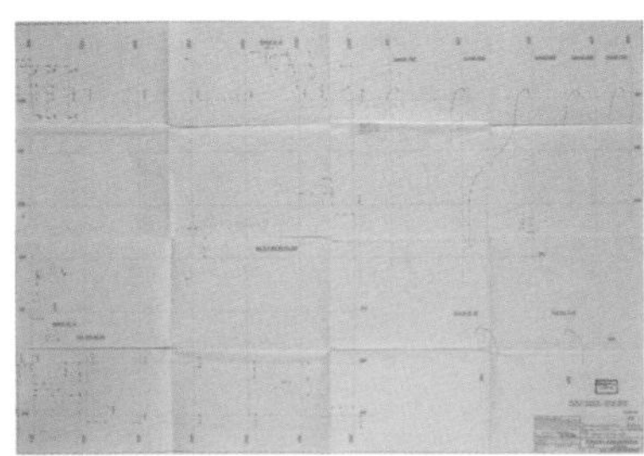

R27-6

Alfa Romeo, 6C 2500 Super Sport Villa d'Este, 1949
p. 246

R28-1
Cut-away drawing for the 6C 2500, views of the coachwork (8.6.1949), 1949
Copy of the original
Arese (Milan), Automobilismo Storico Alfa Romeo, Museo Storico, Centro di Documentazione Storica
Photo © Automobilismo Storico Alfa Romeo, Centro di Documentazione Storica
R28-2
Side elevation drawing for the 2500 SS Villa d'Este, open-top version
Gouache and pencil on paper, 25 x 61 cm
Bianchi Anderloni Collection

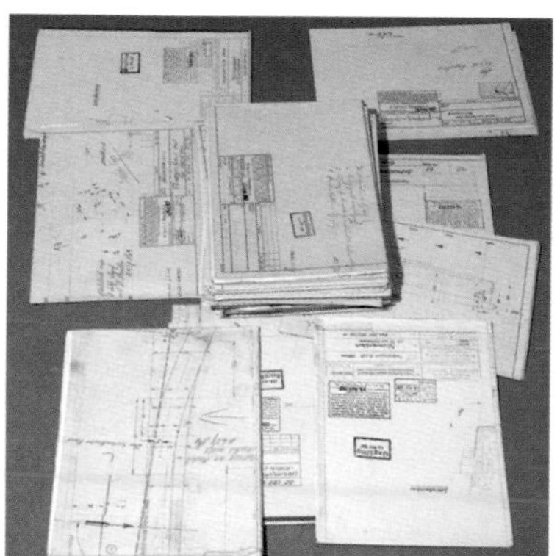
R27-7

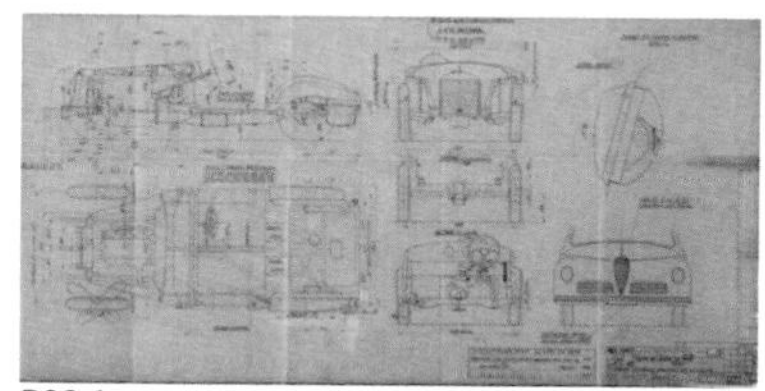
R28-1

Mercedes-Benz, 300 SL Gullwing, 1954
p. 250

R29-1
Four-view drawing for the 300 SL Gullwing (signed Angerhöfer, 20.9.54), 1954
DaimlerChrysler Classic Archive
© DaimlerChrysler AG
R29-2
Four-view drawing for the 300 SL Gullwing (signed Angerhöfer, 20.9.54), 1954
DaimlerChrysler Classic Archive
© DaimlerChrysler AG
R29-3
Plan view of the 300 SL Gullwing, view from above (1954)
DaimlerChrysler Classic Archive
© DaimlerChrysler AG
R29-4
Lateral cross-section of the 300 SL Gullwing (signed W.S.)
(1954)
DaimlerChrysler Classic Archive
© DaimlerChrysler AG
R29-5
Cut-away drawing for the 300 SL Gullwing
(1954)
DaimlerChrysler Classic Archive
© DaimlerChrysler AG
R29-6
Drawing for the 300 SL Gullwing, detail of the doors and of the interior (1954)
DaimlerChrysler Classic Archive
© DaimlerChrysler AG

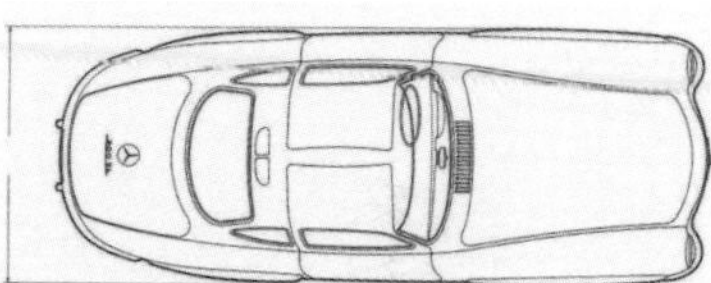
R29-3

R29-4

R29-5

R27-8

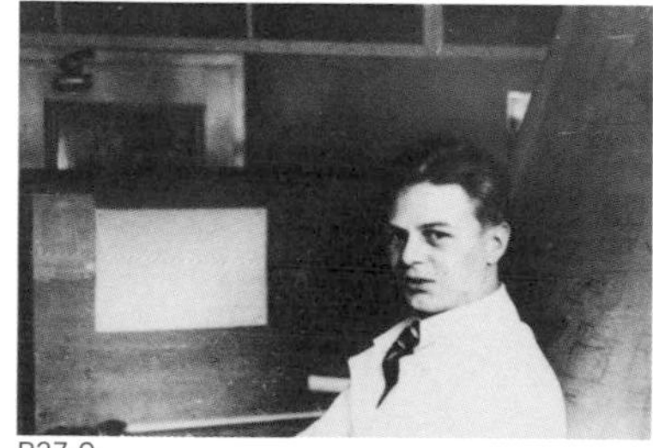
R27-9

R28-2

R29-1

R29-2

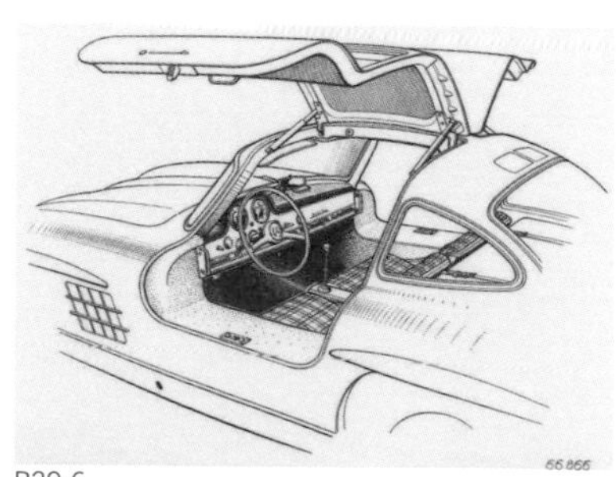
R29-6

Ferrari, 250 GT Berlinetta passo corto, 1959
p. 256

R29-7
Cross-sections of the 300 SL Gullwing (1954)
DaimlerChrysler Classic Archive
© DaimlerChrysler AG
R29-8
Leaflet for the 300 SL Gullwing, 1955
DaimlerChrysler Classic Archive
© DaimlerChrysler AG
R29-9
Leaflet for the 300 SL Gullwing, 1955
DaimlerChrysler Classic Archive
© DaimlerChrysler AG
R29-10
300 SL Gullwing Coupé series W 198
Period photograph
DaimlerChrysler Classic Archive
© DaimlerChrysler AG
R29-11
The 1000th 300 SL Gullwing leaves the assemble line in December 1955
Period photograph
DaimlerChrysler Classic Archive
© DaimlerChrysler AG
R29-12
Presentation of the 190 SL and 300 SL Gullwing at the International Motor Sports, New York, February 1954
Period photograph
DaimlerChrysler Classic Archive
© DaimlerChrysler AG
R29-13
300 SL Gullwing Coupé, 1954
Period photograph
DaimlerChrysler Classic Archive
© DaimlerChrysler AG

R29-8

R29-11

R29-9

R29-12

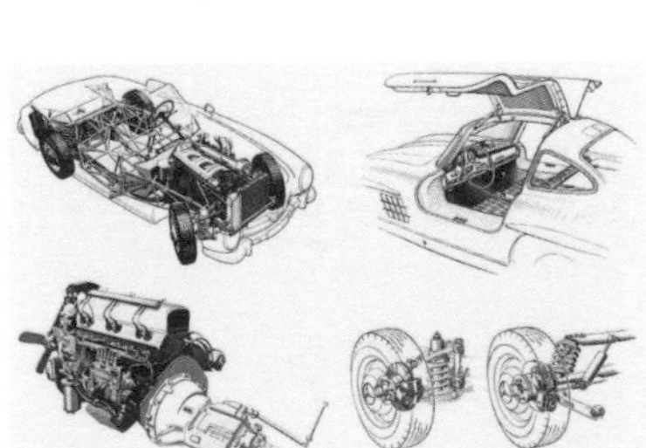
R29-7

R29-10

R29-13

R30-1
Side elevation drawing of a 250 GT, 1960
Copy of the original, 29 x 59.5 cm
Pininfarina SpA

R30-1

Jaguar, E-type coupé, 1961

p. 260

Studebaker, Avanti, 1962

p. 264

Ford, Model T, 1908

p. 270

R33-1
Technical drawing with indications of dimensions for garaging the Model T, 1912
Dearborn, Collections of the Henry Ford
© From the Collections of The Henry Ford

R33-2
Technical drawing of the dimensions of the Model T coupé version, 1912
Dearborn, Collections of the Henry Ford
© From the Collections of The Henry Ford

R33-3
Chassis of the Model T (30.3.1917), 1917
Retouched photograph, 20 x 27 cm
Dearborn, Collections of the Henry Ford
© From the Collections of The Henry Ford

R33-4
Drawings of the Model T of 1919, the Roadster above, the Sedan below (10.2.1919), 1919
Period photograph, 27 x 20 cm
Dearborn, Collections of the Henry Ford
© From the Collections of The Henry Ford

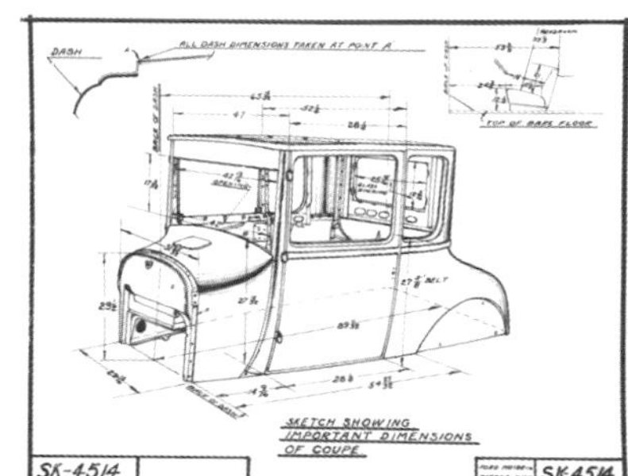

R33-2

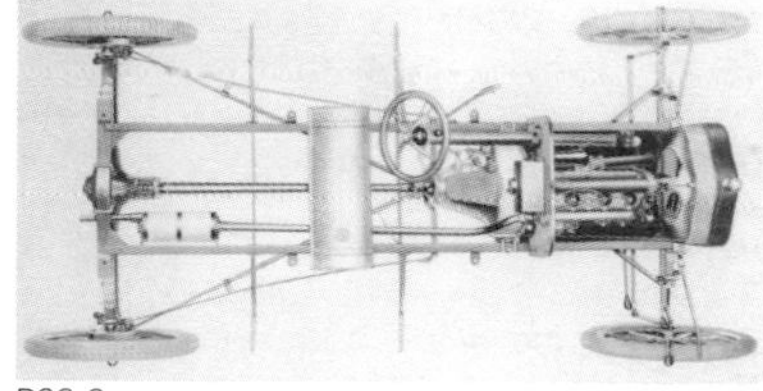
R33-3

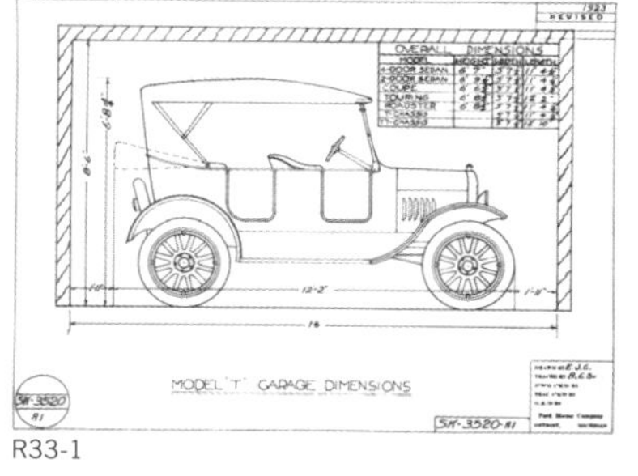

R33-1

R33-4

Ford, Model T, 1908, continued

R33-5
Technical drawing for the interior of the Model T (1921)
Dearborn, Collections of the Henry Ford

R33-6
Illustration for the Coupelet version of the Model T of 1915, 1914
Retouched photograph, 20 x 27 cm
Dearborn, Collections of the Henry Ford

R33-7
Illustration for the Coupé version of the 1917 (21.4.1917), 1917
Retouched photograph, 19 x 28 cm
Dearborn, Collections of the Henry Ford

R33-8
Illustration for the Coupelet version of the Model T of 1917 (16.11.1916), 1916
Retouched photograph, 19 x 28 cm
Dearborn, Collections of the Henry Ford

R33-9
Drawing for the Coupé version of the Model T of 1917 (21.4.1917), 1917
Retouched photograph, 20 x 28 cm
Dearborn, Collections of the Henry Ford

R33-10
Illustration of the chassis for the Model T of 1917 (16.11.1916), 1916
Retouched photograph, 19 x 27 cm
Dearborn, Collections of the Henry Ford

R33-11
Illustration for the Coupé version of the Model T of 1914, front view, 1913
Retouched photograph, 20 x 27 cm
Dearborn, Collections of the Henry Ford

R33-12
Illustration for the Model T Runabout of 1914, with badge 'Ford, The Universal Car,' 1913
Retouched photograph, 18 x 28 cm
Dearborn, Collections of the Henry Ford

R33-13
Illustrations of the Model T models for publication in Ford Times, 1912
Dearborn, Collections of the Henry Ford

R33-14
Illustrations of the Model T models for publication in Ford Times, 1912
Dearborn, Collections of the Henry Ford

R33-15
Model T Coupé version at Belle Isle of Detroit (27.10.1924), 1924
Period photograph, 20 x 27 cm
Dearborn, Collections of the Henry Ford

R33-16
Model T Coupé, rear view (30.8.1917), 1917
Period photograph, 20 x 19 cm
Dearborn, Collections of the Henry Ford

R33-17
Model T Coupé, 1923
Dearborn, Collections of the Henry Ford

R33-18
Chassis for the Model N at the Piquette Ave factory, 1906
Dearborn, Collections of the Henry Ford

R33-19
Coachwork for the Model T at the Highland Park factory, 1913
Dearborn, Collections of the Henry Ford

R33-20
Final part of the Model T Sedan assembly line at the Holden Avenue factory, Detroit (2.4.1923), 1923
Period photograph, 20 x 28 cm
Dearborn, Collections of the Henry Ford

R33-5

R33-8

R33-6

R33-9

R33-7

R33-10

R33-11

R33-14

R33-17

R33-20

R33-12

R33-15

R33-18

R33-13

R33-16

R33-19

Volkswagen, Käfer (Beetle), 1938

p. 274

R34-1
Study for the Käfer (Beetle), lateral cross-section 'Typ KDF' (23.3.39), 1939
Copy of the original, 21 x 30 cm
Ralf J.F. Kieselbach Collection
R34-2
Study for the Käfer (Beetle), lateral cross-section 'Zundapp,' 1932
Copy of the original, 21 x 30 cm
Ralf J.F. Kieselbach Collection
R34-3
Three-view drawing for the Käfer (Beetle), 'Stom-limousine auf Typ 12' (1.12.31), 1931
Copy of the original, 13 x 18 cm
Ralf J.F. Kieselbach Collection
R34-4
Rendering for the Käfer (Beetle), version with opening roof (signed Reuters) (1952)
Mixed media
Ralf J.F. Kieselbach Collection
R34-5
Rendering for the Käfer (Beetle), version with opening roof (signed Reuters) (1952)
Mixed media
Ralf J.F. Kieselbach Collection
R34-6
Side elevation drawimg for the Käfer (Beetle)
Period photograph, 17.5 x 24 cm
Ralf J.F. Kieselbach Collection
R34-7
Rendering for the Käfer (Beetle)
Period photograph, 17.5 x 24 cm
Ralf J.F. Kieselbach Collection
R34-8
Illustration for the Käfer (Beetle)
Period photograph, 17.5 x 24 cm
Ralf J.F. Kieselbach Collection
R34-9
Model of the Käfer (Beetle) for wind tunnel tests
Period photograph, 12.5 x 17.8 cm
Ralf J.F. Kieselbach Collection
R34-10
Prototype for the Käfer (Beetle)
Period photograph, 13 x 17.8 cm
Ralf J.F. Kieselbach Collection
R34-11
Prototype for the Käfer (Beetle)
Period photograph, 13 x 17.8 cm
Ralf J.F. Kieselbach Collection

R34-12
The Käfer (Beetle) production line, enamel bath, 1949
Period photograph
Ralf J.F. Kieselbach Collection
© Verlag Dr. Franz Burda, Offenburg, Baden, 1949 – photo Alfred Tritschler
R34-13
The Käfer (Beetle) production line, 1949
Period photograph
Ralf J.F. Kieselbach Collection
© Verlag Dr. Franz Burda, Offenburg, Baden, 1949 – photo Alfred Tritschler
R34-14
The Käfer (Beetle) production line, testing the bodywork is watertight, 1949
Period photograph
Ralf J.F. Kieselbach Collection
© Verlag Dr. Franz Burda, Offenburg, Baden, 1949 – photo Alfred Tritschler
R34-15
The Käfer (Beetle) production line, 1949
Period photograph
Ralf J.F. Kieselbach Collection
© Verlag Dr. Franz Burda, Offenburg, Baden, 1949 – photo Alfred Tritschler
R34-16
Daily production of the Käfer (Beetle), 1949
Period photograph
Ralf J.F. Kieselbach Collection
© Verlag Dr. Franz Burda, Offenburg, Baden, 1949 – photo Alfred Tritschler

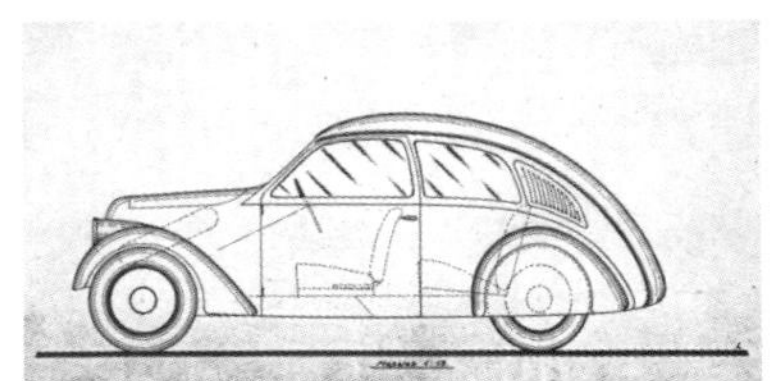
R34-2

R34-5

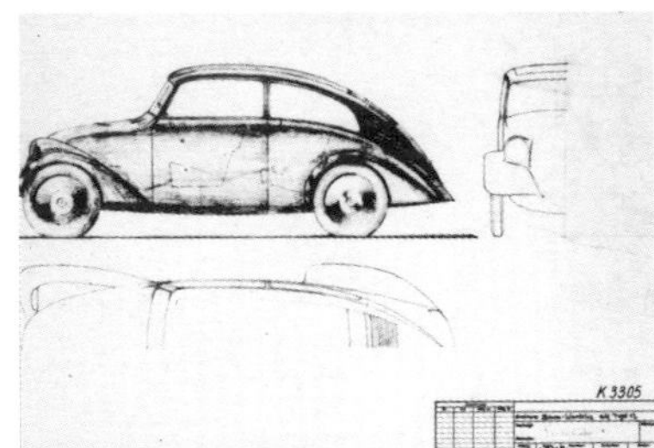
R34-3

R34-6

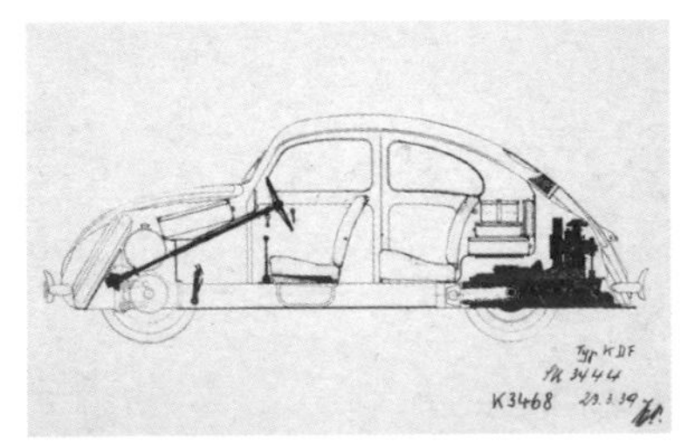
R34-1

R34-4

R34-7

Citroën, T.P.V. (Toute petite voiture), 1939

p. 278

R34-8

R34-11

R34-14

R35-1
Sketches for the bonnet of the 2CV, 1939
Pencil on paper
Citröen
© Citröen Communication
R35-2
Sketch for the bonnet of the 2CV, 1939
Pencil on paper
Citröen
© Citröen Communication

R34-9

R34-12

R34-15

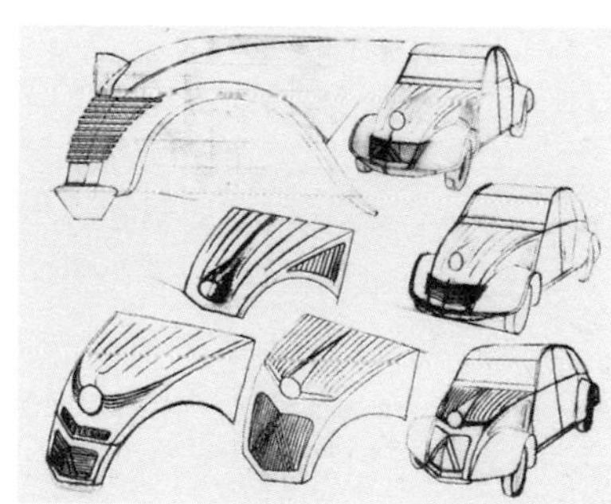

R35-1

R34-10

R34-13

R34-16

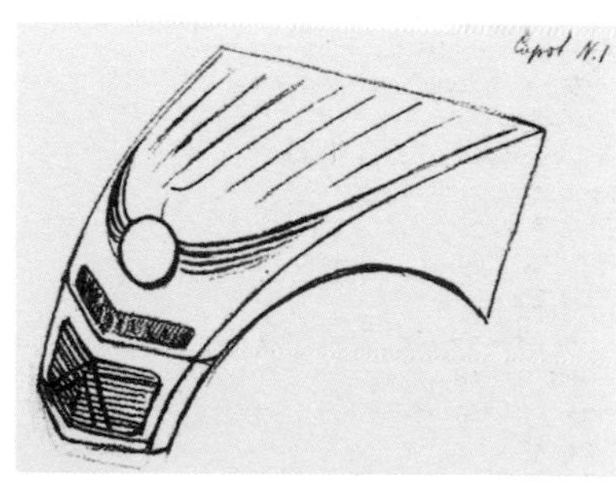

R35-2

Fiat, 600, 1955
p. 282

Trabant, P 600 ('P 60 Kombi-Sonderwunsch'), 1958
p. 284

R37-1
Sketches for the Trabant, three views
Chalk on black paper, 20 x 15 cm
Ingolstadt, AUDI AG-Unternehmensarchiv
R37-2
Sketch for the Trabant
Chalk on black paper, 20 x 15 cm
Ingolstadt, AUDI AG-Unternehmensarchiv
R37-3
Sketch for the Trabant
Indian ink on black paper, 20 x 15 cm
Ingolstadt, AUDI AG-Unternehmensarchiv
R37-4
Sketch for the Trabant
Chalk on black paper, 20 x 15 cm
Ingolstadt, AUDI AG-Unternehmensarchiv

R37-1

R37-3

R37-2

R37-4

Volkswagen, Golf GTI, 1974

p. 200

R38-1
Four-view drawing for the Golf with international requirements
Copy of the original, 50.6 x 70 cm
Italdesign Giugiaro Photographic Archive
© Italdesign Giugiaro Photographic Archive

R38-2
Sketch for the Golf with variants of indicators and detail of the definitive indicator used, three-quarter view from the front
Mixed media on paper, copy of the original, 50.6 x 70 cm
Italdesign Giugiaro Photographic Archive
© Italdesign Giugiaro Photographic Archive

R38-3
Side elevation drawing for the Golf, scale 1:10
Copy of the original, 46.3 x 84 cm
Italdesign Giugiaro Photographic Archive
© Italdesign Giugiaro Photographic Archive

R38-4
Side elevation drawing for the Golf with indications of the wheelbase, scale 1:10
Copy of the original, 50.6 x 70 cm
Italdesign Giugiaro Photographic Archive
© Italdesign Giugiaro Photographic Archive

R38-5
Sketch for the Golf, scale 1:10, three-quarter view from the front
Photographic print on blue Canson paper, 50.6 x 70 cm
Italdesign Giugiaro Photographic Archive
© Italdesign Giugiaro Photographic Archive

R38-6
Side elevation drawing for the Golf, scale 1:10
Photographic print on blue Canson paper, 50.6 x 70 cm
Italdesign Giugiaro Photographic Archive
© Italdesign Giugiaro Photographic Archive

R38-7
Sketch of Golf gear-knobs
Copy of the original, 50.6 x 70 cm
Italdesign Giugiaro Photographic Archive
© Italdesign Giugiaro Photographic Archive

R38-8
Illustration for the Golf, detail of the dashboard
Copy of the original, 50.6 x 70 cm
Italdesign Giugiaro Photographic Archive
© Italdesign Giugiaro Photographic Archive

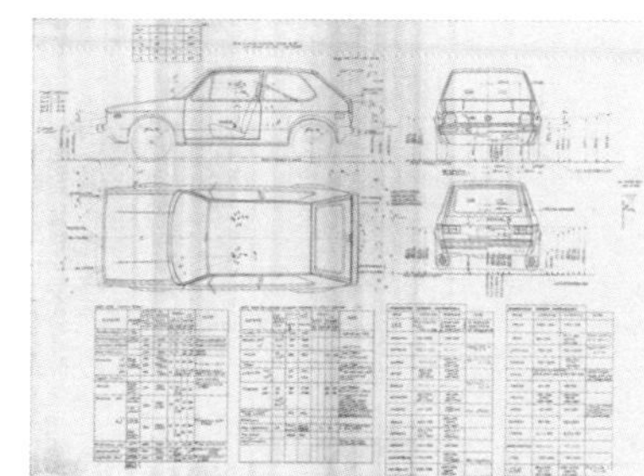

R38-1

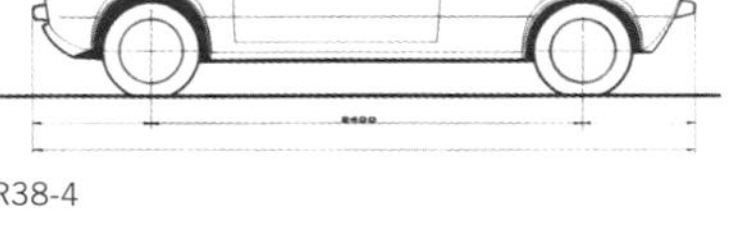

R38-4

R38-7

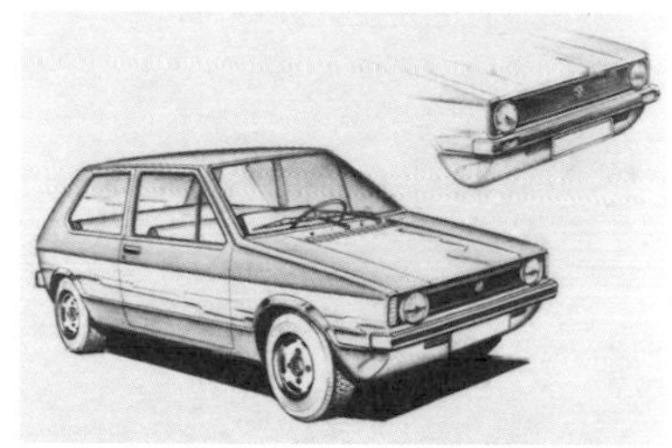

R38-2

R38-5

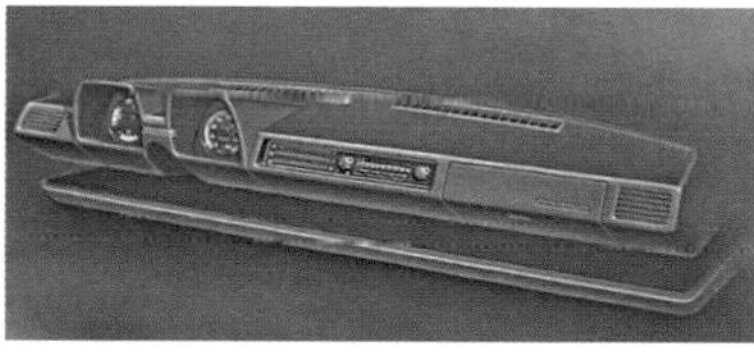

R38-8

R38-3

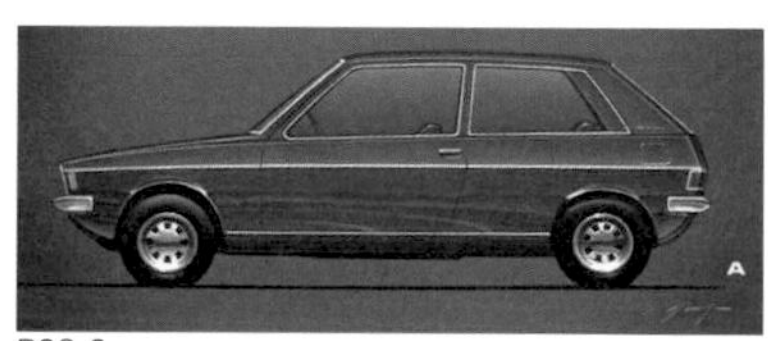

R38-6

Fiat, Panda 30, 1980

p. 292

R39-1
Motor plan, initial study for the Fiat Rustica, the future Panda, 1976
Copy on tracing paper with notes in blue pen, coloured pencils and pencil,
47 x 65.4 cm
Italdesign Giugiaro Photographic Archive
© Italdesign Giugiaro Photographic Archive

R39-2
Technical drawing of the passenger seating for the Panda,scale 1:10, overall view with definition of the passenger space, prepared by Giugiaro before the design phase, 1980
Pencil on paper, 34 x 53.3 cm
Italdesign Giugiaro Photographic Archive
© Italdesign Giugiaro Photographic Archive

R39-3
Technical drawing of the passenger space for the Panda, scale 1:10, side view with definition of the passenger space and outline of external volumes,
1980
Pencil and Indian ink on paper, 28 x 48.8 cm
Italdesign Giugiaro Photographic Archive
© Italdesign Giugiaro Photographic Archive

R39-4
Technical drawing of the passenger space for the Panda, scale 1:10, side view with indication of maximum length, wheelbase and front and rear overhangs, 1976
Pencil on paper, 29.4 x 51 cm
Italdesign Giugiaro Photographic Archive
© Italdesign Giugiaro Photographic Archive

R39-5
Two-view drawing for the Panda, scale 1:10, side and rear view. Above, sketch for the solution for welding the roof to the sides and consequent elimination of the traditional gutters, 1980
Pencil on paper, 34 x 61.6 cm
Italdesign Giugiaro Photographic Archive
© Italdesign Giugiaro Photographic Archive

R39-6
Technical drawing for the Panda, scale 1:10 (6.11.78), 1978
Copy on tracing paper, 60 x 84 cm
Italdesign Giugiaro Photographic Archive
© Italdesign Giugiaro Photographic Archive

R39-7
Study for the interior of the Panda, detail of the seats (1980)
Print on photographic paper, 50 x 70 cm
Italdesign Giugiaro Photographic Archive
© Italdesign Giugiaro Photographic Archive

R39-8
Study for the interior of the Panda, detail of the dashboard with glove compartment (1980)
Print on photographic paper, 50 x 70 cm
Italdesign Giugiaro Photographic Archive
© Italdesign Giugiaro Photographic Archive

R39-9
Rendering for the Panda, scale 1:10, side view (1980)
Photographic print on blue Canson paper, 50 x 70 cm
Italdesign Giugiaro Photographic Archive
© Italdesign Giugiaro Photographic Archive

R39-10
Rendering for the Panda, scale 1:10, three-quarter front and rear views (1980)
Photographic print on blue Canson paper, 50 x 70 cm
Italdesign Giugiaro Photographic Archive
© Italdesign Giugiaro Photographic Archive

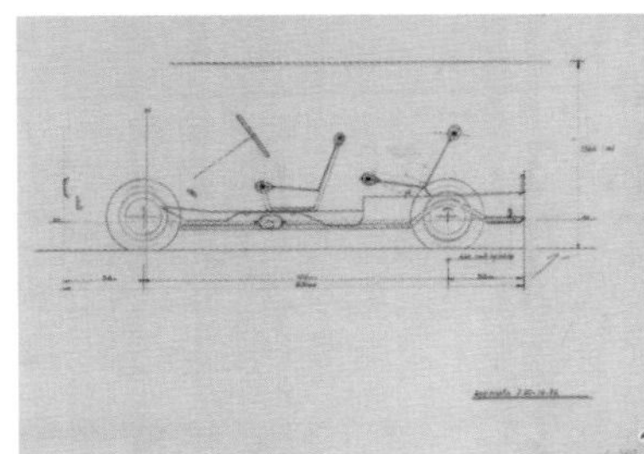
R39-2

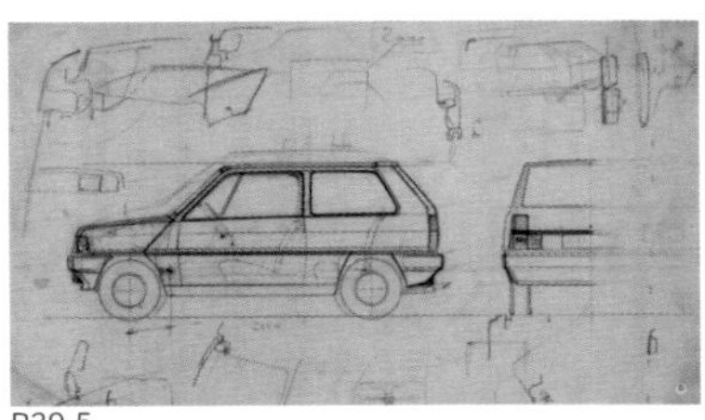
R39-5

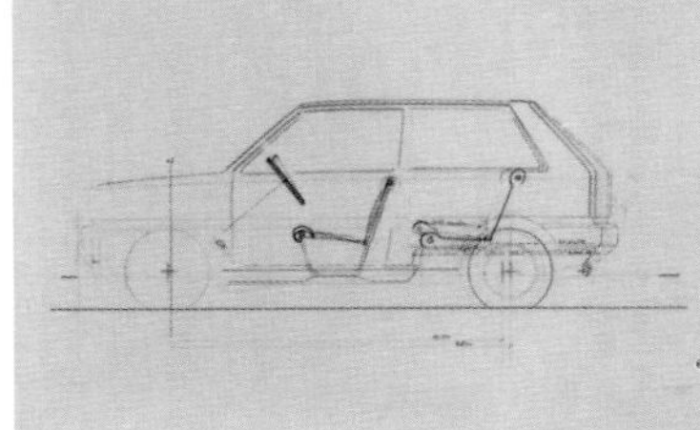
R39-3

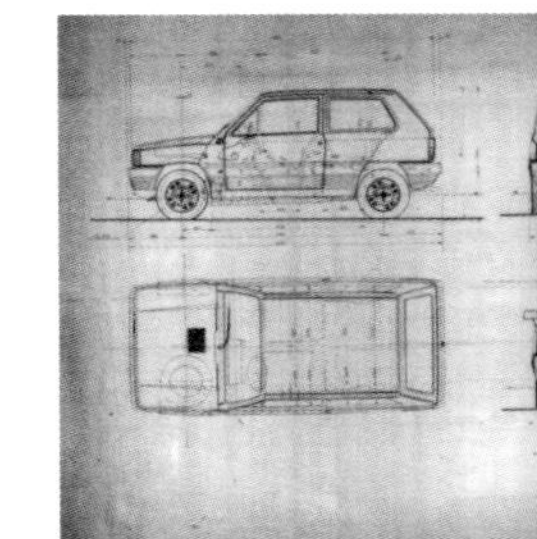

R39-6

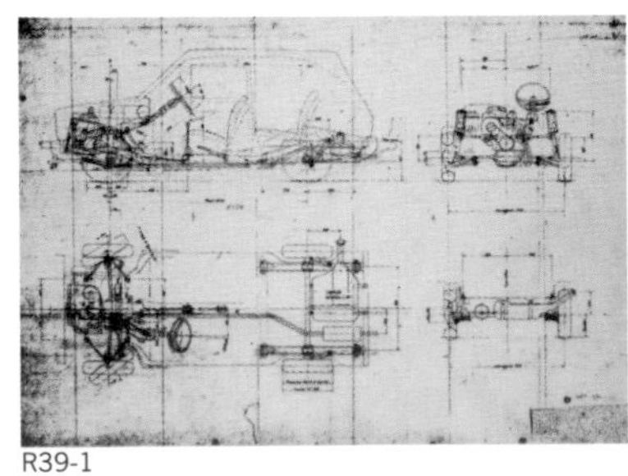
R39-1

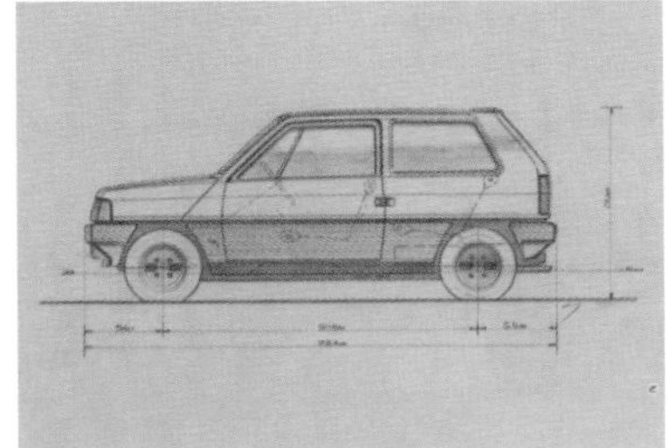
R39-4

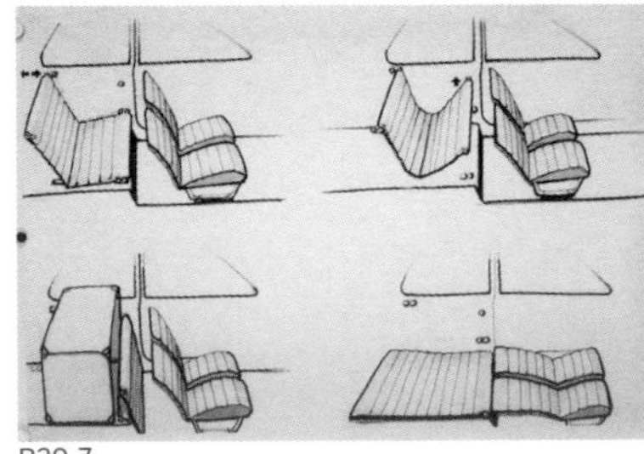
R39-7

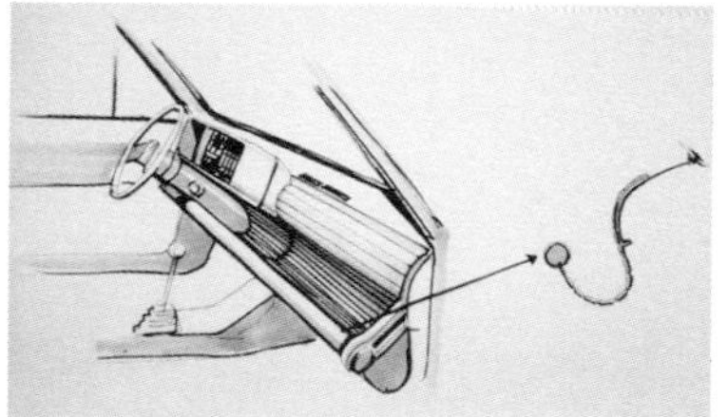

R39-8

R39-9

R39-10

A.L.F.A., 40/60 HP 'Ricotti,' 1914

p. 298

R40-1
Conte Ricotti in the 40/60 HP transformed into a torpedo
Period photograph
Anselmi Archive

R40-1

Projects by Mario Revelli de Beaumont

R41-1
Blueprint for multi-purpose vehicle (studio no. 4, 7.12.33), 1933
Blueprint, 45.5 x 93 cm
Revelli de Beaumont Archive
Photo Franco Turcati
R41-2
Blueprint for multi-purpose vehicle (studio no. 2, 5.12.33), 1933
Blueprint, 45.5 x 94 cm
Revelli de Beaumont Archive
Photo Franco Turcati
R41-3
Blueprint for multi-purpose vehicle (studio no. 3, 5.12.33), 1933
Blueprint, 43.5 x 90 cm
Revelli de Beaumont Archive
Photo Franco Turcati

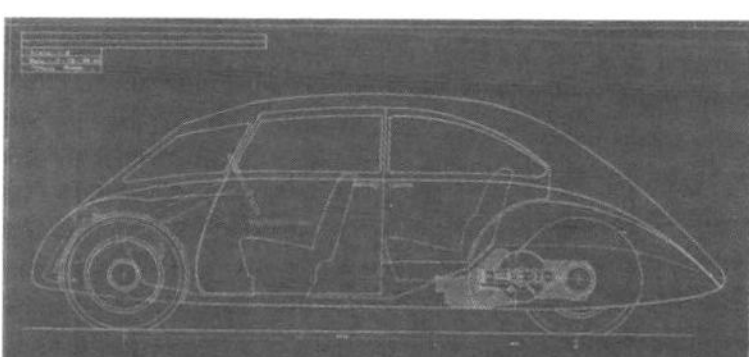

R41-1

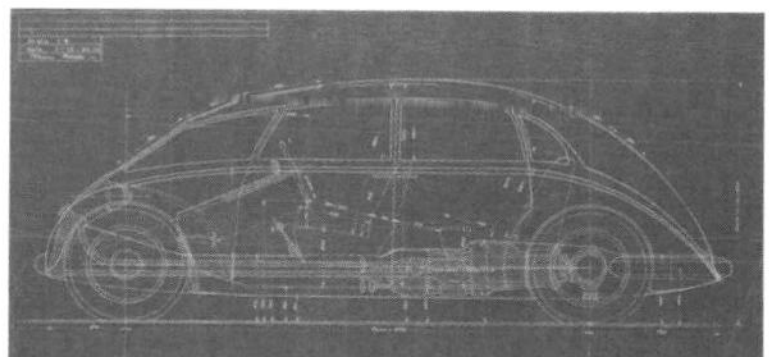

R41-2

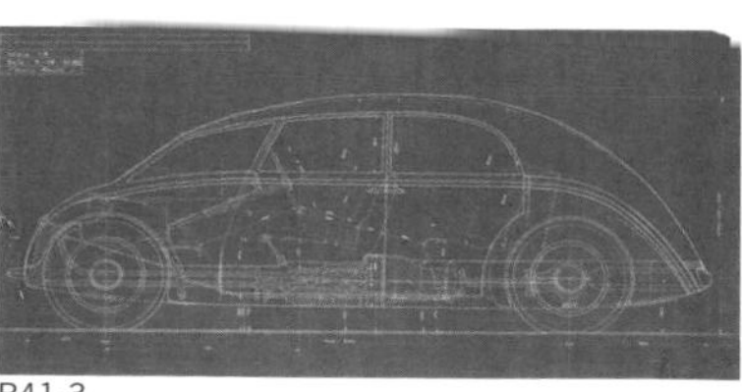

R41-3

The project of Mario Revelli de Beaumont, continued

R41-4
Sketch for the Revelli taxi, 1934
Tempera on paper, 42.5 x 80 cm
Revelli de Beaumont Archive
Photo Franco Turcati
R41-5
Study for the multi-purpose vehicle (studio no. 4, 10.1.34), 1934
Blueprint, 38.5 x 71 cm
Revelli de Beaumont Archive
Photo Franco Turcati
R41-6
Study for the multi-purpose vehicle (model no. 6, 16.1.34), 1934
Blueprint, scale 1:5, 39.5 x 71 cm
Revelli de Beaumont Archive
Photo Franco Turcati
R41-7
Study for the Revelli taxi (1941)
Watercolour on paper, 28.5 x 21 cm
Revelli de Beaumont Archive
Photo Franco Turcati
R41-8
Sketch for the Revelli taxi (three-seater Revelli taxi, the driver isolated in a central cabin at front, 18.3.40), 1940
Pencil on paper, 43.5 x 40 cm
Revelli de Beaumont Archive
Photo Franco Turcati
R41-9
Technical drawing for the Revelli taxi (overall view of the six-seater Revelli taxi, 3+3 alongside, electric propulsion, 5.4.40), 1940
Pencil on paper, 47 x 72 cm
Revelli de Beaumont Archive
Photo Franco Turcati
R41-10
Technical drawing for the Revelli taxi (overall view of the Revelli taxi with three seats in a row, electric propulsion, 18.3.40), 1940
Pencil on paper, 49.5 x 62 cm
Revelli dei Beaumont Archive
Photo Franco Turcati
R41-11
Technical drawing for the Revelli taxi, 1934
Blueprint, 71 x 98 cm
Revelli de Beaumont Archive
Photo Franco Turcati
R41-12
Technical drawing multipurpose vehicle, showing four views (1.8.33), 1933
Pencil on paper, 55.5 x 75 cm
Revelli de Beaumont Archive
Photo Franco Turcati

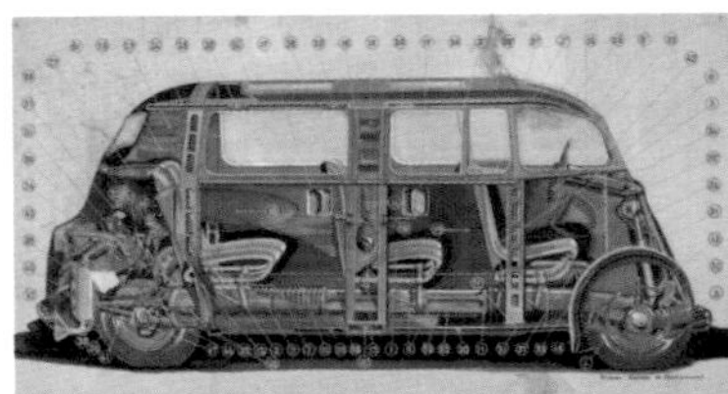
R41-4

R41-7

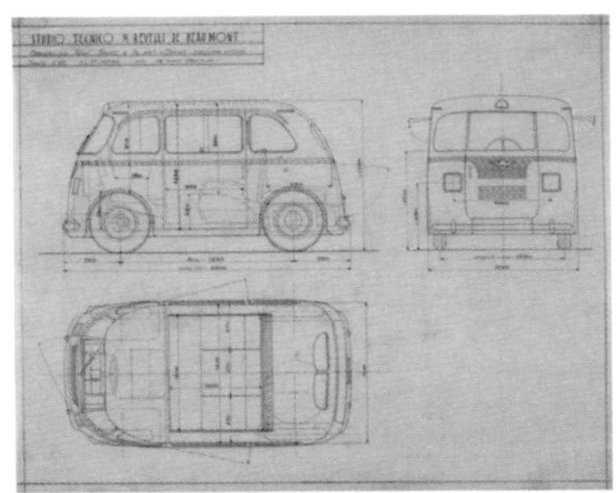
R41-10

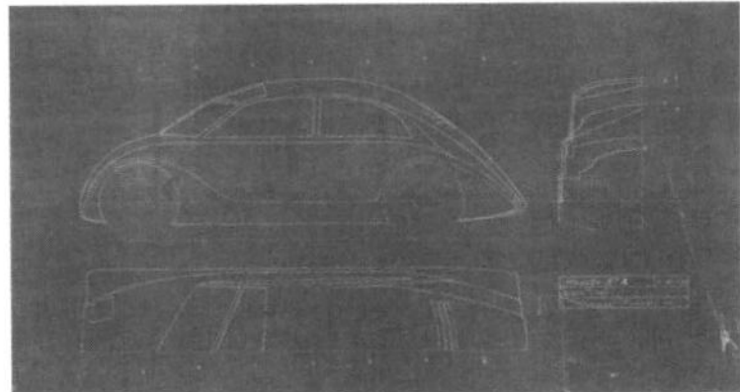
R41-5

R41-8

R41-11

R41-6

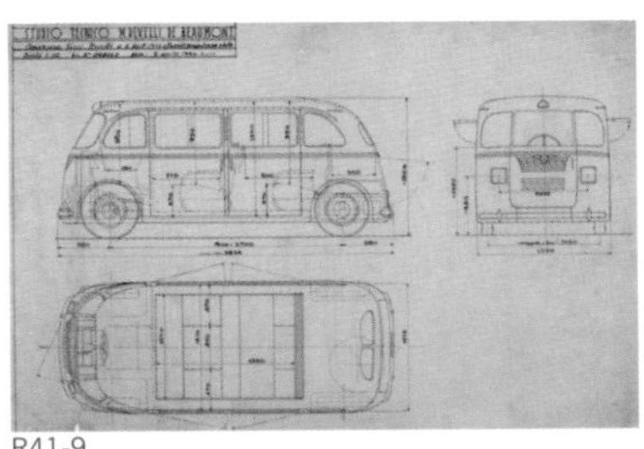
R41-9

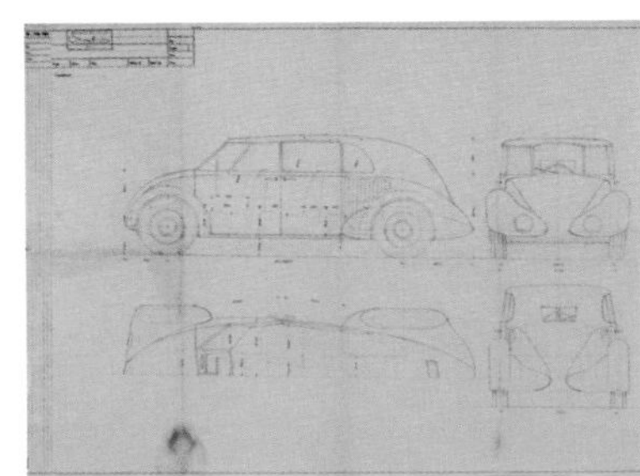
R41-12

R41-13
Four-view drawing for the multipurpose vehicle (16.7.33), 1933
Pencil on paper, 46.5 x 76 cm
Revelli de Beaumont Archive
Photo Franco Turcati

R41-14
Sketch for the Revelli ambulance (ambulance with space for two stretchers and six seats) (1940)
Pencil on paper, 34 x 50 cm
Revelli de Beaumont Archive
Photo Franco Turcati

R41-15
Four-view drawing for the Revelli electric vehicle, 1941
Tracing paper, 44 x 54 cm
Revelli de Beaumont Archive
Photo Franco Turcati

R41 16
Rendering for the Revelli electric vehicle, 1941
Watercolour on card, 33 x 32 cm
Revelli de Beaumont Archive
Photo Franco Turcati

R41-17
Sketch for the Revelli electric vehicle, 1941
Tracing paper, 28 x 31 cm
Revelli de Beaumont Archive
Photo Franco Turcati

R41-18
Rendering for the Revelli electric vehicle (1941)
Copy of the original, 20 x 23 cm
Revelli de Beaumont Archive
Photo Franco Turcati

R41-19
Chassis design of the Revelli electric vehicle (1941)
Copy of the original, 10.5 x 22 cm
Revelli de Beaumont Archive
Photo Franco Turcati

R41-20
Cut-away drawing of the Revelli electric vehicle (1941)
Copy of the original, 18.5 x 23 cm
Revelli de Beaumont Archive
Photo Franco Turcati

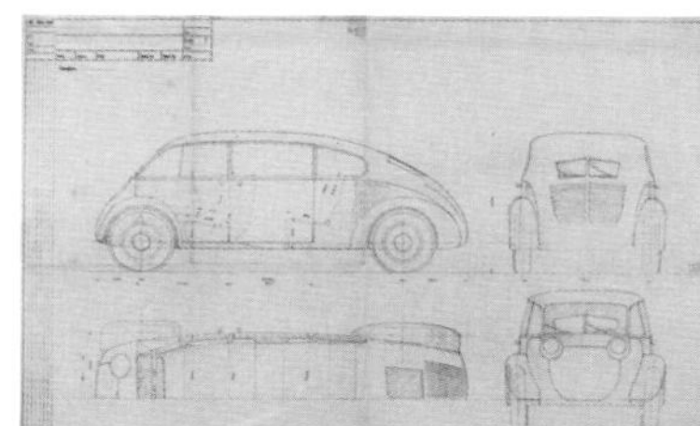
R41-13

R41-16

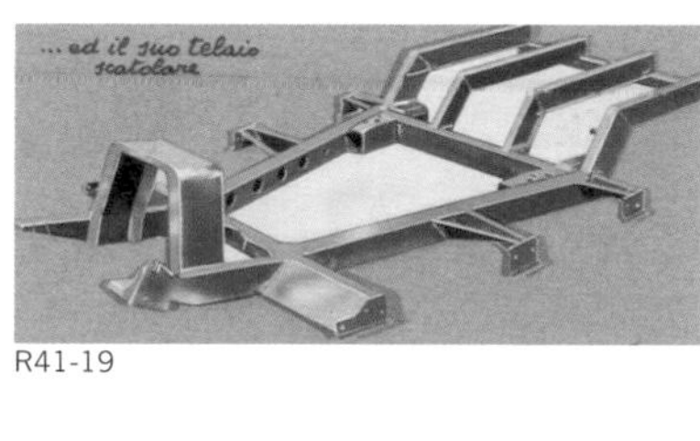

R41-19

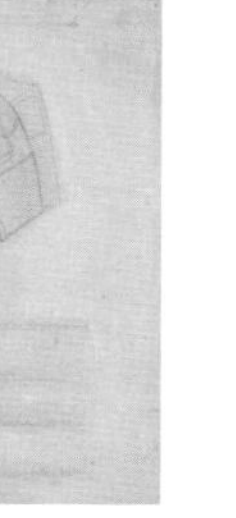
R41-14

R41-17

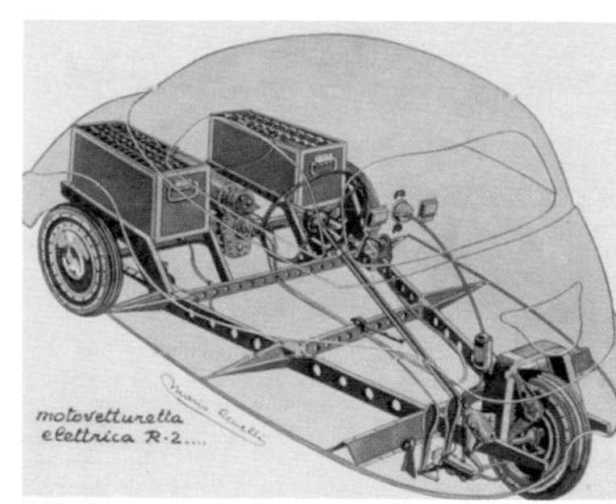

R41-20

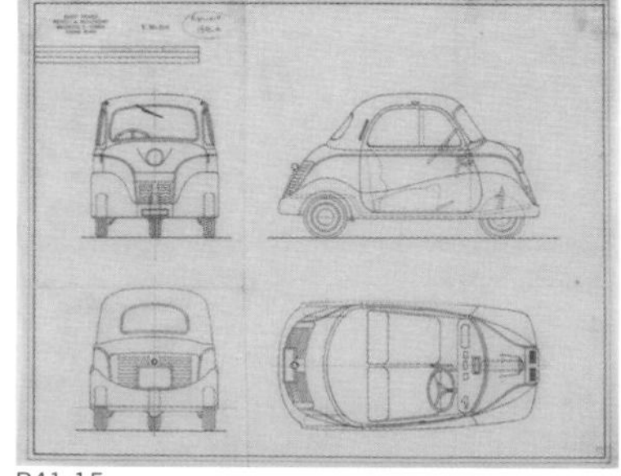
R41-15

R41-18

Fiat, 600 Multipla, 1956

p. 302

R42-1
Four-view drawing for the 600 Multipla (16.9.55), 1955
Ozalid on paper,
59.6 x 84.5 cm
Turin, Archivio Storico Fiat
Photo Franco Turcati
R42-2
600 Multipla
Period photograph
Turin, Archivio Storico Fiat

R42-1

R42-2

Italdesign Giugiaro, Megagamma, 1978

p. 306

R43-1
Four-view drawing for the Megagamma, scale 1:10, 1978
Copy on tracing paper, 34 x 78 cm
Italdesign Giugiaro Photographic Archive
© Italdesign Giugiaro Photographic Archive
R43-2
Rendering of the Megagamma, side view, 1978
Print on photographic paper, 50 x 70 cm
Italdesign Giugiaro Photographic Archive
© Italdesign Giugiaro Photographic Archive
R43-3
Diagram of the passenger space within the Megagamma with indication of space taken up by mechanical components and luggage space, side view, 1978
Print on photographic paper, 50 x 70 cm
Italdesign Giugiaro Photographic Archive
© Italdesign Giugiaro Photographic Archive
R43-4
Diagram of the passenger space within the Megagamma with comparison between the Gamma and Megagamma, side view, 1978
Print on photographic paper, 50 x 70 cm
Italdesign Giugiaro Photographic Archive
© Italdesign Giugiaro Photographic Archive
R43-5
Diagram of the passenger space within the Megagamma with ergonomic study of comparison between entering and exiting the car, 1978
Print on photographic paper, 50 x 70 cm
Italdesign Giugiaro Photographic Archive
© Italdesign Giugiaro Photographic Archive
R43-6
Photograph of the master model for the Megagamma, 1978
Print on photographic paper, 50 x 70 cm
Italdesign Giugiaro Photographic Archive
© Italdesign Giugiaro Photographic Archive

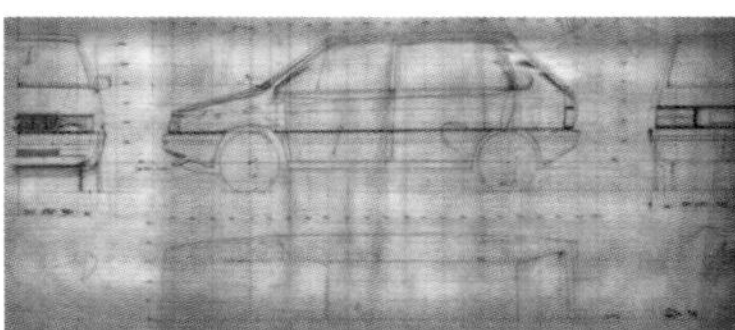

R43-1

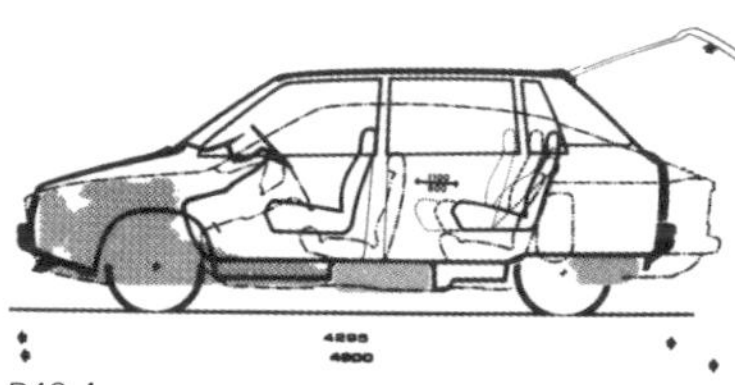

R43-4

R43-2

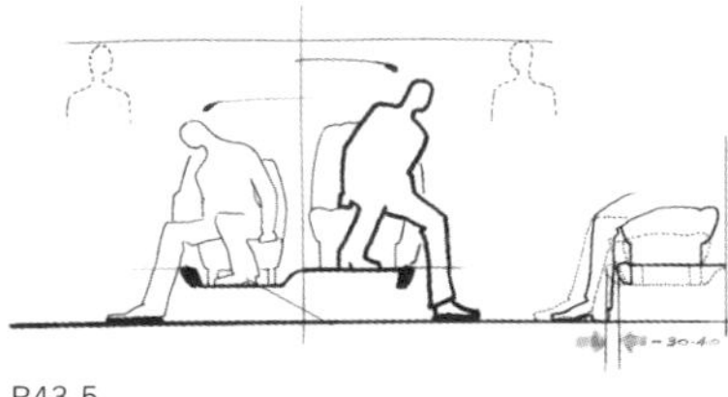

R43-5

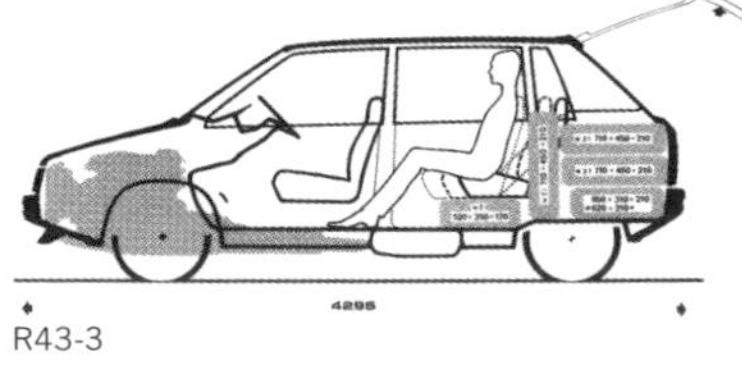

R43-3

R43-6

Renault, Espace, 1984

p. 310

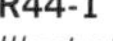

R44-1
Illustration showing use of space in the Espace, with reference especially to the boot area, 1984
Coloured marker pen on paper
Renault Collection
© Renault communication / all rights reserved
Renault Presse
R44-2
Illustration showing use of space in the Espace (1984)
Coloured marker pen on paper
Renault Collection
© Renault communication / all rights reserved
Renault Presse
R44-3
Illustration showing interior of the Espace, 1984
Mixed media
Renault Collection
© Renault communication / all rights reserved
Renault Presse
R44-4
Study for the pre-Espace model (design by Volanis), 1984
Mixed media
Ralf J.F. Kieselbach Collection

R44-2

R44-3

R44-1

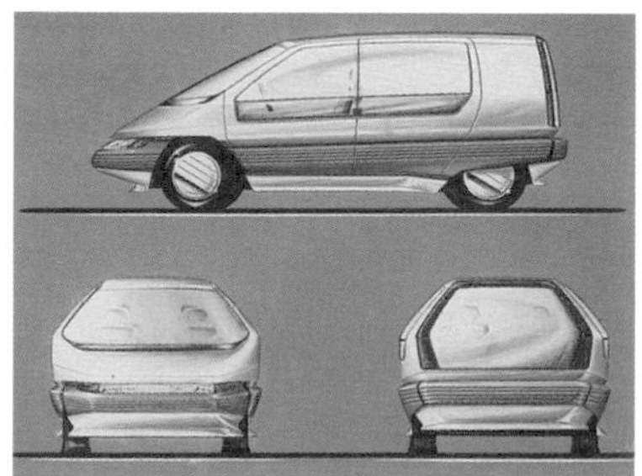

R44-4

Avions Voisin, C6 Laboratoire, 1923

p. 310

R45-1
Study for the C6 Laboratoire
Copy of the original, 30 x 21 cm
Moch Collection
R45-2
Artistic interpretation of the Grand Prix with the C6 Laboratoire in the foreground
Pencil and watercolour on paper
Moch Collection
R45-3
C6 Laboratoire, Grand Prix 1923
Period photograph
Moch Collection

R45-3

R45-1

R45-2

Chrysler, Airflow Series CU, 1934
p. 322

R46-1
Rendering for the Airflow CU, side view
Original leaflet
Ralf J.F. Kieselbach Collection
R46-2
Cut-away drawing of the chassis for the Airflow CU
Original leaflet
Ralf J.F. Kieselbach Collection
R46-3
Rendering of details of the Airflow CU
Original leaflet
Ralf J.F. Kieselbach Collection
R46-4
Cover of the original leaflet
Ralf J.F. Kieselbach Collection

R46-1

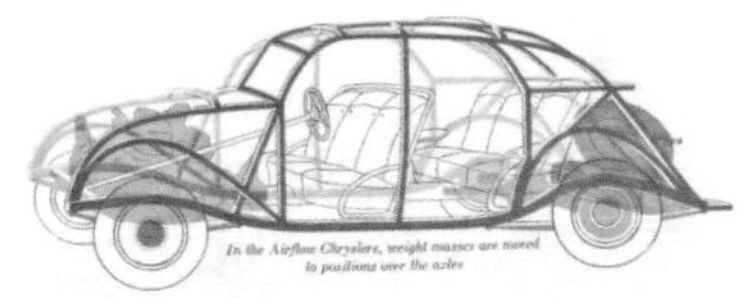

R46-2

R46-3

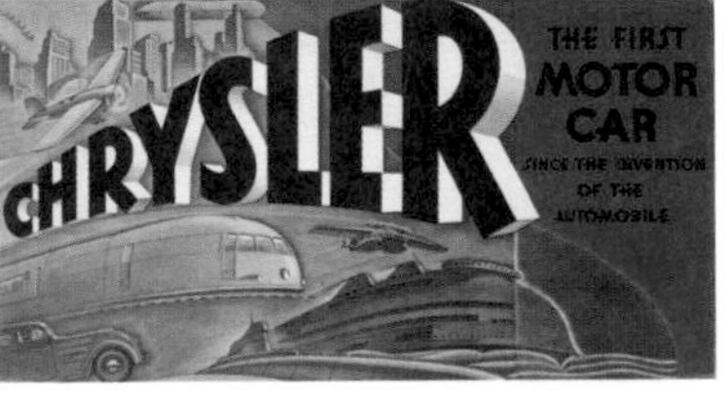

R46-4

Tatra, Type 77, 1934
p. 326

R47-1
Two-view drawing for the Type 77, 1986
Original leaflet
Ralf J.F. Kieselbach Collection
R47-2
Three-view drawing for the Type 77, 1986
Original leaflet
Ralf J.F. Kieselbach Collection
R47-3
Two-view drawing for the Type 77
Period print, 8 x 11 cm
Ralf J.F. Kieselbach Collection
R47-4
Cut-away diagram of the Type 77
Period print, 8 x 16 cm
Ralf J.F. Kieselbach Collection
R47-5
Drawing for the Type 77
Original leaflet
Ralf J.F. Kieselbach Collection
R47-6
Advertisement for the Type 77, 1936
Original leaflet
Ralf J.F. Kieselbach Collection

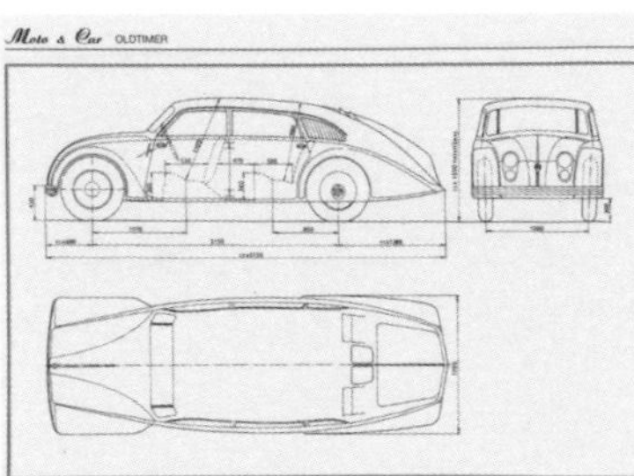

R47-2

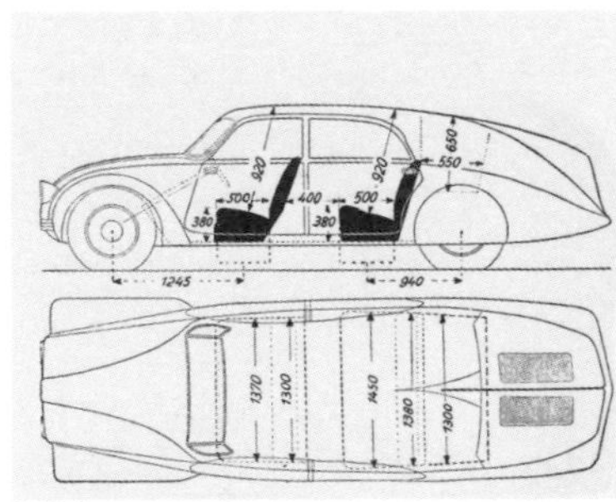

R47-3

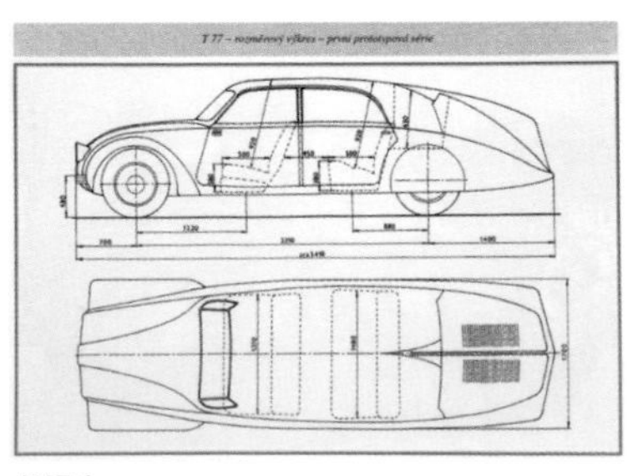

R47-1

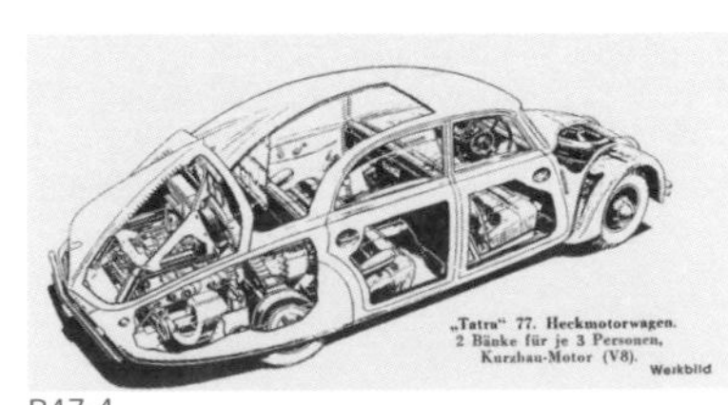

R47-4

Avions Voisin, C 28 Clairière, 1935

p. 330

R47-5

R47-6

R48-1
Three-view drawing for the C 28
(1934)
Copy of the original
Moch Collection
R48-2
Technical drawing of the pedals for the Avion Voisin, 1921
Copy of the original, 21 x 30 cm
Moch Collection
R48-3
Drawing for the C 28 four-seater with two doors
Period print
Moch Collection
R48-4
Drawing for the C 28 four-seater with two doors
Period print
Moch Collection
R48-5
Drawing for the C 28 'berline profilée' with four seats and opening roof
Period print
Moch Collection
R48-6
Period catalogue: 'Voisin vous parle de l'avenir' (Voisin speaks to you of the future)
Period print
Moch Collection

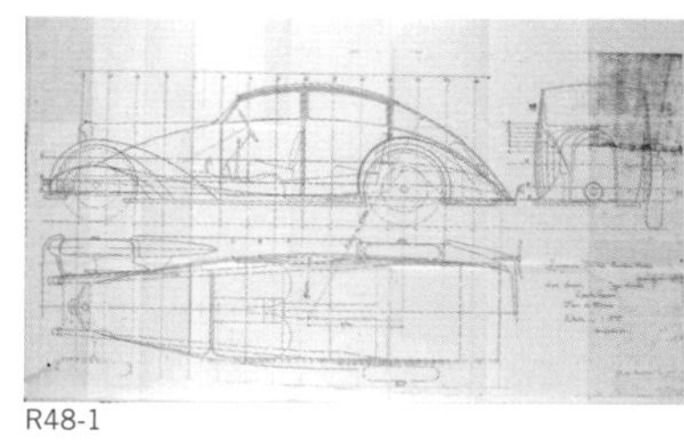

R48-1

R48-2

R48-5

R48-3

R48-6

R48-4

Lancia, Aprilia, 1937
p. 334

R49-1
Three-view drawing for the Aprilia (24.1.39), 1939
Ozalid on plastic-coated paper, 57.5 x 84 cm
Turin, Archivio Storico Fiat
Photo Franco Turcati
R49-2
Technical drawing of the radiator surround for the Aprilia berlina 238, 1936
Ozalid, 83 x 116 cm
Turin, Archivio Storico Fiat
Photo Franco Turcati

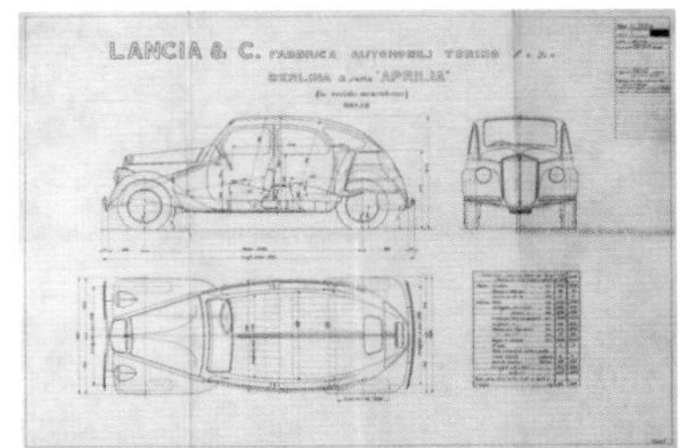

R49-1

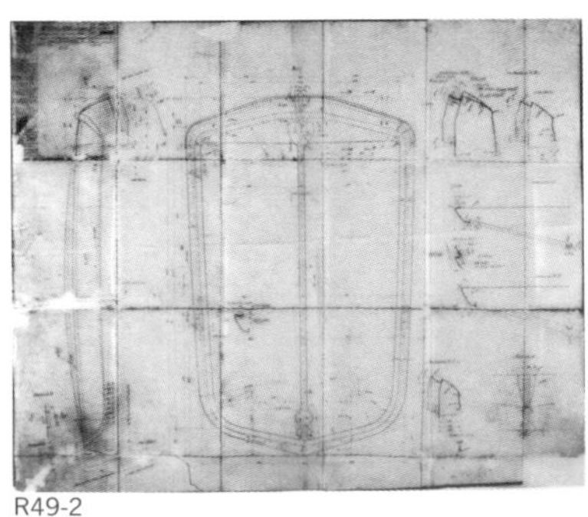
R49-2

Alfa Romeo, 8C 2900 B Berlinetta Aerodinamica Le Mans, 1938
p. 338

R50-1
Regulations for the Le Mans 24-Hours with notes by Enzo Ferrari
Original document
Bianchi Anderloni Collection

LES 24 HEURES DU MANS
XVe GRAND PRIX D'ENDURANCE
organisé par
L'AUTOMOBILE-CLUB DE L'OUEST
18 & 19 JUIN 1938
CIRCUIT PERMANENT DE LA SARTHE

R50-1

MG, EX.181, 1957
p. 342

R51-1
Phil Hill standing next to the EX.181 Record Car, Bonneville Record Run, 1959
Period photograph
British Motor Industry Heritage Trust
© BMIHT – British Motor Industry Heritage Trust Film and Picture Library

R51-1

Bertone, Carabo, 1968
p. 348

R52-1
Sketch for the Carabo, 1968
Indian ink on tracing paper
Bertone_ Public relations department
R52-2
Study for the Carabo, details of the interior and exterior, 1968
Indian ink on tracing paper
Bertone_ Public relations department

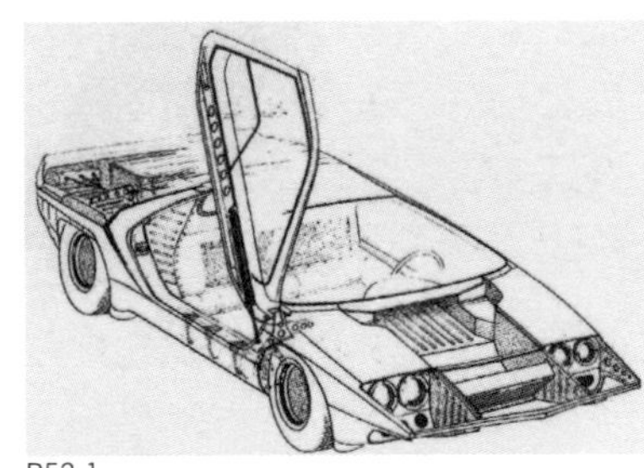
R52-1

R52-2

R52-3
Scale model for the Carabo, with three views, 1968
Period photograph
Bertone_ Public relations department
R52-4
Scale model for the Carabo, seen from above, 1968
Period photograph
Bertone_ Public relations department

R52-3

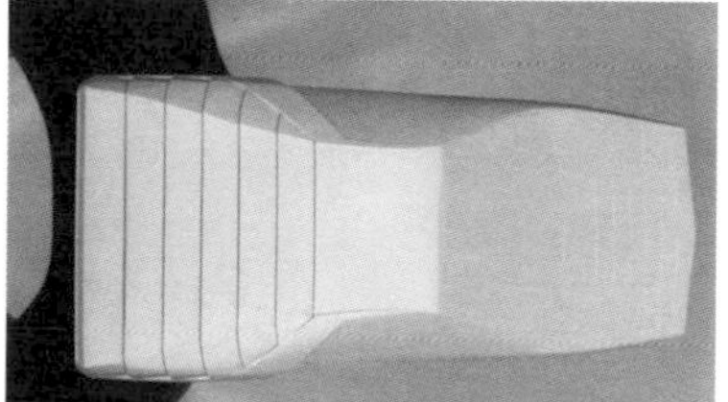

bertone

R52-4

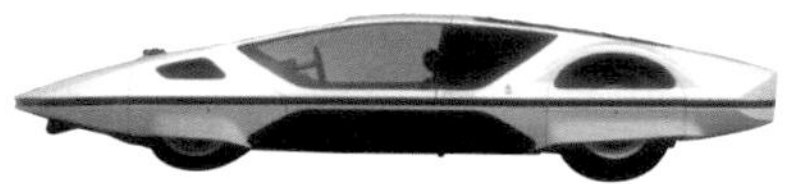

Pininfarina, Modulo, 1970

p. 352

R53-1
Rendering for the Modulo, side view, 1970
Mixed media
Pininfarina SpA
R53-2
Presentation of the Modulo on the Italian stand at the Universal Exposition of Osaka, 1970
Period photograph
Pininfarina SpA
R53-3
Cut-away diagram of the Modulo
Pininfarina SpA

R53-3

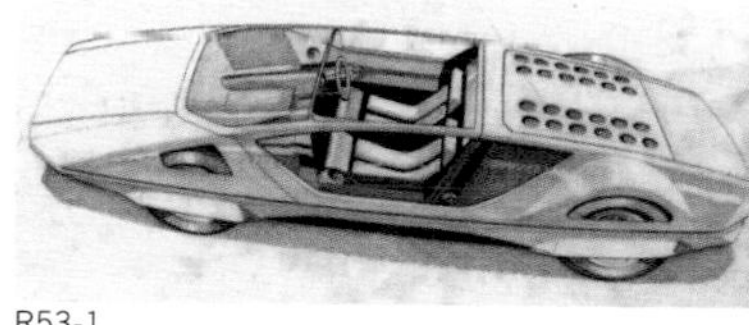

R53-1

R53-2

Italdesign Giugiaro, Boomerang, 1972

p. 356

R54-1
Side elevation drawing for the Tapiro, scale 1:1, 1970
Chalk on card, 180 x 500 cm
Italdesign Giugiaro Photographic Archive

R54-1

Italdesign Giugiaro, Medusa, 1980

p. 360

R55-1
Three-view drawing for the Medusa, scale 1:10, detail of the exterior bodywork with lateral and front view and study for the interior and boot opening (5.7.79), 1979
Blueprint with notes in pencil and ink, 42.5 x 91 cm
Italdesign Giugiaro Photographic Archive
© Italdesign Giugiaro Photographic Archive

R55-2
Three-view drawing for the Medusa, scale 1:10, detail of the exterior bodywork with lateral and front view (5.7.79), 1979
Copy on tracing paper, 40.5 x 98 cm
Italdesign Giugiaro Photographic Archive
© Italdesign Giugiaro Photographic Archive

R55-3
Giorgetto Giugiaro draws himself creating the lifesize plaster model of the Medusa, 1980
Print on photographic paper, 50 x 70 cm
Italdesign Giugiaro Photographic Archive
© Italdesign Giugiaro Photographic Archive

R55-4
'Location' drawing for the Medusa, side view
Print on photographic paper, 70 x 100 cm
Italdesign Giugiaro Photographic Archive
© Italdesign Giugiaro Photographic Archive

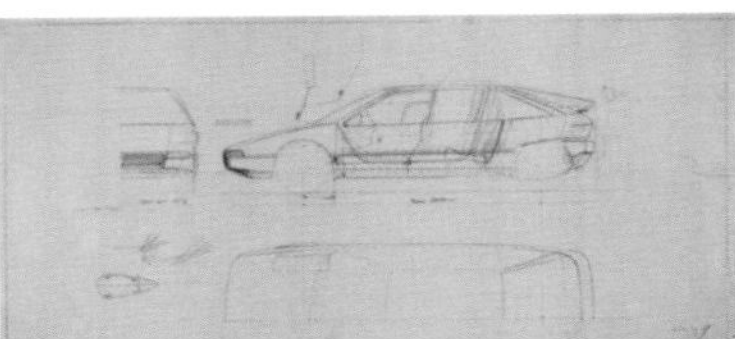
R55-1

R55-2

R55-3

R55-4

Italdesign Giugiaro, Gabbiano, 1983

p. 360

R56-1
Sketch for the Gabbiano, 1983
Copy on photographic paper, 50 x 70.5 cm
Italdesign Giugiaro Photographic Archive
© Italdesign Giugiaro Photographic Archive

R56-2
Gabbiano, 1983
Period photograph, 50 x 70.5 cm
Italdesign Giugiaro Photographic Archive
© Italdesign Giugiaro Photographic Archive

R56-1

R56-2

Fioravanti, LF, 2001

p. 364

Lamborghini, Miura P 400, 1966

p. 370

R58-1
Rendering of the Miura, 1966
Period photograph, 13 x 18 cm
Bertone_ Public relations department
R58-2
Rendering for the Miura, 1966
Period photograph, 13 x 18 cm
Bertone_ Public relations department
R58-3
Drawing for the Miura, view of the interior with details of the dashboard, 1966
Period photograph, 13 x 18 cm
Bertone_ Public relations department
R58-4
Miura, side view with bonnet and boot open, 1966
Period photograph, 13 x 18 cm
Bertone_ Public relations department

R58-2

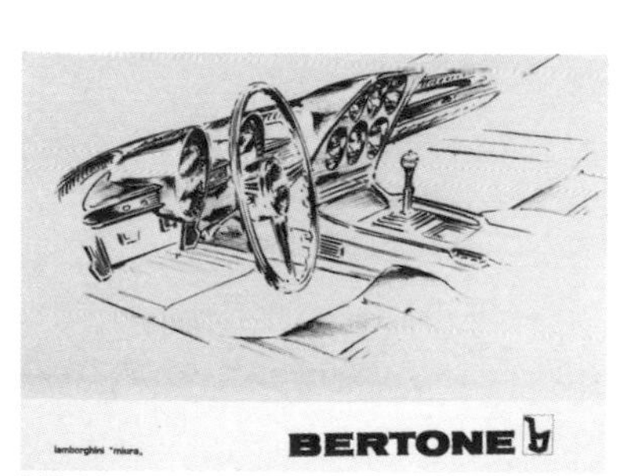

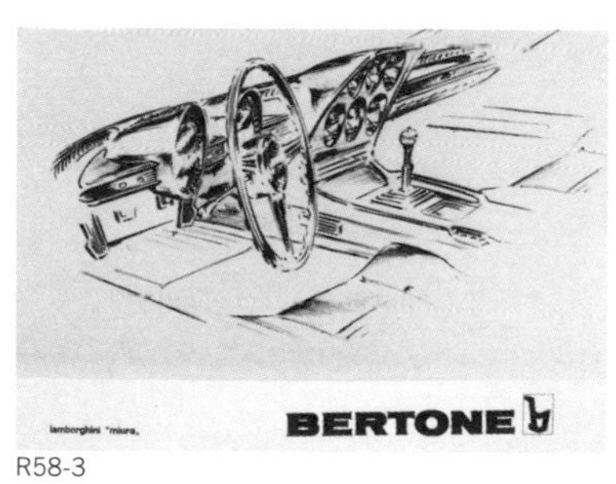

R58-3

R58-1

R58-4

Alfa Romeo, 33 Stradale, 1967

p. 376

R59-1
Exterior bodywork for the 33.2 Stradale prototype, 1969
Arese (Milan), Automobilismo Storico Alfa Romeo, Museo Storico, Centro di Documentazione Storica
Photo © Automobilismo Storico Alfa Romeo, Centro di Documentazione Storica

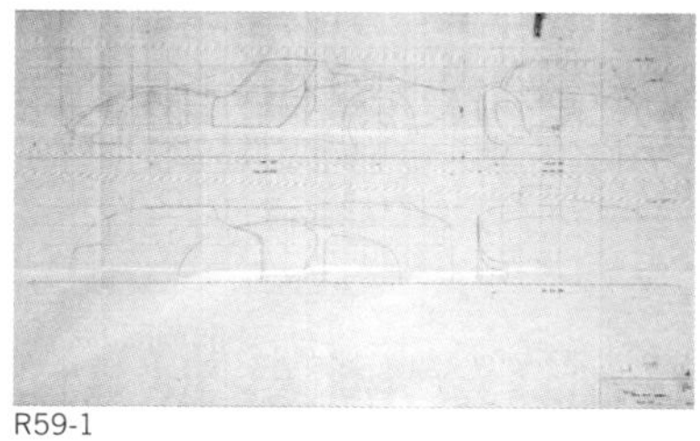

R59-1

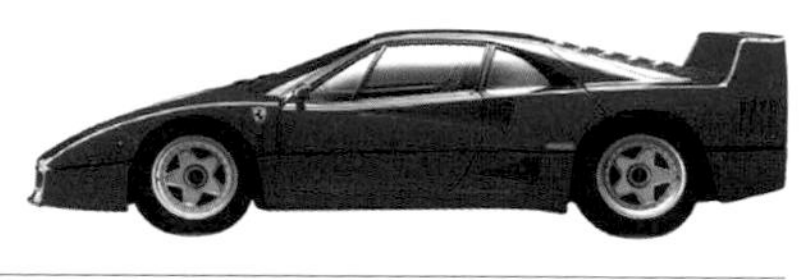

Ferrari, F40, 1987

p. 382

R60-1
Sketches for the F40, three quarter front and rear view, 1987
Galleria Ferrari
© La Presse / Ferrari SpA

R60-1

Pagani, Zonda C12, 2002

p. 388

R61-1
Study for the Zonda, view from above, 2000
Pagani Automobili Spa
Pagani Automobili Communication
R61-2
Study for the Zonda, side view, 2000
Pagani Automobili Spa
Pagani Automobili Communication
R61-3
Sketches for the Zonda, three overlapping views, 2000
Pagani Automobili Spa
Pagani Automobili Communication
R61-4
Sketches of the dashboard and seats for the Zonda, 2000
Pagani Automobili Spa
Pagani Automobili Communication

R61-2

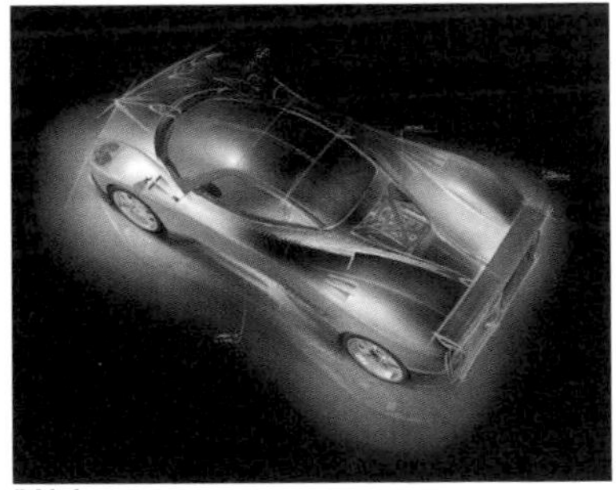

R61-1

R61-3

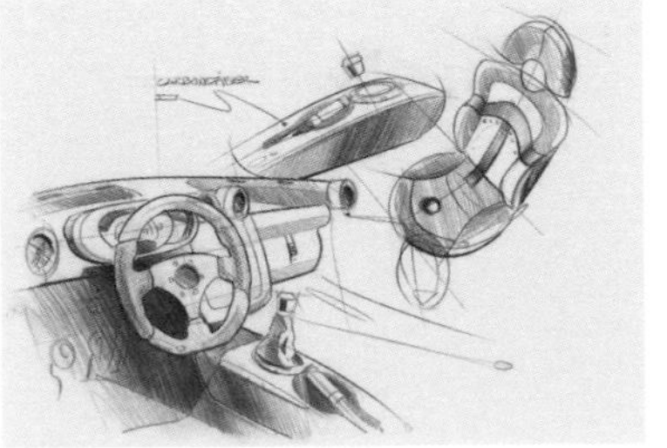

R61-4

Ferrari, 599 GTB Fiorano, 2006

p. 392

R62-1
Rendering for the 599 GTB Fiorano, front three-quarter view, 2006
Maranello (Modena), Galleria Ferrari
© La Presse / Ferrari Spa
R62-2
Rendering for the 599 GTB Fiorano, rear three-quarter view, 2006
Maranello (Modena), Galleria Ferrari
© La Presse / Ferrari Spa

R62-1

R62-2

Lancia, Lambda, 1922

p. 398

R63-1
Study for the Lambda Torpedo, scale 1:10 (15.6.1926), 1926
Pencil on tracing paper, 33 x 57 cm
Turin, Archivio Storico Fiat
Photo Franco Turcati

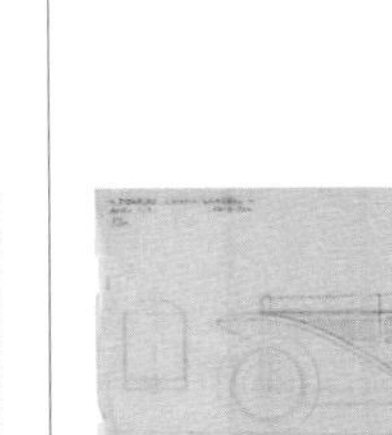

R63-1

Citroën, 7CV Traction Avant, 1934

p. 402

R64-1
Flaminio Bertoni's employment contract at Citroën (8.7.1932), 1932
Original document, 27 x 21 cm
Leonardo Bertoni Archive
R64-2/3
Patent for a photo frame, front and rear (design Flaminio Bertoni), 1955
Original document, 15 x 23 cm
Leonardo Bertoni Archive
R64-4
Original letter by Flaminio Bertoni within book containing correspondence between Bertoni and Carrozzena Baroffio
Original letter – book, 27 x 21 cm
Leonardo Bertoni Archive
R64-5
Flaminio Bertoni with model
Period photograph
Leonardo Bertoni Archive
R64-6
Flaminio Bertoni with his Traction Avant at the Passo della Forcora with his wife, Lucienne, son Serge and aunt Anna
Period photograph
Leonardo Bertoni Archive

Société anonyme ANDRÉ CITROËN
au capital de 400.000.000 de francs
Siège social à Paris : 143, Quai de Javel

CONTRAT D'ENGAGEMENT
DU PERSONNEL AU MOIS

Entre la Société Anonyme ANDRÉ CITROËN, au Capital de 400.000.000 de Frs, Siège social à Paris, 143, Quai de Javel, d'une part
et Monsieur Bertoni Flaminio
né le 10 Janvier 1903 à Masnago (Italie)
demeurant à 46 Avenue de la Marne à Asnières d'autre part
il a été convenu ce qui suit :
Monsieur Bertoni Flaminio
est admis à remplir à la Société Anonyme ANDRÉ CITROËN, à dater du 1 Juillet 1932 les fonctions de Dessinateur d'études dans l'une quelconque de ses Usines ou Succursales, aux appointements mensuels de Dix huit cent francs

Au cours des trois premiers mois qui constituent une période d'essai, il pourra être congédié sans aucun délai de préavis. Par réciprocité, il pourra, dans la même période, quitter ses fonctions à tout moment. Dans l'un ou l'autre cas, le calcul de ses appointements sera fait proportionnellement au nombre de jours du mois pendant lesquels il aura été présent.

Les dits mois d'essai étant écoulés, l'engagement se trouvera régi aux clauses et conditions du droit commun et des usages de la région parisienne. L'une et l'autre parties auront, en conséquence, la faculté de faire cesser le présent contrat en prévenant un mois à l'avance.

En cas de congédiement suivi de son départ immédiat, il lui sera alloué, sauf renvoi justifié, une indemnité forfaitaire d'un mois de traitement, sans prime d'aucune sorte.

Si des avantages (primes, gratifications, traitement de maladie, congé, etc...) lui étaient accordés en sus de son traitement ces avantages, quelle que soit leur importance, devant [illegible] ne pourront jamais faire l'objet de sa part d'aucune réclamation. En particulier, s'il est immatriculé aux Assurances Sociales, aux termes de la Loi du 5 Avril 1928, il ne saurait prétendre au cumul des prestations légales avec des avantages de même nature que peut accorder la Société, à titre bénévole, au personnel non assujetti à la Loi.

Toutes les contestations auxquelles pourra donner lieu le présent engagement, seront exclusivement portées devant les tribunaux compétents de la Seine.

Fait en double exemplaire à Paris, le 8 Juillet 1932

R64-1

INSTRUCTIONS
EN SE SERVANT D'UN COUPE-PAPIER

R64-3

R64-5

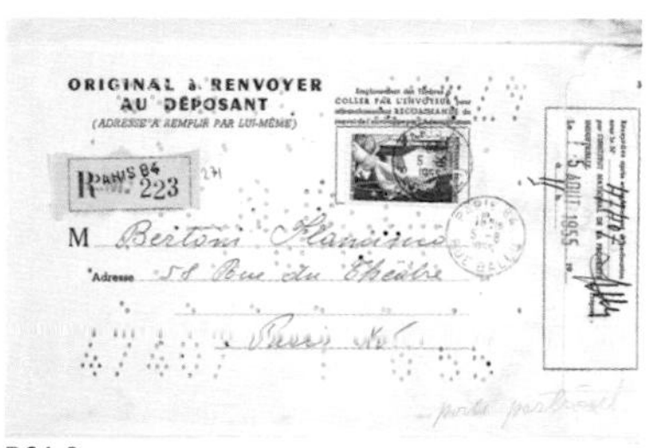

ORIGINAL À RENVOYER AU DÉPOSANT
(ADRESSE À REMPLIR PAR LUI-MÊME)
M Bertoni Flaminio

R64-2

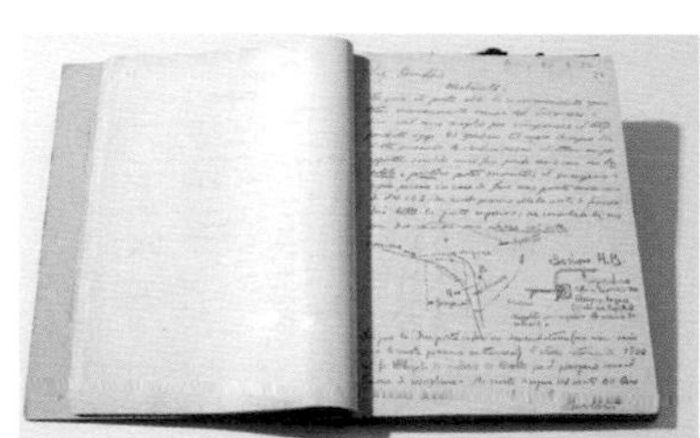

R64-4

R64-6

Panhard, Dynavia, 1948

p. 406

R65-1/2
Model for the Dynavia, scale 1:4, 1949
Wood, 30 x 50 cm
Loan from the Cité de l'Automobile – Musée National – Collection Schlumpf
Photo Fred Hurst

R65-3/4
Model for the Dynavia, scale 1:4, 1949
Wood, 30 x 50 cm
Loan from the Cité de l'Automobile – Musée National – Collection Schlumpf
Photo Fred Hurst

R65-3

R65-1

R65-4

R65-2

Citroën, DS 19, 1955

p. 410

R66-1
Sketch by Bertoni for the four-door saloon, side view
Pencil on paper
Citroën
© Citroën Communication

R66-2
Sketch by Bertoni for the DS convertible, with two doors and four seats, side view
Pencil on paper
Citroën
© Citroën Communication

R66-3
Studies of forms based on the 'tear-drop' drawn by Bertoni in the 1940s
Pastel on paper
Citroën
© Citroën Communication

R66-4
Sketches by Bertoni
Pencil on paper
Citroën
© Citroën Communication

R66-5
Studies by Bertoni for the form of a sports model (S)
Pastel on paper (framed together)
Citroën
© Citroën Communication

R66-6
Study by Bertoni for the DS model
Pencil on paper
Citroën
© Citroën Communication

R66-7
Study by Bertoni for the front of the DS
Pencil on paper
Citroën
© Citroën Communication

R66-8
Study by Bertoni
Pencil on paper
Citroën
© Citroën Communication

R66-9
Study model for the DS
Chalk
Citroën
© Citroën Communication

R66-10
Study model for the DS
Chalk
Citroën
© Citroën Communication

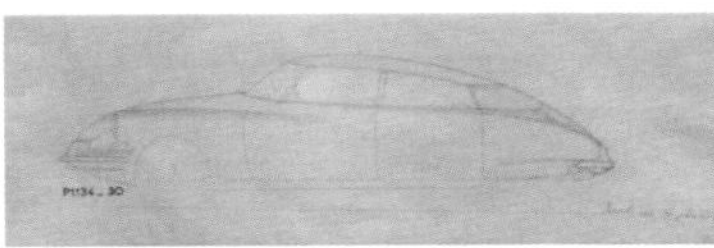

R66-1

R66-2

R66-3

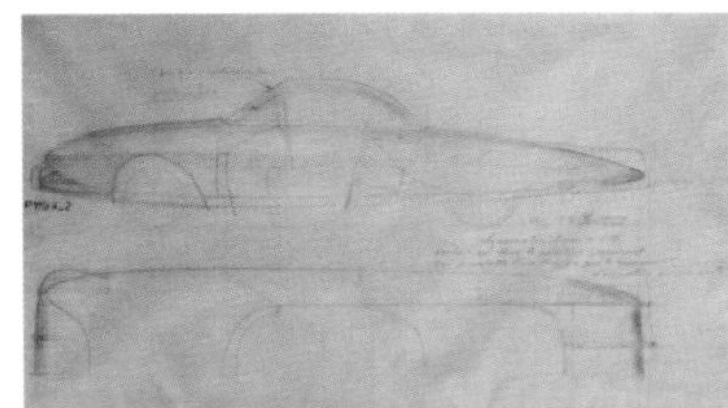

R66-4

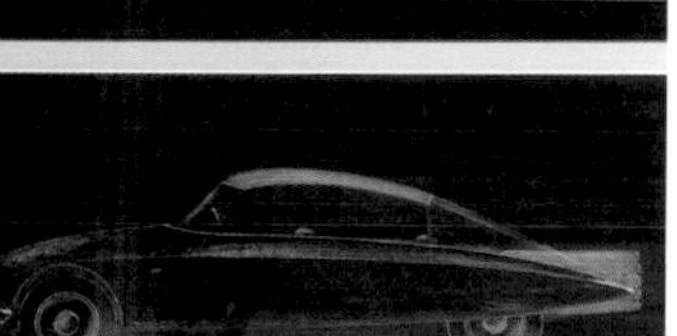
R66-5

R66-8

R66-6

R66-9

R66-7

R66-10

NSU, RO 80, 1967

p. 414

R67-1
Side elevation drawings for the RO 80 (drawing no. 3shows the definitive version)
Copy of the original, 30 x 21 cm
Ralf J.F. Kieselbach Collection
R67-2
Cut-away diagram of the RO 80 (signed Schlenzig) (1967)
Mixed media
Ralf J.F. Kieselbach Collection
R67-3
Cut-away diagram of the RO 80 (signed Schlenzig) (1967)
Mixed media
Ralf J.F. Kieselbach Collection

R67-2

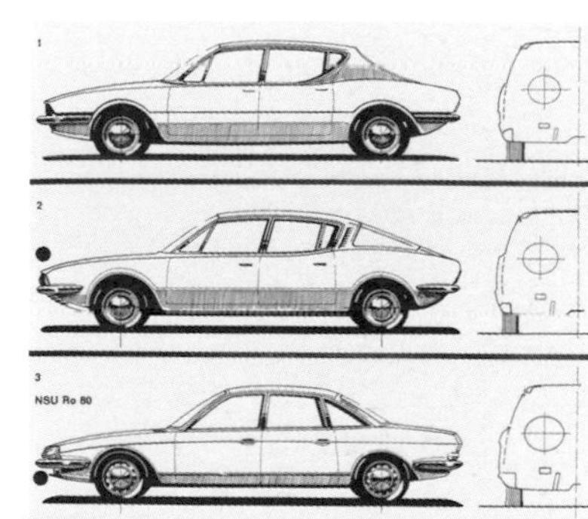
R67-1

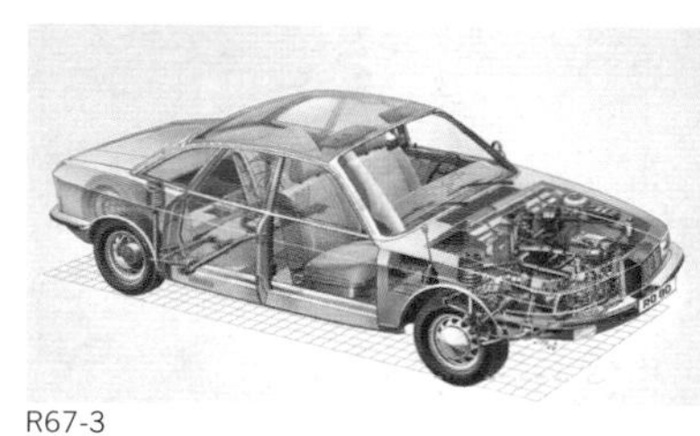
R67-3

La Jamais Contente, 1899

p. 420

R67-4
Claus Luthe, designer of the RO 80 at work
Period photograph, 16.5 x 21 cm
Ralf J.F. Kieselbach Collection
R67-5
Claus Luthe, designer of the RO 80 in his studio
Photograph, 16.5 x 21 cm
Ralf J.F. Kieselbach Collection

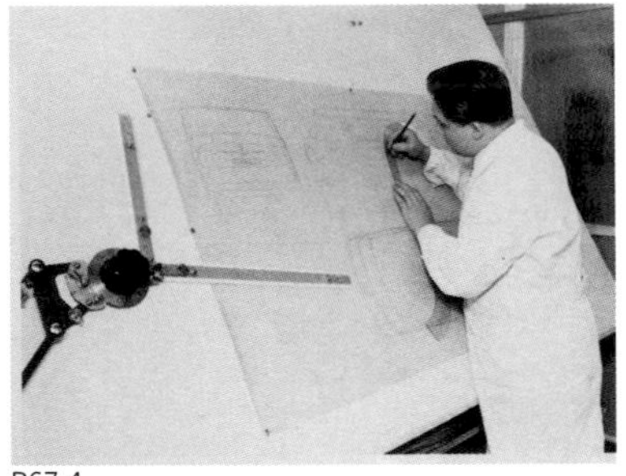
R67-4

R67-5

R68-1
Side view
Copy of the original, 30 x 42 cm
Lions Club International Le Bourget
– Christian Wannyn
R68-2
Four-view drawing
Copy of the original, 21 x 30 cm
Lions Club International Le Bourget
– Christian Wannyn
R68-3
Patent for the Jamais Contente, 1898
Photograph
Lions Club International Le Bourget
– Christian Wannyn
R68-4
The 'Flower Celebration' with Messrs Jenatzy on the Jamais Contente
Period photograph
Lions Club International Le Bourget
– Christian Wannyn
R68-5
Camille Jenatzy's speed record (100 kph – 62 mph) on 29 April 1899
Period photograph
Lions Club International Le Bourget
– Christian Wannyn
R68-6
Camille Jenatzy's speed record (100 kph – 62 mph) on 29 April 1899
Period print
Lions Club International Le Bourget
– Christian Wannyn

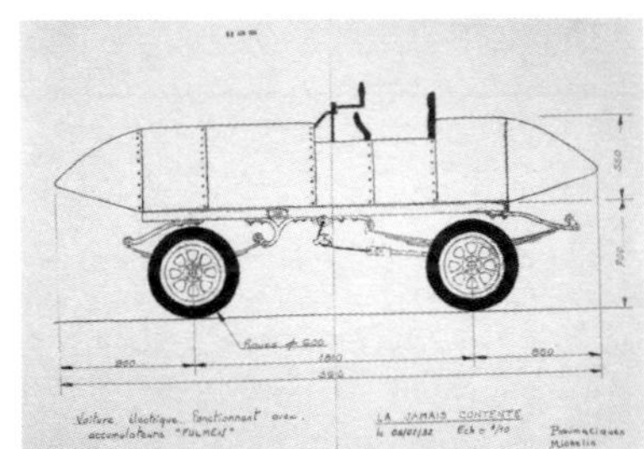
R68-1

R68-4

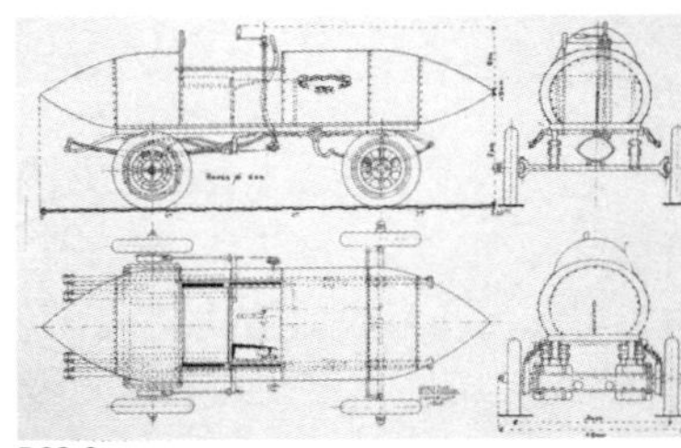
R68-2

R68-5

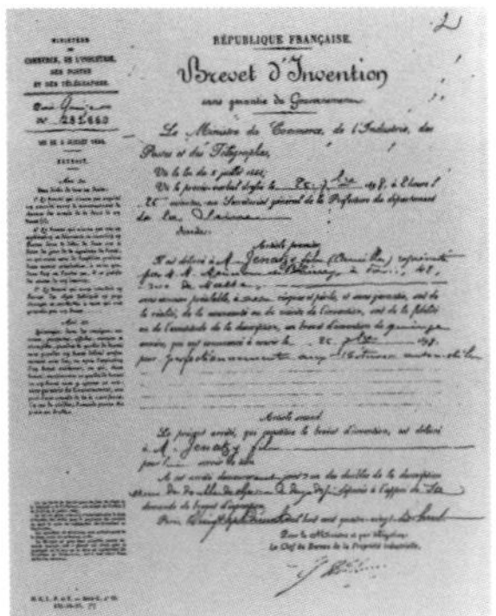

R68-3

R68-6

Fiat, Turbina, 1954

p. 424

R69-1
Presentation of the Turbina, 1954
Period photograph
Turin, Archivio Storico Fiat
R69-2
Presentation of the Turbina, 1954
Period photograph
Turin, Archivio Storico Fiat
R69-3
Presentation of the Turbina, 1954
Period photograph
Turin, Archivio Storico Fiat

R69-1

R69-2

R69-3

Italdesign Giugiaro, Biga, 1992

p. 428

R70-1
Technical drawing for the Biga, scale 1:10, with orthogonal projections, 31.01.92
Ink and pencil on tracing paper, 57 x 96.5 cm
Italdesign Giugiaro Photographic Archive
Photo archivio Italdesign Giugiaro
R70-2
Diagram of the passenger space in the Biga, view from above, 31.01.92
Mixed media, 40 x 70 cm
Italdesign Giugiaro Photographic Archive
Photo archivio Italdesign Giugiaro
R70-3
Diagram of the passenger space in the Biga, side view, 1992
Mixed media, 40 x 60 cm
Italdesign Giugiaro Photographic Archive
Photo archivio Italdesign Giugiaro
R70-4
Diagram of the passenger space in the Biga, side view (with disabled passenger), 1992
Mixed media, 40 x 60 cm
Italdesign Giugiaro Photographic Archive
Photo archivio Italdesign Giugiaro

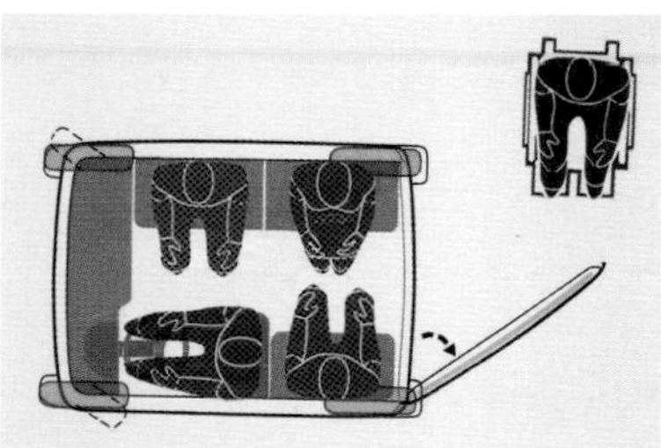

R70-2

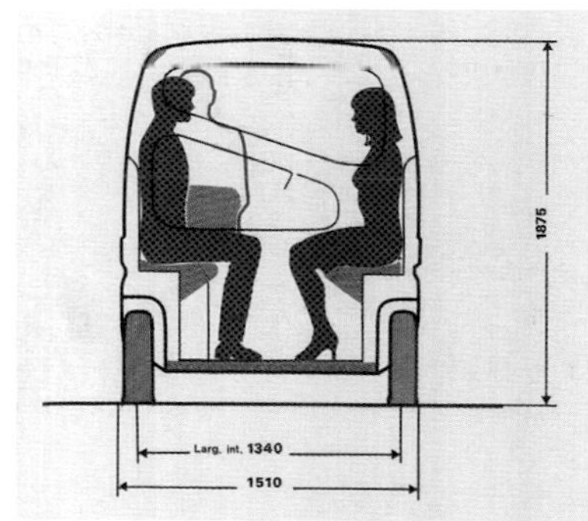

R70-3

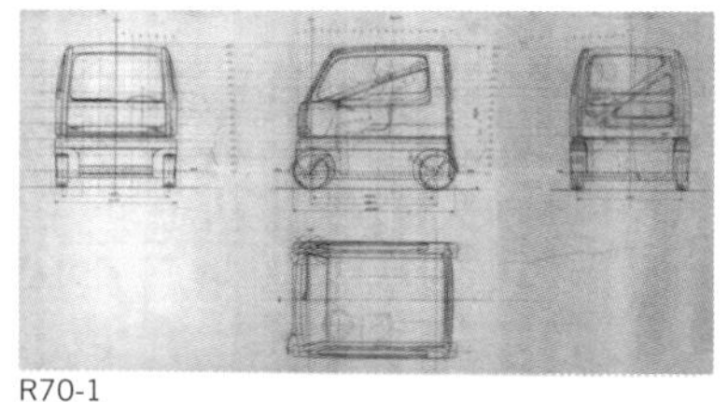

R70-1

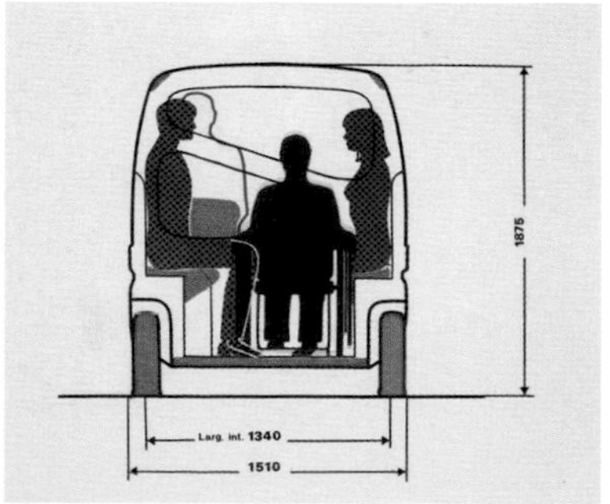

R70-4

Fiat, Vanzic, 1995
p. 432

GM, Hy-wire, 2002
p. 436

Pininfarina, Nido, 2004
p. 440

R70-5
Diagram of the passenger space in the Biga, side views with increased headspace and reduced width, together with side view of entry into vehicle, 1992
Mixed media, 33 x 60.5 cm
Italdesign Giugiaro Photographic Archive
Photo archivio Italdesign Giugiaro
R70-6
Design for the control unit for the Biga, 1992
Mixed media, 35 x 50 cm
Italdesign Giugiaro Photographic Archive
Photo archivio Italdesign Giugiaro

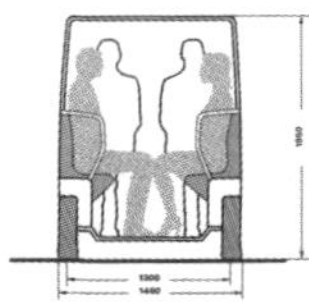

R70-5

R70-6

Mercedes-Benz, F 600 HY, 2005

p. 444

R74-1
Study of the passenger space for the F 600 HY, 2004
Rendering
DaimlerChrysler Advanced Design Italia
© DaimlerChrysler AG
R74-2
Study of the boot lid space for the F 600 HY, 2004
Rendering
DaimlerChrysler Advanced Design Italia
© DaimlerChrysler AG
R74-3
Study of the passenger space for the F 600 HY (pic-nic), 2004
Rendering
DaimlerChrysler Advanced Design Italia
© DaimlerChrysler AG
R74-4
Study for the F 600 HY, detail of the interiors and doors, 2004
Rendering
DaimlerChrysler Advanced Design Italia
© DaimlerChrysler AG
R74-5
Study for the F 600 HY, detail of the central console, 2004
Rendering
DaimlerChrysler Advanced Design Italia
© DaimlerChrysler AG
R74-6
Study for the F 600 HY, detail of the glove compartment, 2004
Rendering
DaimlerChrysler Advanced Design Italia
© DaimlerChrysler AG
R74-7
Study for the F 600 HY, detail of the steering wheel, 2004
Rendering
DaimlerChrysler Advanced Design Italia
© DaimlerChrysler AG

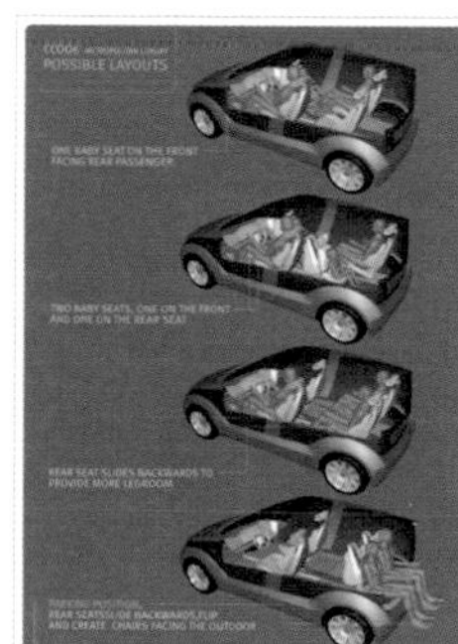

R74-1

R74-4

R74-7

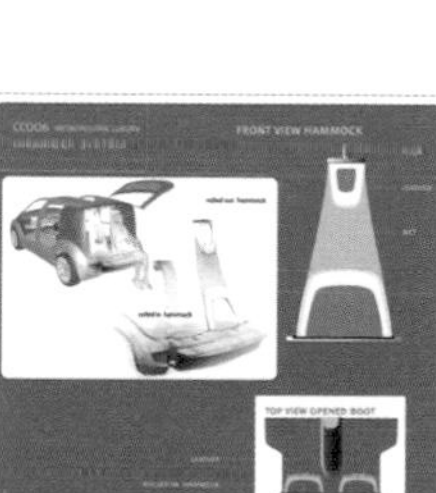

R74-2

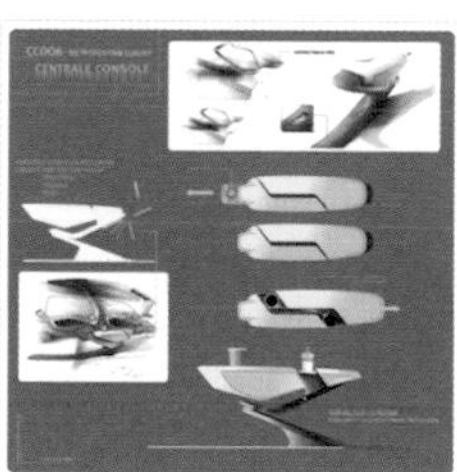

R74-5

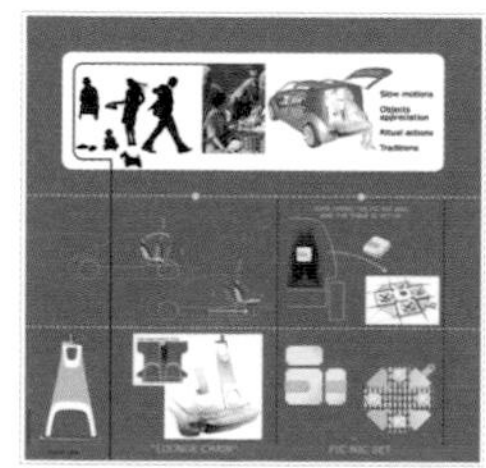

R74-3

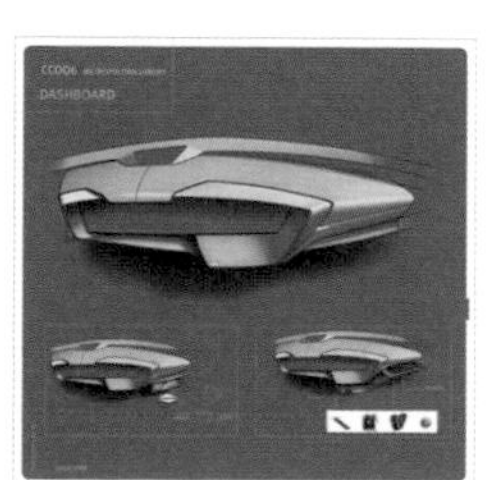

R74-6

Zaha Hadid, Z.CAR, 2005

p. 448

R75-1
Construction of the prototype Z.CAR, 2005
Photograph
Kenny Schachter / ROVE Collection
R75-2
Assembly of the prototype Z.CAR, 2005
Photograph
Kenny Schachter / ROVE Collection

R75-1

R75-2

R75-3
Detail of the prototype Z.CAR during production, 2005
Photograph
Kenny Schachter / ROVE Collection

R75-3

Nissan, Pivo, 2005

p. 452

R76-1
Study for the Pivo, side, three-quarter front and rear views, 2006
Rendering
Nissan Motor Company LTD
R76-2
Rendering for the Pivo, side, three-quarter front view and with door open, 2006
Rendering
Nissan Motor Company LTD
R76-3
Sketch for the interior of the Pivo, 2006
Mixed media
Nissan Motor Company LTD
R76-4
Sketches for the Pivo, 2006
Mixed media
Nissan Motor Company LTD
R76-5
Sketches for the interior of the Pivo, 2006
Mixed media
Nissan Motor Company LTD

R76-1

R76-3

R76-4

R76-2

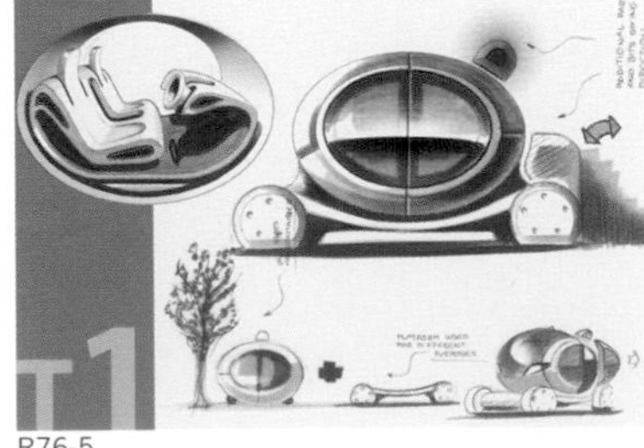

R76-5

Turin, IED, X 1/99, 2005
p. 458

Turin, IED, Ascari, 2005
p. 460

Turin, IED, Millechili, 2005
p. 460

Pforzheim, Hochschule, Project by Patrick Faulwetter, 2004
p. 464

R80-1
Presentation of Patrick Faulwetter's project, 2004
Mixed media
University of Applied Sciences Pforzheim
Transportation Design Department

R80-1

Pforzheim, Hochschule, Project by Jakob Hirzel, 2006
p. 464

R81-1
Presentation of Jakob Hirzel's project, 2006
Mixed media
University of Applied Sciences Pforzheim
Transportation Design Department

R81-1

Pforzheim, Hochschule, Project by Gregory John Paul, 2006
p. 464

R82-1
Presentation of Gregory John Paul's project, 2006
Mixed media
University of Applied Sciences Pforzheim
Transportation Design Department

R82-1

London, Royal College of Arts, Fiat Scratch, 2006
p. 468

R83-1/6
Presentation of Uros Pavasovic's project for the Fiat Scratch, 2006
Mixed media
Uros Pavasovic RCA Collection

R83-1

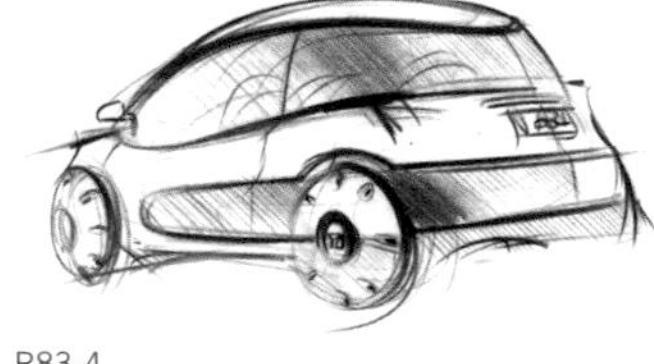
R83-4

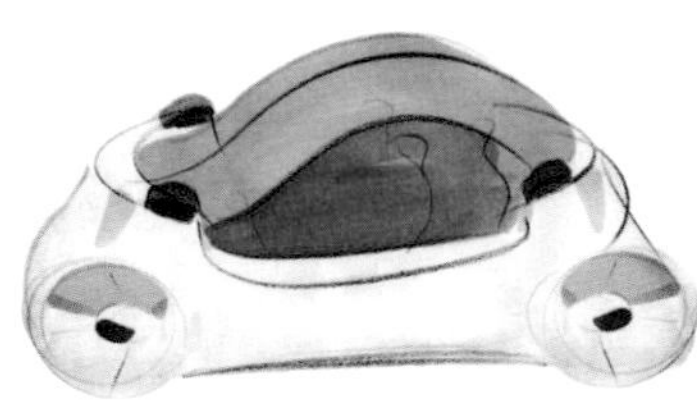

R83-2

R83-5

R83-3

R83-6

London, Royal College of Arts, Post-consumption, 2006

p. 468

R84-1/7
Presentation of Johan Jonsson's Post-consumption project, 2006
Mixed media
Johan Jonsson RCA Collection

R84-1

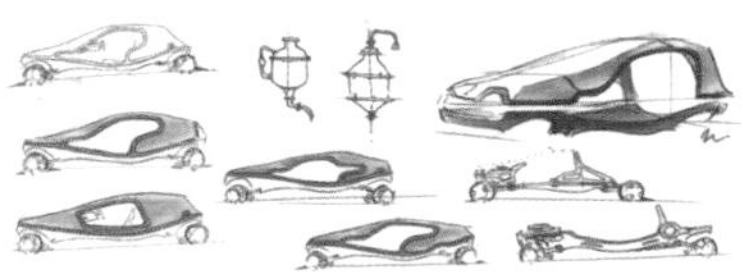

R84-2

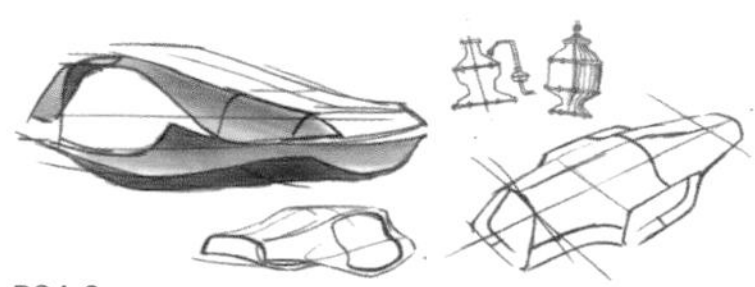

R84-3

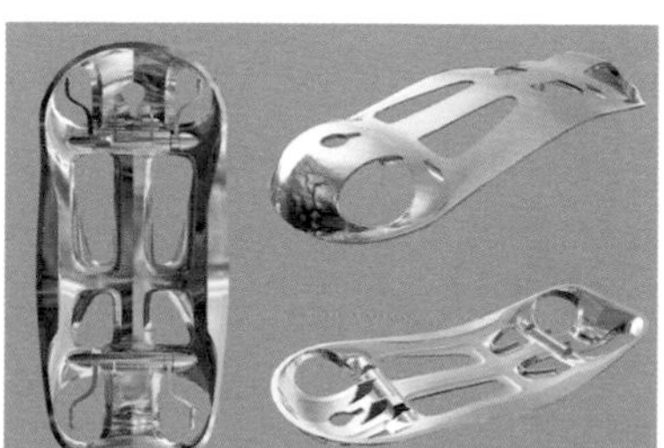

R84-4

R84-5

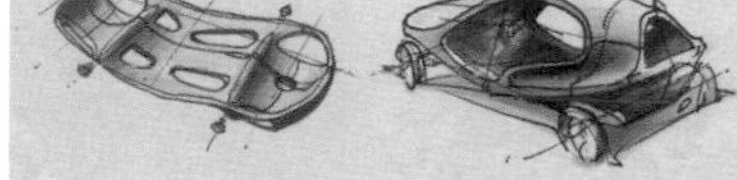

R84-6

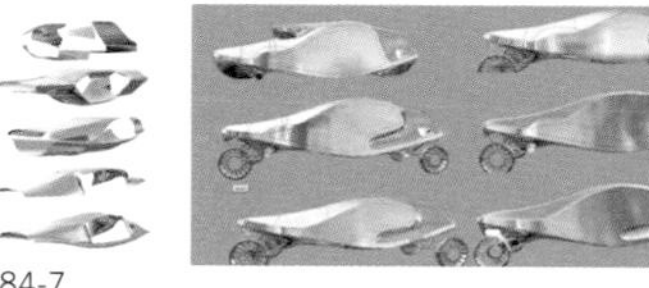

R84-7

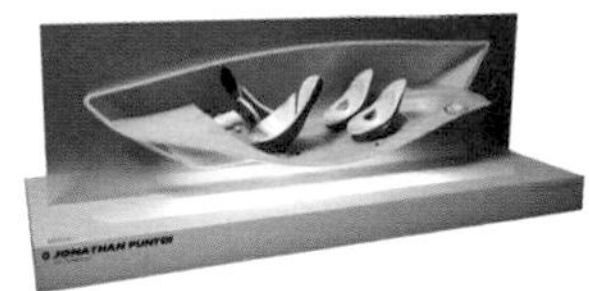

London, Royal College of Arts, Dedalus Concept, 2006

p. 468

R85-1/7
Presentation of Jonathan Punter's Daedalus Concept project, 2006
Mixed media
Jonathan Punter RCA Collection

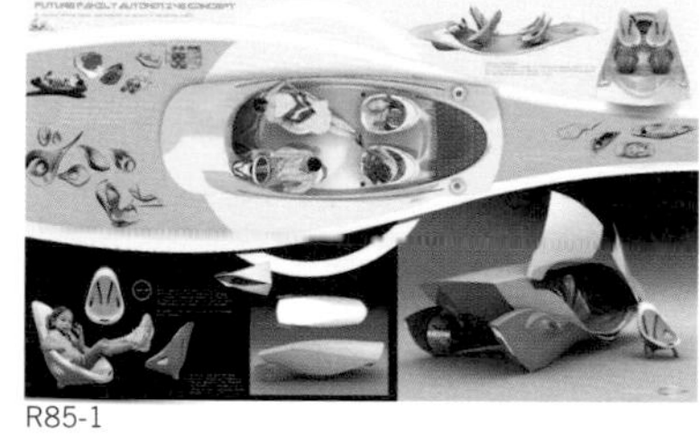

R85-1

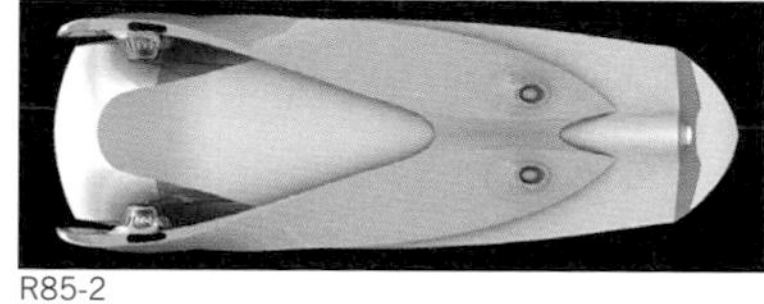

R85-2

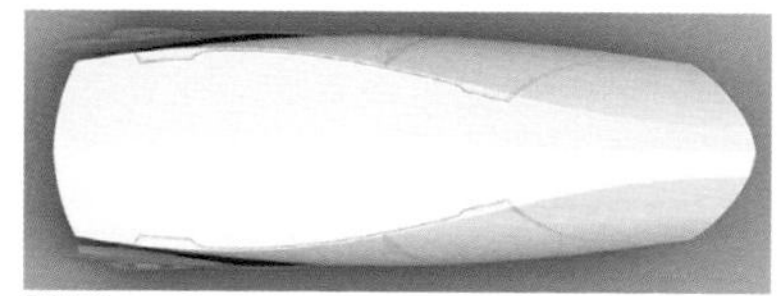

R85-3

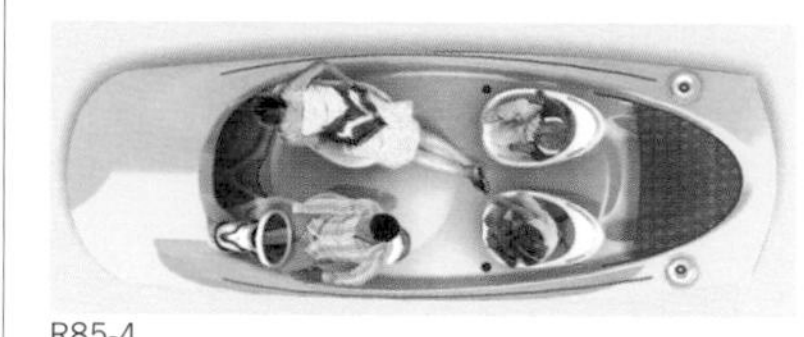

R85-4

R85-5

R85-6

R85-7

The Protagonists

Karl Benz

Karl Benz

Karl Benz's most important contribution to history was designing and building the first functional motor car with internal combustion engine, for the first time conceiving the vehicle in its entirety. Moreover, we must also attribute to Benz the invention of the axle-pivot steering system and of the first 'boxer' engine.
Karl Friedrich Benz was born in Karlsruhe in 1844, the son of a steam locomotive driver. His ancestors came from a small village in the Black Forest.
As a child, he had a passion for trains, but it was decided that he would become a civil servant, so he was sent to secondary school and during his school years, showed a great aptitude for the natural sciences.
He discovered the new, avant-garde art of photography and, using a camera, recorded the characteristic locals from the Black Forest area. In this way, and working also as a watchmaker — one of the typical professions of the region — he began earning a salary. At the age of 17, he entered polytechnic (Technische Hochschule) and later worked in a locomotive factory. He worked as designer at Mannheim and Pforzheim, always in pursuit of his dream of inventing a form of locomotion with an independent propulsive force, and in this he was supported by his enthusiastic wife, Berta.
In 1871, he became proprietor of a foundry and engineering workshop; with these, he became fully independent for the first time. Thanks to the wealth of knowledge he had been able to glean over time, he succeeded in producing a fixed two-stroke gas engine for a public company, Benz & Cie. Rheinische Gasmotorenfabriken, based in Mannheim; its shareholders had no intention of venturing into the production of vehicles. Starting with an Otto-cycle four-stroke engine, Benz developed the propulsion unit for his first car, which in 1885 first moved under its own power around the factory courtyard. The German patent he detained was soon followed by French, British and American patents. With series production of the model called Velo, Benz's company became the largest producer of cars in the world.
Due to internal disagreements, he and his two brothers left the company in 1903 and founded a new company called C. Benz Söhne at Ladenburg, dedicated to the production of aspirated gas engines. However, the company in reality specialized in the construction of cars with its own engines until 1923. The last two cars were for Benz himself, who had left his company in 1912.
In 1925, Benz published his memoirs. On the occasion of the 25th anniversary of the Allgemeine Schnauferl-Club, the 81-year-old inventor personally drove the first car he had produced — owned by the Deutsches Museum — in a parade of cars.
Karl Benz witnessed the merging of the company he founded with the competing company from Stuttgart. He died in 1929 at the age of 85 in Ladenburg.
(R.J.F.K.)

Benz Patent Motorwagen Model 3

Nuccio Bertone

Giovanni Bertone, Nuccio's father, was born in 1884 at Mondovì. He moved to Turin in 1907 and opened a workshop there in 1912 to repair carriages. In 1921, he built the first coachwork for a car, over a Spa chassis, and gained the esteem of Vincenzo Lancia, soon becoming one of his favourite coachbuilders. In 1934, Nuccio, who was born on 4th July 1914, began working for the company after having studied accountancy; his arrival coincided with the transformation of Carrozzeria Bertone from a craftsman's workshop to an industry and its move to a factory in via Peschiera in Turin.
After meeting Mario Revelli de Beaumont, Nuccio Bertone immediately understood both the importance of a collaboration with a skilled designer, and the need for said designer to be given plenty of elbow-room.
And indeed, it was a Revelli design that gave rise to one of Bertone's most successful vehicles, the 'Balilla della Signora,' on a Fiat 508 C, with soft lines, fine interior and a driving position placed well forward. As the name suggests, the model was popular with ladies, who were often unhappy with the long bonnets of those years.
Two important sports cars date from the immediate post-war years, when Nuccio was alone at the helm of the company: the Stanguellini 1100, designed by Fabio Luigi Rapi, and a cabriolet on a Fiat 1100 chassis, which followed the lines of the standard original quite closely, and assured good orders from the Turinese car manufacturer.

In 1952, Franco Scaglione began working with the company and he soon started creating a series of famous dream cars, such as the three B.A.T. models — 5, 7 and 9 — on Alfa Romeo 1900 chassis, and also some standard production vehicles such as the Giulietta Sprint, of which Bertone built more than 36,000 examples.
In 1959, Bertone took on a young designer, Giorgetto Giugiaro, who was to remain until 1965, when he was replaced by another young and talented designer, Marcello Gandini. Among the most representative cars produced by Bertone thanks to them was the Alfa Romeo 2000 and 2600 Sprint, the Giulia Sprint and Montreal, the BMW 3200 CS, the Iso Rivolta GT 300, the Fiat 850 Spider and Dino Coupé, the Lamborghini Miura, Espada and Countach, the Lancia Stratos, and the Maserati Khamsin.
A number of their futuristic concept cars also had a considerable impact. These included the Testudo, Canguro, Marzal, Carabo and Stratos HF.
Nuccio Bertone never retired but continued to frequent the factory until shortly before his death on 26th February 1997. Since October 2006, he has been included in the Automotive Hall of Fame in Detroit with the following motivation: 'For his influence on car design, for having discovered and developed some of the greatest designers in the world, for having contributed for decades to the car industry and for having created some of the most beautiful cars in existence.'
(H.S.)

Giovanni and Nuccio Bertone

Flaminio Bertoni

Flaminio Bertoni was born in Masnago, near Varese, in Northern Italy on 10th January 1903. The death of his father in 1917, forced him to break off his studies and find a job at the Carrozzeria F.lli Macchi. With the war over, he was noticed for his constant proposals for improvements and was transferred to the design department: this was the start of his career as designer. With any financial worries over, he was able to dedicate himself to the one true passion in his life: art, and drawing and sculpture in particular. He began frequenting the art studios of Varese and sketched out his first sculptural models. 1922 marked a turning point: he produced a scale model of his first car and his designs at Macchi were noted by a delegation of French engineers, resulting in his being invited to move to France to gain experience. In April 1923, he moved to Paris, and found work with some coachbuilders until, in January 1925, he was taken on by Citroën.
In May, Macchi offered him the position of chief designer and this, plus his mother's fragile health, caused him to move back to Italy and Masnago. Shortly after, he opened a studio in which he could draw and sculpt in complete freedom.
He dedicated all his time to work and art: in 1929, he left Macchi and began producing industrial designs for third parties; in 1930, he exhibited in Rome and gained his first recognition in the artistic field. But the attraction of Paris and its artistic world was a strong one: in 1931, he returned and found work as a designer at SICAL, which produced coachwork for Citroën. In June 1932, he was again hired by the French manufacturer and this time he remained for life. Lefèbvre joined the company in 1933, and became responsible for the Traction Avant project. One evening, inspiration came to Bertoni and, working through the night, he created a scale model in plasticine and presented it on the following morning to André Citroën. The latter was immediately struck by the idea and ordered that it be continued: the Traction Avant was born and would remain in production until 1957. This was the first production car to be made with a model as the starting point rather than a drawing!
For Bertoni, this was a major turning point. As a result of the excessive investment made in the new factory, Citroën was plunged into a crisis and went into receivership. The staff of the design studio dropped from 40 to six but he, although a foreigner, kept his post. In the meantime, his visits to the Louvre reinforced his desire to leave his mark in the artistic field too, and he began producing sculpture acclaimed by the critics. Over the years, he designed the 2CV and the DS for Citroën; two cars that have marked milestones in the history of the car. His last work would be the Ami 6. Bertoni died on 7th February, 1963.
(H.S.)

(H.S.)

Flaminio Bertoni with a drawing

Flaminio Bertoni and his mother, Angela Mazzola

Felice and Carlo Felice Bianchi Anderloni

In the history of the motor car, there are names of coach-builders that are synonymous with beauty and elegance: the name of Carrozzeria Touring is one of these.
The Milanese workshop (active from 1926 to 1967) was founded by Felice Bianchi Anderloni and Gaetano Ponzoni, two lawyers from the *haute bourgeoisie* with a passion for cars. Bianchi Anderloni was the creative spirit while Ponzoni was to handle all the commercial aspects.
In just a few years, Carrozzeria Touring became a by-word for avant-garde, both in terms of style and construction: the sports car, which until the mid-1920s had generally been a light torpedo, now became a light berlinetta (the future granturismo). Starting with a French patent by Weymann (low road noise and weight achieved through the use of a wooden frame lined with fake leather), Bianchi Anderloni replaced this 'pegamoid' with aluminium panels, which enabled him to produce curved forms. The names of the models were innovative and refined too: 'Royal Touring,' 'Flying Star,' 'Freccia di Belzebù,' 'Fugientem incurro diem,' 'Soffio di Satana.' Bianchi Anderloni's motto was 'weight is the enemy, drag the obstacle.' In 1937, he patented the 'Superleggera' construction process, which was to become the factory's badge. This period saw the creation of the fabulous Alfa Romeo 8C 2900 B and 6C 2300 B MM, genuine masterpieces on wheels.
But Touring models were not only fast and light: part of the weight saved allowed the fitting of accessories that made the cars more comfortable and safer. And it was also thanks to this striving for comfort that the Alfa Romeos built by Touring would win almost all the editions of the most tiring race of all — the Mille Miglia — between 1932 and 1947.
The distinguishing mark of the Touring style was sobriety, the fruit of careful study at the modelling stage. In the lexicon of car design, 'Italian lines' means the rejection of ornamentation, and the Touring cars are the finest expression of this ethos. Felice's son, engineer Carlo Felice Bianchi Anderloni, who took his father's place in 1948, also felt this. His first two creations, a convertible — the Ferrari 166 Barchetta, winner of the 1949 Mille Miglia — and a coupé — the Alfa Romeo 6C 2500 SS Villa d'Este — were extraordinary examples of timeless 'rolling sculpture.' The use of the three-section radiator grille motif for the front of today's Alfa Romeos is testament to the extraordinary mark left by Carrozzeria Touring on the image of the manufacturer. The same may be said of Aston Martin, Lamborghini and Maserati, with which Touring worked until its closure, a terrible event that even today causes regret among enthusiasts of all that is beautiful.
(H.S.)

Felice Bianchi Anderloni

Carlo Felice Bianchi Anderloni

Ettore and Jean Bugatti

Was Ettore Bugatti more of an artist or more of an engineer? He was born in Milan on 15th September 1881 and died in Paris on 21st August 1947. In his 66 years of life he built probably less than 7800 cars, but each of these represent mechanical beauty and all reveal his original touch.
Ettore came from a family of artists (his father, Carlo, designed and made furniture; his brother, Rembrandt, was a noted animal sculptor, and his father's sister had married Giovanni Segantini), and this artistic vision would lead him to imbue cold mechanical creations with his artistic vision of life: the famous front axle of his cars, the design of the straight-8 engine, the wire wheels of the Type 59 are all genuine works of art.
Ettore never surrendered his Italian citizenship except on the point of death so that he could reclaim his factory, which had been requisitioned. This is why we can state that the Bugatti factory, founded in 1909 in Molsheim in Alsace (German territory at the time, then returned to France), was an Italian company on French territory.
Bugatti's first design dates from 1898, when he mounted four single-cylinder De Dion engines on a Prinetti & Stucchi tricycle. Then, in 1901, he presented the Type 2 at the International Motor Show of Milan; this was his first car with a four-cylinder engine. From 1902 to 1909, he worked for a number of different German industries and at the end of 1909 presented the first 'real' Bugatti, the Type 10. But it was racing that made Bugatti famous, with leading drivers and passionate gentleman drivers clocking up hundreds of victories throughout the world. An eclectic figure, Bugatti designed and registered a total of 855 patents.
His designated heir was his son, Jean (born on 15th January 1909 and baptized Gianoberto Carlo Rembrandt), the third-born but first of his sons. From adolescence, he frequented the factory more than his school. It was he who proposed technical innovations, such as the adoption of hemispherical combustion chambers, double camshafts and, in 1932 at the age of just 23, it was he who developed the project for the Type 57. After 1931, Jean was responsible for the coachwork department at the Molsheim factory, and he soon breathed life into what would be called the 'Jean Bugatti style:' the Esder roadster on Royale chassis, the surprofilé coach of the Type 50, the Type 55 Roadster, the Atlantic and the Atalante on Type 57 chassis are just some of the examples of his talent.
Upon the instigation of Jean, Bugatti competed and won in the 1937 and 1939 24-Hours of Le Mans, and it was during a test of the winning 57 C that on 11th August 1939, he lost his life in an accident. And with his death, Bugatti effectively died too.
(H.S.)

Jean Bugatti

Ettore Bugatti

Ercole and Emilio Castagna

The advent of the 'auto-mobile,' whether fitted with an internal combustion, steam or electric engine, brought about a veritable revolution in one industrial sector: that of the construction of carriages. For this revolution, which obliged the carriage-builders to transform themselves into coachwork for cars, only spared those companies most responsive to social change, those who did not consider the car an ephemeral fad, and those who already had directors who were forward-looking *entrepreneurs*, willing to abandon the past and tradition. Among those companies able to make this leap into a new world was Carrozzeria Castagna.

Carlo Castagna began working as an apprentice in 1854 at the age of nine, in the carriage factor of Paolo Mainetti in Milan. He was alert and showed initiative and soon began climbing the career ladder: worker, manager, director. In 1894, he was in charge of the company where had worked for almost 40 years. In 1906, he set up S.A. Carlo Castagna & C., of which he held almost all the shares. Upon the death of Carlo, his son, Ercole, was ready to step in and completely industrialize the factory, which during the Great War also produced trucks, ambulances and even fuselages and wings for Caproni aircraft.

After the war, the far-sighted Ercole drew out licences for special construction methods, such as the Baehr and Hibbard & Darrin patents for transformable cars and, much later, Labourdette's Vutotal patent (which Ercole called Vistotal) for windscreens.

His younger brother, Emilio, who had studied art, dedicated himself to designing coachwork, of a generally classical style but of a construction and attention to detail of the highest order.

The 'Commodore' roadster, presented at the Commodore Hotel in New York in 1928, marked the high point of Emilio's creativity and enabled Carrozzeria Castagna, which had already provided coachwork for the most important Italian chassis (Alfa Romeo, Isotta Fraschini, Lancia) to see its skills rewarded by being given car chassis from other prestigious international marques, such as Mercedes-Benz and the American Duesenberg. Unfortunately, first the Wall Street crisis, followed by that of Isotta Fraschini and, finally, the retirement of Emilio in 1933, were all blows that left a profound mark and the second half of the 1930s proved rather meagre for the Castagna company. Decline set in, and with the bombings of Milan, which caused the destruction of the factory, this only became worse.

At the end of the war, Castagna rose again in a new plant at Venegono Superiore, near Varese, but times had changed and the company ceased trading in 1954.

(H.S.)

Ercole, Savinio, Cipriano and Carlo Castagna

Colin Chapman

Colin Chapman was born on 19th May 1928 at Richmond, on the outskirts of London; in 1948, he took a degree in engineering, modified an old Austin 7 of 1930 and so created his first car, the Lotus Mark 1, which he used in rallying.
In 1952, he set up Lotus Engineering Co., and built the first car to have a chassis designed by him, the Mark 6. The name, Lotus, began to circulate in the racing world and in 1955 the Mark 9, a small, light sports car with 1100 cc Coventry-Climax engine, participated in the 24-Hours of Le Mans. In 1956, it was the turn of the Eleven, driven by racers of such calibre as Mike Hawthorn and Graham Hill, while Vanwall commissioned him to design a chassis for Formula 1. The first single-seater Lotus, the Type 12, was built in 1957 for Formula 2, while Chapman debuted in Formula 1 with Lotus the following year, with the same Type 12 powered by a 2 and 2.2-litre Climax engine, as well as with the new Type 16. Success came in 1960, when a Type 18, with rear-mounted engine, won the Monaco and the United States Grands Prix with Stirling Moss behind the wheel. Colin Chapman was by now, and rightly, considered one of the greatest car designers of all time; in the 25 years Lotus participated in F1, it won 72 victories and took 88 pole positions, 7 world constructors' titles and six drivers' titles. Quite apart from this extraordinary success, Chapman is remembered as the engineer who did most to develop the modern racing car as regards chassis and aerodynamics. His innovations were so efficient that his rivals were often forced to copy him in order to remain competitive.
In the 1960s, he was the first to win with a monocoque chassis and the first to use spoilers on single-seaters. In the 1970s, he showed the way forward by placing all the weight at the rear, with the Lotus 78 'wing car', was the first to anticipate the ground effect in F1. In the 1980s he was the first to consider active suspension. But his fruitful mind also produced other significant developments in car engineering, such as the bodyshell of the Elite, a small and extremely light two-seater sports car of 1958, made entirely of reinforced fibreglass, and the VARI system (Vacuum-Assisted Resin Injection).
On 15th December 1982, on his way home from a FISA meeting in Paris, Colin Chapman suffered a heart attack and died in the night. The first tests of the Lotus 92, the first single-seater in the world with active suspension and electronic control, were to take place the following morning, on 16th December. Formula 1 lost its most creative mind and the car industry one of its strongest personalities of the post-war years.
(H.S.)

Colin Chapman

André Citroën

Born in Paris on 5th February 1878, André Citroën is one of the most important French industrialists of the first half of the 20th century; always forward-looking in terms of research and the application of new techniques, he constantly pushed his industries to production levels that were unmatchable for his competitors. During the Great War, his arms factory on the outskirts of Paris produced 50,000 shells a day, while other factories barely succeeded in making 5,000 and when, at the end of the war, all the industries, and not just in France, were reconverted to civil production, he, who had never built cars, was ready to launch his first model by 1919, the Type A. This was no coincidence but the application of his principles that led him to undertake a long tour in the United States to study the major car industries and Ford in particular, before embarking on the production of his Type A, the first to be built in Europe with an eye to large-scale manufacture.
It was also the first car to offer left-hand drive, the first cheap model to offer electric starting and a spare wheel. Citroën was innovative in everything, not only in the product, but also in production methods, trade union relations (he was the first French industrialist to pay a month's bonus at the end of the year), the distribution of spare parts and after-sales assistance (he was the first to introduce a one-year guarantee and a free service after running-in). He was also the first European to sell by instalment and to rent out his own cars. Despite having started production only in 1919, by 1929 he was Europe's first manufacturer to break through the threshold of 100,000 cars a year. Citroën was also a master in public relations: he exhibited his cars in major department stores, sponsored the signpost system in France, produced miniature cars for children that in every way resembled their parents' full-size models, and paid for the illumination of Place de la Concorde and the Arc de Triomphe from his own pocket. On the evening of 4th July 1925, the letters of his name illuminated the Eiffel Tower thanks to 200,000 light bulbs and over 600 kilometres of wiring. In the wake of this promotional strategy, which was innovative in every field, Citroën launched himself into three raids: the first crossing of the Sahara by car in 1922 and 1923, the 'Croisère Noire' in Africa in 1924 and 1925, and the 'Croisière Jaune' in Asia in 1931 and 1932. The vehicles used were the 'chenillettes,' tracked vehicles made using standard parts and fitted with rubber tracks.
In the 1930s, Citroën was also hit by financial problems, despite good sales; in January 1935, Michelin acquired control of the company and began putting the books back in order. On 3rd July 1935, André Citroën died of a terminal illness.
(H.S.)

André Citroën

Rudolf Diesel

Rudolf Diesel was one of the most notable inventors in the field of engineering but at the same time one of the most controversial. He dedicated a large part of his life to research in a completely different direction to that which would give him world-wide fame, working on the newly-invented refrigerator. Endowed with remarkable talent, over the course of his lifetime he received many awards and honours.

Diesel was born into a family that had settled in Thuringia (Germany) centuries earlier, but he was himself born in Paris in 1858, a city his parents were forced to leave following the outbreak of the Franco-Prussian war in 1870. After moving to Augsburg, he frequented some technical schools and finally entered the Technische Hochschule to become a mechanical engineer.

At that time, with Europe undergoing major industrialization, there were continuous discoveries in the technical and scientific field. Among these discoveries was the refrigerator functioning through the compression of ammonia, invented by Carl Linde, who had Diesel as one of his pupils at the school. It was Diesel who developed the projects for a high-yield steam engine, but he was so taken with Linde's refrigerators that he sought out employment in this field, making considerable advances first in Switzerland and then in Paris. He also had the opportunity to meet the director of Augsburg's mechanical industry, the original nucleus of today's MAN.

In the meantime, he patented the Diesel cycle for internal combustion engines which he invented himself, and offered it without success to Germany's oldest gas motor manufacturer, Deutz of Cologne. He then turned to the mechanical engineering industry in Augsburg, which was working on a new engine with the financial support of Krupp. In the wake of the first licensing contracts between Deutz, Augsburg's mechanical engineering company and Krupp, companies were founded in Germany and elsewhere to produce Diesel engines. Ships, locomotives, small engines and large commercial vehicles bearing his name began to appear. In 1913, he received an invitation to participate in the Universal Exhibition of San Francisco for 1915, and he also published a volume: *Die Entstehung des Dieselmotors* (The birth of the Diesel engine).

The first car powered by a Diesel engine was only produced in 1936, however, many years after his death. In a number of books his youngest son, Eugen, has described the life of his father and the situation that led him to commit suicide in 1913 during a crossing to England. *(R.J.F.K.)*

Rudolf Diesel

Enzo Ferrari

Enzo Ferrari and Gilles Villeneuve

Thanks to his cars, Enzo Ferrari has become one of the most influential figures in post-war Italy and one of the most well-known Italians in the world. He was born in Modena on 18th February 1898; his father, owner of a metalworking plant, was prosperous and in 1903 already possessed a motor car, a De Dion Bouton.
In 1908, the young Enzo was in Bologna for the Coppa Florio, and he saw his idols, Nazzaro and Lancia, race by. By the age of ten, he had decided he would become a racing driver. In 1919, he was hired as tester for a small company, CMN, and had his racing debut in the Parma – Poggio di Berceto hill climb. In 1920, he raced with an Isotta Fraschini, was noted by Alfa Romeo and taken on as an official racing driver. He also began a professional activity in Modena, first with Carrozzeria Emilia and then as sales agent for Alfa Romeo.
In 1923, he won the Circuito del Savio at Ravenna and met the parents of Francesco Baracca: this was the first contact that would lead to the adoption of the prancing horse as the emblem of his future company.
At the end of 1929, he founded the Scuderia Ferrari, which became operative in 1930 and for which such aces as Campari, Fagioli, Moll, Varzi and Nuvolari would race.
In 1933, Alfa Romeo came under the control of the IRI and officially retired from racing; Scuderia Ferrari became its motor sports division.
The partnership was successful but these were difficult years because of the overwhelming domination of Mercedes and AutoUnion in Grand Prix racing. Alfa decided to return to the fray and transferred the racing division back to Milan with Ferrari as sports director. However, the latter found himself unsuited to being an employee once more and in 1939 set himself up on his own. In 1940, he built his first car, the 815, but he was as yet unable to use his own name because of a non-competition agreement with Alfa, so he used the Auto Avio Costruzioni lodge.
During the war, he moved the factory from Modena to Maranello and built tooling machines. Then, at last, in 1947, he presented the 125 S, the first car with the Ferrari label, and the first with the glorious twelve-cylinder engine which would give the marque world-wide fame and make it a symbol of motor sports success, as well as mechanical refinement and elegance. Enzo Ferrari's number one aim was to be first — on the track and off.
He was not an engineer but a savvy organiser, endowed with great intuitive capacity, a profound knowledge of men and extraordinary charisma. His cars were almost always present at the start of great international races and often first at the finish line. Loaded with victories and championship titles, these became the object of growing attention from the mass media. This eventually led to the Modena-born constructor becoming legendary. He died in Modena on 14th August, 1988.
(H.S.)

Enzo Ferrari as racing driver

Henry Ford

Henry Ford, Frank Vivian and a Model T engine

Henry Ford was little more than an adolescent when he came across a steam-powered vehicle on a road he was travelling with his father aboard a cart. He was so fascinated that he forced his father to stop and began questioning the driver of the strange machine. It was love at first sight. He already had a passion for mechanics, although of a different sort, given that he enjoyed himself dismantling, assembling and repairing watches and clocks he found at home and those of his neighbours. But his attraction for engines was so strong that in 1880, he left the family farm and moved to Detroit to work in a company specializing in shipbuilding.

At the outset, his father did not approve: he had emigrated to America from his native Ireland in 1840 and had bought some land in Michigan which he had started to cultivate and on which he had built a house for the whole family.

It was natural, therefore, that he should see a future in farming for his son, born on the farm on 30th July 1863. However, in 1888, Henry married and in 1892 found employment in the Edison Illuminating Company.

His only son, Edsel, was born in 1893.

The house Henry lived in had a basement in which he began building a motor-driven quadricycle during his evenings after work. By 1896, the vehicle was ready and he drove it around the streets of Detroit. In 1899, he found some backers and created the Detroit Automobile Company, of which he was the chief engineer. Not only was this the first of Ford's initiatives, but also the first car company in Detroit, which would later become the car capital of the world.

Detroit Automobile had a short history but Henry did not give up. He built a racing car, the 999, with a 70 b.h.p. engine and in 1901 won the first race he participated in. In the same year, he founded the Henry Ford Company, but again his business failed because, instead of dedicating himself to the construction of cars to sell to the public, he built a racing car; his partners forced him to resign.

Finally, on 16th June 1903, he founded the Ford Motor Company, which was destined to make history.

By 1904, the company already had three models in its catalogue, and in 1905 there were no less than 450 dealers dotted around the neighbouring states.

He announced his future aims in 1907: the result was the Ford T, first produced in 1908, and the first assembly line for cars, opened in 1913. Henry's idea was a winner: no longer would the workers go to fetch the pieces to assemble on a car; rather, the car would go to the worker, where the piece to be mounted was ready for assembly.

In 1923, more than 50% of the cars circulating on America's roads were Fords, namely the legendary and indestructible Model T.

The world had lost a farmer but acquired an industrialist who transformed the car into a vehicle available to all.

Henry Ford died on 7th April 1947.

(H.S.)

Henry Ford with the '1896 Quadricycle,' his first car, and the ten millionth Ford Model T, 25th July 1924

Dante Giacosa

Born in Rome into a Piedmontese family on 3rd January 1905, Dante Giacosa returned to Turin, took a degree in engineering in 1927 and began working in 1928 for SPA, a car manufacturing company acquired by Fiat in 1926. He always remained faithful to the Turinese group, even after retiring in 1969, after 41 years spent as a designer; he carried working as a consultant until the day of his death on 31st March 1996.
Giacosa arrived at Fiat itself, at Lingotto, in 1929, where he began designing tractors. He then passed to the technical aircraft engine division but finally the great day came: his immediate superior, Antonio Fessia, told him that Senator Agnelli wanted a small, cheap car costing no more than 5000 lire. 'Do you feel up to designing the chassis and the engine?' Giacosa accepted and began work on the 'Progetto Zero/A,' the future Topolino.
The success of the Topolino was also the success of Giacosa as a designer, and he was thus given the task of working on the new Balilla, the 508 C 1100, presented in 1937. This was followed by the large Fiat that was intended to compete with the Lancia Astura and Alfa Romeo 6C 2500, for which Giacosa designed a 2.8 litre six-cylinder engine During the war, he returned to aircraft engines and modified a Topolino for his personal use, fitting it with an electric engine. At the end of 1944, with the approval of Fiat, he gave way to the request of Piero Dusio and designed the D46, the single-seater (built using parts of the 500 and of the 1100), which put Cisitalia in the public eye. However, when it came to defining a permanent contract, he refused and returned full-time to Lingotto.
In the immediate post-war years, he brought the Nuova Balilla up to date, which became the 1100. He also designed the first monocoque Fiat, the 1400. In 1952, he designed a car destined mainly for GT races, the 8V, fitted with a 70° V8 engine displacing two litres.
With the 1100/103 of 1953, together with the 600 of 1955 and the Nuova 500 of 1957, he helping motorize the Italy of the boom years.
In the early 1960s, Giacosa directed projects for the six-cylinder 1800, 2100 and 2300 and for the four-cylinder 1300 and 1500, the little 850 and the new medium-sized car, the 124. He also designed a front-wheel-drive car, but Fiat's directors opted not to manufacture it; the model was passed on to Autobianchi, a group company, and successfully produced with the name of Primula. It would take until 1969 before Giacosa could persuade Fiat that front-wheel drive was a good thing, with the production of the 128, heir to the glorious 1100 and the first Fiat of the modern era.
(H.S.)

Dante Giacosa at work for the launch of the Fiat 125, 1967
Turin, Archivio Storico Fiat

Dante Giacosa at the Styling Centre, 1986
Turin, Archivio Storico Fiat

Giorgetto Giugiaro

Born on 7th August 1938 at Garessio, near Cuneo, Giorgetto Giugiaro was predestined: his grandfather and father were painters who executed frescos for houses and churches, and from them he learned to draw; his mother was a dressmaker and from her he learned to turn a sketch into a three-dimensional object. At the age of 14, he moved to Turin and frequented the Academy of Fine Arts, together with evening classes in a technical school because, as he was to recount later, 'in industrial design the technical element is no less important than the artistic one.'

Giugiaro's drawings for his end-of-year coursework for 1955 were noted by engineer Dante Giacosa, who had him taken on at Fiat at the age of just 17. But 'in four years, I never had the satisfaction of seeing any of my designs transformed into a model.' He felt frustrated and at the Turin Show of 1959 introduced himself to Nuccio Bertone, a man with a flair for finding talent, who immediately sensed his skills and soon after put Giugiaro in charge of his styling department. Giugiaro's first design was for the Alfa Romeo 2000 Sprint, followed by — amongst the production cars — the BMW 3200 CS, the Simca 1000 coupé, the Iso Rivolta 300 GT and the Giulia GT. Among his one-off cars were the Aston Martin DB4 GT Jet and the Chevrolet Testudo, the undisputed star of the Geneva Show of 1963.

At the end of 1965, he moved to Carrozzeria Ghia and in 1966 presented two cars at the Turin Show which he admits have remained in his heart: the Maserati Ghibli with front-mounted engine, and the De Tomaso Mangusta, with rear-mounted engine. Both designs remain modern to this day.

1966 was also the year of the arrival of De Tomaso at Ghia and relations between the two were sometimes less than cordial. Giugiaro resisted for a year, but then in 1968 founded SIRP Spa with Aldo Mantovani; this would later become Italdesign. The first commission came from Alfa Romeo, for which he designed and handled the industrialization of the Alfasud, presented at the Turin Show of 1971. Later contacts with Volkswagen, which urgently needed to replace its ageing Beetle, led to the Golf, destined to become a dynasty that still today ranks amongst the top sellers. For BMW, he designed the sporty M1, and over the years, for the Fiat group, the Delta, Panda, Uno, Thema, Punto; for Maserati, the Bora and 3200 GT. Through Giugiaro Design, he is also active in other sectors. For instance, he designed the Nikon F3. Giugiaro has designed hundreds of cars and of these, over a hundred have been put into mass production. However, it is not the numbers that decree the greatness of a designer so much as the impact his innovations have brought to the sector. And it is for this reason that an expert jury in 1999, comprising more than 120 international journalists, elected him 'Car Designer of the 20th Century.'

(H.S.)

Giorgetto Giugiaro
Photo Italdesign Giugiaro archive
© Italdesign Giugiaro

Giorgetto Giugiaro
Photo Italdesign Giugiaro archive
© Italdesign Giugiaro

Albrecht Goertz

In order to become a great designer, one can start drawing cars as a child, work as a bank apprentice or move to the United States from the German provinces at the age of 22. Count Albrecht Goertz, a member of the northern German aristocracy who became famous for having designed the BMW 507, did all of these. The United States had not lured him with an appetizing opportunity; indeed, Goertz began work as a humble car washer.
The great passion for cars in the country where Henry Ford was born took Goertz in 1938 to San Francisco at the age of 24, to transform old Ford models A and B into hot-rods. In his workshop, he also built a model he had designed himself, the Paragon, which stands out for its eccentric design. In post-war New York, this would prove fundamental for the development of Goertz's career. By pure coincidence, he met one of the most important industrial designers of the period, Raymond Loewy, in a car park in 1947.
This event later proved fundamental for the life of the young Count. Goertz became a designer while Loewy, impressed by the model designed by Goertz, offered him a place in his studio, while also undertaking to perfect his training. After a period as his employee — working on the Studebaker Champion in a studio in Indiana — Goertz left Loewy to set himself up on his own and present himself as an independent figure in the design market.
His company, Goertz Industrial Design Inc., produced designs of all sorts on commission from international clients: ballpoint pens, office equipment, kitchen utensils, radios and televisions, cameras, and also furniture, musical instruments, stands for trade fairs, bicycles and motor boats.
Among his customers was the Italian Carrozzeria Motto, producer of splendid coachwork for cars. After designing the famous 503 and 507 for BMW in Munich, other car companies sought his assistance, including Datsun of Japan for the Z series. Goertz subsequently worked for Porsche, British Leyland and some French brands, and in the 1970s again for BMW.
Until 1989, his studio was constantly busy and only in 1990 did he decide to close its premises on New York's 36th Street.
Subsequently, he stayed in touch internationally as a welcome guest of BMW and of exclusive events such as the Concours d'Elégance at Villa d'Este on the Lago di Como. Albrecht Goertz died on 27th October 2006 at the age of 92.
(R.J.F.K.)

Albrecht Goertz alongside the first 507

Alec Issigonis

'A camel is a horse designed by a committee;' 'All creative people hate mathematics. It is the least creative subject one can study, unless one becomes an Einstein or one studies it in an abstract, philosophical manner.' These are just two quotations by 'Mister Mini,' as Alec Issigonis is often called today.
Studying his biography, it is no surprise that he should have fared badly with mathematics (and indeed, was failed three times in his exams to become an engineer), that he should hate to be boxed in a large corporation with limited brief (he left Morris after it merged with Austin to form BMC in 1952), and that for his whole life he would sketch out his designs on any paper that came to hand, without ever dedicating himself to detailed technical drawings, which he regarded tedious and of no interest to him.
He was the prototype 'lateral thinker' with many of the defects typical of this race: megalomania, arrogance, eccentricity, sudden changes of humour. But he also had undoubted talent, as three of his projects reveal: the 'Lightweight Special,' the Morris Minor and the Mini.
The 'Lightweight Special' was a racing car designed by him and made entirely (bar the engine) in his spare time between 1933 and 1937 in his garage at home.
In a nutshell, it contained all the basic ingredients of his design philosophy: a rigid structure, independent suspension with rubber springs, low weight. He himself drove this little car, built around an aluminium monocoque chassis, in club races, and it was in this way that he met John Cooper, who would later be one of the vital parts of the future success of the Mini.
During the war, he developed the Mosquito project at Morris. This was launched as the Minor in 1948 and was a revolutionary car in its time, with a small exterior in comparison to the unusually spacious interior, and offering unusually good roadholding and ease of driving. The Minor was the first car to enjoy widespread distribution in Britain, with a million examples being built until 1971.
The birth of the Mini is associated with the Suez crisis of 1956-1957 and the need to put a small car with low fuel consumption rapidly into production. Issigonis's lateral thinking came up with a form that had 80% of its space dedicated to the passengers and their baggage. That project paved the way to the modern front-wheel-drive car with transverse engine. Not bad for a boy born on 18th November 1906 at Izmir, a city that was first Turkish and then Greek, of Greek father and German mother and evacuated by the Royal Navy in 1923. Sir Alexander Arnold Constantine Issigonis died on 2nd October 1988.
(H.S.)

Alec Issigonis

Vittorio Jano

Describing the professional career of Vittorio Jano means covering the entire history of Italian racing from the 1920s to the 1960s and of its most prestigious cars. Born in Turin on 22nd April 1891, Jano frequented the Istituto Professionale and in 1909, at the age of 18, was taken on as assistant designer at Rapid, a car manufacturer founded by Giovanni Battista Ceirano. In 1911, he moved to Fiat, where he worked on the project for the extremely competitive Fiat 801, 803, 804 and 805 Grand Prix cars, which took first and second place at the Italian Grand Prix in Monza in 1923. Alfa Romeo wanted to make a name for itself in racing and Enzo Ferrari, its driver at the time, convinced Jano to leave Fiat and move to Milan. Here, in just five months, he designed the P2, which won the French and Italian Grands Prix in 1924 and in 1925 conquered the world championship for Alfa (a victory recalled ever since then by the presence of the laurel crown in the Alfa Romeo badge). Jano remained with Alfa until 1937 and under his direction, standard production cars such as the 6C 1500, 1750, 1900 and 2300, the 8C 2300 and 2900 were designed, as well as all the Grand Prix racing cars: the Tipo A, Tipo B (P3), the 8C 1935, the 12C and the 12C 1937. Moreover, between 1927 and 1933, he was also responsible for the aircraft engine and industrial vehicles division. Unfortunately, following a period of great triumphs on the racetrack with the immortal P3, and of good commercial success, above all with the 6C, some bad times followed for Alfa Romeo, which in 1933 passed into the control of the IRI (Istituto di Ricostruzione Industriale – Institute for Industrial Recovery). Jano was blamed for the lack of success on the tracks against the Mercedes 'Silver arrows' and AutoUnion, and in October was removed from his post, whereupon he returned to Turin. Taken on by Lancia in 1939, Jano headed the team responsible for the Ardea project, and for the Aurelia after the war, as well as for the D50, the Formula 1 car commissioned by Gianni Lancia, which first raced in 1954. Sadly, in 1955, Alberto Ascari, Lancia's leading racing driver, was killed while testing in Monza and Lancia withdrew from racing, giving all the D50s and spare parts to Ferrari.

Jano became a consultant to Enzo Ferrari and thus revived the old collaboration between the designer and the manufacturer who had, in the meantime, become one of the most famous car makers in the world. The association resulted in two Formula 1 world championships, in 1956 with the Ferrari-Lancia and in 1961 with the Tipo 156, fitted with the Dino engine designed by the Piedmontese designer. After retiring, Jano suffered the loss of his son and on 13th February 1965 took his own life.

(H.S.)

Vittorio Jano in front of an Alfa Romeo P2, 1924/1930

Vincenzo Lancia

Vincenzo Lancia at the wheel

Vincenzo Lancia was one of the great innovators in the history of the motor car.
Born on 24th August 1881 at Fobello (Vercelli), he attended the Technical Institute of Turin, where the family owned a house in which it passed the winter months. A part of it was let to Giovanni Battista Ceirano (one of the pioneers of the Italian car industry, together with his brothers, Giovanni and Matteo), who at the time was a manufacturer of bicycles. The young Lancia was attracted to mechanical engineering; moreover, Ceirano was designing a car. Lancia succeeded in getting himself taken on and soon had himself noticed for his undoubted skills. Ceirano's company, together with the finished design for the new car, was taken over by the newly-founded Fiat. Very soon, Lancia rose to become the chief tester of the new company and racing driver in the competitive works team. His first race took place in July 1900. Lancia would eventually take part in 40 races and win 18. This experience enabled him to refine that special sensitivity that would then be transposed to the design of his cars. The last race to see him at the start was the Record del Miglio di Modena (Modena Record Mile) in 1910, but this time, he was driving a Lancia. For indeed, he had founded Lancia & C. in 1906, with Claudio Fogolin, a work colleague and friend from Fiat, as co-founder.
The first car to bear the Lancia badge was finished in September 1907. As he was about to drive out for the first test drive, Lancia noticed that the car was wider than the workshop doors, which he promptly had widened with pickaxes. The name of Lancia, a bold and fast driver, was already well-known to car enthusiasts, who soon also came to appreciate the superior quality of his creations and ensured the success of the new marque, whose cars were always full of innovative, bold ideas. The same quality was discernible in his aircraft engines, lorries for military and civilian use and armoured vehicles. During the course of his life, with the collaboration of skilled engineers chosen by himself, Vincenzo Lancia wrote some important pages in the history and evolution of the car, with the adoption of independent front wheels, the monocoque chassis and engines with unusual narrow vee angles. In 1922, the Lambda was the first car with a monocoque chassis, the Augusta in 1932 the first with an integral body and chassis,a concept perfected with the Aprilia in 1936, the last car to be designed by Lancia, who died at the age of just 56 on 15th February 1937.
But Lancia also made some innovations with his engines, introducing a narrow vee architecture (with four, six and eight cylinders with the Trikappa in 1922).
This architecture was to be maintained by the company after its founder's death.
(H.S.)

Vincenzo Lancia aboard a Lancia
Anselmi archive

Hans Ledwinka

Hans Ledwinka was born in 1878 at Klosterneuburg, near Vienna. He spent almost all his working life employed in a single company, Tatra, famous throughout the world for the extraordinary cars designed by Ledwinka. Yet he abandoned them twice in his lifetime, only to return and be promoted once more.
After completing his studies at the Technische Fachschule für Maschinenbau (Technical Institute for Mechanical Engineering), in Vienna, he began working for Wagenbau-Fabriks-Gesellschaft (Company for the Construction of Road Vehicles) in Nesselsdorf — the company that would later be transformed into Tatra — and began working on the construction of the first motorized vehicles to be made by the company.
In 1902, he returned to Vienna and found a job with a steam engine company but his original director, who had hired him in 1897 and saw his great potential, managed to tempt him back in 1905. Between 1917 and 1921, as director of the car division of the Österreichische Waffenfabrikgesellschaft (Austrian Company for the Manufacture of Arms), later to become Steyr, Ledwinka succeeded in launching a series of projects that brought him the title of engineer in 1920, as special recognition for his work. During that period, he also developed a project for a small, innovative car, from which derived the Tatra Type 11, after the director of the Nesselsdorf plant had 'forced' him to return to 'his' company, this time as chief designer and technical director. Ledwinka designed not just cars and industrial vehicles, but also a locomotive that bore the seeds for major future technical developments. Ledwinka always sought to incorporate new advances, and in recognition of this he was given an honorary degree at the Technische Hochschule of Vienna.
A tragic event in his life was his incarceration between 1945 and 1951 by the communist regime for his being a non-Czech and despite his internationally-recognized merits as a designer. From his prison cell, he collaborated on a project for a new aerodynamic form, but once out of jail, he refused any new offers of work from Tatra.
From Vienna, he moved to Munich in 1954 and worked as designer for a company producing small cars, with the satisfaction of seeing his son, Erich, follow his steps as car designer in Austria. The car he owned, an aerodynamic Type 87 Tatra was donated by Ledwinka in 1965 to the Deutsches Museum in Munich, the city in which he died in 1967 at the age of 89.
(R.J.F.K.)

Hans Ledwinka

The Maserati brothers

The story of the Maserati brothers — Carlo, Bindo, Alfieri, Ettore and Ernesto — the sons of a railway employee from Voghera, is little-known, perhaps because, driven by innate modesty, they have always maintained a low profile, but it is important and significant. The eldest brother, Carlo, designed and built a single-cylinder to be fitted to any bicycle in 1898, when he was just 17. He developed his technical knowledge further at Fiat, Isotta Fraschini, Bianchi and Junior. Carlo was a shooting star: he died in 1910 but he was a great teacher to his brothers. Alfieri, born in 1887, took over the leadership. An official driver for Isotta Fraschini, he became its representative in Britain, the United States and Argentina. On 1st December 1914, he opened his own workshop in Bologna with his younger brothers, Ettore and Ernesto, and during the war patented and made a spark plug. In 1926, he produced the T26, the first car to wear the trident badge, designed by the sixth brother, Mario, who was an artist.

The car debuted with Alfieri at the wheel at the Targa Florio and won its class. The Type 26 inaugurated that series of technical innovations characterizing the history of Maserati: its eight-cylinder engine, for instance, had the shortest piston travel of any engine produced in the world. Maserati would be the first to use magnesium alloy, the first to bring a 16-cylinder engine to the race-track, the first in Europe to adopt a hydraulic braking system, the first to build a Grand Prix car propelled by a V8.

Fate was not kind, however, and turned on the Maserati brothers once more: 1932 saw the death of Alfieri, the charismatic leader, endowed with great qualities as engineer, racing driver and public relations man. In order to enable the company to continue, Bindo, at the time with Isotta, joined his brothers and began handling the commercial side of things. Ernesto, an excellent driver, left the driver's seat and became designer; Ettore handled the workshop. Maserati cars were made in small numbers and treated like jewels. Borzacchini, Campari, Varzi and Nuvolari contributed to the foundation of the legend of this small factory, a David against the Goliath of AutoUnion and Mercedes, sponsored by the Führer, and Alfa Romeo, supported by the Duce. There were no sponsors: Maserati dedicated itself to smaller engines which it sold to gentlemen drivers, but in 1937 the Maserati brothers were obliged to sell the company to the Orsi group. Freed of financial constraints, they designed masterpieces of engineering, including the 8CTF which won the 500 Miles at Indianapolis, the most famous race in the world, in 1939 and 1940. In 1947 in their beloved Bologna, they founded OSCA, which produced sports cars with small engines, much favoured by gentlemen drivers in the 1950s. *(H.S.)*

Bindo, Ernesto and Ettore Maserati with the portrait of Alfieri Maserati on the wall

Giovanni Michelotti

Born in Turin on 8th October 1921, Giovanni Michelotti began working very young, in 1937, as a designer in the Stabilimenti Farina, a coachworks founded in 1906 by Giovanni Farina, the elder brother of 'Pinin.' By 1939, he had become chief designer but in 1947, wishing to achieve greater freedom in his work, without the constraints of company requirements, he decided to open his own studio. Active until the mid-1970s, Michelotti was perhaps the most prolific designer of cars and one of the forebears of the Italian style of the post-war years, collaborating with manufacturers and coachworks around the world. Able constantly to adjust to the new needs of industries as a result of technical advances, or because of shifts in taste and lifestyle of customers, he remained in the forefront, ready to interpret the trends of the moment in his own key. He constantly renewed himself, without remaining anchored to obsolescent styles as occurred with some of his colleagues. Shy and reserved, Michelotti was not well-known to the general public, partly because very few of his creations bear his name: very few people know that no less than 160 of the first Ferraris (with coachwork by Vignale, Allemano and Ghia) and several Maseratis (such as the 5000 GT Allemano, the Sebring and the 3500, GT Vignale Spyder) were his. However, he was well-known to the manufacturers and coachbuilders, who were well-pleased by his shyness; it is no cioncidence that at the Turin Show of 1958, 40 of the cars displayed on the stands of various manufacturers were designed by him. If BMW today is one of the manufacturers with the strongest and most recognizable images, the merit lies in part with Michelotti. In 1959, he designed the 700 coupé and two-door saloon, the model that marked the resurgence of the Bavarian company. In 1962, he designed the 1500, the series of 2000 CS coupés, the two-door 1600 and the 2500/2800 flagships and coupés variants. All of these models provided the inspiration for today's models. Among his most important and long-lasting collaborations with foreign companies is his association with Triumph (for them he designed the Herald, the TR4 and the Spitfire), as well as Ford (the Anglia Torino, initially only for the Italian market), Alpine (the A110 Berlinette). Giovanni Michelotti was also the first European designer to collaborate on a long-term basis with the emerging Japanese car industry. Edgardo Michelotti, his son, began cataloguing his father's œuvre following his death on 23rd January 1980. He arrived at over 1200 projects relative to cars produced in series and prototypes that remained unique examples.
(H.S.)

Giovanni Michelotti

Battista ‘Pinin’ Farina

Battista Farina, known as ‘Pinin,’ was born in Turin on 2nd November 1893 and began working at the age of 12 in the bodywork repair shop of his brother Giovanni (the future Stabilimenti Farina). At 18, he first met with Senator Giovanni Agnelli, who chose the radiator Battista had designed for his new Fiat Zero, and gave Giovanni Farina the task of building the torpedo coachwork, also designed by Pinin. After becoming the company’s designer in 1920, he went to America to learn about the new construction methods. He met Henry Ford who, after seeing his designs, offered him a job, which Pinin turned down. The 1920s brought great commercial success to the Stabilimenti Farina and fame to Pinin, who in 1930 set up his own company called ‘Carrozzeria Pinin Farina.’ Customers appreciated the balance of forms in his creations, the innovations (such as the sloping windscreen), and the care over construction details, but Pinin was not fazed by this glory and was always ready to take on new stylistic trends and stay a step ahead of them. In 1933, he created a sensational aerodynamic saloon using a Lancia Astura chassis, and in the following years developed this idea until he arrived at the Lancia Aprilia Berlinetta Aerodynamica in 1936, one of the most advanced designs of the period.
Recovery from the war was hard for the Italian car manufacturers, as they were not permitted to participate in the European shows of 1946, but Pinin managed to circumvent the obstacle: he arrived in Paris with his son, Sergio, in two cars, an Alfa Romeo 6C 2500 and a Lancia Aprilia, which he parked in front of the main entrance to the Salon, thereby achieving a great success. In 1947, he designed the Maserati A6 1500, with wings within the bodywork, and the Cisitalia 202 Gran Sport, which the Americans called ‘rolling sculpture.’ In 1951 came his first direct encounter with the American industry:
he designed the Nash Healey roadster. His collaboration with Ferrari started in 1952 with a cabriolet over a 212 chassis, a collaboration that continues to this day. He also continued to work for Lancia, for which he designed the B24 spider in 1954. This same year saw another of his masterpieces, the Maserati A6GCS Berlinetta, a racing car that also won concours d’élégance. 1955 saw another great product in the Florida: from its highly advanced lines sprang the new Lancia saloon, the Flaminia, in 1956.
In the meantime, he he was accompanied in his work by his son, Sergio, and by his brother-in-law, Renzo Carli, who introduced new stylistic and industrial ideas.
The fame of Pinin was world-wide by now and in 1961, with a decree issued by the president of the republic, Giovanni Gronchi, his surname was changed from Farina to Pininfarina. Battista Pininfarina, the man who brought ‘Italian style’ to the world, died on 3rd April 1966 in Lausanne.
(H.S.)

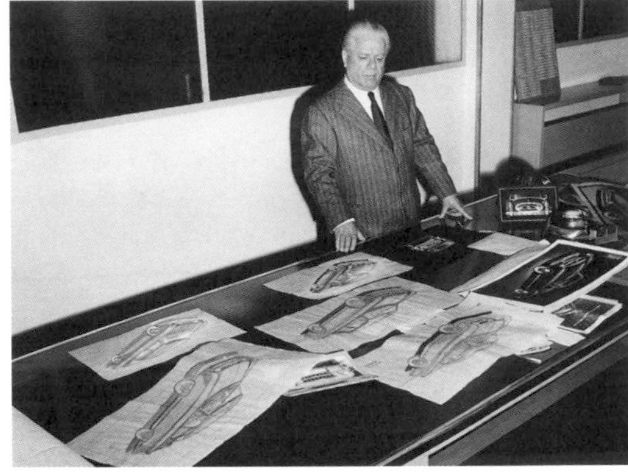

Battista ‘Pinin’ Farina at work

Battista ‘Pinin’ Farina with his son, Sergio, and Mr Curtice, President of General Motors Corp

Ferdinand Porsche

Ferdinand Porsche was born in 1875 at Maffersdorf in Bohemia. His extraordinary technical talent enabled him to think up new solutions in the car industry that would eventually make him famous.
After working as an apprentice in his father's installations company and frequenting evening school at the Industrial and Technical Institute of Reichenberg, and as non-examination student at the Technische Hochschule in Vienna, he began working at the age of 18 for the Bela Egger electricity company in Vienna. He began as a mechanic and became director of the testing department. In 1906, he was nominated director of the development section with the Austrian Daimler company, which later became Austro-Daimler, for which he worked on aircraft, cars, locomotive engines, vehicles for the fire brigade, electric trolley-buses and petrol and electric military vehicles.
As director general of the company, he was given an honorary degree. Following the reduction in funds for the racing division, a passion shared by Porsche as a racing driver, in 1923, he moved to Daimler in Stuttgart as director of the design department and member of the board of directors.
After his efficient development of the supercharged engine, in 1924 Ferdinand Porsche was awarded a second honorary degree. In 1929, following internal disagreements, he left the company.
He was then nominated technical director of Steyr in Austria and after having worked for the Austro-Daimler group, founded his own design studio in Stuttgart.
The commission for the development of the Silberpfeil (Silver arrow) for AutoUnion and the realization of the centrally-mounted engine brought him worldwide fame, and an honorary university seat. There was a sense that there was a genius at work every time he was observed concentrating on every detail as his cars raced around a circuit. The crowning of a lifetime's work was the design of a mass-produced car, the Volkswagen (people's car), following a commission from the German government.
In 1945, the Americans sought to arrest Porsche and unprisoned him. The French military authorities subsequently led him to believe in a possible contract for an automotive contract in order to bring him to trial. In the meantime, his team, under the direction of his son, Ferry, produced the Cisitalia racing car for Piero Dusio in Gmünd, Austria, where the company had moved for reasons of security.
Thanks to the payment received, Ferdinand Porsche was able to bring his legal problems to an end and began to consider the construction of a new sports car based on the Volkswagen. The brilliant designer died in Stuttgart in 1951.
(R.J.F.K.)

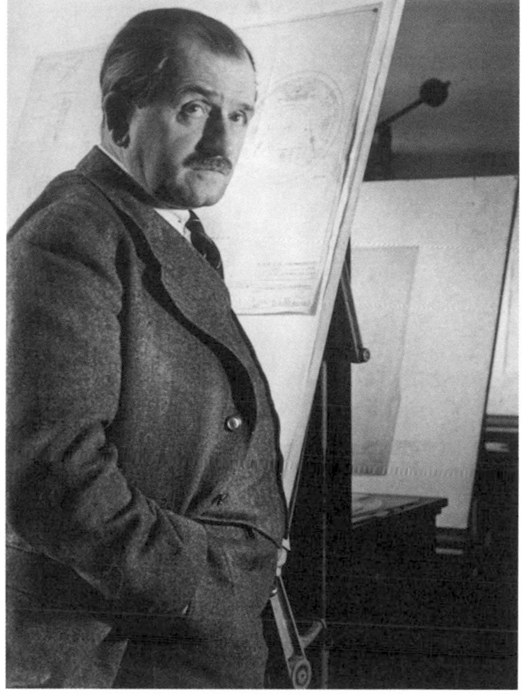

Ferdinand Porsche at the age of 62
in his studio at 24 Kronenstrasse, Stuttgart

Ferdinand Porsche and his grandchildren,
holding a model of the Number 1

Mario Revelli de Beaumont

Born in Rome in 1907 into a noble Piedmontese family, Mario Revelli de Beaumont was the forebear of the modern independent designer. Indeed, although he spent all his life in the car sector, he always preferred working as a consultant rather than as employee.
After gaining early experience in the motorcycle sector, Revelli, a cultured, elegant man with refined tastes, began designing for leading Italian coachbuilders. Particularly fruitful was his early collaboration with Carrozzeria Viotti, for which he designed traditional models and sports cars, especially on Fiat chassis, such as the beautiful roadster using 525 SS components of 1929, by many considered to be the most attractive car built by Fiat in the 1930s. But equally important was his work for Stabilimenti Farina, Ghia (for which he created the 508 Balilla Sport roadster, known as 'Coppa d'oro,' later adopted by Fiat), Bertone and Pinin Farina. Equally significant was his work using Isotta Fraschini Tipo 8, Lancia Astura and Aprilia chassis.
The coachwork designed by him denoted attention to formal elegance but also to aerodynamic research, which began to dominate in the 1930s even in standard production cars. And it is perhaps for this capacity for innovation and research that Revelli was invited by Fiat to take the post of creative director of the project group for the new mid-size saloon, the 1500 with six-cylinder engine, whose aerodynamic lines would become a point of reference for all car manufacturers. Subsequently he became part of the group that worked on the design of the new utility car, the 500 'Topolino.' But apart from the special or series-production cars he worked on, Revelli also confirmed his talent and fantasy in the design of accessories, such as the adjustable quarter-light, the window winder and transparent roof panels. Some of his ideas were way ahead of his time: between 1934 and 1941 he came up with a number of advanced ideas that, regrettably, were never to see the light of day. These included cab-forwards taxis, with internal combustion or electric engines, and room for four or six passengers, and a small two-seater car with electric engine, the forebear of today's city-car. In the post-war years, he worked with Italian car-makers once more, with Fiat particularly, but also with Simca (for which he designed the 1000) and General Motors in the United States, before becoming self-employed in Grugliasco, on the outskirts of Turin, where he died in 1985.
(H.S.)

Mario Revelli de Beaumont

Charles Stewart Rolls and Frederick Henry Royce

Frederick Henry Royce was born into an extremely humble family on 25th March 1863 and was obliged to abandon school after just a year for a job, but he continued studying in the evening after a hard day's work. When he was little more than 20, he set himself up on his own making electrical components. In the space of a few years, his business grew, acquiring him peace of mind and prosperity; indeed, at the turn of the century, he was able to buy a second-hand French motor car, a Decauville. Royce was a perfectionist and the poor construction of the French car encouraged him to explore the trappings of the car from closer-to and to make some modifications to improve it.
The next step came almost automatically and between 1903 and early 1904, he built three prototypes of cars with internal combustion engines in the little free time he had.
Born on 27th August 1877, Charles Stewart Rolls was of aristocratic origins. He was passionate about cars from the outset and thanks to his family's considerable wealth, owned a Peugeot in 1896, a French car like Royce's. With it, he took part in the Emancipation Run.
He decided to cultivate his passion by turning it into a career and in 1903 founded C.S. Rolls & Co., to import and sell various European marques in Britain. At this point, despite the difference in age and social extraction, the meeting with Royce was inevitable. The reciprocal diffidence soon evaporated and an agreement was signed in 1904 whereby Rolls would sell the cars built by Royce through his distribution channels. In 1906, the construction and sales activities merged and Rolls-Royce Ltd was formed. That same year saw the launch of the 40/50 HP, the legendary Silver Ghost, the first of a series of cars that would enjoy the fame of being 'the best cars in the world.' The Silver Ghost remained in production until 1925. All Rolls-Royces have been expensive, exclusive cars, but as Royce himself said, 'The quality remains long after the price has been forgotten.'
In later years, Charles Rolls developed a passion for aircraft (which is why the company became an aircraft engine manufacturer) and lost his life on 12th July 1910 in an unsuccessful landing. In the same year, Royce began to have serious health problems and was practically forced to move to the south of France to seek a better climate. From here, he continued to keep an eye on his company until his death on 22nd April 1933.
(H.S.)

Frederick Henry Royce

Charles Stewart Rolls

Giovanni Savonuzzi

Born in Ferrara on 28th February 1911, Giovanni Savonuzzi graduated in engineering and began his professional career with Fiat, in the aircraft engine testing department, where he met another engineer, Dante Giacosa, who would have a fundamental role to play in his future career. In 1944, Piero Dusio, an industrialist and Turinese gentleman driver, founded Cisitalia and, thanks to his good relations with the Agnelli family, he sought and obtained the collaboration of Giacosa who, in his free time, began working on a single-seater, the future D46. When Dusio sought to have him full-time to work on a two-seater, Giacosa was reluctant to leave Fiat and recommended that Giovanni Savonuzzi take his place instead. Giacosa felt he would be able to bring to Cisitalia the required technical organization for the realization of its projects. In the years immediately following the war, Savonuzzi designed the first two-seater cars for Cisitalia: the so-called 'Cassone,' the Spider Miller Miglia 'Nuvolari' and the 'Aerodinamica Savonuzzi,' a light and aerodynamic (Cx 0.19) coupé able to reach a top speed of over 200 kph despite its little 1.1-litre engine developing only 60 b.h.p. The lines of the Cisitalia 202 are also by Savonuzzi: the great Pinin Farina intervened with his great mastery and thus was born one of the masterpieces of car design.

In 1949, Savonuzzi left Cisitalia and created SVA with the idea of producing a single-seater with four-cylinder 813 cc engine which, with a supercharger, could deliver over 150 b.h.p. The idea never took off, however, and in 1954, Savonuzzi joined Carrozzeria Ghia as technical director. Knowing the working methods of the major car manufacturers, he transformed Ghia from the point of view of organization, but above all brought his ideas of style. He began with the Supersonic series, an elegant, aerodynamic coupé built in small numbers over a Fiat 8V chassis and, as a prototype, over Jaguar XK 120 and Aston Martin Mark II chassis. The Supersonic also saw the start of the collaboration between Ghia and Chrysler, which reached its high point at the Turin Show of 1955 with the presentation of the prototype Gilda, a dream car on which both Chrysler and Savonuzzi drew for the realization of other cars.

In 1957, Savonuzzi moved to Chrysler where he first worked in the turbine engine department and then became manager of the whole car research division. In 1969, he returned to Fiat to head the research department and then he became an external consultant for Fiat Aviazione.

A university lecturer and member of the National Research Institute, Savonuzzi died in Turin on 18th February 1986. *(H.S.)*

Giovanni Savonuzzi next to the Cisitalia 'Cassone'

Franco Scaglione

The three B.A.T.s are not just cars but also cult objects. When they are displayed, they still provoke wonder, astonishment and admiration. Anyone can see that whoever designed them was a visionary artist. This artist was called Franco Scaglione. He appeared only briefly on the scene but he fully deserves a place in the firmament of designers who created the image of Italian coachwork around the world. He worked for less than 20 years — his first known work, the Fiat-Abarth 1500 (characterized by the large headlight at the centre of the radiator) dates from 1952 and his last, the IMX Italia, from 1971 — but has nevertheless left an indelible mark, opening new horizons with his inimitable designs.

Born on 26th September 1916 in Florence of a father who was a military doctor and a mother who was an officer in the Red Cross, Franco Scaglione had a rebellious character that led him several times during the course of his career to clash with his seniors, to refuse to accept compromises and, finally, suddenly to leave a world that had deluded and abandoned him. But not forgotten, since at every congress on coachwork, in every exhibition on car design, in every concours d'élégance, the cars designed by him are always at the centre of attention. Intelligent, gifted, full of fantasy, and an erratic genius: this was how Bertone described him. An independent spirit, Scaglione always worked as a consultant, although on a long-term basis.

His first major project was immediately an eye-opener: the Fiat-Abarth 1500, which Bertone presented at the Turin Show of 1952, was acquired by Packard, which took it to America to study its lines. A 'Scaglione' style was born, distinguished by a downward sloping the nose, almost scraping the asphalt, a concave section behind the front wings, the use of fins, and large, curved rear windscreens.

The 1950s were golden years, the years of the famous B.A.T.s (which stood for Berlinetta Aerodinamica Tecnica rather than the English 'bat'): the 5, 7 and 9, designed between 1953 and 1955. But also of the 2000 Sportiva, of the Giuletta Sprint and SS, which made an entire generation of Italians dream. All were built using Alfa Romeo running gear for Bertone. In the 1960s, he designed the ATS 2500 for Allemano and the first 350 GTV for Lamborghini. His 'swansong' in 1967 was the Alfa Romeo 33 Stradale, one of the most admired sports cars even today. It is no coincidence that, 40 years later, today's 8C borrows from its lines. These years were followed by the dark ones of the collaboration with Intermeccanica, an adventure in which Scaglione lost everything, including any financial prosperity.

In the early 1970s, he moved to Suvereto, in Tuscany, where he subsequently died, almost forgotten by the automotive world, on 15th June 1993.

(H.S.)

Franco Scaglione

Gabriel Voisin

Vive la différence. This might be the motto of Gabriel Voisin, a pioneer of aviation and the air industry, but remembered above all for his cars.

Born at Belleville-sur-Saône on 5th February 1880, he studied architecture but developed a passion for aviation. His first designs date from 1905, when he founded an aviation company with Louis Blériot. These were early days: the Wright brothers had flown only in 1903 but their aircraft had not been able to take off on its own. Voisin sensed that a more powerful engine was required, and on 15th March 1907, one of his aircraft, flown by his brother Charles, flew for 80 m after having taken off under its own power. On 13th January, Voisin took off and landed in the same point after flying in a circle for a kilometre; in 1909, Blériot flow over the English Channel; in 1914, Voisin designed the first all-metal plane and presented it to the armed forces. During the Great War, the Société des Aéroplanes G. Voisin produced about 11,000 aircraft, including the first bombers. At the end of the war, Voisin abandoned aviation — according to some, because of the harm caused by his aircraft, according to others, because he had foreseen a long but difficult future for commercial aviation. In response to the housing crisis, he designed a type of prefabricated home, which could be erected anywhere in just a few hours and cost little. But he found his way made difficult by traditional builders and he abandoned the project.

He then dedicated himself to the car. His aim was to build luxurious touring cars that were fast and reliable. The first Voisin, the M1, was ready by May 1919. To publicize the project, Voisin considered racing and he thus built the revolutionary Laboratoire. Later, he left the race-track in favour of speed records: in 1930, every record over distances between 500 and 50,000 km were held by Voisin cars. In 1927, he abandoned his aerodynamic research and designed cars with square forms and with sensational Art Déco interiors. The handles and other details were by Le Corbusier. These Voisin cars were successful, but in the wake of the crisis resulting from the Wall Street crash, decline set in. Production dropped from 1004 units in 1929 to 300 in 1932. The company was sold to a Belgian consortium but had to close soon after. In 1934, Voisin returned to the company and in 1935 presented the last cars, the C28s, characterized by very aerodynamic lines. However, this was not enough to save the factory, which closed after producing a total of about 9,000 cars.

After the war, Voisin designed the Biscooter, a little two-seater vehicle with aluminium bodywork, two-stroke 125 cc single-cylinder engine and front-wheel drive. A total of around 20,000 of these were later built in Spain in the 1950s. Voisin died on Christmas Day, 1973.

(H.S.)

Gabriel Voisin

Felix Wankel

Felix Wankel was born in 1902 in Lahr, in Baden. The diploma he acquired and his apprenticeship as salesman for a publishing house were not central to his life as his one sole passion was the cars and engines in his workshop. Here, he would dedicate his spare time to the construction of cars such as the three-wheeled racing car baptized the Teufelskäfer (devilish beetle).
At the time, he already cherished the notion of developing an engine based on rotary movements. He was convinced that the perfect sealing of the combustion chamber constituted the first step to the creation of a new generation of engines. Despite the fact Wankel represented the perfect example of the head-in-the-clouds type of inventor, he always succeeded in stimulating the interest of people and companies in his ideas. He could thus always count on trusted friends and collaborators able to build his inventions.
An important aspect of his story results from the fact that he had no academic training behind him and he had constantly to battle against mathematical problems. But his obstinately fussy nature helped him find a solution to the problems he met while elaborating his ideas. Important support came to him from companies, which arranged for him to have a laboratory or placed a workshop at his disposal. For instance, in 1934 BMW decided to support his research into gaskets. Moreover, in 1936, following an agreement with the Ministry for Aviation, he was able to build a test centre for developing his research. This was located on Lake Constance in southern Germany.
This research centre produced rotating chambers for aircraft engines, internal combustion engines for torpedoes or for hydrofoils and, in 1944, the first supercharger with rotating pistons.
The Wankel institute was requisitioned by the French occupying forces in 1945. After negotiations and highly complex legal actions, a new institute for motoring research was finally able to open its doors. The NSU motorcycle factory in Neckarsulm, with its exceptional and innovative research department, supported Wankel's research too, partly because the then car factory was also restarting its production. In 1954, NSU was able to present a prototype of a volumetric rotating engine, and in 1958, the first functioning engine with rotating pistons. An engine with a piston with planetary movement, a further development of the earlier model, was mounted on a small NSU model and put into production from 1963. The final result of the collaboration between Wankel and NSU was the design of the famous NSU RO 80 model.
Undaunted, Wankel continued the research into his engines and in 1982 offered his latest invention, a two-stroke engine with rotating pistons.
NSU was the only company to continue to provide finance for Wankel's research for a long time, and it was subsequently sold, while the now prosperous Wankel, endowed with an honorary degree, was able to afford a luxurious car and chauffeur, a necessary luxury because this brilliant inventor remained without a driving licence until the day of his death in 1988.
(R.J.F.K.)

Felix Wankel

Ugo Zagato

Elio and Gianni Zagato

Ugo Zagato, born in Gavello (near Rovigo) on 25th June 1890 (at the age of 15), emigrated to Germany, where he found work in a mechanical engineering company. After returning to Italy, he was taken on by Carrozzeria Varesina, which built buses, and then by Officine Aeronautiche O. Pomilio of Turin. This latter experience was especially fundamental for his development as he learned here how to keep weight down, using light metals such as aluminium, and drag, both enemies reduce of speed. At the end of the Great War, he opened his first coachworks in Milan.
His background was different to that of nearly every other coachbuilder for cars, as he had not undertaken an apprenticeship with any company having a history in building horse-drawn carriages. His designs were characterized by research into lightness and simplicity of form. He established a name for himself in the sports car sector after designing the body of the Alfa Romeo RL SS in 1926. In 1927, he bodied a number of 6C 1500 chassis (Giuseppe Campari would win the second edition of the Mille Miglia with one of these in 1928) and 6C 1750 Gran Sports, a milestone for both the Milanese car manufacturer and for Zagato.
As a result of financial difficulties, Zagato closed the company in 1932 and became a consultant to Carrozzeria Brianza. Then he set himself up on his own once more and successfully: the 1938 edition of the Mille Miglia saw 36 Zagato cars at the start. During the war, with racing suspended, he worked for Isotta Fraschini and introduced the first forward-mounted driving cabin for lorries into Italy. After the conflict, which saw his factory destroyed by bombing, he relaunched his activity and built the rear-engined Monterosa for Isotta Fraschini and several small saloons in the 'Panoramica' series. He was assisted by his sons, Gianni and Elio, the latter a keen racing driver who made a name for himself at the wheel of Zagato's small, light and fast cars. Towards the middle of the 1950s, Zagato built a fair number of small coupés for racing on Alfa Romeo 1900, Fiat 8V and Maserati A6G/54 chassis, followed by the Abarth 750 and 1000, the Lancia Appia, Flaminia, Flavia and Fulvia and others. Among these was the celebrated coupé on an Aston Martin DB4 GT chassis, considered (rightly) one of the masterpieces of the post-war era.
The Zagato style paved the way not only because of the low weight of the vehicles but also because of their superior aerodynamics, as in the case of the Giulietta SZ, first fitted with a rounded tail and later modified with the famous cut-off tail that later distinguished a series of models, such as the TZ and TZ2. The double-bubble roof is an unmistakable sign of Zagato's touch. According to his son, Elio, this came about only to satisfy a customer who was taller than average and had too little space in such a tiny cabin. Ugo Zagato died on 31st October, 1968.
(H.S.)

Ugo Zagato

Photographic credits
For the photographs of the Alfa Romeo models of Arese we wish to thank Automobilismo Storico Alfa Romeo, Museo Storico, Centro di Documentazione Storica
Automobilia srl Milano
© BMIHT – British Motor Industry Heritage Trust Film and Picture Library
BMW AG Konzernarchiv
Nick Brändli
British Motor Industry Heritage Trust
DaimlerChrysler Advanced Design Italia
© DaimlerChrysler AG
© Diego Cassetta – Mart
Chip Riegel Photography
© Citröen Communication
Ralf J.F. Kieselbach Collection
Moch Collection
Christian Wannyn Collection
Xavier De Nobel
Nicola Eccher
Tina Eggert
Photo Andrew Cross
Photo archivio Italdesign Giugiaro
Photo Deutsches Museum
Photo Neutral
Photo Systematica
© From the Collections of The Henry Ford
Frederic Hurst
Familie Böhler
Familie Knotter-Meer
Christian Jäger
Johan Jonsson
Keller Collection
Intertrab e.V.
La Presse / Ferrari Spa
La Presse Maranello
La Presse Torino
Michael Mende
Musée de l'Air et de l'Espace Lions Club Le Bourget © MAE/ Alexandre Fernandes
Pagani Automobili Communication
Pagani Automobili Communication / photo Roberto Morelli
Uros Pavasovic
© Dr. Ing. h.c.f. Porsche AG
© Renault communication / all rights reserved Renault Presse
Smart
Franco Turcati
© Verlag Dr. Franz Burda, Offenburg, Baden, 1949 – photo Alfred Tritschler
© Villafranca di Verona, Museo Nicolis